THE 8086 MICROPROCESSOR
Architecture, Software, and Interfacing Techniques

WALTER A. TRIEBEL
Intel Corporation

AVTAR SINGH
Anderson Jacobson Inc.

PRENTICE-HALL, INC.
Englewood Cliffs, New Jersey 07632

Library of Congress Cataloging in Publication Data

Triebel, Walter A.
The 8086 microprocessor.

Bibliography: p.
Includes index.
1. Intel 8086 (Microprocessor) 2. Microcomputers.
I. Singh, Avtar, 1947- . II. Title. III. Title:
The eight thousand eighty six microprocessor.
QA76.8.I292T76 1985 001.64 84-18332
ISBN 0-13-246695-3

Editorial/production supervision: *Lynn Frankel*
Cover design: *Photo Plus Art*
Manufacturing buyer: *Gordon Osbourne*

Walter A. Triebel
To my daughter, Lindsey

Avtar Singh
To my uncle, Daya Singh Bhogal

Printed in the United States of America

10 9 8 7 6 5 4 3 2 1

ISBN 0-13-246695-3 01

Prentice-Hall International, Inc., *London*
Prentice-Hall of Australia Pty. Limited, *Sydney*
Editora Prentice-Hall do Brasil, Ltda., *Rio de Janeiro*
Prentice-Hall Canada Inc., *Toronto*
Prentice-Hall of India Private Limited, *New Delhi*
Prentice-Hall of Japan, Inc., *Tokyo*
Prentice-Hall of Southeast Asia Pte. Ltd., *Singapore*
Whitehall Books Limited, *Wellington, New Zealand*

Contents

Preface

Today, the 8086 family is the most widely used family of 16-bit microprocessors in modern microcomputer-based products. The 8088 8-bit bus version of the 8086 is the microprocessor employed in the popular IBM personal computer, and the 8086 is used in a number of other personal computers, as well as in a wide variety of other electronic equipment. Individuals involved in the design of this equipment need a systems level understanding of the 8086 microcomputer system. That is, a thorough knowledge of both its software and hardware is required.

This book presents an extensive study of the architecture, software, and interfacing techniques used in the design of 8086-based systems. This material is developed in Chapter 2, The 8086 Microprocessor; Chapters 3 and 4, 8086 Microprocessor Programming 1 and 2; Chapter 6, Memory Interface of the 8086 Microprocessor; Chapter 7, Input/Output Interface of the 8086 Microprocessor, and Chapter 8, Interrupt Interface of the 8086 Microprocessor.

In these chapters we first develop a thorough understanding of the internal architecture of the 8086 microprocessor and show how it executes instructions. This includes material on its pipelined instruction prefetch. Next, we present in detail software issues such as addressing modes, the instruction set, and the analysis and writing of assembly language programs. A large number of practical applications are illustrated through example programs.

The latter three chapters concern hardware and introduce architectural features and circuit design techniques for the memory, input/output, and interrupt interfaces of the 8086 microcomputer. Extensive coverage of bus cycles, address maps, bus demultiplexing techniques, program memory subsystems, data storage memory subsystems, input/output interface circuits, and interrupt interface circuits is included. Extensive material is also provided on large-scale integrated (LSI) peripheral controllers such as the 8255A (parallel peripheral interface), 8251A (universal synchronous/asynchronous receiver/transmitter), 8279 (keyboard/display controller), and the 8259A (programmable interrupt controller).

Two additional chapters are included that introduce Intel's 8086 Microcomputer System Design Kit (SDK-86). The SDK-86 is an educational microcomputer system that can be used to execute and debug programs written for the 8086 microprocessor. Chapter 5 introduces the SDK-86 microcomputer and the commands that can be issued to the microcomputer from its keypad. Moreover, examples are used to show how programs are entered, verified, executed, and debugged on the SDK-86 microcomputer.

Chapter 9 is a hardware study of the microcomputer in the SDK-86. This chapter illustrates a practical application of the material on interfacing techniques studied in Chapters 6, 7, and 8. The architecture and circuit design of the 8086-based microcomputer is described in detail. Some elementary troubleshooting and diagnostic techniques are introduced.

This book is written for use as a textbook in the electrical engineering technology curricula offered at universities and community colleges. Use of the book does require prior knowledge of basic digital electronics. This background is at a level consistent with but not necessarily as extensive as the material presented in the earlier Prentice-Hall books: *Integrated Digital Electronics*, 2nd ed. Walter A. Triebel, 1985 and *Handbook of Semiconductor and Bubble Memories*, Walter A. Triebel and Alfred E. Chu, 1981. The book does include a large amount of practical information that also makes it a valuable reference for practicing engineers and technicians.

WALTER A. TRIEBEL
AVTAR SINGH

1

Introduction to Microprocessors and Microcomputers

1.1 INTRODUCTION

The most recent advances in computer system technology have been closely related to the development of high-performance 16-bit microprocessors and their microcomputer systems. During the last three years, the 16-bit microprocessor market has matured significantly. Today, several complete 16-bit microprocessor families are available. They include support products such as large-scale integrated (LSI) peripheral devices, development systems, emulators, and high-level software languages. Over the same period of time, these higher-performance microprocessors have become more widely used in the design of new electronic equipment and computers. This book presents a detailed study of one of the most popular 16-bit microprocessors, the 8086 by Intel Corporation.

In this chapter we begin our study of microprocessors and microcomputers. The following topics are discussed:

1. The digital computer
2. Mainframe computers, minicomputers, and microcomputers
3. Hardware elements of the digital computer system
4. General architecture of a microcomputer system
5. Types of microprocessors and single-chip microcomputers

1.2 THE DIGITAL COMPUTER

As a starting point, let us consider what a *computer* is, what it can do, and how it does it. A computer is a digital electronic data processing system. Data are input to the computer in one form, processed within the computer, and the information that results is either output or stored for later use. Figure 1.1 shows a modern computer system.

Computers cannot think about how to process the data that were input. Instead, the user must tell the computer exactly what to do. The procedure by which a computer is told how to work is called *programming* and the person who writes programs for a computer is known as a *programmer*. The result of the programmer's work is a set of instructions for the computer to follow. This is the computer's *program*. When the computer is operating, the instructions of the program guide it step by step through the task that is to be performed.

For example, a large department store can use a computer to take care of bookkeeping for its customer charge accounts. In this application, data about items purchased by the customers, such as price and department, are entered into the computer by an operator. These data are stored in the computer under the customer's account number. On the next billing date, the data are processed and a tabular record of each customer's account is output by the computer. These statements are mailed to the customers as a bill.

In a computer, the program controls the operation of a large amount of electronic circuitry. It is this circuitry that actually does the processing of data. Electronic computers first became available in the 1940s. These early computers were built with vacuum-tube electronic circuits. In the 1950s, a second generation of computers was built. During this period, transistor electronic circuitry, instead of tubes, was used to produce more compact and more reliable computer systems. When the *integrated circuit* (IC) came into the electronic market during the 1960s, a third generation of computers appeared. With ICs, industry could manufacture more complex, higher-speed, and very reliable computers.

Today, the computer industry is continuing to be revolutionized by the advances made in integrated-circuit technology. It is now possible to manufacture *large-scale integrated circuits* (LSI) that can form a computer with just a small group of ICs. In fact, in some cases, a single IC can be used. These new technologies are rapidly advancing the low-performance, low-cost part of the computer marketplace by permitting simpler and more cost-effective designs.

1.3 MAINFRAME COMPUTERS, MINICOMPUTERS, AND MICROCOMPUTERS

For many years the computer manufacturers' aim was to develop larger and more powerful computer systems. These are what we call *large-scale* or *mainframe computers*. Mainframes are always *general-purpose computers*. That is, they are designed with the ability to run a large number of different types of programs. For this reason, they can solve a wide variety of problems.

Figure 1.1 Modern large-scale computer *(Courtesy of International Business Machines Corp.)*.

For instance, one user can apply the computer in an assortment of scientific applications where the primary function of the computer is to solve complex mathematical problems. A second user can apply the same basic computer system to perform business tasks such as accounting and inventory control. The only difference between the computer systems used in these two applications could be their programs. In fact, today many companies use a single general-purpose computer to resolve both their scientific and business needs.

Figure 1.1 is an example of a mainframe computer manufactured by International Business Machine Corporation (IBM). Because of their high cost, mainframes find use only in central computing facilities of large businesses and institutions.

The many advances that have taken place in the field of electronics over the past two decades have led to rapid advances in computer system technology. For instance, the introduction of *small-scale integrated* (SSI) *circuits*, followed by *medium-scale integrated* (MSI) *circuits*, and *large-scale integrated* (LSI) *circuits*, has led the way in expanding the capacity and performance of large mainframe computers. But at the same time, these advances have also permitted the introduction of smaller, lower-performance, and lower-cost computer systems.

As computer use grew, it was recognized that the powerful computing capability of a mainframe was not needed by many customers. Instead, they desired easier access to a machine with smaller capacity. It was to satisfy this requirement that the *minicomputer* was developed. Minicomputers, such as that shown in Fig. 1.2, are also digital computers and are capable of performing the same basic operations as the earlier, larger systems. However, they are designed to provide a smaller functional capability. The processor section of this type of computer is typically manufactured using SSI and MSI electronic circuitry.

Minicomputers have found wide use as general-purpose computers, but their lower cost also allows their use in dedicated applications. A computer used in a dedicated application represents what is known as a *special-purpose computer*. By "special-purpose computer" we mean a system that has been tailored to meet the needs of a specific application. Examples are process control computers for industrial facilities, data processing systems for retail stores, and medical analysis systems for patient care. Figure 1.3 shows a minicomputer-based retail store data processing system.

The newest development in the computer industry is the *microcomputer*. Today, the microcomputer represents the next step in the evolution of the computer world. It is a computer that has been designed to provide reduced size and capability from that of a minicomputer, with a much lower cost.

The heart of the microcomputer system is the *microprocessor*. A microprocessor is a general-purpose processor built into a single IC. It is an example of an LSI device. Through the use of LSI circuitry in the microcomputer have come the benefits of smaller size, lighter weight, lower cost, reduced power requirements, and higher reliability.

The low cost of microprocessors, which can be as low as $1, has opened the use of computer electronics to a much broader range of products. Figures 1.4 through

Figure 1.2 Minicomputer system *(Courtesy of Digital Equipment Corp.).*

Figure 1.3 Retail store data processing system *(Courtesy of Sweda International Incorporated).*

Figure 1.4 Calculator *(Courtesy of Texas Instruments, Incorporated).*

1.6 show some typical systems in which a microcomputer is used as a special-purpose computer.

Microcomputers are also finding wide use as general-purpose computers. Figure 1.7 is an example of a personal computer system. In fact, microcomputer systems designed for the high-performance end of the microcomputer market are rivaling the performance of the lower-performance minicomputers and at a much lower cost to the user.

Figure 1.5 Compact computer *(Courtesy of Texas Instruments, Incorporated).*

Figure 1.6 Home computer *(Courtesy of International Business Machines Corp.).*

Figure 1.7 Personal computer *(Courtesy of International Business Machines Corp.).*

1.4 HARDWARE ELEMENTS OF THE DIGITAL COMPUTER SYSTEM

The hardware of a digital computer system is divided into four functional sections. The block diagram of Fig. 1.8 shows the four basic units of a simplified computer: the *input unit, central processing unit, memory unit,* and *output unit*. Each section has a special function in terms of overall computer operation.

The *central processing unit* (CPU) is the heart of the computer system. It is responsible for performing all arithmetic operations and logic decisions initiated by the program. In addition to arithmetic and logic functions, the CPU controls overall system operation.

On the other hand, the input and output units are the means by which the CPU communicates with the outside world. The *input unit* is used to input information and commands to the CPU for processing. For instance, a Teletype terminal can be used by the programmer to input a new program.

After processing, the information that results must be output. This output of data from the system is performed under control of the *output unit*. Example of ways of outputting information are as printed pages produced by a high-speed printer or displayed on the screen of a video display terminal.

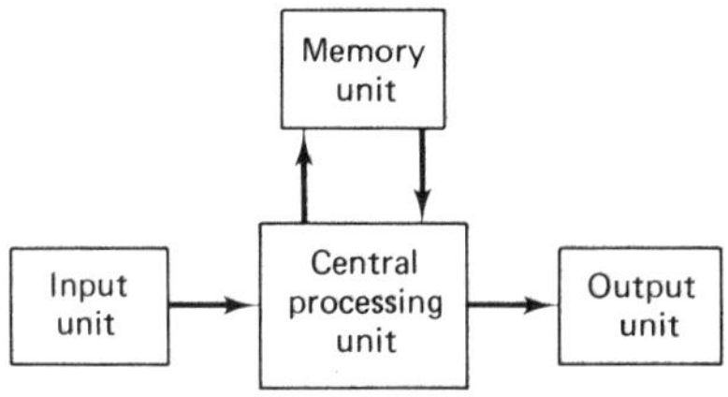

Figure 1.8 Block diagram of a digital computer (Walter A. Triebel, *Integrated Digital Electronics,* © 1979. Adapted by permission of Prentice-Hall, Inc., Englewood Cliffs, N.J.).

The *memory unit* of the computer is used to store information such as numbers, names, and addresses. By "store," we mean that memory has the ability to hold this information for processing or for outputting at a later time. The programs that define how the computer is to process data also reside in memory.

In computer systems, memory is divided into two different sections, known as *primary storage* and *secondary storage*. They are also sometimes called *internal memory* and *external memory*, respectively. *External memory* is used for long-term storage of information that is not in use. For instance, it holds programs, files of data, and files of information. In most computers, this part of memory employs storage on magnetic media such as magnetic tapes, magnetic disks, and magnetic drums. This is because they have the ability to store large amounts of data.

Internal memory is a smaller segment of memory used for temporary storage of programs, data, and information. For instance, when a program is to be executed, its instructions are first brought from external memory into internal memory together with the files of data and information that it will affect. After this, the program is executed and its files updated while they are held in internal memory. When the processing defined by the program is complete, the updated files are returned to external memory. Here the program and files are retained for use at a later time.

The internal memory of a computer system uses electronic memory devices instead of storage on a magnetic media memory. In most modern computer systems, semiconductor read-only memory (ROM) and random access read/write memory (RAM) are in use. These devices make internal memory much faster-operating than external memory.

Neither semiconductor memory nor magnetic media memory alone can satisfy the requirements of most general-purpose computer systems. Because of this fact, both types are normally present in the system. For instance, in a personal computer system, working storage is typically provided with RAM, while long-term storage is provided with floppy disk memory. On the other hand, in special-purpose computer systems, such as a video game, semiconductor memory is used. That is, the program that determines how the game is played is stored in ROM, and data storage, such as for graphic patterns, is in RAM.

1.5 GENERAL ARCHITECTURE OF A MICROCOMPUTER SYSTEM

Now that we have introduced the *general architecture* of a digital computer, let us look at how a microcomputer fits this model. Looking at Fig. 1.9, we find that the architecture of the microcomputer is essentially the same as that of the digital computer in Fig. 1.8. It has the same function elements: input unit, output unit, memory unit, and in place of the CPU, a *microprocessor unit* (MPU). Moreover, each element serves the same basic function relative to overall system operation.

The difference between minicomputers, mainframe computers, and microcomputers does not lie in the fundamental blocks used to build the computer; instead, it relates to the capacity and performance of the electronics used to implement their blocks and the resulting overall system capacity and performance. As indicated earlier, microcomputers are designed with smaller capacity and lower performance than either minicomputers or mainframes.

Unlike the mainframe and minicomputer, a microcomputer can be implemented with a small group of components. Again the heart of the computer system is the MPU (CPU) and it performs all arithmetic, logic, and control operations. However, in a microcomputer the MPU is implemented with a single microprocessor chip instead of a large assortment of SSI and MSI logic functions such as in minicomputers and mainframes. Notice that correct use of the term "microprocessor" restricts its use to the central processing unit in a microcomputer system.

Notice that we have partitioned the memory unit into an internal memory section for storage of active data and instructions and an external memory section for long-term storage. As in minicomputers, the long-term storage medium in a microcomputer is frequently a floppy disk. However, Winchester rigid disk drives are becoming popular when storage requirements are higher than those provided by floppy disks. In industrial applications, where the environment for the equipment is rugged, bubble memories are also employed as long-term storage devices.

Internal memory of the microcomputer is further subdivided into *program storage memory* and *data storage memory*. Typically, internal memory is implemented with both ROM and RAM ICs. Data, whether they are to be interpreted as numbers, characters, or instructions, can be stored in either ROM or RAM. But in most microcomputer systems, instructions of the program and data such as lookup tables are stored in ROM. This is because this type of information does not normally change. By using ROM, its storage is made *nonvolatile*. That is, if power is lost, the information is retained.

On the other hand, the numerical and character data that are to be processed by the microprocessor change frequently. These data must be stored in a type of

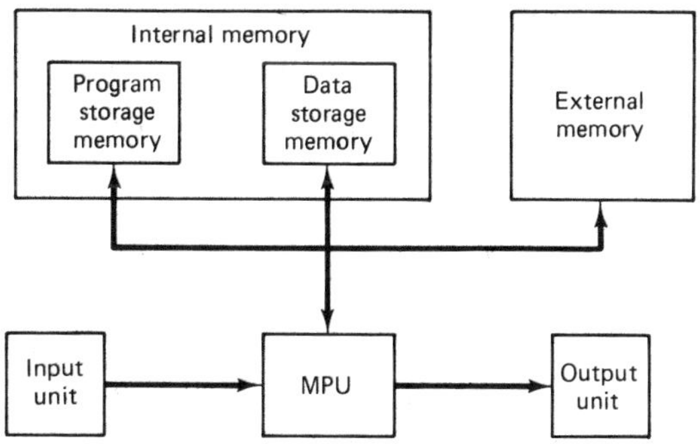

Figure 1.9 General microcomputer system architecture.

memory from which they can be read by the microprocessor, modified through processing, and written back for storage. For this reason, they are stored in RAM instead of ROM.

Depending on the application, the input and output sections can be implemented with something as simple as a few switches for inputs and a few light-emitting diodes (LEDs) for outputs. In other applications, for example in a personal computer, the input/output (I/O) devices can be more sophisticated, such as video display terminals and printers, just like those employed in minicomputer systems.

Up to this point, we have been discussing what is known as a *multichip microcomputer system*, that is, a system implemented with a microprocessor and an assortment of support circuits, such as ROMs, RAMs, and I/O peripherals. This architecture makes for a very flexible system design. Its ROM, RAM, and I/O capacity can be easily expanded by just adding more devices. This is the circuit configuration used in most larger microcomputer systems. An example is the personal computer system shown in Fig. 1.10(a).

Devices are now being made that include all the functional blocks of a microcomputer in a single IC. This is called a *single-chip microcomputer*. Unlike the multichip microcomputer, single-chip microcomputers are limited in capacity and not as easy to expand. For example, a microcomputer device can have 4K bytes of ROM, 128 bytes of RAM, and 32 lines for use as inputs or outputs. Because of this limited capability, single-chip microcomputers find wide use in special-purpose computer applications. A block diagram of a calculator implemented with a single-chip microcomputer is shown in Fig. 1.10(b).

1.6 TYPES OF MICROPROCESSORS AND SINGLE-CHIP MICROCOMPUTERS

The principal way in which microprocessors and microcomputers are categorized is in terms of the number of binary bits in the data they process, that is, their word length. Figure 1.11 shows that the three standard organizations used in the design of microprocessors and microcomputers are 4-bit, 8-bit, and 16-bit data words.

The first microprocessors and microcomputers, which were introduced in the early 1970s, were all designed to process data that were arranged 4 bits wide. This organization is frequently referred to as a *nibble* of data. Many of the early 4-bit devices, such as the PPS-4 microprocessor made by Rockwell International Incorporated and the TMS1000 single-chip microcomputer made by Texas Instruments Incorporated, are still in wide use today.

The low performance and limited system capabilities of 4-bit microcomputers limits their use to simpler, special-purpose applications. Some common uses are in calculators and electronic toys. In this type of equipment, low cost, not high performance, is the overriding requirement in the selection of a processor.

In the 1973–1974 period, second-generation microprocessors were introduced. These devices, such as Intel Corporation's 8008 and 8080, were 8-bit microproces-

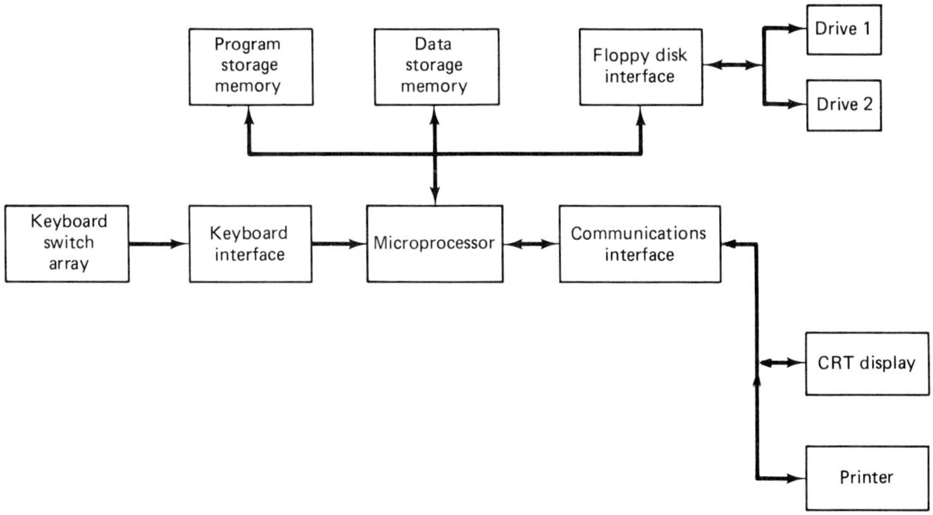

(a)

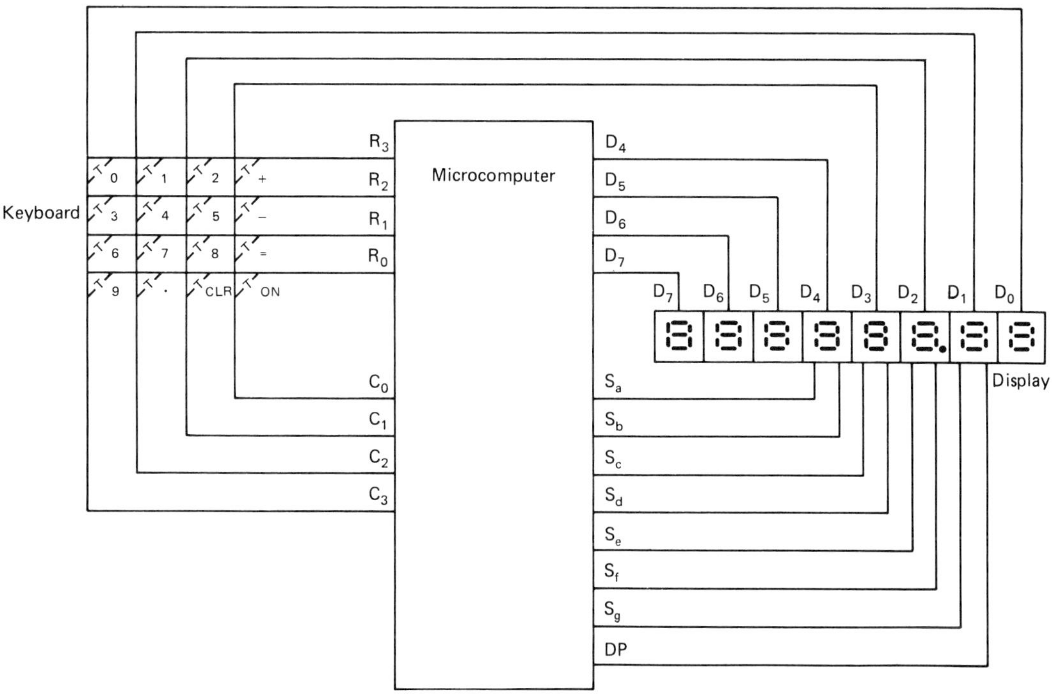

(b)

Figure 1.10(a) Block diagram of a personal computer; **(b)** block diagram of a calculator.

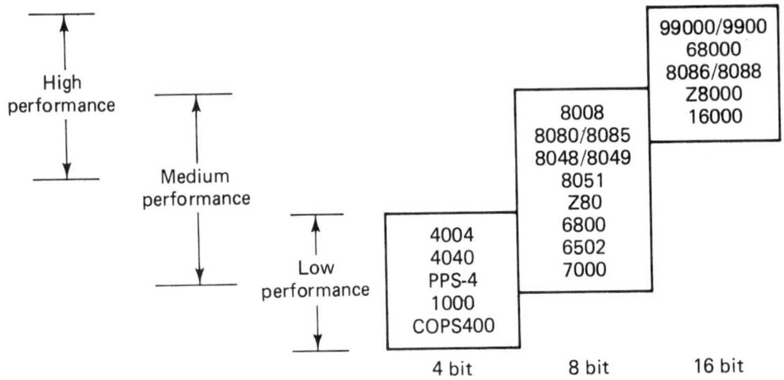

Figure 1.11 Microprocessor and single-chip microcomputer categories and relative performance.

sors. That is, they were designed to process 8-bit (one-byte-wide) data instead of 4-bit data.

The newer 8-bit microprocessors exhibited higher-performance operation, larger system capabilities, and greater ease of programming. They were able to provide the system requirements for many applications that could not be satisfied by 4-bit microcomputers. These extended capabilities led to widespread acceptance of multichip 8-bit microcomputers for special-purpose system designs. Examples of some of these dedicated applications are electronic instruments, cash registers, and printers.

Somewhat later, 8-bit microprocessors began to migrate into general-purpose microcomputer systems. In fact, the Z-80A is the host MPU in a number of personal computers.

Late in the 1970s, 8-bit single-chip microcomputers, such as Intel's 8048, became available. The full microcomputer capability of this single chip further reduces the cost of implementing designs for smaller, dedicated digital systems. In fact, 8-bit microcomputers are still being designed for introduction into the marketplace. An example is Intel's new 8051 family of 8-bit microcomputers. Newer devices, such as the 8051, offer a one-order-of-magnitude-higher performance, more powerful instruction sets, and special on-chip functions such as interval/event timers and universal asynchronous receiver/transmitters (UARTs).

The plans for development of third-generation 16-bit microprocessors were announced by many of the leading semiconductor manufacturers in the mid-1970s. The 9900 was introduced in 1977, followed by a number of other key devices, such as the 9981, 8086, 8088, Z8000, 68000, 99000, and 16000. These devices all provide high performance and have the ability to satisfy a broad scope of special-purpose and general-purpose microcomputer applications. All of the devices have the ability to handle 8-bit as well as 16-bit data words. Some can even process data organized as 32-bit words. Moreover, their powerful instruction sets are more in line with those provided by minicomputers instead of those of 8-bit microprocessors.

In terms of special-purpose applications, 16-bit microprocessors are replacing 8-bit processors in applications that require very high performance: for example, certain types of electronic instruments. A single-chip 16-bit microcomputer, the 8096 is also available for use in this type of application.

16-bit microprocessors are also being used in applications that can benefit from some of their extended system capabilities. For instance, they are beginning to be used in word-processing systems. This type of system requires a large amount of character data to be temporarily active; therefore, it can benefit from the ability of a 16-bit microprocessor to access a much larger amount of data storage memory.

Most new personal computer designs are being done with 16-bit microprocessors. For instance, IBM in its personal computer, the PC, uses the 8088 microprocessor to implement the microcomputer. The 8088 is an 8-bit bus version of the 8086 microprocessor that we cover in this book.

ASSIGNMENT

Section 1.2

1. What guides the computer as to how it is to process data?
2. What type of electronic devices are revolutionizing the low-performance, low-cost computer market today?

Section 1.3

3. What is the key difference between mainframe, mini-, and microcomputers?
4. What is meant by "general-purpose computer"?
5. What is meant by "special-purpose computer"?

Section 1.4

6. What are the building blocks of a general computer system?
7. What is the difference between primary and secondary storage?

Section 1.5

8. What are the basic building blocks of a microcomputer system?
9. What is the difference between program storage and data storage memory in a microcomputer?
10. What is the difference between internal and external storage memory in a microcomputer?

Section 1.6

11. What are the standard data word lengths of microprocessors and microcomputers available today?
12. What is the difference between a multichip microcomputer and a single-chip microcomputer?
13. Name five 16-bit microprocessor families.

2

The 8086 Microprocessor

2.1 INTRODUCTION

In Chapter 1 some general aspects of microprocessors and microcomputers were introduced. With the present chapter we begin our study of Intel's 8086 microprocessor. In this chapter, the general architectural aspects of the 8086 are covered. The next seven chapters are devoted to other aspects such as instruction set, programming, memory interface, input/output interface, and interrupt handling. Specifically, this chapter deals with:

1. The 8086 microprocessor
2. Minimum- and maximum-mode systems and interfaces
3. Internal architecture of the 8086 microprocessor
4. The 8284 clock generator and 8086 bus cycle
5. Instruction execution in the 8086 system

2.2 THE 8086 MICROPROCESSOR

The 8086, first announced in 1978, was the first 16-bit microprocessor introduced by Intel Corporation. It has been followed by a steady stream of family components such as the 8088 microprocessor, the 8087 numeric coprocessor, and the 8089 I/O processor.

The 8086 is manufactured using *high-performance metal-oxide-semiconductor* (HMOS) *technology* and the circuitry on its chip is equivalent to approximately 29,000 transistors. It is enclosed in a 40-pin package as shown in Fig. 2.1. Many of its pins

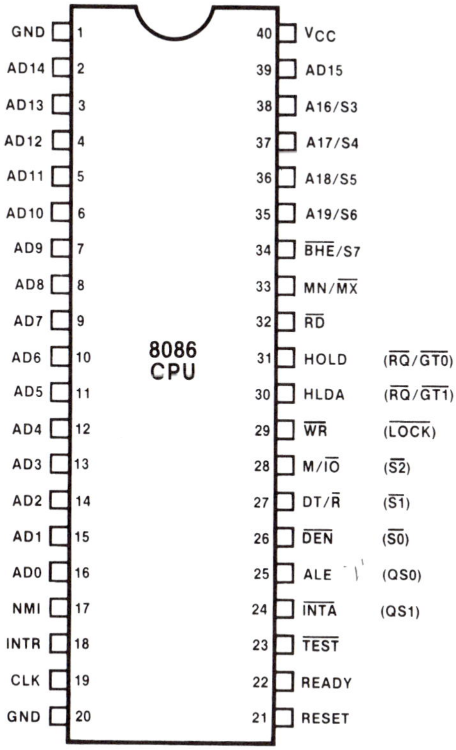

Figure 2.1 Pin layout of the 8086 *(Courtesy of Intel Corporation).*

have multiple functions. For example, in the pin layout we see that address lines A_0 through A_{15} and data bus lines D_0 through D_{15} are multiplexed. For this reason, these leads are labeled AD_0 through AD_{15}.

The 8086 is a true 16-bit microprocessor with 16-bit internal and external data paths. It has the ability to address up to 1M byte of memory via a 20-bit-wide address bus. Moreover, it can address up to 64K of byte-wide input/output ports or 32K of word-wide ports.

2.3 MINIMUM-MODE AND MAXIMUM-MODE SYSTEMS

The 8086 microprocessor can be configured to work in either of two modes. These modes are known as the *minimum system mode* and the *maximum system mode*. The minimum system mode is selected by applying logic 1 to the MN/$\overline{\text{MX}}$ input lead. Minimum 8086 systems are typically smaller and contain a single microprocessor. Changing MN/$\overline{\text{MX}}$ to logic 0 selects the maximum mode of operation. This configures the 8086 system for use with multiple processors. This mode-selection feature lets the 8086 better meet the needs of a wide variety of system requirements.

Depending on the mode of operation selected, the assignments for a number of the pins on the 8086's package are changed. As shown in Fig. 2.1, the pin functions specified in parentheses are those that pertain to a maximum mode system.

The signals that are common to both modes of operation, those unique to minimum mode, and those unique to maximum mode are listed in Fig. 2.2(a), (b), and (c), respectively. Here we find the name, function, and type for each signal. For example, the signal $\overline{RD}$ is in the common group. It functions as a read control output and is used to signal memory or I/O devices when the 8086's system bus is set up

Common Signals		
Name	**Function**	**Type**
AD15-AD0	Address/Data Bus	Bidirectional, 3-State
A19/S6-A16/S3	Address/Status	Output, 3-State
$\overline{BHE}$/S7	Bus High Enable/Status	Output, 3-State
MN/$\overline{MX}$	Minimum/Maximum Mode Control	Input
$\overline{RD}$	Read Control	Output, 3-State
$\overline{TEST}$	Wait On Test Control	Input
READY	Wait State Control	Input
RESET	System Reset	Input
NMI	Non-Maskable Interrupt Request	Input
INTR	Interrupt Request	Input
CLK	System Clock	Input
V_{CC}	+5V	Input
GND	Ground	

(a)

Minimum Mode Signals (MN/$\overline{MX}$ = V_{CC})		
Name	**Function**	**Type**
HOLD	Hold Request	Input
HLDA	Hold Acknowledge	Output
$\overline{WR}$	Write Control	Output, 3-State
M/$\overline{IO}$	Memory/IO Control	Output, 3-State
DT/$\overline{R}$	Data Transmit/Receive	Output, 3-State
$\overline{DEN}$	Data Enable	Output, 3-State
ALE	Address Latch Enable	Output
$\overline{INTA}$	Interrupt Acknowledge	Output

(b)

Figure 2.2(a) Signals common to both minimum and maximum mode *(Intel Corporation);* **(b)** unique minimum mode signals *(Intel Corporation);* **(c)** unique maximum mode signals *(Intel Corporation).*

Maximum Mode Signals ($MN/\overline{MX}$ = GND)		
Name	Function	Type
$\overline{RQ}/\overline{GT1}$, 0	Request/Grant Bus Access Control	Bidirectional
$\overline{LOCK}$	Bus Priority Lock Control	Output, 3-State
$\overline{S2}$-$\overline{S0}$	Bus Cycle Status	Output, 3-State
QS1, QS0	Instruction Queue Status	Output

(c)

Figure 2.2(c)

for input of data. Moreover, notice that the signals hold request (HOLD) and hold acknowledge (HLDA) are produced only in the minimum-mode system. If the 8086 is set up for maximum mode, they are replaced by the request/grant bus access control lines $\overline{RQ}/\overline{GT}_0$ and $\overline{RQ}/\overline{GT}_1$.

2.4 MINIMUM-SYSTEM-MODE INTERFACE

When the minimum system mode of operation is selected, the 8086 itself provides all the control signals needed to implement the memory and I/O interfaces. Figure 2.3 shows a block diagram of a minimum-mode configuration of the 8086. The minimum-mode signals can be divided into the following basic groups: address/data bus, status, control, interrupt, and DMA. For simplicity in the diagram, multiplexed signal lines are shown to be independent.

Address/Data Bus

Let us first look at the address/data bus. In an 8086-based system these lines serve two functions. As an *address bus*, they are used to carry address information to the memory and I/O ports. The address bus is 20 bits long and consists of signal lines A_0 through A_{19}. Of these, A_{19} represents the MSB and A_0 the LSB. A 20-bit address gives the 8086 a 1M-byte memory address space. Moreover, it has an independent I/O address space which is 64K bytes in length.

The 16 *data bus* lines D_0 through D_{15} are actually multiplexed with address lines A_0 through A_{15}, respectively. By "multiplexed" we mean that the bus works as an address bus during one period of time and as a data bus during another period. D_{15} is the MSB and D_0 the LSB. When acting as a data bus, they carry read/write data for memory, input/output data for I/O devices, and interrupt-type codes from an interrupt controller.

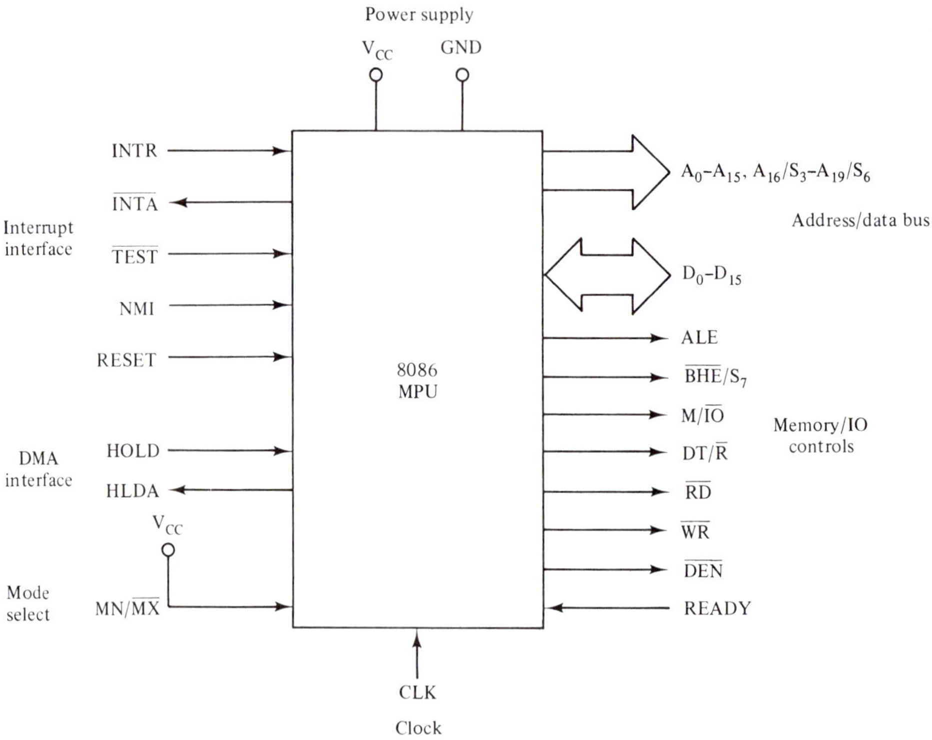

Figure 2.3 Block diagram of the minimum mode 8086 MPU.

Status Signals

The four most significant address lines, A_{19} through A_{16} are also multiplexed, but in this case with status signals S_6 through S_3. These status bits are output on the bus at the same time that data are transferred over the other bus lines. Bits S_4 and S_3 together form a 2-bit binary code that identifies which of the 8086's internal segment registers was used to generate the physical address that was output on the address bus during the current bus cycle. These four codes and the register they represent are shown in Fig. 2.4. Notice that the code $S_4S_3 = 00$ identifies a register known as the *extra segment register* as the source of the segment address.

Status line S_5 reflects the status of another internal characteristic of the 8086. It is the logic level of the internal interrupt enable flag. The last status bit S_6 is always at the 0 logic level.

Control Signals

The *control signals* are provided to support the 8086's memory and I/O interfaces. They control functions such as when the bus is to carry a valid address, in which direction data are to be transferred over the bus, when valid write data are on the

S_4	S_3	Segment register
0	0	Extra
0	1	Stack
1	0	Code/none
1	1	Data

Figure 2.4 Memory segment status codes.

bus, and when to put read data on the system bus. For example, *address latch enable* (ALE) is a pulse to logic 1 that signals external circuitry when a valid address word is on the bus. This address must be latched in external circuitry on the 1-to-0 edge of the pulse at ALE.

Another control signal that is produced during the bus cycle is $\overline{\text{BHE}}$ (*bank high enable*). Logic 0 on this line is used as a memory enable signal for the most significant byte half of the data bus, D_8 through D_{15}. This line also serves a second function, which is as the S_7 status line.

Using the M/$\overline{\text{IO}}$ (*memory/IO*) and DT/$\overline{\text{R}}$ (*data transmit/receive*) lines, the 8086 signals which type of bus cycle is in progress and in which direction data are to be transferred over the bus. The logic level of M/$\overline{\text{IO}}$ tells external circuitry whether a memory or I/O transfer is taking place over the bus. Logic 1 at this output signals a memory operation, and logic 0 an I/O operation. The direction of data transfer over the bus is signaled by the logic level output at DT/$\overline{\text{R}}$. When this line is logic 1 during the data transfer part of a bus cycle, the bus is in the transmit mode. Therefore, data are either written into memory or output to an I/O device. On the other hand, logic 0 at DT/$\overline{\text{R}}$ signals that the bus is in the receive mode. This corresponds to reading data from memory or input of data from an input port.

The signals *read* ($\overline{\text{RD}}$) and *write* ($\overline{\text{WR}}$), respectively, indicate that a read bus cycle or a write bus cycle is in progress. The 8086 switches $\overline{\text{WR}}$ to logic 0 to signal external devices that valid write or output data are on the bus. On the other hand, $\overline{\text{RD}}$ indicates that the 8086 is performing a read of data off the bus. During read operations, one other control signal is also supplied. This is $\overline{\text{DEN}}$ (*data enable*), and it signals external devices when they should put data on the bus.

There is one other control signal that is involved with the memory and I/O interface. This is the READY signal. It can be used to insert wait states into the bus cycle such that it is extended by a number of clock periods. This signal is provided by way of an external clock generator device and can be supplied by the memory or I/O subsystem to signal the 8086 when they are ready to permit the data transfer to be completed.

Interrupt Signals

The key interrupt interface signals are *interrupt request* (INTR) and *interrupt acknowledge* ($\overline{\text{INTA}}$). INTR is an input to the 8086 that can be used by an external device to signal that it needs to be serviced. This input is sampled during the final clock period of each *instruction acquisition cycle*. Logic 1 at INTR represents an active interrupt request. When an interrupt request has been recognized by the 8086, it indicates this fact to external circuits with pulses to logic 0 at the $\overline{\text{INTA}}$ output.

The $\overline{\text{TEST}}$ input is also related to the external interrupt interface. Execution of a WAIT instruction causes the 8086 to check the logic level at the $\overline{\text{TEST}}$ input. If logic 1 is found, the MPU suspends operation and goes into what is known as the *idle state*. The 8086 no longer executes instructions; instead, it repeatedly checks the logic level of the $\overline{\text{TEST}}$ input waiting for its transition back to logic 0. As $\overline{\text{TEST}}$ switches to 0, execution resumes with the next instruction in the program. This feature can be used to synchronize the operation of the 8086 to an event in external hardware.

There are two more inputs in the interrupt interface: the *nonmaskable interrupt* (NMI) and the *reset interrupt* (RESET). On the 0-to-1 transition of NMI, control is passed to a nonmaskable interrupt service routine. The RESET input is used to provide a hardware reset for the 8086. Switching RESET to logic 0 initializes the internal registers of the 8086 and initiates a reset service routine.

DMA Interface Signals

The *direct memory access* (DMA) interface of the 8086 minimum-mode system consists of the HOLD and HLDA signals. When an external device wants to take control of the system bus, it signals this fact to the 8086 by switching HOLD to the 1 logic level. At the completion of the current bus cycle, the 8086 enters the hold state. When in the hold state, signal lines AD_0 through AD_{15}, A_{16}/S_3 through A_{19}/S_6, $\overline{\text{BHE}}$, $M/\overline{\text{IO}}$, $DT/\overline{\text{R}}$, $\overline{\text{RD}}$, $\overline{\text{WR}}$, $\overline{\text{DEN}}$, and INTR are all in the high-Z state. The 8086 signals external devices that it is in this state by switching its HLDA output to the 1 logic level.

2.5 MAXIMUM-SYSTEM-MODE INTERFACE

When the 8086 is set for the maximum-mode configuration, it produces signals for implementing a *multiprocessor/coprocessor system environment*. By "multiprocessor environment" we mean that more than one microprocessor exists in the system and that each processor is executing its own program. Usually in this type of system environment, there are some system resources that are common to all processors. They are called *global resources*. There are also other resources that are assigned to specific processors. These dedicated resources are known as *local* or *private resources*.

Coprocessor also means that there is a second processor in the system. However, in this case, the two processors do not access the bus at the same time. One passes control of the system bus to the other and then may suspend its operation. In the maximum-mode 8086 system, facilities are provided for implementing allocation of global resources and passing bus control to other microcomputers or coprocessors.

8288 Bus Controller—Bus Commands and Control Signals

Looking at the maximum-mode block diagram in Fig. 2.5, we see that the 8086 does not directly provide all the signals that are required to control the memory, I/O, and interrupt interfaces. Specifically, the $\overline{\text{WR}}$, M/$\overline{\text{IO}}$, DT/$\overline{\text{R}}$, $\overline{\text{DEN}}$, $\overline{\text{ALE}}$, and $\overline{\text{INTA}}$ signals are no longer produced by the 8086. Instead, it outputs three status signals $\overline{S}_0$, $\overline{S}_1$, and $\overline{S}_2$ prior to the initiation of each bus cycle. This 3-bit *bus status code* identifies which type of bus cycle is to follow. $\overline{S}_2\overline{S}_1\overline{S}_0$ are input to the external *bus controller* device, the 8288, which decodes them to identify the type of MPU bus cycle. In response, the bus controller generates the appropriately timed command and control signals.

Figure 2.6 shows the relationship between the bus status codes and the types of bus cycles. Also shown are the output signals that are generated to tell external circuitry which type of bus cycle is taking place. These output signals are: *memory read command* ($\overline{\text{MRDC}}$), *memory write command* ($\overline{\text{MWTC}}$), *advanced memory write command* ($\overline{\text{AMWC}}$), *I/O read command* ($\overline{\text{IORC}}$), *I/O write command* ($\overline{\text{IOWC}}$), *advanced I/O write command* ($\overline{\text{AIOWC}}$), and *interrupt acknowledge command* ($\overline{\text{INTA}}$).

The 8288 produces one or two of these eight command signals for each bus cycle. For instance, when the 8086 outputs the code $\overline{S}_2\overline{S}_1\overline{S}_0$ equals 001, it indicates that an I/O read cycle is to be performed. In turn, the 8288 makes its $\overline{\text{IORC}}$ output switch to logic 0. On the other hand, if the code 111 is output by the 8086, it is signaling that no bus activity is to take place.

The control outputs produced by the 8288 are DEN, DT/$\overline{\text{R}}$, and ALE. These three signals provide the same functions as those described for the minimum system mode. This set of bus commands and control signals is compatible with the *Multibus*, an industry standard for interfacing microprocessor systems.

The 8289 Bus Arbiter—Bus Arbitration and Lock Signals

Looking at Fig. 2.5, we see that an 8289 *bus arbiter* has also been added in the maximum-mode system. It is this device that permits multiple processors to reside on the system bus. It does this by implementing the *Multibus arbitration protocol* in an 8086-based system.

Addition of the 8288 bus controller and 8289 bus arbiter frees a number of the 8086's pins for use to produce control signals that are needed to support multiple processors. *Bus priority lock* ($\overline{\text{LOCK}}$) is one of these signals. It is input to the bus arbiter together with status signals $\overline{S}_0$ through $\overline{S}_2$. The outputs of the 8289 are bus arbitration signals: *bus busy* ($\overline{\text{BUSY}}$), *common bus request* ($\overline{\text{CBRQ}}$), *bus priority out* ($\overline{\text{BPRO}}$), *bus priority in* ($\overline{\text{BPRN}}$), *bus request* ($\overline{\text{BREQ}}$), and *bus clock* ($\overline{\text{BCLK}}$). They correspond to the *bus exchange* signals of the Multibus and are used to lock other processors off the system bus during the execution of an instruction by the 8086. In this way the processor can be assured of uninterrupted access to *common system resources* such as *global memory*.

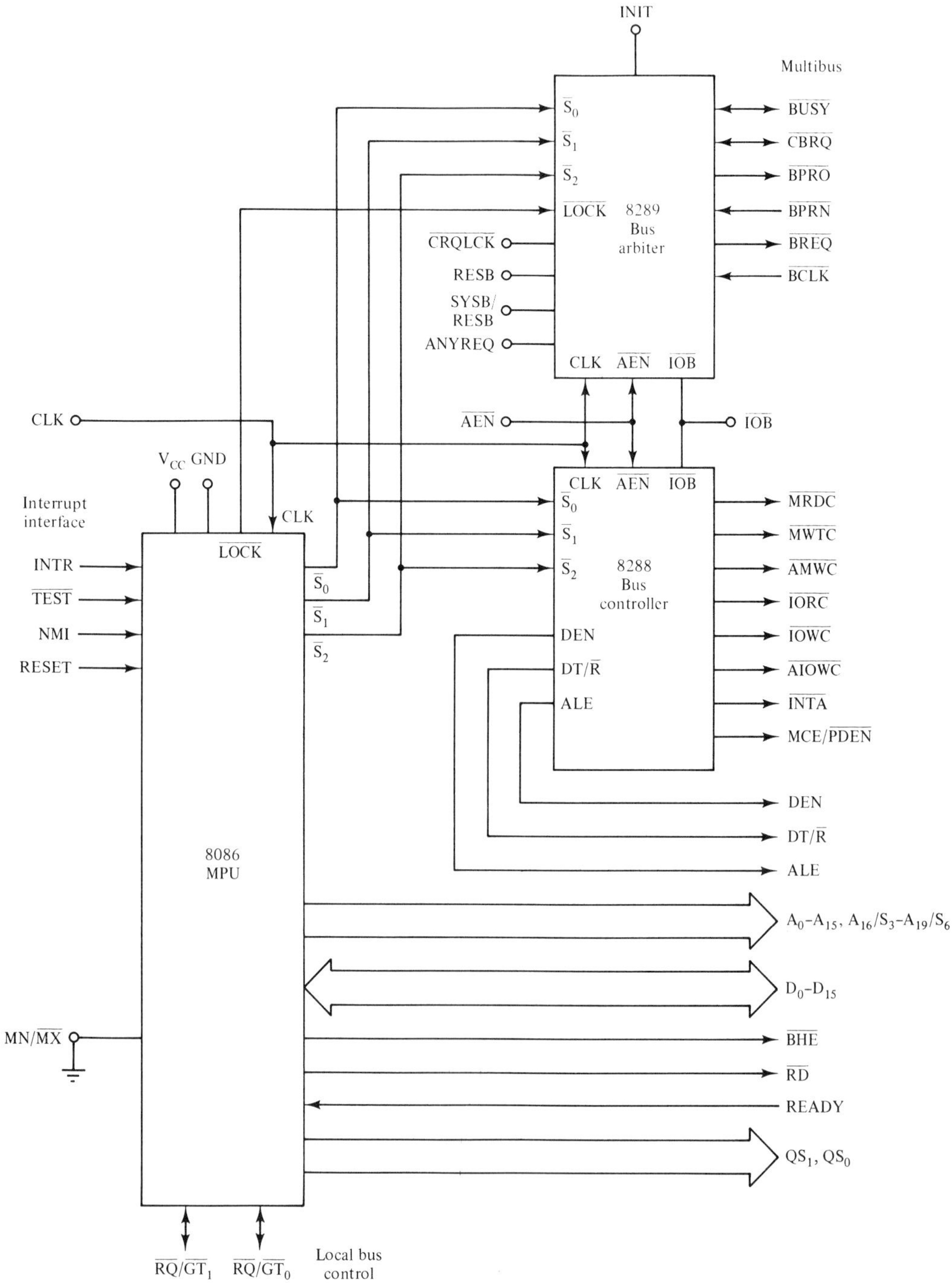

Figure 2.5 8086 maximum mode block diagram.

Status Inputs			CPU Cycle	8288 Command
$\overline{S2}$	$\overline{S1}$	$\overline{S0}$		
0	0	0	Interrupt Acknowledge	$\overline{INTA}$
0	0	1	Read I/O Port	$\overline{IORC}$
0	1	0	Write I/O Port	$\overline{IOWC}$, $\overline{AIOWC}$
0	1	1	Halt	None
1	0	0	Instruction Fetch	$\overline{MRDC}$
1	0	1	Read Memory	$\overline{MRDC}$
1	1	0	Write Memory	$\overline{MWTC}$, $\overline{AMWC}$
1	1	1	Passive	None

Figure 2.6 Bus status codes *(Courtesy of Intel Corporation).*

Queue Status Signals

Two new signals that are produced by the 8086 in the maximum-mode system are queue status outputs QS_0 and QS_1. Together they form a 2-bit *queue status code*, QS_1QS_0. This code tells the external circuitry what type of information was removed from the queue during the previous clock cycle. Figure 2.7 shows the four different queue statuses. Notice that $QS_1QS_0 = 01$ indicates that the first byte of an instruction was taken off the queue. As shown, the next byte of the instruction that is fetched is identified by the code 11. Whenever the queue is reset due to a transfer of control, the reinitialization code 10 is output.

Local Bus Control Signals—Request/Grant Signals

In a maximum-mode configuration, the minimum-mode HOLD, HLDA interface is also changed. These two signals are replaced by *request/grant lines* $\overline{RQ}/\overline{GT}_0$ and $\overline{RQ}/\overline{GT}_1$, respectively. They provide a prioritized bus access mechanism for accessing the *local bus.*

QS1	QS0	Queue Status
0 (low)	0	No Operation. During the last clock cycle, nothing was taken from the queue.
0	1	First Byte. The byte taken from the queue was the first byte of the instruction.
1 (high)	0	Queue Empty. The queue has been reinitialized as a result of the execution of a transfer instruction.
1	1	Subsequent Byte. The byte taken from the queue was a subsequent byte of the instruction.

Figure 2.7 Queue status codes *(Courtesy of Intel Corporation).*

2.6 INTERNAL ARCHITECTURE OF THE 8086

The internal architecture of a microprocessor describes its functional components and their interaction. Figure 2.8 shows a block diagram of the internal architecture of the 8086 microprocessor.

Internal Blocks of the 8086

Within the 8086 microprocessor, the internal functions are divided between two separate processing units. They are the *bus interface unit* (BIU) and the *execution unit* (EU). In general, the BIU is responsible for performing all bus operations, such as instruction fetching, reading and writing operands for memory, and inputting or outputting of data for peripherals. On the other hand, the EU is responsible for executing instructions.

Both units operate asynchronously to give the 8086 an overlapping instruction fetch and instruction execution mechanism. In essence, this parallel processing of the BIU and EU eliminates the time needed to fetch many of the instructions. This results in efficient use of the system bus and significantly improved system performance.

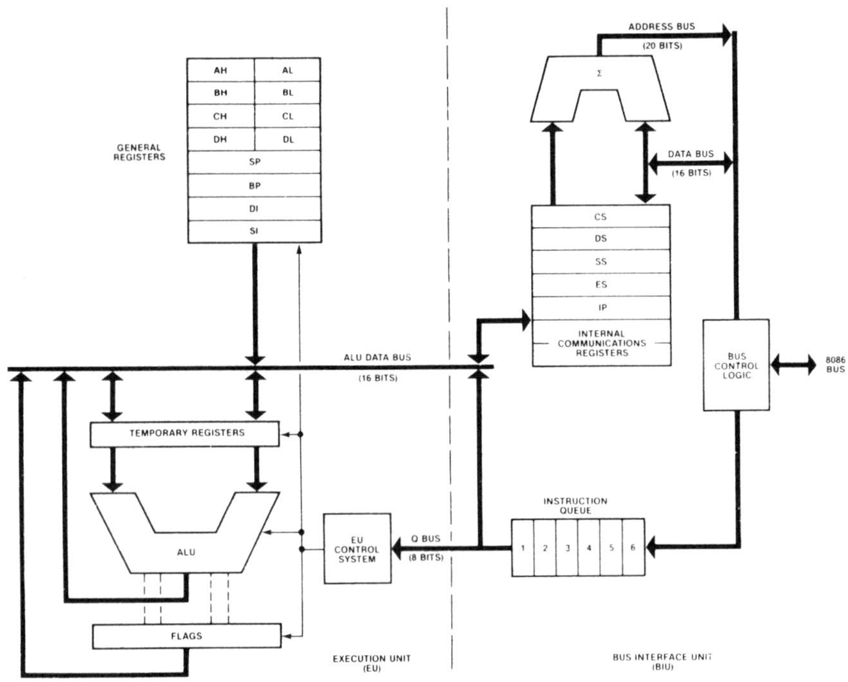

Figure 2.8 Internal architecture of the 8086 *(Courtesy of Intel Corporation).*

Bus Interface Unit

The bus interface unit is the 8086's interface to the outside world. It provides a full 16-bit bidirectional data bus and 20-bit address bus. The bus interface unit is responsible for performing all external bus operations. Specifically, it has the following functions: *instruction fetch, instruction queueing, operand fetch and storage, address relocation*, and *bus control*. To implement these functions, the BIU contains the *segment registers, internal communication registers, instruction pointer, instruction object code queue, address summer*, and *bus control logic*. These components are identified in Fig. 2.8.

The BIU uses a mechanism known as an *instruction stream queue* to implement a *pipeline architecture*. This queue permits prefetch of up to six bytes of instruction code. Whenever the queue of the BIU is not full, that is, it has room for at least two more bytes, and at the same time, the EU is not requesting it to read or write operands from memory, the BIU is free to look ahead in the program by prefetching the next sequential instruction. These prefetched instructions are held in its *first in, first out (FIFO) queue*. With its 16-bit data bus, the BIU fetches two instruction bytes in a single memory cycle. After a byte is loaded at the input end of the queue, it automatically shifts up through the FIFO to the empty location nearest the output. The EU accesses the queue from the output end. It reads one instruction byte after the other from the output of the queue.

If the queue is full and the EU is not requesting access to operands in memory, the BIU does not perform any bus cycles. These intervals of no bus activity, which may occur between bus cycles, are known as *idle states*. Moreover, if the BIU is already in the process of fetching an instruction when the EU requests it to read or write operands from memory or I/O, the BIU first completes the instruction fetch bus cycle before initiating the operand read/write cycle.

The BIU also contains a dedicated adder which is used to generate the 20-bit *physical address* that is output on the address bus. This address is formed by adding an appended 16-bit segment address and a 16-bit offset address. For example, the physical address of the next instruction to be fetched is formed by combining the current contents of the code segment (CS) register and the current contents of the instruction pointer (IP) register.

The BIU is also responsible for generating bus control signals such as those for memory read or write and I/O read or write. These signals are needed for control of the circuits in the memory and I/O subsystems.

Execution Unit

The execution unit is responsible for *decoding* and *executing* all instructions. Notice in Fig. 2.8 that it consists of an *ALU, status and control flags, eight general-purpose registers, temporary registers*, and *queue control logic*.

The EU extracts instructions from the top of the queue in the BIU, decodes them, generates operand addresses if necessary, passes them to the BIU and requests it to perform the read or write bus cycles to memory or I/O, and performs the operation specified by the instruction on the operands. During execution of the instruction, the EU tests the status and control flags and updates them based on the results of executing the instruction. If the queue is empty, the EU waits for the next instruction byte to be fetched and shifted to the top of the queue.

When the EU executes a branch or jump instruction, it transfers control to a location corresponding to another set of sequential instructions. Whenever this happens, the BIU automatically resets the queue and then begins to fetch instructions from this new location to refill the queue.

2.7 INTERNAL REGISTERS OF THE 8086

The 8086 has four groups of user-accessible internal registers. They are the *instruction pointer, four data registers, four pointer and index registers*, and *four segment registers*. They represent a total of thirteen 16-bit registers. In addition to these registers, there is another 16-bit register called the *status register*, with 9 of its bits implemented for *status* and *control flags*.

Instruction Pointer

The *instruction pointer* (IP) is a 16-bit register within the 8086 that identifies the location of the next instruction to be executed in the current code segment. It is similar to a program counter (PC); however, IP contains an offset pointer instead of the physical address of the next instruction. This is because the 8086 contains 16-bit registers and memory, but requires a 20-bit address. The offset must be combined with the contents of another register, in this case the code segment register (CS), to generate the physical address of the instruction. This register is physically located in the BIU.

Every time an instruction word is fetched from memory, the BIU updates the value in IP such that it points to the next sequential instruction word in memory.

Data Registers

As shown in Fig. 2.8, there are four general-purpose data registers that are located within the EU of the 8086. During program execution, they are used for temporary storage of frequently used intermediate results. The advantage of storing these data in internal registers instead of memory is that they can be accessed much faster.

The *data registers* are shown in more detail in Fig. 2.9(a). Here we see that the four data registers are referred to as the *accumulator register* (A), the *base register* (B), the *count register* (C), and the *data register* (D). Each register can be accessed either as a 16-bit word or as two 8-bit bytes. References to a register as a word are identified by an X after the register letter. For instance, the accumulator is referenced as AX. In a similar way, the other three registers are referred to as BX, CX, and DX.

On the other hand, when referencing one of these registers on a byte-wide basis, its high byte and low byte are identified by following the register name with the letter H or L, respectively. For the A register, the most significant byte is referred to as AH and the least significant byte as AL. The other byte-wide register pairs are BH and BL, CH and CL, and DH and DL.

Any of the general-purpose data registers can be used for arithmetic or logic operations such as add or AND. However, for some operations, such as those performed by string instructions, specific registers are used. In the case of a string instruction, register C is used to store a count representing the number of bytes to be moved. This is the reason it is given the name "count register."

Another example of dedicated use of data registers is that all I/O operations require the data that are to be input or output to be in the A register, while register DX holds the address of the I/O port. Figure 2.9(b) summarizes the dedicated functions of the general-purpose data registers.

Pointer and Index Registers

There are four other general-purpose registers shown in Fig. 2.8, two *pointer registers* and two *index registers*. They are used to store offset addresses of memory locations relative to the segment registers. The values held in these registers can be loaded or modified through software. This is done prior to executing the instruction that references the register for address offset. In this way, the instruction simply specifies which register contains the offset address.

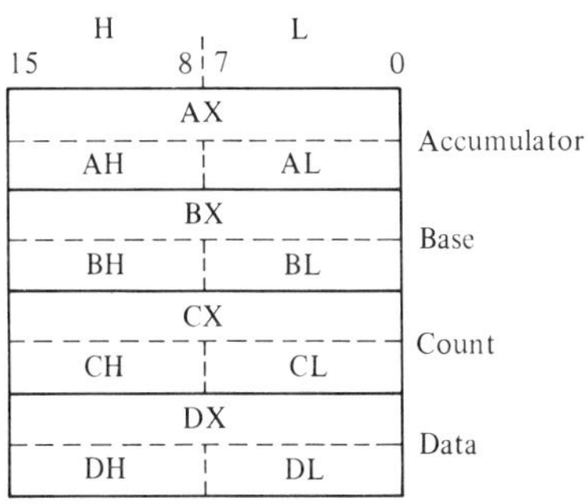

(a)

Register	Operations
AX	Word multiply, word divide, word I/O
AL	Byte multiply, byte divide, byte I/O, translate, decimal arithmetic
AH	Byte multiply, byte divide
BX	Translate
CX	String operations, loops
CL	Variable shift and rotate
DX	Word multiply, word divide, indirect I/O

(b)

Figure 2.9(a) General purpose data registers (*Courtesy of Intel Corporation*); **(b)** dedicated register functions (*Courtesy of Intel Corporation*).

Figure 2.10 shows that the two pointer registers are the *stack pointer* (SP) and *base pointer* (BP). The stack pointer permits easy access to locations in the stack segment of memory. The value in SP represents the offset of the next stack location which can be accessed relative to the current address in the stack segment (SS) register; that is, it always points to the top of the stack.

BP also represents an offset from the SS register. However, it is used to access data within the stack segment.

The index registers are used to hold offset addresses for instructions that access data stored in the data segment of memory. For this reason, they are always referenced to the value in the data segment (DS) register. The *source index* (SI) register is used to store an offset address for a source operand and the *destination index* (DI) register is used for storage of an offset that identifies the location of a destination operand. For example, a string instruction that requires an offset to the location of a source or destination operand would use these registers.

Segment Registers

As we indicated earlier, the physical address of the 8086 is 20 bits wide, but its registers and memory locations which contain logical addresses are just 16 bits wide. This gives a 1M-byte address space. However, the address space is segmented into 64K-byte segments and just four segments can be active at a time. It is for selection of the four active segments that the 16-bit *segment registers* are provided within the BIU of the 8086.

These four registers are the *code segment* (CS) *register*, the *data segment* (DS) *register*, the *stack segment* (SS) *register*, and the *extra segment* (ES) *register*. These registers are shown in Fig. 2.11. They are loaded with 16-bit addresses that identify which segments of memory are active. For example, the value in CS identifies the starting address of the 64K-byte segment known as the code segment. By "starting address," we mean the lowest-addressed byte in the active code segment. The values held in these registers for instance, the current code segment address, are frequently referred to as the current segment register values.

Code segments of memory contain instructions of the program. The contents of CS identify the starting location of the current code segment in memory. To access the storage location of an instruction in the active code segment, the 8086 must

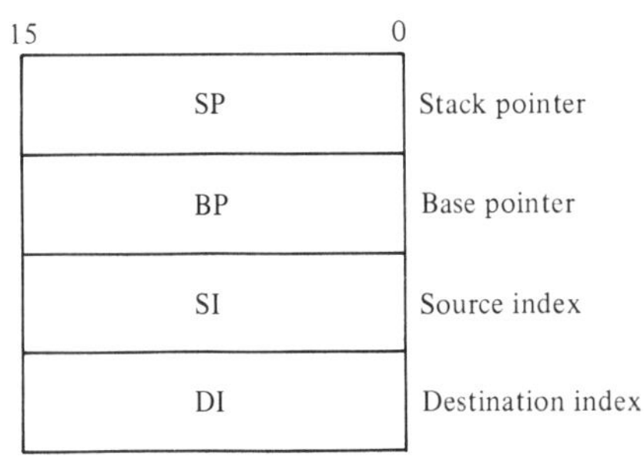

Figure 2.10 Pointer and index registers *(Courtesy of Intel Corporation).*

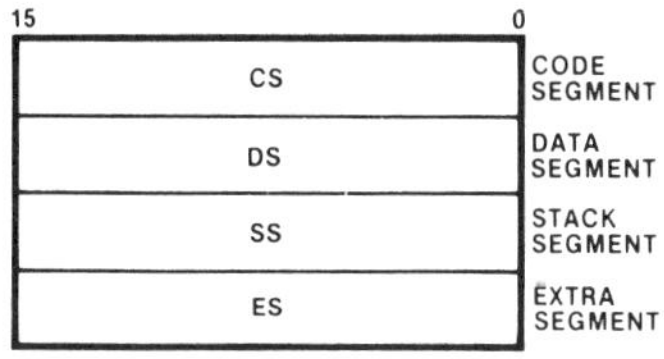

Figure 2.11 Segment registers *(Courtesy of Intel Corporation).*

generate its 20-bit physical address. To do this, it combines the contents of the instruction pointer (IP) register with the value in CS to produce the physical address that will be output on the address bus.

The active code segment can be changed by simply executing an instruction that loads a new value into the CS register. For this reason, we can use any of the 16 independent 64K-byte segments of memory for storage of code.

The contents of the data segment (DS) register identify the starting location of the current data segment in memory. This is a second active 64K segment that provides a read/write memory space in which data can be stored. Operands for most instructions are fetched from this segment. However, a prefix may be included with the instruction to obtain operands from any of the other segments. Values in the source index (SI) register or destination index (DI) register are combined with the value in DS to form the 20-bit physical address of the source or destination operand in the data segment.

The stack segment (SS) register contains a logical address that identifies the starting location of the current stack segment in memory. It is the 64K segment to which the values of the instruction pointer (IP), status flags, and other registers are pushed whenever a hardware interrupt, software interrupt, or subroutine call occurs. After the service routine or subroutine is complete, the original system status is restored from the stack by executing pop instructions and the return instruction. The next location to which a word is to be pushed or from which a word is to be popped is identified by combining the current value in SS with the stack pointer (SP).

The last segment register identifies the fourth active 64K-byte memory area. This area is called the *extra segment* (ES). The extra segment is usually used for data storage. For instance, the string instructions use the value in ES with the contents of DI as an offset to specify the destination address.

Flag Register

The *flag register* is a 16-bit register within the EU. However, as shown in Fig. 2.12, just 9 of its bits are implemented. Six of these bits represent status flags. They are the *carry flag* (CF), the *parity flag* (PF), the *auxiliary carry flag* (AF), the *zero flag* (ZF), the *sign flag* (SF), and the *overflow flag* (OF).

The *status flags* indicate conditions that are produced as the result of executing an arithmetic or logic instruction. That is, specific flag bits are reset (logic 0) or set (logic 1) at the completion of execution of the instruction.

Let us first summarize the operation of these status flags:

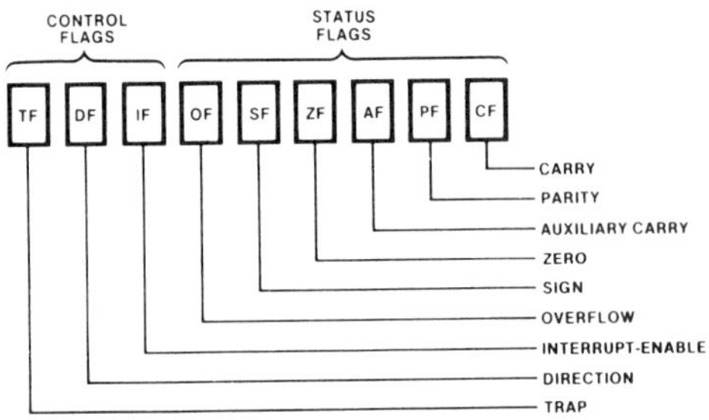

Figure 2.12 Status flags *(Courtesy of Intel Corporation).*

1. The *carry flag* (CF): CF is set if there is a carryout or a borrow in for the most significant bit of the result during the execution of an arithmetic instruction. Otherwise, CF is reset.
2. The *parity flag* (PF): PF is set if the result produced by the instruction has even parity, that is, if it contains an even number of bits at the 1 logic level. If parity is odd, PF is reset.
3. The *auxiliary carry flag* (AF): AF is set if there is a carryout from the low nibble into the high nibble or a borrow in from the high nibble into the low nibble of the lower byte in a 16-bit word. Otherwise, AF is reset.
4. The *zero flag* (ZF): ZF is set if the result of an arithmetic or logic operation is zero. Otherwise, ZF is reset.
5. The *sign flag* (SF): The MSB of the result is copied into SF. Thus SF is set if the result is a negative number or reset if it is positive.
6. The *overflow flag* (OF): When OF is set, it indicates that the signed result is out of range. If the result is not out of range, OF remains reset.

For example, at the completion of execution of a byte addition instruction, the carry flag (CF) could be set to indicate that the sum of the operands caused a carryout condition. The auxiliary carry flag (AF) could also be set due to the execution of the instruction. This depends on whether or not a carryout occurred from the least significant nibble to the most significant nibble when the byte operands are added. The sign flag (SF) is also affected and it will reflect the logic level of the MSB of the result.

The status flags are read only; therefore, they can only be tested. The 8086 provides instructions within its instruction set which are able to use these flags to alter the sequence in which the program is executed. For instance, ZF equal to logic 1 could be tested as the condition that would initiate a jump to another part of the program.

The other three implemented flag bits are *control flags*. They are the *direction flag* (DF), the *interrupt enable flag* (IF), and the *trap flag* (TF). These three flags control functions of the 8086 as follows:

1. The *trap flag* (TF): If TF is set, the 8086 goes into the single-step mode. When in the single-step mode, it executes one instruction at a time. This type of operation is very useful for debugging programs.

2. The *interrupt flag* (IF): For the 8086 to recognize maskable interrupt requests at its INT input, the IF flag must be set. When IF is reset, requests at INT are ignored and the maskable interrupt interface is disabled.
3. The *direction flag* (DF): The logic level of DF determines the direction in which string operations will occur. When it is reset, the string instruction automatically decrements the address. Therefore, the string data transfers proceed from high address to low address. On the other hand, setting DF causes the string address to be incremented. In this way, transfers proceed from low address to high address.

Bits CF, DF, IF, and TF of the flag register can be modified at any point in the program through user software. That is, special instructions are provided in the instruction set of the 8086 such that they can be set or cleared. For instance, at the beginning of an interrupt service routine, IF could be reset. This locks out the occurrence of another maskable interrupt. At the end of the service routine, it could be set once again to enable the maskable interrupt interface.

2.8 SYSTEM CLOCK

The time base for synchronization of the internal and external operations of the 8086 microprocessor is provided by the CLK input signal. At present, the 8086 is available in two different speeds. The standard part operates at 5 MHz and the 8086-2 operates at 8 MHz. CLK is externally generated by the 8284 clock generator and driver IC. Figure 2.13 is a block diagram of this device.

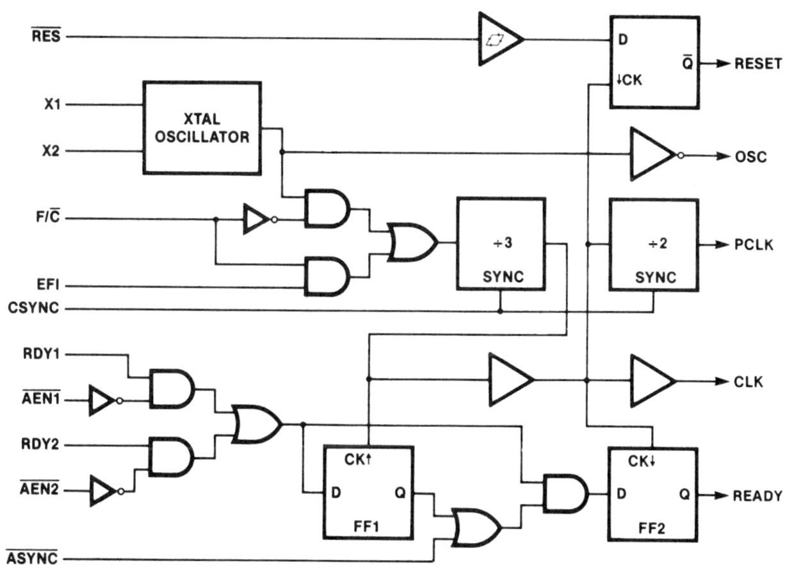

Figure 2.13 Block diagram of the 8284 clock generator *(Courtesy of Intel Corporation).*

The normal way in which this clock chip is used is to connect either a 15-MHz or a 24-MHz crystal between its X_1 and X_2 inputs. This circuit connection is shown in Fig. 2.14. Notice that a series capacitor C_L is also required. Its typical value when used with the 15-MHz crystal is 12 pF. The *fundamental crystal frequency* is divided by 3 within the 8284 to give either a 5-MHz or a 8-MHz clock signal. This signal is buffered and output at CLK. CLK can be directly connected to CLK of the 8086.

The waveform of CLK is shown in Fig. 2.15. Here we see that the signal is at *MOS-compatible voltage levels* and not TTL levels. Its minimum and maximum low logic levels are $V_{Lmin} = -0.5$ V and $V_{Lmax} = 0.6$ V, respectively. Moreover, the minimum and maximum high logic levels are $V_{Hmin} = 3.9$ V and $V_{Hmax} = V_{CC} + 1$ V, respectively. The *period* of the 5-MHz clock signal can range from a minimum of 200 ns to a maximum of 500 ns, and the maximum *rise* and *fall times* of its edges equal 10 ns.

In Fig. 2.13 we see that there are two more clock outputs on the 8284. They are *peripheral clock* (PCLK) and *oscillator clock* (OSC). These signals are provided to drive peripheral ICs. The clock signal output at PCLK is always half the frequency of CLK. That is, it is either 2.5 MHz or 4 MHz. Also, it is at TTL-compatible levels rather than MOS levels. On the other hand, the OSC output is at the fundamental clock frequency, which is three times that of CLK. These relationships are illustrated in Fig. 2.16.

The 8284 can also be driven from an external clock source. The external clock signal is applied to the external frequency input (EFI). Input $F/\overline{C}$ is provided for clock source selection. When it is strapped to the 0 logic level, the crystal between X_1 and X_2 is used. On the other hand, applying logic 1 to $F/\overline{C}$ selects EFI as the source of the clock. The clock sync (CSYNC) input can be used for external synchronization in systems that employ multiple clocks.

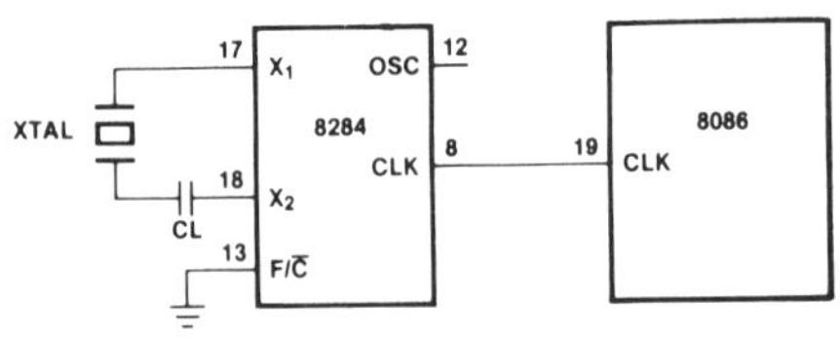

Figure 2.14 Connecting the 8284 to the 8086 *(Courtesy of Intel Corporation).*

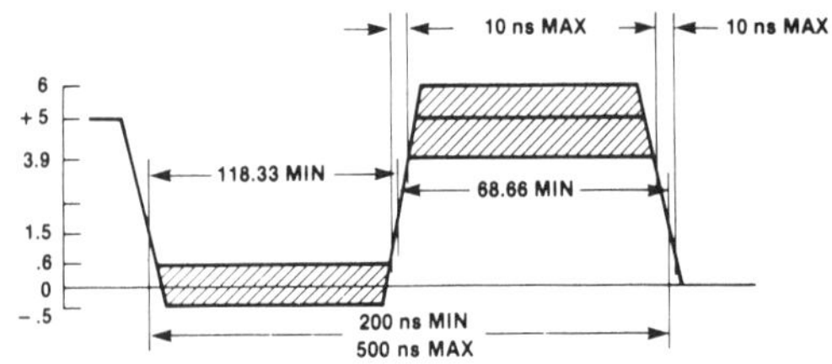

Figure 2.15 CLK voltage and timing characteristics *(Courtesy of Intel Corporation).*

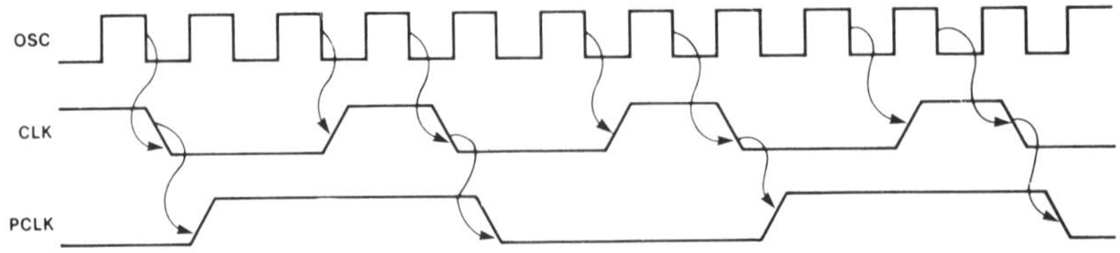

Figure 2.16 Relationship between CLK and PCLK *(Courtesy of Intel Corporation).*

2.9 BUS CYCLE

The *bus cycle* of the 8086 is used to access memory, I/O devices, or the interrupt controller. As shown in Fig. 2.17(a), it corresponds to a sequence of events that starts with an address being output on the system bus followed by a read or write data transfer. During these operations, a series of control signals are also produced by the 8086 to control the direction and timing of the bus.

The bus cycle of the 8086 processor consists of at least four clock periods. These four time states are called T_1, T_2, T_3, and T_4. During T_1, the BIU puts an address on the bus. For a write memory cycle, data are put on the bus during period T_2 and maintained through T_3, and T_4. When a read cycle is to be performed, the bus is first put in the high-Z state during T_2 and then the data to be read must be put on the bus during T_3 and T_4. These four clock states give a *bus cycle duration* of 125 ns $\times$ 4 = 500 ns in an 8-MHz 8086 system.

If no bus cycles are required, the BIU performs what are known as *idle states*. During these states no bus activity takes place. Each idle state is one clock period long and any number of them can be inserted between bus cycles. Figure 2.17(b) shows two bus cycles separated by idle states. Idle states are also performed if the queue is full and the EU does not require the BIU to read or write operands from memory.

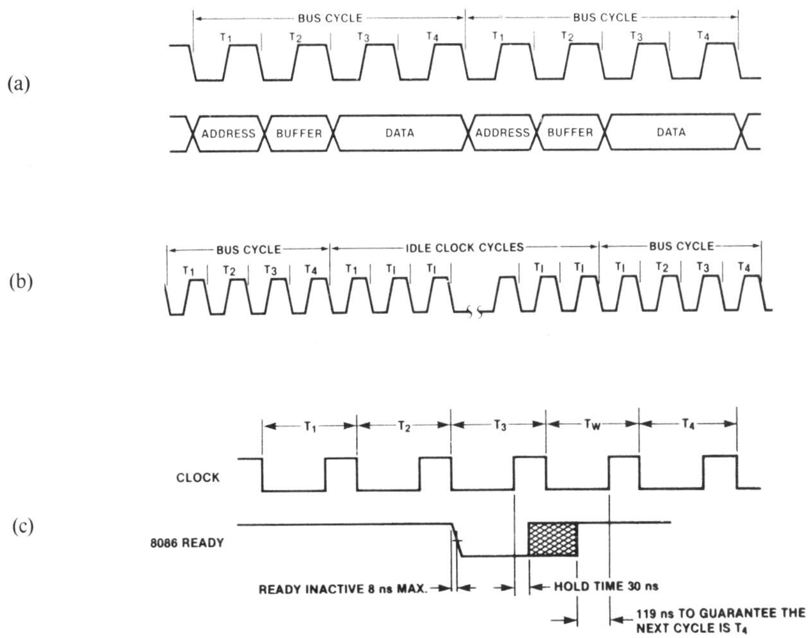

Figure 2.17(a) Bus cycle clock periods *(Courtesy of Intel Corporation);* **(b)** bus cycle with idle states *(Courtesy of Intel Corporation);* **(c)** bus cycle with wait states *(Courtesy of Intel Corporation).*

Wait states can also be inserted into a bus cycle. This is done in response to a request by an event in external hardware instead of an internal event such as a full queue. In fact, the READY input of the 8086 is provided specifically for this purpose. Figure 2.17(c) shows that logic 0 at this input indicates that the current bus cycle should not be completed. As long as READY is held at the 0 level, wait states are inserted between periods T_3 and T_4 of the current bus cycle and the data that were on the bus during T_3 are maintained. The bus cycle is not completed until the external hardware returns READY back to the 1 logic level. This extends the duration of the bus cycle, thereby permitting the use of slower memory devices in the system.

2.10 INSTRUCTION EXECUTION SEQUENCE

During normal system operation, the 8086 fetches instructions one after the other from program memory and executes them. After an instruction is fetched it must be decoded within the 8086 and if necessary its operands read from either data memory or from internal registers. The operation specified in the instruction is performed on the operands and the results written back to either an internal register or a location in data memory. The 8086 is now ready to execute the next instruction.

Figure 2.18 shows in detail the overlapping of instruction fetch and execution by the 8086. Notice that as the EU is executing the previously fetched first instruction, the BIU fetches the second sequential instruction over the system bus. After this, a third instruction is fetched and put in the queue. During the third period, the second instruction is available at the output of the queue. It is extracted from the queue by the EU and executed. At the same time, the BIU uses the bus to write the result of the first instruction into memory. In the next period, a fourth instruction is fetched by the BIU and put into its queue. During the fifth period, an operand required by the third instruction is read over the bus. Finally, the third instruction is executed and a fifth instruction fetched. Notice that during this interval of time four new instructions were fetched and loaded into the queue and three instructions were executed.

An assembly language program and its equivalent 8086 machine code are shown in Fig. 2.19(a). This program is a loop that executes repeatedly. Notice that the instructions are coded using one, two, three, or four bytes. For example, the instruction MOV AX,0F802H is represented with the three bytes $B8_{16}$, 02_{16}, and $F8_{16}$. On the other hand, PUSH AX takes up just one byte, which is 50_{16}.

The program is stored in the code segment of memory as consecutive bytes as shown in Fig. 2.19(b). Notice that it takes 16 byte addresses to hold the complete program.

Remember that the queue status and bus status are output signals of the maximum-mode 8086. QS_1QS_0 identifies the instruction queue status initiated by the EU during the previous clock period. Moreover, the code at $\overline{S}_2\overline{S}_1\overline{S}_0$ tells an external 8288 bus controller which type of bus cycle is currently in progress.

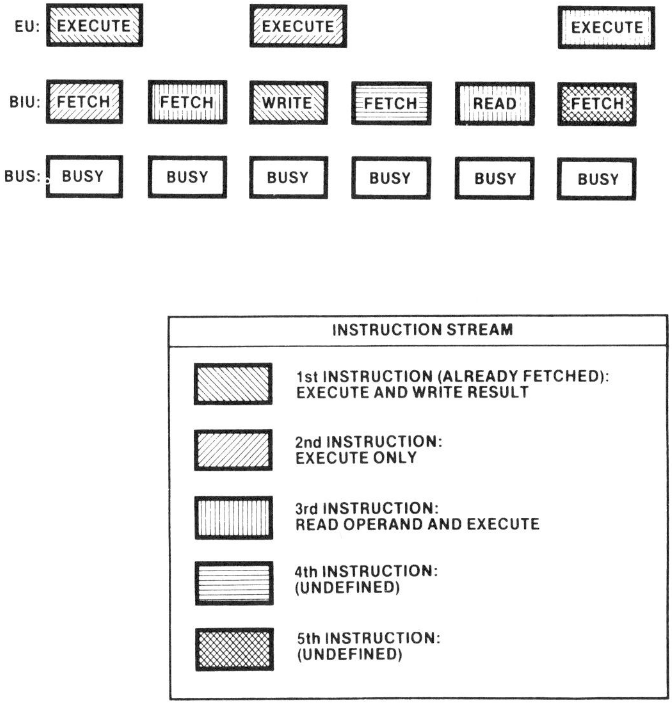

Figure 2.18 Overlapping instruction fetch and execution (*Courtesy of Intel Corporation*)

Also remember that the interaction between the BIU and EU is by way of the queue for prefetched instruction opcodes and immediate operands. On the other hand, bus cycles must be requested of the BIU by the EU for accessing data operands in memory.

Figure 2.19(c) shows in detail the relationships between signals, bus activity, and internal queue status that are important to understand the instruction execution sequence of the 8086. This diagram includes the clock periods (CLK), bus status codes ($\overline{S}_2\overline{S}_1\overline{S}_0$), types of bus cycle (BIU activity), contents of the queue (QUEUE), queue status codes (QS_1QS_0), and instruction execution cycle (EU instruction execution).

Let us now trace the operation of the 8086 step by step through the execution of an instruction from the program in Fig. 2.19(a). In this example we will assume that the jump instruction JMP $-14 has already been read out of the queue by the EU. Therefore, during clock periods 1 through 7 the EU is performing this operation. At clock period 1 in Fig. 2.19(c), we see that the queue has been initialized and contains no valid opcodes. Therefore, during this period, queue sotatus QS_1QS_0 = 10 is output. This indicates that the queue is empty. Moreover, the bus is idle (TI) for clock periods 1 and 2.

The next four clock periods, 3 through 6, represent a code fetch bus cycle. Notice that the bus activity identifies the four clock periods T_1 through T_4 of a read bus cycle. During this bus cycle, $B802_{16}$ is fetched from program storage memory and loaded into the queue. The code fetch status code $\overline{S}_2\overline{S}_1\overline{S}_0 = 100$ is output by the 8086 during periods T_1 and T_2 of the bus cycle.

The next four clock periods, 7 through 10, represent another read bus cycle. This cycle corresponds to the fetch of $F850_{16}$ and its placement in the queue. But at the same time, the EU reads the first two bytes of the MOV instruction from the queue. The first byte, which is $B8_{16}$, is accompanied by the first byte queue status code, $QS_1QS_0 = 01$, and the second byte, 02_{16}, is accompanied by the $QS_1QS_0 = 11$ status code. Remember that this is a three-byte instruction and the last byte, which is $F8_{16}$, was just fetched into the queue. At the end of this second instruction fetch bus cycle, we find that just two bytes, $F8_{16}$ and 50_{16}, remain in the queue. They represent the last byte of the MOV instruction and the complete PUSH instruction.

During clock periods 11 through 14, another code fetch bus cycle takes place. Moreover, during the first half of the bus cycle, the EU removes the third byte of the MOV instruction from the queue. This completes execution of the MOV AX,0F802H instruction. Execution of the remaining instructions proceeds similarly.

ASSEMBLY LANGUAGE	MACHINE CODE
MOV AX, 0F802H	B802F8
PUSH AX	50
MOV CX, BX	8BCB
MOV DX, CX	8BD1
ADD AX, [SI]	0304
ADD SI, 8086H	81C68680
JMP $ -14	EBF0

(a)

B8
02
F8
50
8B
CB
8B
D1
03
04
81
C6
86
80
EB
F0

(b)

Figure 2.19(a) Example program *(Courtesy of Intel Corporation);* **(b)** code storage in memory; **(c)** execution sequence *(Courtesy of Intel Corporation).*

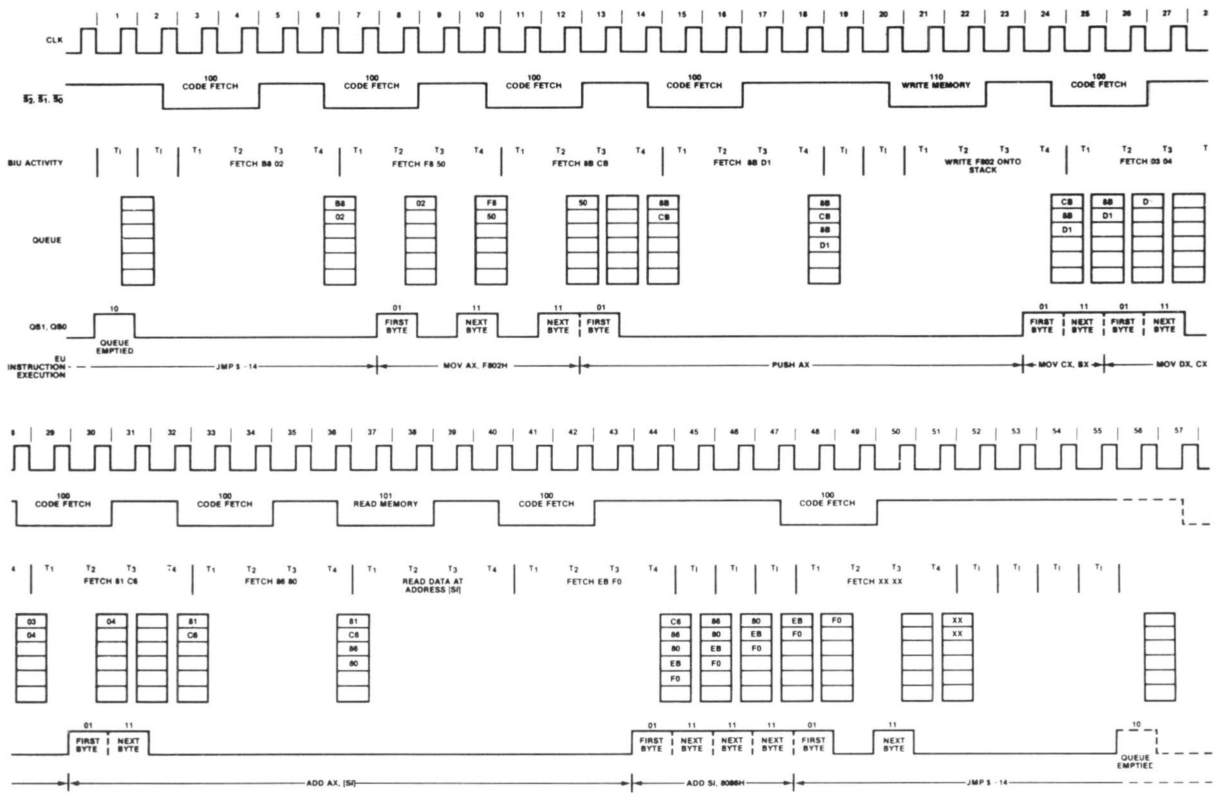

(c)

Figure 2.19 *(continued)*

ASSIGNMENT

Section 2.2

1. Name the technology used to fabricate the 8086 microprocessor.
2. What is the difference between the 8086 and 8088 MPUs?
3. How much memory can the 8086 directly address?
4. How large is the I/O address space of the 8086?

Section 2.3

5. How is the minimum or maximum mode of operation selected?
6. Describe the differences between the minimum-mode 8086 system and the maximum-mode 8086 system.

Section 2.4

7. What are the word lengths of the 8086's address bus and data bus?
8. What does "the status code $S_6S_5S_4S_3$ equals 0001" mean in terms of the memory segment that is being accessed and the interrupt enable/disable status?
9. What signal does the 8086 respond with when it acknowledges an active interrupt request?
10. List the signals that go to the high-Z state in response to a DMA request.

Section 2.5

11. Identify the signal lines of the 8086 that are different for the minimum-mode and maximum-mode interfaces.
12. What control signals are generated by the 8288 bus controller in a maximum-mode system? Which input signals does the 8288 accept from the 8086?
13. What function is served by the 8289 bus arbiter in a maximum-mode 8086 system?
14. If the 8086 executes a jump instruction, what queue status code would be output?
15. Which pins provide signals for local bus control in a maximum-mode 8086 system?

Section 2.6

16. Specify the basic functions served by the bus interface unit and execution unit of the 8086.
17. Describe the internal interface between the BIU and EU.

Section 2.7

18. Make a list of the general-purpose registers of the 8086 and specify their lengths.
19. What dedicated operations are assigned to the general-purpose register?
20. What is the difference between an instruction pointer and a program counter?
21. Identify the pointer and index registers of the 8086. In what way are they different from the general-purpose registers?
22. Why are segment registers provided in the 8086? State the function of each segment register.
23. What is the difference between the functions of status and control flags? Make a list of the status and control flags provided in the 8086. Describe the function of each of these flags.

Section 2.8

24. What is the primary function of the clock generator in an 8086 system? Which signals that are produced by the clock generator are applied to the 8086 MPU?

25. What are the voltage levels of the clock waveform supplied to the 8086 MPU?

Section 2.9

26. Whenever the 8086 reads from or writes to memory, what signal must be received before the bus cycle will run to completion?

27. What is the difference between an idle state and a wait state?

Section 2.10

28. Explain why and how the execution time of the current instruction will be affected by the previous instruction.

3

8086 Microprocessor Programming 1

3.1 INTRODUCTION

Chapter 2 was devoted to the general architectural aspects of the 8086 microprocessor. In this chapter we introduce a large part of its instruction set. These instructions provide the ability to write simple straight-line programs. Chapter 4 covers the rest of the instruction set and some more sophisticated programming concepts. The following topics are presented in this chapter:

1. Software model of the 8086 microprocessor
2. Assembly language and machine language
3. The 8086 addressing modes
4. The 8086 instruction set
5. Data transfer instructions
6. Arithmetic instructions
7. Logic instructions
8. Shift instructions
9. Rotate instructions

3.2 SOFTWARE MODEL OF THE 8086 MICROPROCESSOR

The purpose of developing a *software model* is to aid the programmer in understanding the operation of the microcomputer system from a software point of view. To be able to program a microprocessor, one does not need to know all of its hardware features. For instance, we do not necessarily need to know the function of the signals at its various pins, their electrical connections, or their switching characteristics. Moreover, the function, interconnection, and operation of the internal circuits of the microprocessor also need not normally be considered.

What is important to the programmer is to know the various registers within the device and to understand their purpose, functions, and operating capabilities and limitations. Furthermore, it is essential to know how external memory is organized and how it is addressed to obtain instructions and data.

The software architecture of the 8086 is illustrated with the model in Fig. 3.1. Looking at the model, we see that it includes the 13 internal registers and flags of the 8086 and 1M byte of external memory. Our concern here is with what can be done with this architecture and how to do it through software. For this purpose, let us review briefly the elements of the model. Moreover, this time we concentrate on their relationship to software.

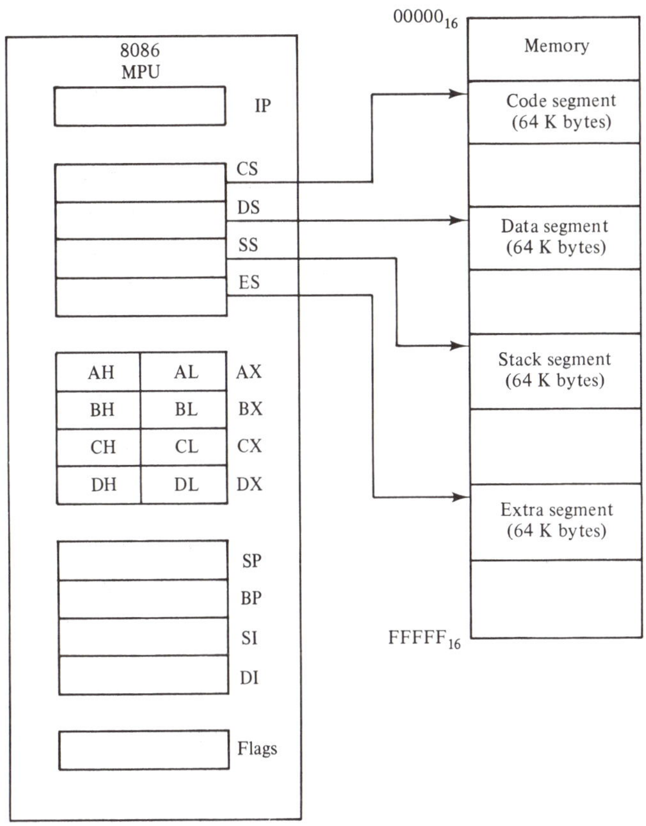

Figure 3.1 Software model of the 8086 microprocessor.

Memory Structure and the Segment Registers

As shown in Fig. 3.1, the 8086 microprocessor supports 1M byte of external memory. This memory space is organized as bytes over the address range 00000_{16} to $FFFFF_{16}$. From an addressing point of view, even- or odd-addressed bytes of data can be independently accessed. Information in the form of 16-bit words can also be stored and accessed. For words of data, the most significant byte is stored at the higher byte address and the least significant byte at the lower byte address.

Notice in Fig. 3.1 that just four 64K-byte segments of memory are active at a time. These segments are called the *code segment, stack segment, data segment*, and *extra segment*. Instructions and data operands in these segments are referenced with the help of the 16-bit segment registers CS, SS, DS, and ES that are located within the microprocessor. Each of these registers contains a 16-bit base address that is used in the generation of the physical memory address that points to the start of the corresponding segment in memory. For example, the code segment register (CS) points to the lowest-addressed location in the current code segment. It is this segment of memory that contains instructions of the program.

The offset of the next instruction that is to be fetched from the current code segment is identified by instruction pointer IP. That is, the contents of CS and IP are combined to form the 20-bit address of the next instruction. After the instruction is fetched, IP is incremented such that it points to the next sequential instruction.

The data segment register (DS) points to the segment of memory in which data to be processed are typically stored. The locations of this segment can be accessed by instructions for use as source or destination operands.

The programmer has the ability to change the values in the segment registers under software control. For example, a new data segment can be established by simply changing the value in DS. This can be done by executing just one or two instructions.

The General-Purpose Registers

The general-purpose group of registers consists of four 16-bit registers called AX, BX, CX, and DX. Each of these registers is addressable as a whole for 16-bit operations or as two 8-bit registers to handle byte operations. For instance, the register AX is a 16-bit register for word operations. But for byte operations, it is considered as two separate 8-bit registers, AH for the high byte and AL for the low byte. In a similar way, word registers BX, CX, and DX are also addressable as byte-wide register pairs BH,BL, CH,CL and DH,DL.

The registers in this group are known as the *accumulator register* (AX or AL,AH), *base register* (BX or BH,BL), *count register* (CX or CH,CL), and the *data register* (DX or DH,DL). These names imply special functions that are performed by each register.

Each of the four general-purpose registers can be used as the source or destination of an operand during an arithmetic, logic, shift, or rotate operation. The use of the accumulator register is also assumed by some instructions. For example, it is either the source or destination register for data during all I/O-mapped input and output operations. Furthermore, multiplication and division arithmetic operations, translate-table operations, and string operations also always use part of the AX register.

During the execution of instructions using what is called the *based addressing mode*, base register BX is used as a pointer to an operand in the current data segment. Thus it contains a memory offset address, not a source or destination operand.

The count register gets its name from the fact that it is used as a counter by some instructions. For instance, its lower byte, CL, contains the count of the number of bits by which the contents of the operand must be rotated or shifted by multiple-bit rotate or shift instructions. It is also used as a counter by string and loop instructions.

The data register, DX, is used in all multiplication and division operations. It must also contain an input/output port address for some types of input/output operations.

Pointer and Index Registers

The next group of four registers consists of two pointer and two index registers. The two pointer registers are the *stack pointer* (SP) and *base pointer* (BP).The contents of the stack pointer are used as an offset from the current value of SS during the execution of instructions that involve the stack segment in external memory. It identifies the location of the top of the stack in the current stack segment. The value in SP is automatically incremented or decremented, respectively, whenever a POP or a PUSH instruction is executed.

The base pointer also contains an offset address into the current stack segment. This offset address is employed when using the based addressing mode and is commonly used by instructions in a subroutine that reference parameters that were passed by way of the stack.

The *source index register* (SI) and the *destination index register* (DI) are used to hold offset addresses for use in indexed addressing of operands in memory. In instructions that use the indexed type of addressing, the source index is generally with reference to the current data segment, and the destination index is with reference to the current extra segment.

The index registers can also be used as source or destination registers in arithmetic and logical operations. Unlike the general-purpose registers, these registers must always be used for 16-bit information and cannot be accessed as two separate bytes.

Flags

The 8086 microprocessor also contains nine 1-bit flags. These flags, identified in Chapter 2, are CF, PF, AF, ZF, SF, TF, IF, DF, and OF. The states of most of these flags reflect the result of the instruction just executed. Specifically, these are the carry, auxiliary carry, zero, sign, parity, and overflow flags. These flag bits can be tested under software control to determine the sequence in which the program should be executed.

The rest of the flags control operating features of the 8086. For instance, the logic level of DF determines whether the contents of the count register are to be incremented or decremented during string operations. Similarly, the flags IF and TF are used to enable/disable interrupts and the single-step mode of operation, respectively. The instruction set of the 8086 includes instructions for saving, loading, and manipulating these flags.

3.3 ASSEMBLY LANGUAGE AND MACHINE LANGUAGE

Now that we have introduced the software model of the 8086, let us continue with the concepts of *assembly language* and *machine language* instructions and programs. It is essential to become familiar with these ideas before attempting to learn the functions of the instructions in the instruction set and their use in writing programs.

Assembly Language Instructions

Assembly language instructions are provided to describe each of the basic operations that can be performed by a microprocessor. They are written using *alphanumeric symbols* instead of the 0s and 1s of the microprocessor's machine code. An example of a short assembly language program is shown in Fig. 3.2(a). The assembly language statements are located on the left. Frequently, comments describing the statements are included on the right. This type of documentation makes it easier for programmers to write, read, and debug code. By the term ''code'' we mean programs written in the language of the microprocessor. Programs written in assembly language are called *source code*.

Each instruction in the source program corresponds to one assembly language statement. The statement must specify which operation is to be performed and what data operands are to be processed. For this reason, an instruction can be divided into two separate parts: its *opcode* and its *operands*. The opcode is the part of the instruction that identifies the operation that is to be performed. For example, typical operations are add, subtract, and move.

In assembly language, we assign a unique one-, two-, or three-letter combination to each operation. This letter combination is referred to as a *mnemonic* for the instruction. For instance, the 8086 assembly language mnemonics for add, subtract, and move are ADD, SUB, and MOV, respectively.

Operands identify the data that are to be processed by the microprocessor as it carries out the operation specified by the opcode. For instance, in an instruction that adds the contents of the base register to the accumulator, BX and AX are the operands. An assembly language description of this instruction is

```
ADD AX,BX
```

In this example, the contents of BX and AX are added together and their sum is put in AX. Therefore, BX is considered to be the *source operand* and AX the *destination operand*.

Here is another example of an assembly language statement:

```
LOOP: MOV AX,BX        ;COPY BX INTO AX
```

```
NAME    EXAMPLE←1

ASSUME  CS:PROG←CODE, DS:MAIN←DATA

MAIN←DATA   SEGMENT

        NUMBERS      DW  10,30,53,72,233,51,122
        SUM          DW  ?

MAIN←DATA   ENDS

PROG←CODE   SEGMENT

PROG←START: MOV     AX,MAIN←DATA
            MOV     DS,AX              ;LOAD DS WITH SEG ADDRESS OF DATA
            MOV     BX,OFFSET NUMBERS  ;LOAD BX WITH OFFSET
            MOV     CX,7               ;LOAD CX WITH COUNT
            MOV     AX,0               ;CLEAR AX
LOOP1:      ADD     AX,[BX]            ;ADD DATA POINTED TO BY BX TO AX
            INC     BX                 ;INC POINTER
            LOOPNZ  LOOP1              ;LOOP UNTIL DONE
            MOV     SUM,AX             ;STORE RESULT
            HLT                        ;HALT
PROG←CODE   ENDS
END PROG←START
```

(a)

```
LOC  OBJ              LINE   SOURCE

                        1    NAME    EXAMPLE←1
                        2
                        3    ASSUME  CS:PROG←CODE, DS:MAIN←DATA
                        4
----                    5    MAIN←DATA   SEGMENT
                        6
0000 0A00               7            NUMBERS      DW  10,30,53,72,233,51,122
0002 1E00
0004 3500
0006 4800
0008 E900
000A 3300
000C 7A00
000E ????               8            SUM          DW  ?
                        9
----                   10    MAIN←DATA   ENDS
                       11
----                   12    PROG←CODE   SEGMENT
                       13
0000 B8----      R     14    PROG←START: MOV     AX,MAIN←DATA
0003 8ED8              15                MOV     DS,AX              ;LOAD DS WITH SEG ADDRESS OF DATA
0005 BB0000            16                MOV     BX,OFFSET NUMBERS  ;LOAD BX WITH OFFSET
0008 B90700            17                MOV     CX,7               ;LOAD CX WITH COUNT
000B B80000            18                MOV     AX,0               ;CLEAR AX
000E 0307              19    LOOP1:      ADD     AX,[BX]            ;ADD DATA POINTED TO BY BX TO AX
0010 43                20                INC     BX                 ;INC POINTER
0011 E0FB              21                LOOPNZ  LOOP1              ;LOOP UNTIL DONE
0013 A30E00            22                MOV     SUM,AX             ;STORE RESULT
0016 F4                23                HLT                        ;HALT
----                   24    PROG←CODE   ENDS
                       25    END PROG←START
```

(b)

Figure 3.2(a) Typical 8086 assembly language program *(Courtesy of Intel Corporation);* **(b)** assembled machine code *(Courtesy of Intel Corporation).*

This instruction statement starts with the word LOOP. It is an address identifier for the instruction MOV AX,BX. This type of identifier is called a *label* or *tag*. The instruction is followed by "COPY BX INTO AX." This part of the statement is called a *comment*. Thus a general format for writing an assembly language statement is

LABEL: INSTRUCTION ;COMMENT

Machine Language Instructions

Before a source program can be executed by the microprocessor, it must first be run through a process known as *assembling*. This is normally done on a minicomputer or microcomputer with a program called an *assembler*. The result produced by this step is an equivalent program expressed in the *machine code* that is executed by the microprocessor. That is, it is the equivalent of the source program but now written in 0s and 1s. This program is also referred to as *object code*.

Figure 3.2(b) is a listing that includes the machine language program for the assembly language program in Fig. 3.2(a). It was produced by an 8086 assembler. Reading from left to right, this listing contains addresses of memory locations, followed by the machine code instructions, the original assembly language statements, and comments. Notice that for simplicity the machine code instructions are expressed in hexadecimal notation and not as binary numbers.

3.4 THE 8086 ADDRESSING MODES

When the 8086 executes an instruction, it performs the specified function on data. These data are called its *operands* and may be part of the instruction, reside in one of the internal registers of the 8086, stored at an address in memory, or held at an I/O port. To access these different types of operands, the 8086 is provided with various *addressing modes*. Here are the modes available on the 8086: *register addressing, immediate addressing, direct addressing, register indirect addressing, based addressing. indexed addressing, based indexed addressing, string addressing*, and *port addressing*.

Of these nine modes, all but register addressing and immediate addressing make reference to an operand stored in memory. Therefore, they require the BIU to initiate a read or write bus cycle to the memory subsystem. Thus the addressing modes provide different ways of computing the address of the operand that is output on the address bus during the bus cycle. Let us now consider in detail each of these addressing modes.

Register Addressing Mode

With the register addressing mode, the operand to be accessed is specified as residing in an internal register of the 8086. An example of an instruction that uses this addressing mode is

MOV AX,BX

This stands for move the contents of BX, the *source operand*, to AX, the *destination operand*. Both the source and destination operands have been specified as the contents of internal registers of the 8086.

Let us now look at the effect of executing the register addressing mode MOV instruction. In Fig. 3.3(a) we see the state of the 8086 just prior to fetching the instruction. Notice that IP and CS point to the MOV AX,BX instruction at address 01000_{16}. Prior to execution of this instruction, the contents of BX are $ABCD_{16}$ and the contents of AX represent a don't-care state. As shown in Fig. 3.3(b), the result of executing the instruction is that $ABCD_{16}$ is copied into AX.

Immediate Addressing Mode

If a source operand is part of the instruction instead of the contents of a register or memory location, it represents what is called an *immediate operand* and is accessed using the immediate addressing mode. Typically, immediate operands represent constant data.

Immediate operands can be either a byte or word of data. In the instruction

MOV AL,015H

the source operand 15_{16} is an example of a byte-wide immediate source operand. Note that the value of the immediate operand must always be preceded by a zero. The destination operand, which is the contents of AL, uses register addressing. Thus this instruction employs both the immediate and register addressing modes.

Figure 3.4(a) and (b) illustrate fetch and execution of this instruction. Here we find that the immediate operand 15_{16} is stored in program storage memory in the byte location immediately following the opcode of the instruction. This value is also fetched into the instruction queue in the BIU. When the EU performs the MOV operation, the source operand is fetched from the instruction queue; therefore, no external memory bus cycle is initiated. The result of executing this instruction is that the immediate operand is loaded into the lower byte part (AL) of the accumulator register.

Direct Addressing Mode

Direct addressing differs from immediate addressing in that the locations following the instruction opcode hold an *effective memory address* (EA) instead of data. This effective address is a 16-bit offset of the storage location of the operand from the current value in the data segment (DS) register. EA is combined with the contents of DS in the BIU to produce the *physical address* of the operand.

An example of an instruction that uses direct addressing for its source operand is

MOV CX,BETA

This stands for "move the contents of the memory location which is offset by BETA from the current value in DS into internal register CX."

In Fig. 3.5(a) we find that the value of the offset is stored in the two byte locations that follow the instruction. It is also known as the *displacement*. Notice that the value assigned to constant BETA is 1234_{16}. As the instruction is executed, the

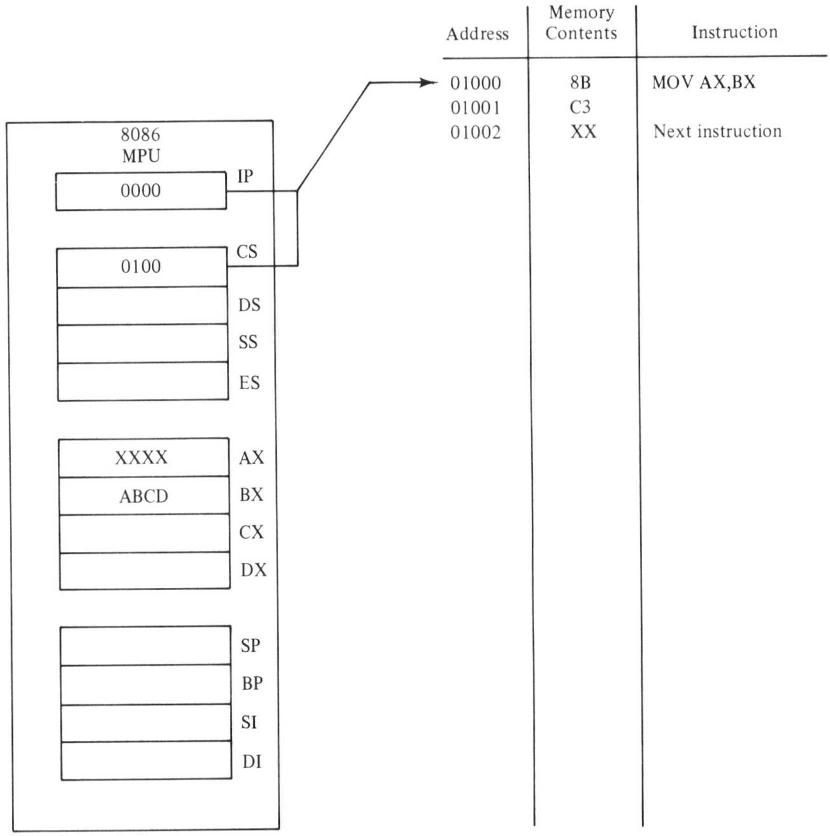

(a)

Figure 3.3(a) Register addressing mode instruction before execution; **(b)** after execution.

BIU combines 1234_{16} with 0200_{16} to set the physical address of the source operand. This gives

$$PA = 02000_{16} + 1234_{16}$$
$$= 03234_{16}$$

Then it initiates an external memory bus cycle to read the word of data starting at this address. This value is $BEED_{16}$. The execution unit causes this value to be loaded in the CX register. This result is illustrated in Fig. 3.5(b).

Register Indirect Addressing Mode

Register indirect addressing is similar to direct addressing in that an effective address is combined with the contents of DS to obtain a physical address. However, it differs in the way the offset is specified. This time EA resides in either a pointer register

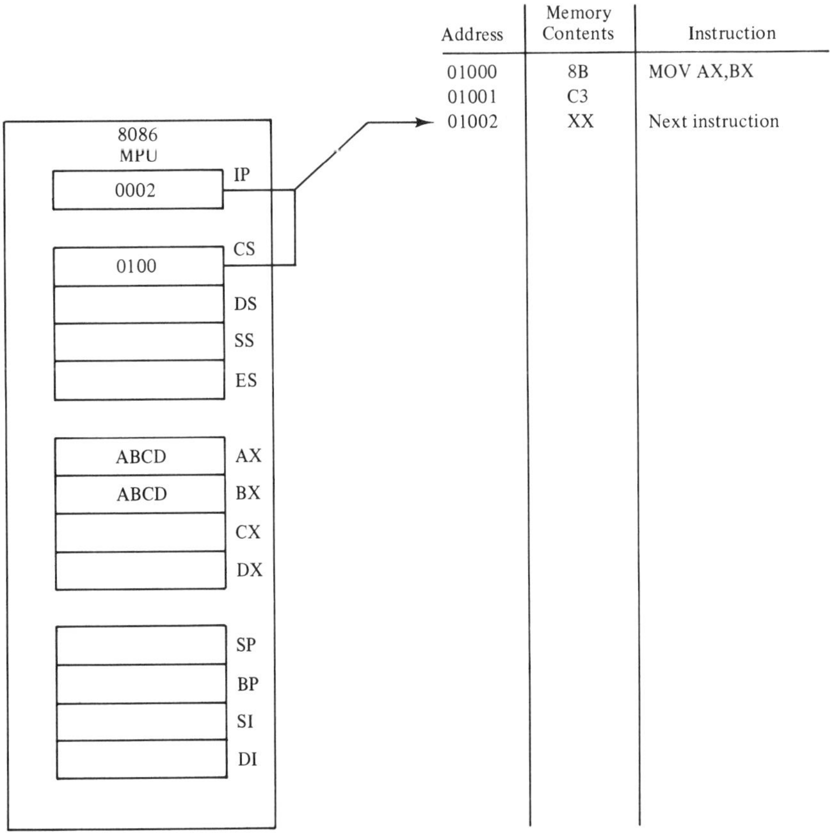

(b)

Figure 3.3 *(continued)*

or an index register within the 8086. The pointer register can be either base register BX or base pointer register BP, and the index register can be source index register SI, or destination index register DI.

An example of an instruction that uses register indirect addressing is

MOV AX,[SI]

This instruction moves the contents of the memory location offset by the value of EA in SI from the current value in DS to the AX register.

For instance, as shown in Fig. 3.6(a) and (b), if SI contains 1234_{16} and DS contains 0200_{16}, the result produced by executing the instruction is that the contents of memory location

$$PA = 02000_{16} + 1234_{16}$$
$$= 03234_{16}$$

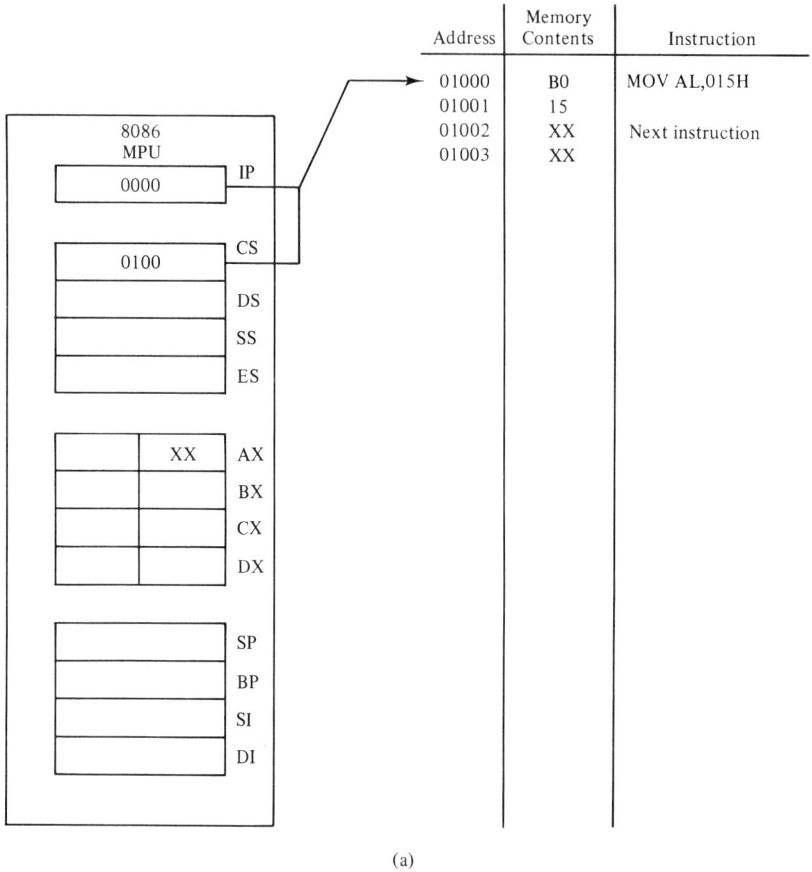

Figure 3.4(a) Immediate addressing mode instruction before execution; **(b)** after execution.

are moved to the AX register. Notice in Fig. 3.6(b) that this value is $BEED_{16}$. In this example, the value 1234_{16} that was found in the SI register must be loaded with another instruction prior to the MOV instruction.

Notice that the result produced by executing this instruction and the example for the direct addressing mode are the same. However, they differ in the way in which the physical address was generated. The direct addressing method lends itself to applications where the value of EA is a constant. On the other hand, register indirect addressing can be used when the value of EA is calculated and stored for example in SI by a previous instruction. That is, EA is a variable.

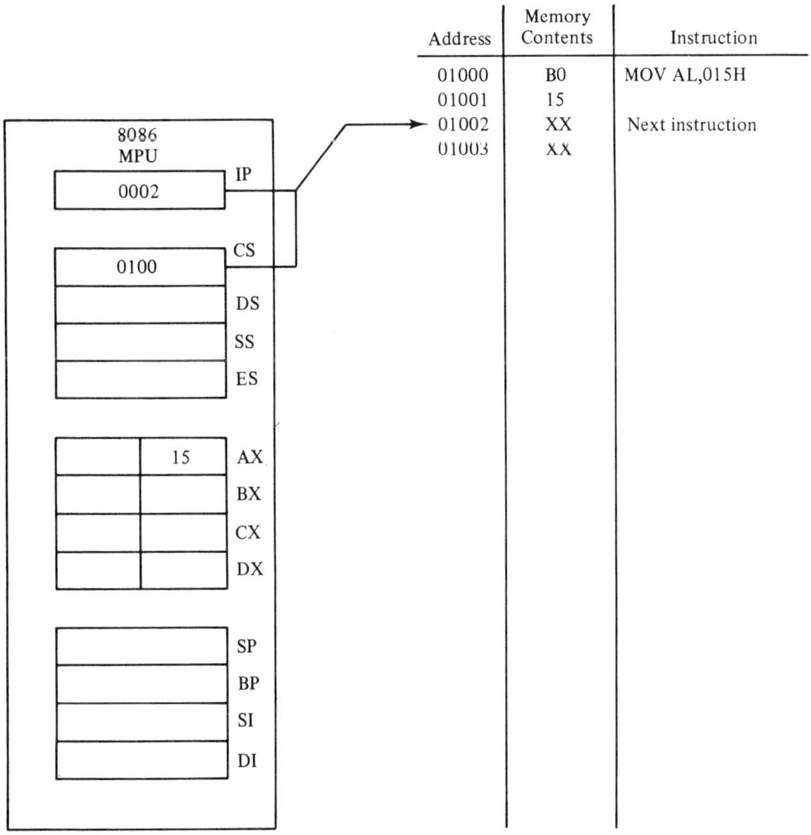

(b)

Figure 3.4 *(continued)*

Based Addressing Mode

In the based addressing mode, the physical address of the operand is obtained by adding a direct or indirect displacement to the contents of either base register BX or base pointer register BP and the current value in DS and SS, respectively. A MOV instruction that uses based addressing to specify the location of its destination operand is as follows:

MOV [BX].BETA,AL

This instruction uses base register BX and direct displacement BETA to derive the EA of the destination operand. The based addressing mode is implemented by specify-

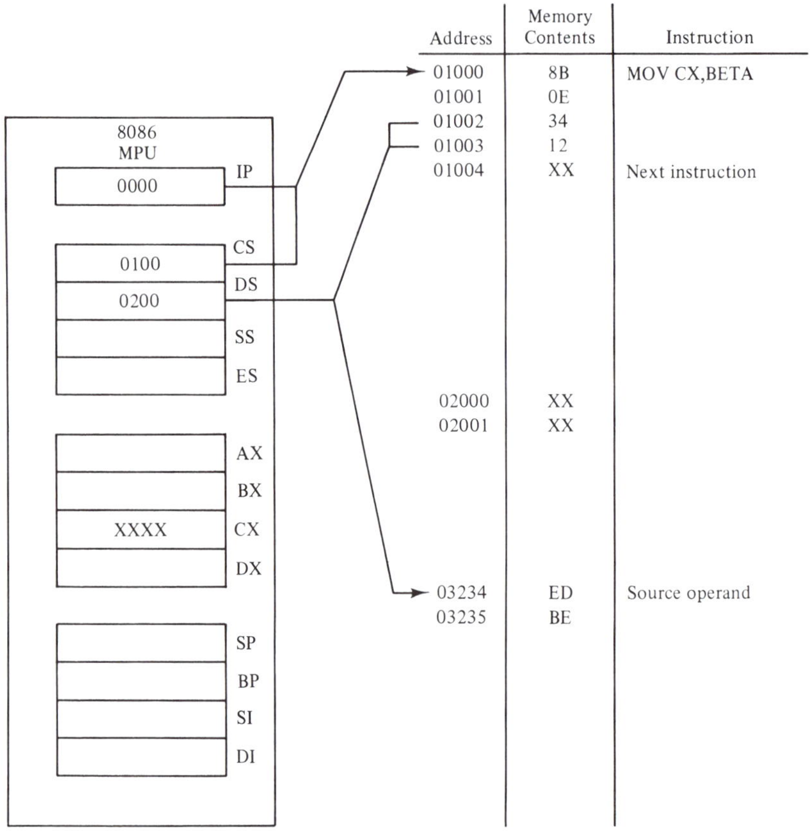

(a)

Figure 3.5(a) Direct addressing mode instruction before execution; **(b)** after execution.

ing the base register in brackets followed by a period and the direct displacement. The source operand in this example is located in byte accumulator AL.

As shown in Fig. 3.7(a) and (b), the fetch and execution of this instruction causes the BIU to calculate the physical address of the destination operand from the contents of DS, BX, and the direct displacement. The result is

$$PA = 02000_{16} + 1000_{16} + 1234_{16}$$
$$= 04234_{16}$$

Then upon request of the EU it initiates a write bus cycle such that the source operand, AL, is written into the storage location at 04234_{16}. The result is that ED_{16} is copied into the destination memory location.

If BP is used instead of BX, the calculation of the physical address is performed using the contents of the stack segment (SS) register instead of DS. This permits access to data in the stack segment of memory.

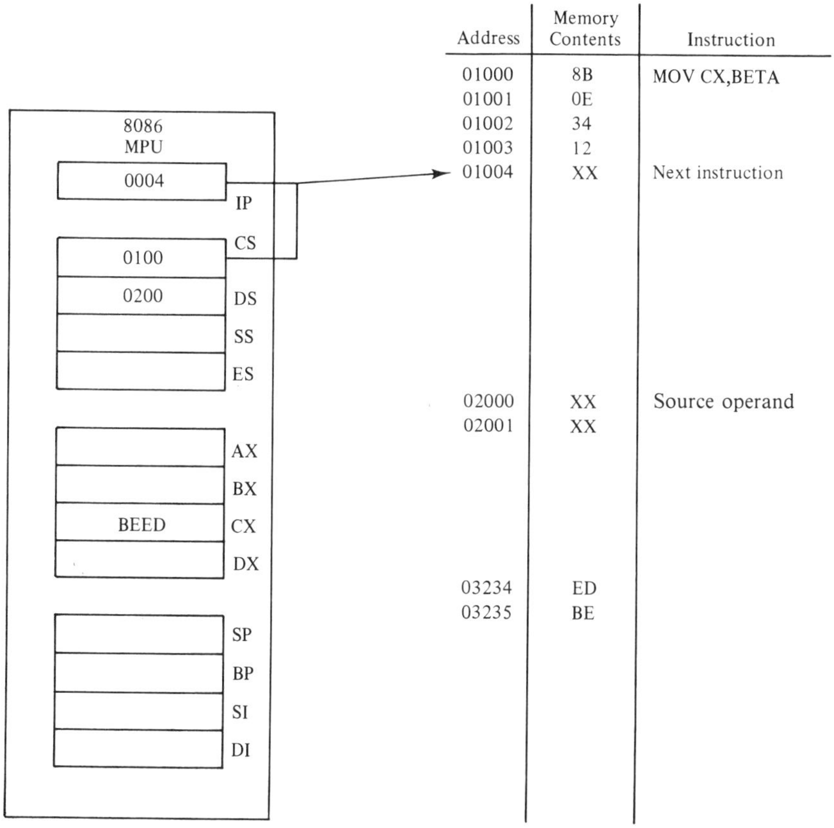

(b)

Figure 3.5 *(continued)*

Indexed Addressing Mode

Indexed addressing works identically to the based addressing we just described; however, it uses the contents of one of the index registers, instead of BX or BP, in the generation of the physical address. Here is an example:

MOV AL,ARRAY[SI]

The source operand has been specified using direct indexed addressing. Notice that the notation this time is such that ARRAY, which is a direct displacement, prefixes the selected index register, SI. Just like for the base register in based addressing, the index register is enclosed in brackets.

The effective address is calculated as

$$EA = (SI) + ARRAY$$

and the physical address is obtained by combining the contents of DS with EA.

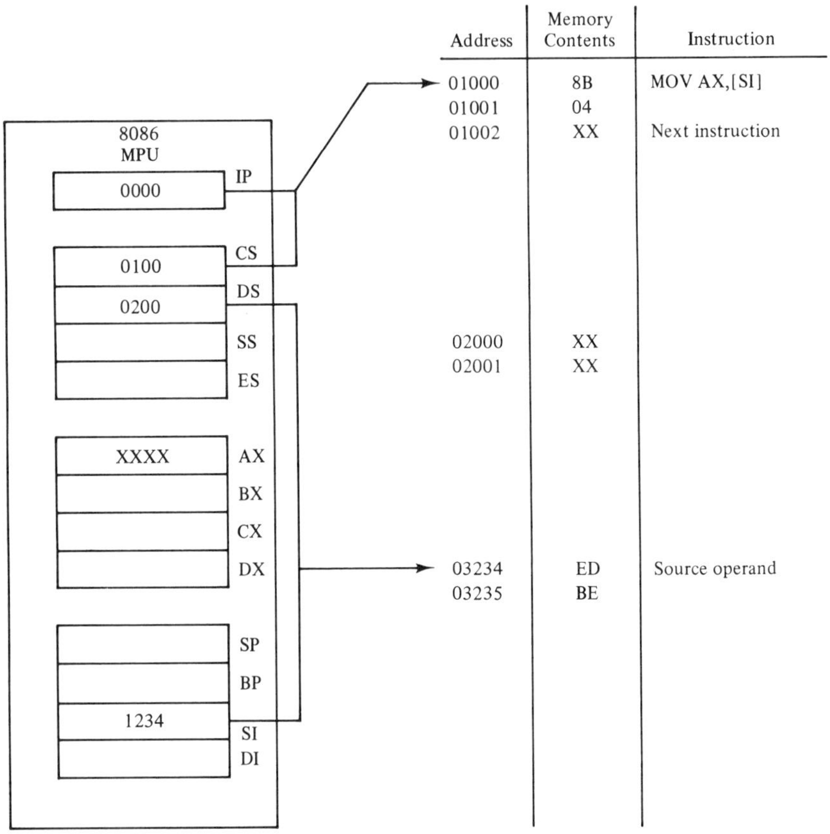

(a)

Figure 3.6(a) Instruction using register indirect addressing before execution; **(b)** after execution.

The example in Fig. 3.8(a) and (b) shows the result of executing the MOV instruction. First the physical address of the source operand is calculated from DS, SI, and the direct displacement.

$$PA = 02000_{16} + 2000_{16} + 1234_{16}$$
$$= 05234_{16}$$

Then the byte of data stored at this location, which is BE_{16}, is read into lower byte AL of the accumulator register.

Based Indexed Addressing Mode

Combining the based addressing mode and the indexed addressing mode together results in a new, more powerful mode known as based indexed addressing. Let us consider an example of a MOV instruction using this type of addressing.

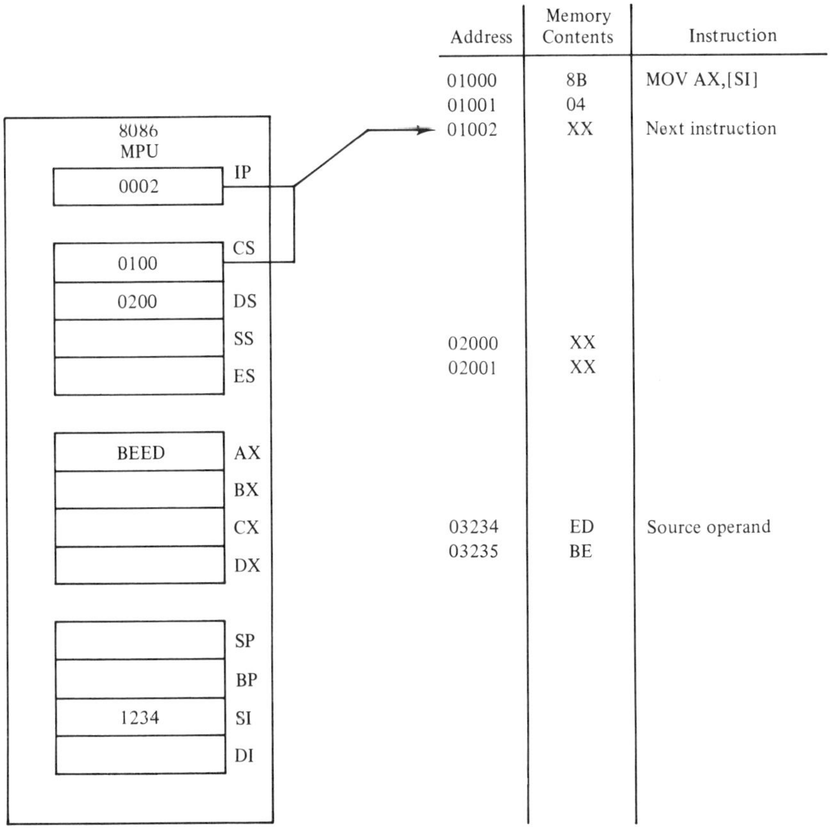

(b)

Figure 3.6 *(continued)*

MOV AH,[BX].BETA[SI]

Notice that the source operand is accessed using based indexed addressing mode. Therefore, the effective address of the source operand is obtained as

$$EA = (BX) + BETA + (SI)$$

and the physical address of the operand from the current DS and the calculated EA.

An example of executing this instruction is illustrated in Fig. 3.9(a) and (b). The address of the source operand is calculated as

$$\begin{aligned} PA &= 02000_{16} + 1000_{16} + 1234_{16} + 2000_{16} \\ &= 6234_{16} \end{aligned}$$

Execution of the instruction causes the value stored at this location to be written into AH.

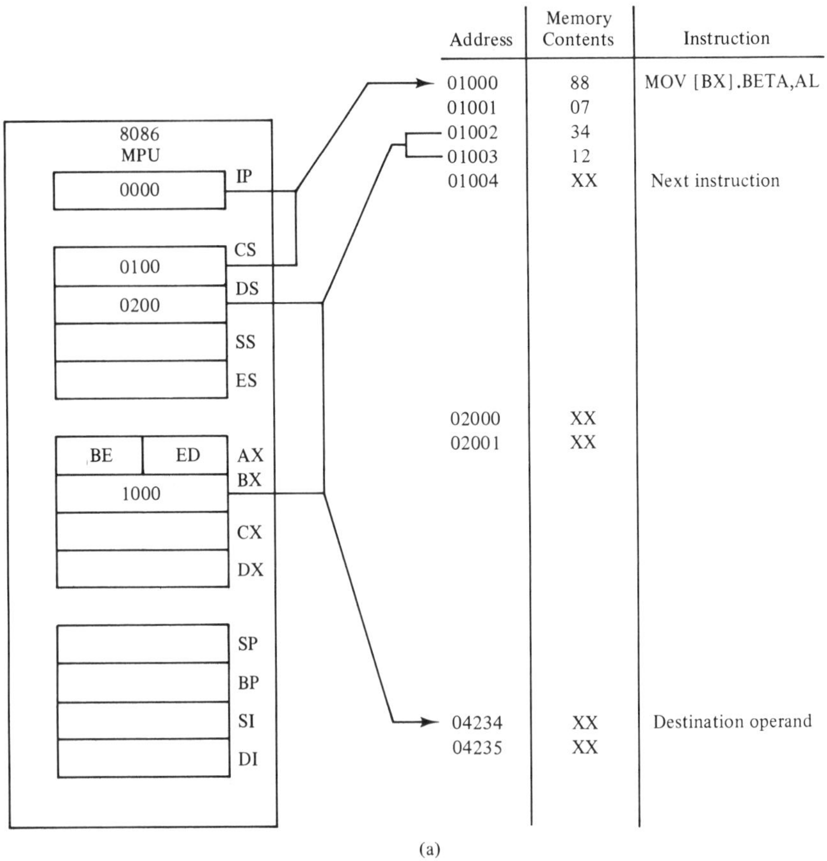

Figure 3.7(a) Instruction using direct base pointer addressing before execution; **(b)** after execution.

String Addressing Mode

The string instructions of the 8086's instruction set automatically use the source and destination index registers to specify the effective addresses of the source and destination operands, respectively. The move string instruction

MOVS

is an example. Notice that neither SI nor DI appears in the string instruction, but both are used during its execution.

Port Addressing Mode

Port addressing is used in conjunction with the IN and OUT instructions to access input and output ports. Any of the memory addressing modes can be used for the port address for memory-mapped ports. For ports in the I/O address space, only

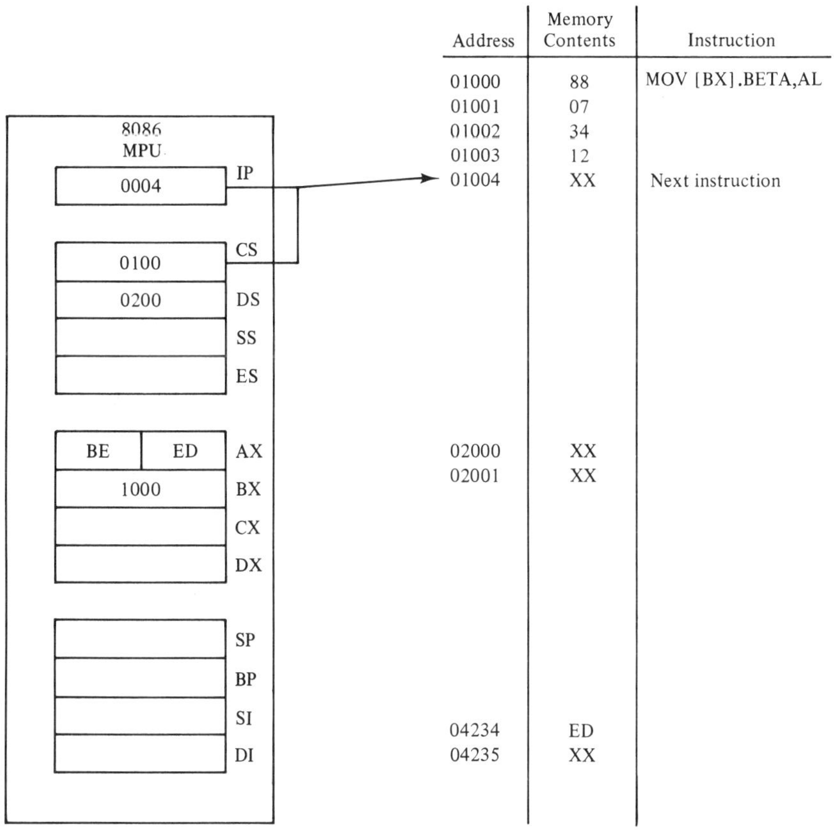

(b)

Figure 3.7 *(continued)*

the direct addressing mode and an indirect addressing mode using DX are available. For example, direct addressing of an input port is used in the instruction

IN AL,15H

This stands for "input the data from the byte wide input port at address 15_{16} of the I/O address space to register AL."

Next, let us consider another example. Using indirect port addressing for the source operand in an IN instruction, we get

IN AL,DX

It means "input the data from the byte-wide input port whose address is specified by the contents of register DX." For instance, if (DX) equals 1234_{16}, the contents of the port at this I/O address are loaded into AL.

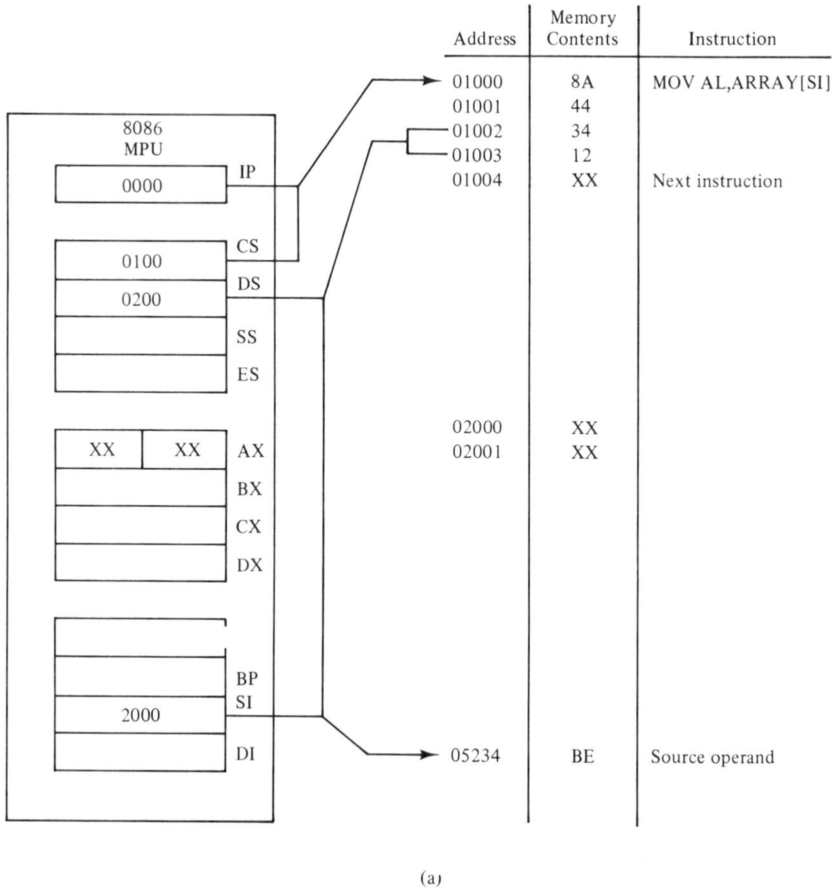

Figure 3.8(a) Instruction using direct indexed addressing before execution; **(b)** after execution.

3.5 INSTRUCTION SET

Having introduced a software model and the various addressing modes of the 8086 microprocessor, we will now continue with its *instruction set*.

The 8086 microprocessor provides a powerful instruction set containing 117 basic instructions. The wide range of operands and addressing modes permitted for use with these instructions further expand the instruction set into many more instructions executable at the machine code level. For instance, the basic MOV instruction expands into 28 different machine level instructions.

For the purpose of discussion, the instruction set will be divided into a number of groups of functionally related instructions. In this chapter we consider the data transfer instructions, arithmetic instructions, logic instructions, shift instructions, and

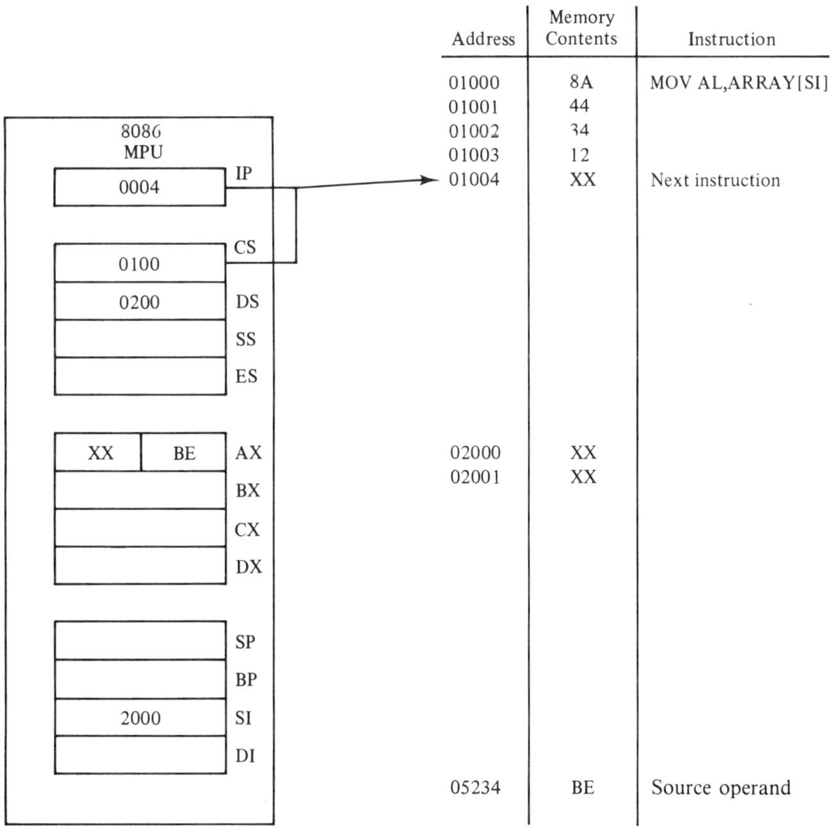

(b)

Figure 3.8 *(continued)*

rotate instructions. Advanced instructions such as those for program and processor control are described in Chapter 4.

3.6 DATA TRANSFER INSTRUCTIONS

The 8086 microprocessor has a group of *data transfer instructions* that are provided to move data either between its internal registers or between an internal register and a storage location in memory. This group includes the *move byte or word* (MOV) instruction, *exchange byte or word* (XCHG) instruction, *translate byte* (XLAT) instruction, *load effective address* (LEA) instruction, *load data segment* (LDS) instruction, and *load extra segment* (LES) instruction. These instructions are discussed in this section.

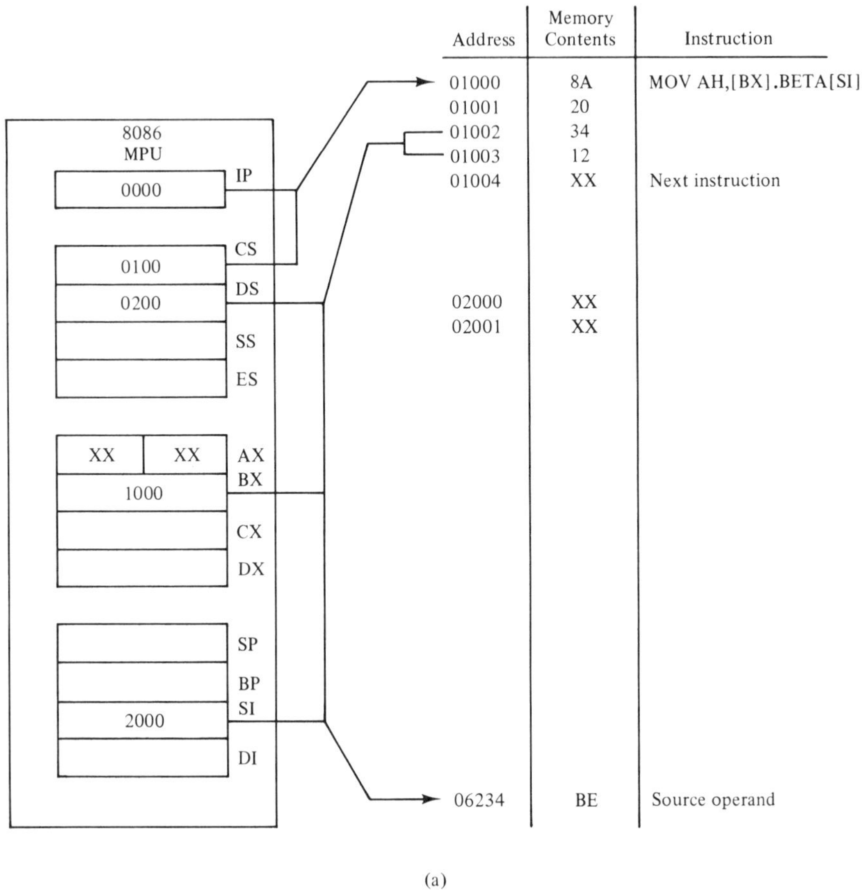

Figure 3.9(a) Instruction using based indexed addressing before execution; **(b)** after execution.

The MOV Instruction

The MOV instruction of Fig. 3.10(a) is used to transfer a byte or a word of data from a source operand to a destination operand. These operands can be internal registers of the 8086 and storage locations in memory. Figure 3.10(b) shows the valid source and destination operand variations. This large choice of operands results in many different MOV instructions. Looking at this list of operands, we see that data can be moved between general-purpose registers, between a general-purpose register and a segment register, between a general-purpose register or segment register and memory, or between a memory location and the accumulator.

Notice that the MOV instruction cannot transfer data directly between a source and a destination that both reside in external memory. Instead, the data must first be moved from memory into an internal register, such as to the accumulator (AX),

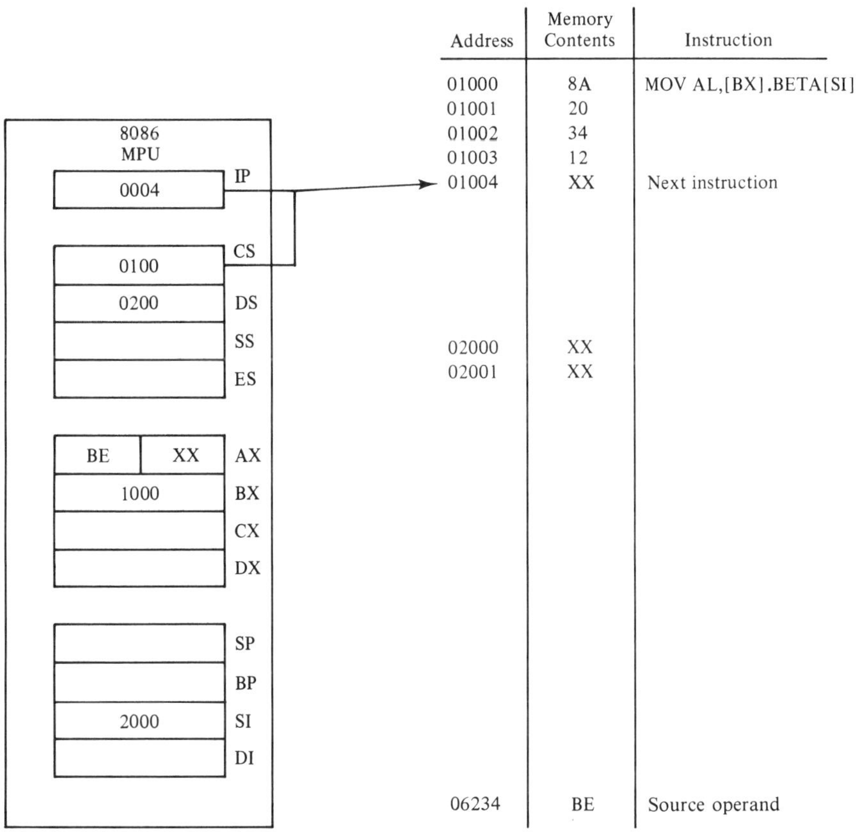

(b)

Figure 3.9 *(continued)*

with one move instruction and then moved to the new location in memory with a second move instruction.

All transfers between general-purpose registers and memory can involve either a byte or word of data. The fact that the instruction corresponds to byte or word data is designated by the way in which its operands are specified. For instance, AL or AH would be used to specify a byte operand, and AX a word operand. On the other hand, data moved between one of the general-purpose registers and a segment register or between a segment register and a memory location must always be word-wide.

In Fig. 3.10(a) we also find additional important information. For instance, flag bits within the 8086 are not modified by execution of a MOV instruction.

An example of a segment register to general-purpose register MOV instruction shown in Fig. 3.10(c) is

Mnemonic	Meaning	Format	Operation	Flags Affected
MOV	Move	MOV D,S	(S) → (D)	None

(a)

Destination	Source
Memory	Accumulator
Accumulator	Memory
Register	Register
Register	Memory
Memory	Register
Register	Immediate
Memory	Immediate
Seg-reg	Reg16
Seg-reg	Mem16
Reg16	Seg-reg
Mem16	Seg-reg

(b)

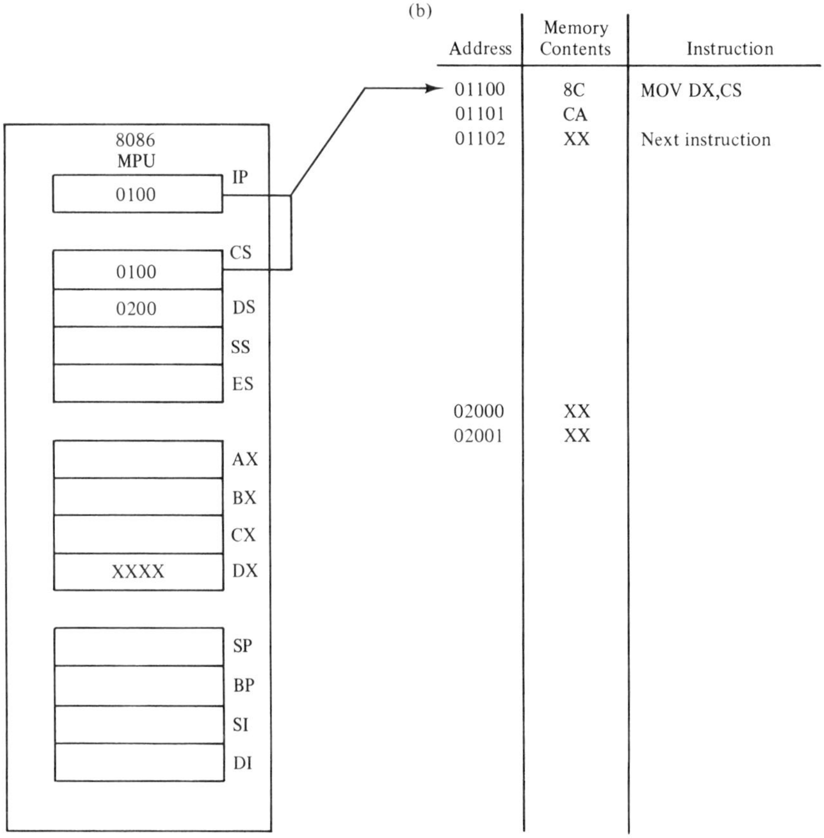

(c)

Figure 3.10(a) MOV data transfer instruction; **(b)** allowed operands; **(c)** MOV DX,CS instruction before execution; **(d)** after execution.

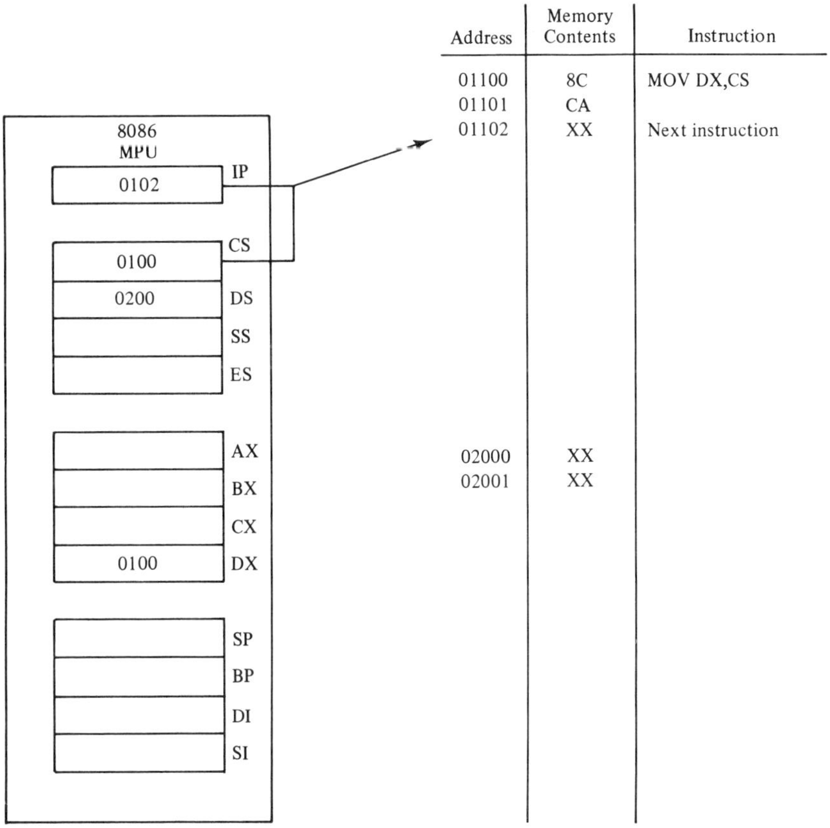

(d)

Figure 3.10 *(continued)*

MOV DX,CS

In this instruction, the code segment register is the source operand and the data register is the destination. It stands for "move the contents of CS into DX." That is,

$$(CS) \longrightarrow (DX)$$

For example, if the contents of CS are 0100_{16}, execution of the instruction MOV DX,CS as shown in Fig. 3.10(d) makes

$$(DX) = (CS) = 0100_{16}$$

In all memory reference MOV instructions, the machine code for the instruction includes an offset address relative to the contents of the data segment register. An example of this type of instruction is

MOV SUM,AX

In this instruction, the memory location identified by the variable SUM is specified using direct addressing. That is, the value of the offset is included in the two byte locations that follow its opcode in program memory.

Let us assume that the contents of DS equals 0200_{16} and that SUM corresponds to a displacement of 1212_{16}; then this instruction means "move the contents of accumulator AX to the memory location offset by 1212_{16} from the starting location of the current data segment." The physical address of this location is obtained as

$$PA = 02000_{16} + 1212_{16} = 03212_{16}$$

Thus the effect of the instruction is

$$(AL) \longrightarrow (\text{MEMORY LOCATION } 03212_{16})$$
$$(AH) \longrightarrow (\text{MEMORY LOCATION } 03213_{16})$$

Example 3.1

If the DS register contains 1234_{16}, what is the effect of executing the instruction:

MOV CX,[0ABCDH]

Solution. Execution of this instruction has the following results:

$$((DS)0_{16} + ABCD_{16}) \quad (CL)$$
$$((DS)0_{16} + ABCD_{16} + 1_{16}) \quad (CH)$$

In other words, CL is loaded with the contents of memory location

$$12340_{16} + ABCD_{16} = 1CF0D_1$$

and CH is loaded with the contents of memory location

$$12340_{16} + ABCD_{16} + 1_{16} = 1CF0E_{16}$$

In example 3.1, source operand $ABCD_{16}$ has been considered to be the direct address of a memory location. The question is why $ABCD_{16}$ does not represent immediate data that are to be loaded into CX. The answer to this question is given by how the 8086's assembler codes instructions. An immediate mode transfer is specified by enclosing $0ABCD_{16}$ with brackets. Therefore, the instruction would have to have been written as

MOV CX,0ABCD

to represent an immediate data operand. The result produced by this instruction is

$$ABCD_{16} \longrightarrow (CX)$$

The XCHG Instruction

In our study of the move instruction, we found that it could be used to copy the contents of a register or memory location into a register or contents of a memory location to a register. In all cases, the original contents of the source location are preserved and the original contents of the destination are destroyed. In some applications, it is required to interchange the contents of two registers. For instance, we might want to exchange the data in the AX and BX registers.

This could be done using multiple move instructions and storage of the data in a temporary register such as DX. However, to perform the exchange function more efficiently, a special instruction has been provided in the instruction set of the 8086. This is the exchange (XCHG) instruction. The forms of the XCHG instruction and its allowed operands are shown in Fig. 3.11(a) and (b). Here we see that it can be used to swap data between two general-purpose registers or between a general-purpose register and a storage location in memory. In particular, it allows for the exchange of words of data between one of the general-purpose registers, including the pointers and index registers, and the accumulator (AX); exchange of a byte or word of data between one of the general-purpose registers and a location in memory; or between two of the general-purpose registers.

Let us consider an example of an exchange between two internal registers. Here is a typical instruction:

XCHG AX,DX

Its execution by the 8086 swaps the contents of AX with that of DX. That is,

$$(\text{AX original}) \rightarrow (\text{DX})$$

$$(\text{DX original}) \rightarrow (\text{AX})$$

or

$$(\text{AX}) \leftrightarrow (\text{DX})$$

Example 3.2

For the data shown in Fig. 3.11(c), what is the result of executing the instruction

XCHG SUM,BX ?

Solution. Execution of this instruction performs the function

$$((\text{DS})0 + \text{SUM}) \leftrightarrow (\text{BX})$$

In Fig. 3.11(c) we see that (DS) = 0200_{16} and the direct address SUM = 1234_{16}. Therefore, the physical address is

$$\text{PA} = 02000_{16} + 1234_{16} = 03234_{16}$$

Notice that this location contains FF_{16} and the address that follows contains 00_{16}. Moreover, note that BL contains AA_{16} and BH contains 11_{16}.

Execution of the instruction performs the following 16-bit swap.

$$(03234_{16}) \leftrightarrow (\text{BL})$$

$$(03235_{16}) \leftrightarrow (\text{BH})$$

As shown in Fig. 3.11(d), we get

$$(\text{BX}) = 00FF_{16}$$

$$(\text{SUM}) = 11AA_{16}$$

Mnemonic	Meaning	Format	Operation	Flags Affected
XCHG	Exchange	XCHG D,S	(D) ↔ (S)	None

(a)

Destination	Source
Accumulator	Reg16
Memory	Register
Register	Register

(b)

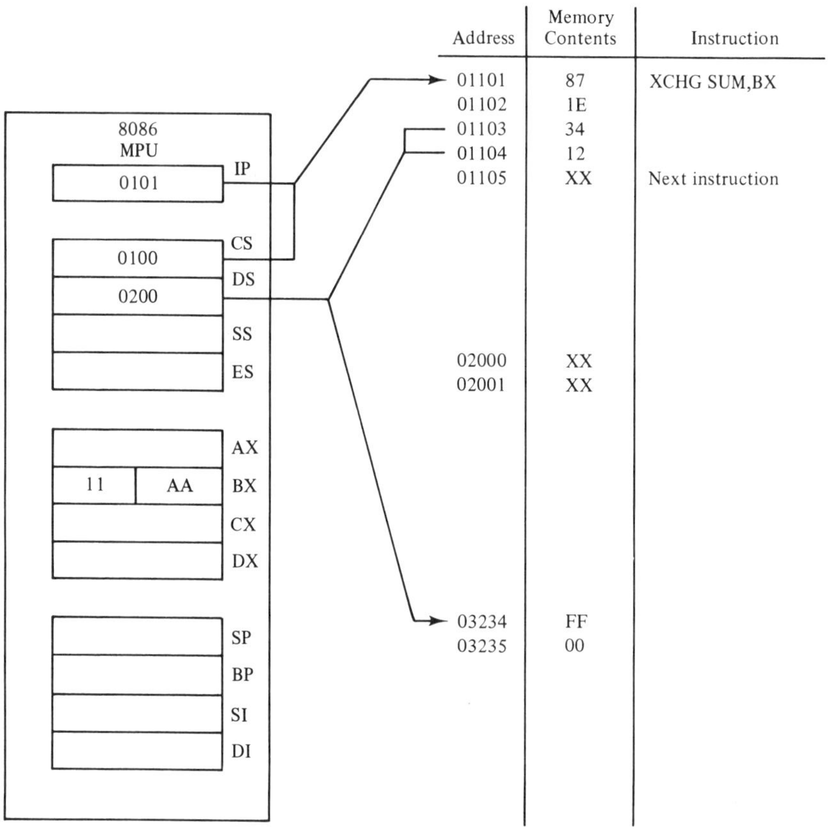

(c)

Figure 3.11(a) Exchange data transfer instruction; **(b)** allowed operands; **(c)** XCHG SUM, AX instruction before execution; **(d)** after execution.

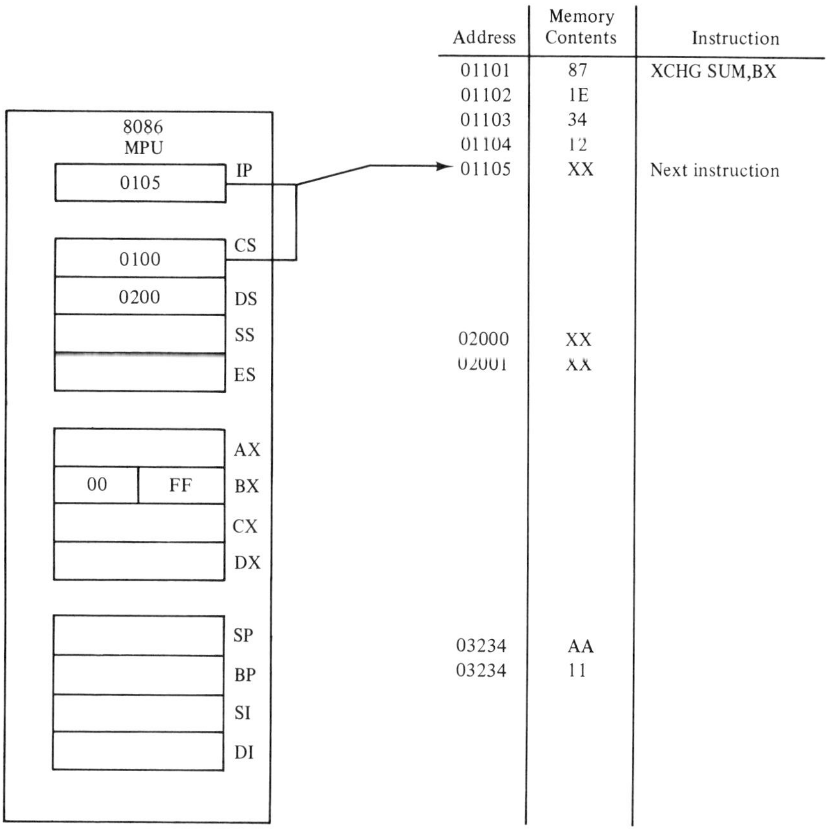

(d)

Figure 3.11 *(continued)*

The XLAT Instruction

The translate (XLAT) instruction has been provided in the instruction set of the 8086 to simplify implementation of the lookup-table operation. This instruction is described in Fig. 3.12. When using XLAT, the contents of register BX represent the offset of the starting address of the *lookup table* from the beginning of the current data segment. Also the contents of AL represent the offset of the element to be accessed from the beginning of the lookup table. This 8-bit element address permits a table with up to 256 elements. The values in both of these registers must be initialized prior to execution of the XLAT instruction.

Execution of XLAT replaces the contents of AL by the contents of the accessed lookup-table location. The physical address of this element in the table is derived as

$$PA = (DS)0 + (BX) + (AL)$$

An example of the use of this instruction would be for software *code conver-*

Mnemonic	Meaning	Format	Operation	Flags Affected
XLAT	Translate	XLAT Source-table	$((AL) + (BX) + (DS)0) \rightarrow (AL)$	None

Figure 3.12 Translate data transfer instruction.

sions: for instance, an ASCII-to-EBCDIC conversion. This requires an EBCDIC table in memory. The individual EBCDIC codes are located in the table at element displacements (AL) equal to their equivalent ASCII character value. That is, the EBCDIC code $B1_{16}$ for letter A would be positioned at displacement 41_{16}, which equals ASCII A, from the start of the table. The start of this ASCII-to-EBCDIC table in the current data segment is identified by the contents of BX.

As an illustration of XLAT, let us assume that the $(DS) = 0300_{16}$, $(BX) = 0100_{16}$, and $(AL) = 0D_{16}$. $0D_{16}$ represents the ASCII character CR (carriage return). Execution of XLAT replaces the contents of AL by the contents of the memory location given by

$$
\begin{aligned}
PA &= (DS)0 + (BX) + 0(AL) \\
&= 03000_{16} + 00100_{16} + 0000D_{16} \\
&= 0310D_{16}
\end{aligned}
$$

Thus the execution can be described by

$$(0310D_{16}) \longrightarrow (AL)$$

Assuming that this memory location contains 52_{16}, this value is placed in AL.

$$(AL) = 52_{16}$$

The LEA, LDS, and LES Instructions

Another type of data transfer operation that is important is to load a segment or general-purpose register with an address directly from memory. Special instructions are provided in the instruction set of the 8086 to give a programmer this capability. These instructions are described in Fig. 3.13(a). They are load register with effective address (LEA), load register and data segment register (LDS), and load register and extra segment register (LES).

Looking at Fig. 3.13(a), we see that these instructions provide the ability to manipulate memory addresses by loading a specific register with a 16-bit offset address or a 16-bit offset address together with a 16-bit segment address into either DS or ES.

The LEA instruction is used to load a specified register with a 16-bit offset address. An example of this instruction is

LEA SI,INPUT

When executed, it loads the SI register with an offset address value. The value of this offset is represented by the value of contant INPUT. INPUT is stored following the instruction opcode in program memory. This value is prefetched by the BIU; therefore, the instruction does not require any external bus cycles during its execution.

The other two instructions, LDS and LES, are similar to LEA except that they load the specified register as well as the DS or ES segment register.

Example 3.3

Assuming that the 8086 is set up as shown in Fig. 3.13(b), what is the result of executing the instruction:

LDS SI,[200H]

Mnemonic	Meaning	Format	Operation	Flags Affected
LEA	Load effective address	LEA Reg16,Mem16	(Mem 16) → (Reg 16)	None
LDS	Load register and DS	LDS Reg16,Mem32	(Mem32) → (Reg16) (Mem32+2) → (DS)	None
LES	Load register and ES	LES Reg16,Mem32	(Mem32) → (Reg16) (Mem32+2) → (ES)	None

(a)

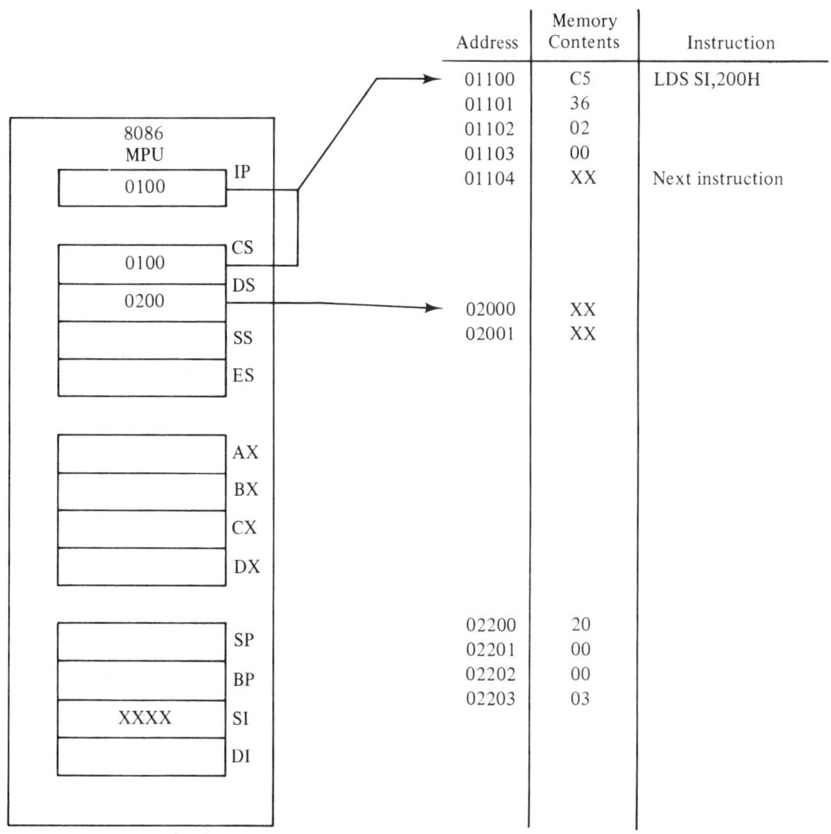

(b)

Figure 3.13(a) LEA, LDS, and LES data transfer instructions; **(b)** LEA SI, 200H instruction before execution; **(c)** after execution.

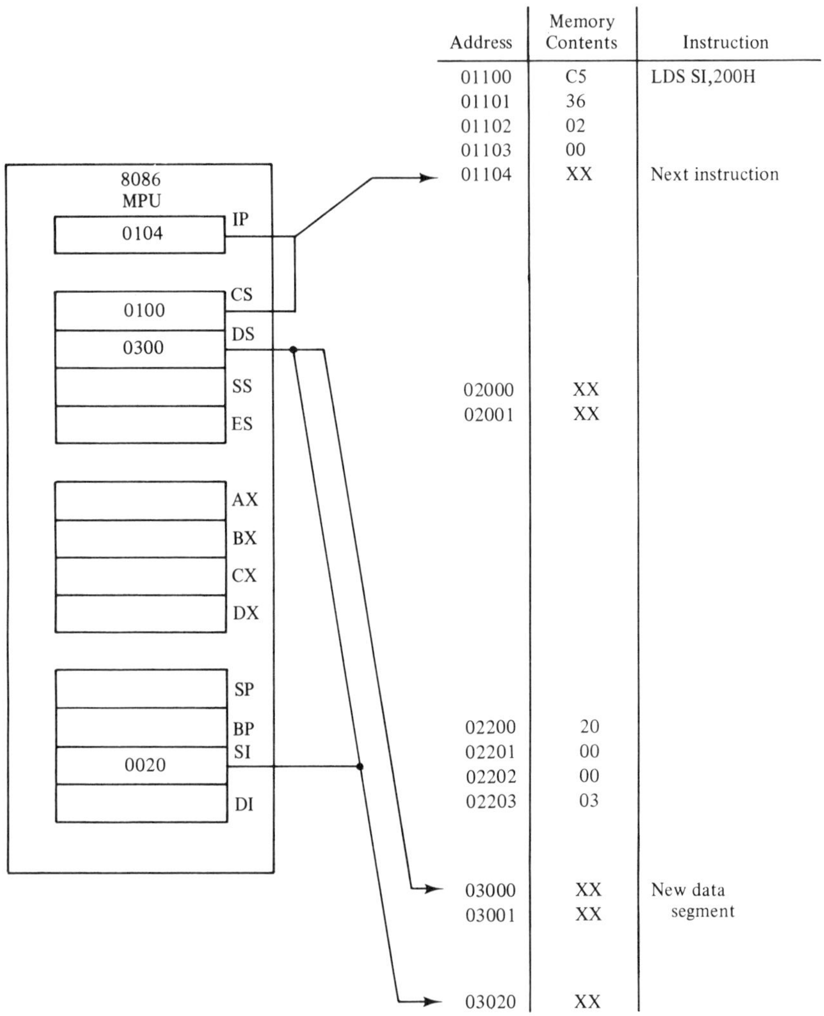

(c)

Figure 3.13 *(continued)*

Solution. Execution of the instruction loads the SI register from the word location in memory whose offset address with respect to the current data segment is 200_{16}. Figure 3.13(b) shows that the contents of DS are 0200_{16}. This gives a physical address of

$$PA = 02000_{16} + 0200_{16} = 02200_{16}$$

It is the contents of this location and the one that follows that are loaded into SI. Therefore, in Fig. 3.13(c), we find that SI contains 0020_{16}. The next two bytes, that is, the contents of addresses 2202_{16} and 2203_{16}, are loaded into the DS register. As shown, this defines a new data segment address of 03000_{16}.

3.7 ARITHMETIC INSTRUCTIONS

The instruction set of the 8086 microprocessor contains an extensive complement of *arithmetic instructions*. They include instructions for the *addition, subtraction, multiplication*, and *division* operations. Moreover, these operations can be performed on numbers expressed in a variety of numeric data formats. They include: *unsigned or signed binary bytes or words, unpacked or packed decimal bytes*, or *ASCII numbers*. By "packed decimal," we mean that two BCD digits are packed into a byte register or memory location. Unpacked decimal numbers are stored one BCD digit per byte. These decimal numbers are always unsigned. Moreover, ASCII numbers are expressed in ASCII code and stored one number per byte.

The status that results from the execution of an arithmetic instruction is recorded in the flags of the 8086. The flags that are affected by the arithmetic instructions are: carry flag (CF), auxiliary flag (AF), sign flag (SF), zero flag (ZF), parity flag (PF), and overflow flag (OF). Each of these flags was discussed in Chapter 2.

For the purpose of discussion, we will divide the arithmetic instructions into the subgroups shown in Fig. 3.14.

Addition Instructions—ADD, ADC, INC, AAA, and DAA

The form of each of the instructions in the *addition group* is shown in Fig. 3.15(a) and their allowed operand variations, for all but the INC instruction, are shown in Fig. 3.15(b). Let us begin by looking more closely at the *add* (ADD) instruction. Notice

Addition	
ADD	Add byte or word
ADC	Add byte or word with carry
INC	Increment byte or word by 1
AAA	ASCII adjust for addition
DAA	Decimal adjust for addition
Subtraction	
SUB	Subtract byte or word
SBB	Subtract byte or word with borrow
DEC	Decrement byte or word by 1
NEG	Negate byte or word
AAS	ASCII adjust for subtraction
DAS	Decimal adjust for subtraction
Multiplication	
MUL	Multiply byte or word unsigned
IMUL	Integer multiply byte or word
AAM	ASCII adjust for multiply
Division	
DIV	Divide byte or word unsigned
IDIV	Integer divide byte or word
AAD	ASCII adjust for division
CBW	Convert byte to word
CWD	Convert word to doubleword

Figure 3.14 Arithmetic instructions *(Courtesy of Intel Corporation).*

in Fig. 3.15(b) that it can be used to add to the contents of the accumulator an immediate operand, the contents of another register, or the contents of a storage location in memory. It also allows us to add the contents of two registers or the contents of a register and a memory location.

In general, the result of executing the instruction is expressed as

$$(S) + (D) \longrightarrow (D)$$

That is, the contents of the source operand are added to those of the destination operand and the sum that results is put into the location of the destination operand.

Example 3.4

Assume that the AX and BX registers contain 1100_{16} and $0ABC_{16}$, respectively. What are the results of executing the instruction ADD AX,BX?

Solution. Execution of the ADD instruction causes the contents of source operand BX to be added to the contents of destination register AX. This gives

$$(BX) + (AX) = 0ABC_{16} + 1100_{16} = 1BBC_{16}$$

This sum ends up in destination register AX.

$$(AX) = 1BBC_{16}$$

Execution of this instruction is illustrated in Fig. 3.16(a) and (b).

Mnemonic	Meaning	Format	Operation	Flags Affected
ADD	Addition	ADD D, S	(S) + (D) → (D) Carry → (CF)	OF, SF, ZF, AF, PF, CF
ADC	Add with carry	ADC D, S	(S) + (D) + (CF) → (D) Carry → (CF)	OF, SF, ZF, AF, PF, CF
INC	Increment by 1	INC D	(D) + 1 → (D)	OF, SF, ZF, AF, PF, CF
AAA	ASCII adjust for addition	AAA		OF, SF, ZF, AF, PF, CF
DAA	Decimal adjust for addition	DAA		OF, SF, ZF, AF, PF, CF

(a)

Destination	Source
Register	Register
Register	Memory
Memory	Register
Register	Immediate
Memory	Immediate
Accumulator	Immediate

(b)

Destination
Reg16
Reg8
Memory

(c)

Figure 3.15(a) Addition arithmetic instructions; **(b)** allowed operands for ADD and ADC; **(c)** allowed operands for INC.

The instruction *add with carry* (ADC) works similarly to ADD. But in this case, the content of the carry flag is also added; that is,

$$(S) + (D) + (CF) \longrightarrow (D)$$

The valid operand combinations are the same as those for the ADD instruction.

Another instruction that can be considered as part of the addition subgroup of arithmetic instructions is the *increment* (INC) instruction. As shown in Fig. 3.15(c), its operands can be the contents of a 16-bit internal register, an 8-bit internal register, or a storage location in memory. Execution of the INC instruction adds 1 to the specified operand. An example of an instruction that increments the high byte of AX is

INC AH

Looking at Fig. 3.15(a), we see that execution of any one of these three instructions affects all six of the flags mentioned earlier.

Example 3.5

The original contents of AX, BL, memory location SUM, and carry flag (CF) are 1234_{16}, AB_{16}, $00CD_{16}$, and 0_{16}, respectively. Describe the results of executing the following sequence of instructions:

```
ADD  AX,SUM
ADC  BL,05H
INC  SUM
```

Solution. By executing the first instruction, we add the word in the accumulator to the contents of the memory location identified as SUM. The result is placed in the accumulator. That is,

$$(AX) \longleftarrow (AX) + (SUM)$$
$$= 1234_{16} + 00CD_{16} = 1301_{16}$$

The carry flag remains reset.

The second instruction adds the lower byte of the base register (BL), immediate operand 5_{16}, and the carry flag, which is 0_{16}. This gives

$$(BL) \longleftarrow (BL) + IOP + (CF)$$
$$= AB_{16} + 5_{16} + 0_{16} = B0_{16}$$

Again CF stays reset.

The last instruction increments the contents of memory location SUM by 1. That is,

$$(SUM) \longleftarrow (SUM) + 1_{16}$$
$$= 00CD_{16} + 1_{16} = 00CE_{16}$$

These results are summarized in Fig. 3.17.

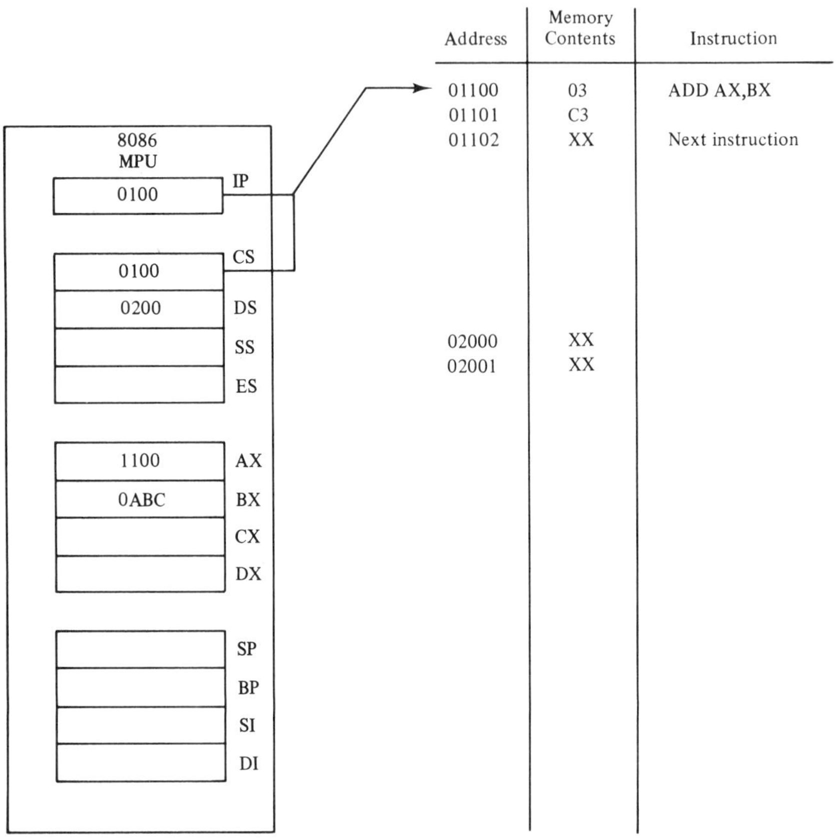

(a)

Figure 3.16(a) ADD instruction before execution; **(b)** after execution.

The addition instructions we just covered can also be used directly to add numbers expressed in ASCII code. This eliminates the need for doing a code conversion on ASCII form data prior to processing it with addition operations. Whenever the 8086 does an addition on ASCII format data, an adjustment must be performed on the result to convert it to a decimal number. It is specifically for this purpose that the *ASCII adjust for addition* (AAA) instruction is provided in the instruction set of the 8086. The AAA instruction should be executed immediately after the instruction that adds ASCII data.

Assuming that AL contains the result produced by adding two ASCII-coded numbers, execution of the AAA instruction causes the contents of AL to be replaced by its equivalent decimal value. If the sum is greater than 9, AL contains the LSDs, and AH is incremented by 1. Otherwise, AL contains the sum and AH is cleared. Both the AF and CF flags can get affected. Since AAA can only adjust data that are in AL, the destination register for ADD instructions that process ASCII numbers should be AL.

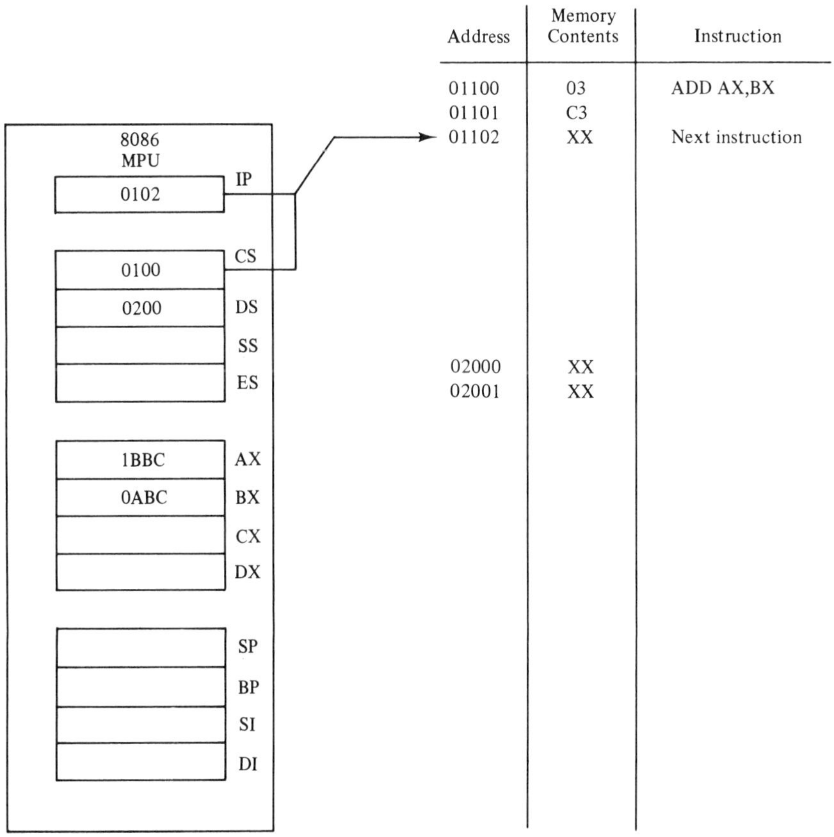

(b)

Figure 3.16 *(continued)*

Instruction	(AX)	(BL)	(SUM)	(CF)
Initial state	1234	AB	00CD	0
ADD AX,SUM	1301	AB	00CD	0
ADC BL,05H	1301	B0	00CD	0
INC SUM	1301	B0	00CE	0

Figure 3.17 Results due to execution of arithmetic program.

Example 3.6

What is the result of executing the following instruction sequence?

ADD AL,BL

AAA

Assume that AL contains 32_{16}, which is the ASCII code for number 2, BL contains 34_{16}, which is the ASCII code for number 4, and AH has been cleared.

Solution. Executing the ADD instruction gives

$$(AL) \leftarrow (AL) + (BL)$$
$$= 32_{16} + 34_{16} = 66_{16}$$

Next the result is adjusted to give its equivalent decimal number. This is done by execution of the AAA instruction. The equivalent of adding 2 and 4 is decimal 6 with no carry. Therefore, the result after the AAA instruction is

$$(AL) = 06_{16}$$
$$(AH) = 00_{16}$$

and both AF and CF remain cleared.

The instruction set of the 8086 includes another instruction, called *decimal adjust for addition* (DAA). This instruction is used to perform an adjust operation similar to that performed by AAA but for the addition of packed BCD numbers instead of ASCII numbers. Information about this instruction is also provided in Fig. 3.15. Similar to AAA, DAA performs an adjustment on the value in AL. A typical instruction sequence is

```
ADD AL,BL
DAA
```

Remember that the contents of AL and BL must be packed BCD numbers. That is, two BCD digits packed into a byte. The adjusted result in AL is again a packed BCD byte.

Subtraction Instructions—SUB, SBB, DEC, AAS, DAS, and NEG

The instruction set of the 8086 includes an extensive set of instructions provided for implementing subtraction. As shown in Fig. 3.18, the subtraction subgroup is similar to the addition subgroup. It includes instructions for subtracting a source and destination operand, decrementing an operand, and for adjusting subtractions of ASCII and BCD data. An additional instruction in this subgroup is negate.

The *subtract* (SUB) instruction is used to subtract the value of a source operand from a destination operand. The result of this operation in general is given as

$$(D) \leftarrow (D) - (S)$$

As shown in Fig. 3.18(b), it can employ the identical operand combinations as the ADD instruction.

The *subtract with borrow* (SBB) instruction is similar to SUB; however, it also subtracts the content of the carry flag from the destination. That is,

$$(D) \leftarrow (D) - (S) - (CF)$$

Example 3.7

Assume that the contents of registers BX and CX are 1234_{16} and 0123_{16}, respectively, and the carry flag is 0. What will be the result of executing the instruction

Mnemonic	Meaning	Format	Operation	Flags affected
SUB	Subtract	SUB D,S	(D) − (S) → (D) Borrow → (CF)	OF, SF, ZF, AF, PF, CF
SBB	Subtract with borrow	SBB D,S	(D) − (S) − (CF) → (D)	OF, SF, ZF, AF, PF, CF
DEC	Decrement by 1	DEC D	(D) − 1 → (D)	OF, SF, ZF, AF, PF, CF
NEG	Negate	NEG D	0 − (D) → (D) 1 → (CF)	OF, SF, ZF, AF, PF, CF
DAS	Decimal adjust for subtraction	DAS		OF, SF, ZF, AF, PF, CF
AAS	ASCII adjust for subtraction	AAS		OF, SF, ZF, AF, PF, CF

(a)

Destination	Source
Register	Register
Register	Memory
Memory	Register
Accumulator	Immediate
Register	Immediate
Memory	Immediate

(b)

Destination
Reg16
Reg8
Memory

(c)

Destination
Register
Memory

(d)

Figure 3.18(a) Subtraction arithmetic instructions; **(b)** allowed operands for SUB and SBB; **(c)** allowed operands for DEC; **(d)** allowed operands for NEG.

SBB BX,CX?

Solution. Since the instruction implements the operation,

$$(BX) - (CX) - (CF) \longrightarrow (BX)$$

we get

$$(BX) = 1234_{16} - 0123_{16} - 0_{16}$$
$$= 1111_{16}$$

Just as the INC instruction could be used to add 1 to an operand, the *decrement* (DEC) instruction can be used to subtract 1 from its operand. The allowed operands are shown in Fig. 3.18(c).

In Fig. 3.18(d) we see that the *negate* (NEG) instruction can operate on operands in a general-purpose register or a storage location in memory. Execution of this instruction causes the value of its operand to be replaced by its negative. The way this is actually done is through subtraction. That is, the contents of the specified operand are subtracted from zero using 2's-complement arithmetic and the result is returned to the operand location.

Example 3.8

Assuming that register BX contains $3A_{16}$, what is the result of executing the instruction

NEG BX ?

Solution. Executing the NEG instruction causes the 2's-complement subtraction that follows:

$$00_{16} - (BX) = 0000_{16} + \text{2's complement of } 3A_{16}$$
$$= 0000_{16} + FFC6_{16}$$
$$= FFC6_{16}$$

This value is returned to BX.

$$(BX) = FFC6_{16}$$

In our study of the addition instruction subgroup, we found that the 8086 was capable of directly adding ASCII and BCD numbers. The SUB and SBB instructions can also subtract numbers represented in these formats. Just as for addition, the results that are obtained must be adjusted to produce their corresponding decimal numbers. In the case of ASCII subtraction, we use the *ASCII adjust for subtraction* (AAS) instruction, and for packed BCD subtraction we use the *decimal adjust for subtract* (DAS) instruction.

An example of an instruction sequence for direct ASCII subtraction is

```
SUB AL,BL
AAS
```

ASCII numbers must be loaded into AL and BL before the execution of the subtract instruction. Notice that the destination of the subtraction should be AL. After execution of AAS, AL contains the difference of the two numbers and AH is cleared if no borrow takes place or is decremented by 1 if a borrow occurs.

Multiplication and Division Instructions—MUL, DIV, IMUL, IDIV, AAM, AAD, CBW, and CWD

The 8086 has instructions to support multiplication and division of binary and BCD numbers. Two basic types of multiplication and division instructions, those for the processing of unsigned numbers and signed numbers, are available. To do these operations on unsigned numbers, the instructions are MUL and DIV. On the other hand, to multiply or divide signed numbers, the instructions are IMUL and IDIV.

Figure 3.19(a) describes these instructions. Notice in Fig. 3.19(b) that only a byte-wide or word-wide operand is specified in a multiplication instruction. It is the source operand. As shown in Fig. 3.19(a), the other operand, which is the destination, is assumed already to be in AL for 8-bit multiplications or in AX for 16-bit multiplications.

The result of executing a MUL or IMUL instruction on byte data can be represented as

$$(AX) \longleftarrow (AL) \times (\text{8-BIT OPERAND})$$

Mnemonic	Meaning	Format	Operation	Flags Affected
MUL	Multiply (unsigned)	MUL S	(AL) · (S8) → (AX) (AX) · (S16) → (DX),(AX)	OF, SF, ZF, AF, PF, CF
DIV	Division (unsigned)	DIV S	(1) Q((AX)/(S8)) → (AL) R((AX)/(S8)) → (AH) (2) Q((DX,AX)/(S16)) → (AX) R((DX,AX)/(S16)) → (DX) If Q is FF_{16} in case (1) or $FFFF_{16}$ in case (2), then type 0 interrupt occurs	OF, SF, ZF, AF, PF, CF
IMUL	Integer multiply (signed)	IMUL S	(AL) · (S8) → (AX) (AX) · (S16) → (DX),(AX)	OF, SF, ZF, AF, PF, CF
IDIV	Integer divide (signed)	IDIV S	(1) Q((AX)/(S8)) → (AX) R((AX)/(S8)) → (AH) (2) Q((DX,AX)/(S16)) → (AX) R((DX,AX)/(S16)) → (DX) If Q is $7F_{16}$ in case (1) or $7FFF_{16}$ in case (2), then type 0 interrupt occurs	OF, SF, ZF, AF, PF, CF
AAM	Adjust AL for multiplication	AAM	Q((AL)/10) → AH R((AL)/10) → AL	OF, SF, ZF, AF, PF, CF
AAD	Adjust AX for division	AAD	(AH) · 10 + AL → AL 00 → AH	OF, SF, ZF, AF, PF, CF
CBW	Convert byte to word	CBW	(MSB of AL) → (All bits of AH)	None
CWD	Convert word to double word	CWD	(MSB of AX) → (All bits of DX)	None

(a)

Source
Reg8
Reg16
Mem8
Mem16

(b)

Figure 3.19(a) Multiplication and division arithmetic instructions; **(b)** allowed operands.

That is, the resulting 16-bit product is produced in the AX register. On the other hand, for multiplications of data words, the 32-bit result is given by

$$(DX,AX) \longleftarrow (AX) \times (16\text{-BIT OPERAND})$$

where AX contains the 16 LSBs and DX the 16 MSBs.

For the division operation, again just the source operand is specified. The other operand is either the contents of AX for 16-bit dividends or the contents of both DX and AX for 32-bit dividends. The result of a DIV or IDIV instruction for an 8-bit divisor is represented by

$$(AH),(AL) \leftarrow (AX)/(8\text{-BIT OPERAND})$$

where (AH) is the remainder and (AL) the quotient. For 16-bit divisions, we get

$$(DX),(AX) \leftarrow (DX,AX)/(16\text{-BIT OPERAND})$$

Here AX contains the quotient and DX contains the remainder.

Example 3.9

If the contents of AL equal -1_{10} and the contents of CL are -2_{10}, what will be the result produced in AX by executing the instructions

MUL CL

and

IMUL CL

Solution. The first instruction multiplies the contents of AL and CL as unsigned numbers.

$$-1_{10} = 11111111_2 = FF_{16}$$
$$-2_{10} = 11111110_2 = FE_{16}$$

Thus, executing the MUL instruction, we get

$$(AX) = (11111111_2) \times (11111110_2) = 1111110100000010_2$$
$$= FD02_{16}$$

The second instruction multiplies the same two numbers as signed numbers and gives

$$(AX) = 1_{16} \times 2_{16}$$
$$= 2_{16}$$

As shown in Fig. 3.19(a), adjust instructions for BCD multiplication and division are also provided. They are *adjust AX for multiply* (AAM) and *adjust AX for divide* (AAD). The multiplication performed just before execution of the AAM instruction is assumed to have been performed on two unpacked BCD numbers with the product produced in AL. The AAD instruction assumes that AH and AL contain unpacked BCD numbers.

The division instructions can also be used to divide an 8-bit dividend in AL by an 8-bit divisor. However, to do this, the sign of the dividend must first be extended to fill the AX register. That is, AH is filled with zeros if the number in AL is positive or with ones if it is negative. This conversion is automatically done by executing the *convert byte to word* (CBW) instruction.

In a similar way, the 32-bit by 16-bit division instructions can be used to divide a 16-bit dividend in AX by a 16-bit divisor. In this case, the sign bit of AX must be extended by 16 bits into the DX register. This can be done by another instruction, which is known as *convert word to double word* (CWD). These two sign-extension instructions are also shown in Fig. 3.19(a).

Notice that the CBW and CWD instructions are provided to handle operations where the result or intermediate results of an operation cannot be held in the correct word length for use in other arithmetic operations. Using these instructions, we can extend a byte or word of data to its equivalent word or double word.

Example 3.10

What is the result of executing the following sequence of instructions?

```
MOV   AL,0A1H
CBW
CWD
```

Solution. The first instruction loads AL with $A1_{16}$. This gives

$$(AL) = A1_{16} = 10100001_2$$

Executing the second instruction extends the most significant bit of AL, which is 1, into all bits of AH. The result is

$$(AH) = 11111111_2 = FF_{16}$$

$$(AX) = 1111111110100001_2 = FFA1_{16}$$

This completes conversion of the byte in AL to a word in AX.

The last instruction loads each bit of DX with the most significant bit of AX. This bit is also 1. Therefore, we get

$$(DX) = 1111111111111111_2 = FFFF_{16}$$

Now the word in AX has been extended to the double word

$$(AX) = FFA1_{16}$$

$$(DX) = FFFF_{16}$$

3.8 LOGIC INSTRUCTIONS

The 8086 has instructions for performing the logic operations *AND, OR, exclusive-OR*, and *NOT*. As shown in Fig. 3.20(a), the AND, OR, and XOR instructions perform their respective logic operations bit by bit on the specified source and destination operands, the result being represented by the final contents of the destination operand. Figure 3.20(b) shows the allowed operand combinations for the AND, OR, and XOR instructions.

For example, the instruction

```
AND AX,BX
```

causes the contents of BX to be ANDed with the contents of AX. The result is reflected by the new contents of AX. If AX contains 1234_{16} and BX contains $000F_{16}$, the result produced by the instruction is

$$1234_{16} \bullet 000F_{16} = 0001001000110100_2 \bullet 0000000000001111_2$$

$$= 0000000000000100_{16}$$

$$= 0004_{16}$$

Mnemonic	Meaning	Format	Operation	Flags Affected
AND	Logical AND	AND D,S	$(S) \cdot (D) \rightarrow (D)$	OF, SF, ZF, AF, PF, CF
OR	Logical Inclusive-OR	OR D,S	$(S) + (D) \rightarrow (D)$	OF, SF, ZF, AF, PF, CF
XOR	Logical Exclusive-OR	XOR D,S	$(S) \oplus (D) \rightarrow (D)$	OF, SF, ZF, AF, PF, CF
NOT	Logical NOT	NOT D	$(\bar{D}) \rightarrow (D)$	None

(a)

Destination	Source
Register	Register
Register	Memory
Memory	Register
Register	Immediate
Memory	Immediate
Accumulator	Immediate

(b)

Destination
Register
Memory

(c)

Figure 3.20(a) Logic instructions; **(b)** allowed operands for AND, OR, and XOR; **(c)** allowed operands for NOT.

This result is stored in the destination operand.

$$(AX) = 0004_{16}$$

In this way we see that the AND instruction was used to mask off the 12 most significant bits of the destination operand.

The NOT logic instruction differs from those for AND, OR, and exclusive-OR in that it operates on a single operand. Looking at Fig. 3.20(c), which shows the allowed operands of the NOT instruction, we see that this operand can be the contents of an internal register or a location in memory.

Example 3.11

Describe the result of executing the following sequence of instructions.

```
MOV  AL,01010101B
AND  AL,00011111B
OR   AL,11000000B
XOR  AL,00001111B
NOT  AL
```

Solution. The first instruction moves the immediate operand 01010101_2 into the AL register. This loads the data that are to be manipulated with the logic instructions. The next instruction performs a bit-by-bit AND operation of the contents of AL with immediate operand 00011111_2. This gives

$$01010101_2 \cdot 00011111_2 = 00010101_2$$

This result is produced in destination register AL. Note that this operation has masked off the 3 most significant bits of AL.

The next instruction performs a bit-by-bit logical OR of the present contents of AL with immediate operand $C0_{16}$. This gives

$$00010101_2 + 11000000_2 = 11010101_2$$
$$(AL) = 11010101$$

This operation is equivalent to setting the two most significant bits of AL.

The fourth instruction is an exclusive-OR operation of the contents of AL with immediate operand 00001111_2. We get

$$11010101_2 \oplus 00001111_2 = 11011010_2$$
$$(AL) = 11011010$$

Note that this operation complements the logic state of those bits in AL that are ones in the immediate operand.

The last instruction, NOT AL, inverts each bit of AL. Therefore, the final contents of AL become

$$(AL) = \overline{11011010_2} = 00100101_2$$

These results are summarized in Fig. 3.21.

Instruction	(AL)
MOV AL,01010101B	01010101
AND AL,00011111B	00010101
OR AL,11000000B	11010101
XOR AL,00001111B	11011010
NOT AL	00100101

Figure 3.21 Results of example program using logic instructions.

3.9 SHIFT INSTRUCTIONS

The four *shift instructions* of the 8086 can perform two basic types of shift operations. They are the *logical shift* and the *arithmetic shift*. Moreover, each of these operations can be performed to the right or to the left. The shift instructions are *shift logical left* (SHL), *shift arithmetic left* (SAL), *shift logical right* (SHR), and *shift arithmetic right* (SAR).

The logical shift instructions, SHL and SHR, are described in Fig. 3.22(a). Notice in Fig. 3.22(b) that the destination operand, the data whose bits are to be shifted, can be either the contents of an internal register or a storage location in memory. Moreover, the source operand can be specified in two ways. If it is assigned the value 1, a 1-bit shift will take place. For instance, as illustrated in Fig. 3.23(a), executing

```
SHL AX,1
```

Mnemonic	Meaning	Format	Operation	Flags Affected
SAL/SHL	Shift arithmetic left/shift logical left	SAL/SHL D,Count	Shift the (D) left by the number of bit positions equal to Count and fill the vacated bits positions on the right with zeros	OF, CF
SHR	Shift logical right	SHR D,Count	Shift the (D) right by the number of bit positions equal to Count and fill the vacated bit positions on the left with zeros	OF, CF
SAR	Shift arithmetic right	SAR D,Count	Shift the (D) right by the number of bit positions equal to Count and fill the vacated bit positions on the left with the original most significant bit	OF, SF, ZF, AF, PF, CF

(a)

Destination	Count
Register	1
Register	CL
Memory	1
Memory	CL

(b)

Figure 3.22(a) Shift instructions; **(b)** allowed operands.

causes the 16-bit content of the AX register to be shifted one bit position to the left. Here we see that the vacated LSB location is filled with 0 and the bit shifted out of the MSB is saved in CF.

On the other hand, if the source operand is specified as CL instead of 1, the count in this register represents the number of bit positions the operand is to be shifted. This permits the count to be defined under software control and allows a range of shifts from 1 to 256 bits.

An example of an instruction specified in this way is

SHR AX,CL

Assuming that CL contains the value 02_{16}, the logical shift right that occurs is shown in Fig. 3.23(b). Notice that the two MSBs have been filled with 0s and the last bit shifted out at the LSB, which is 0, is maintained in the carry flag.

In an arithmetic shift to the left, SAL operation, the vacated bits at the right of the operand are filled with zeros, whereas in an arithmetic shift to the right, SAR operation, the vacated bits at the left are filled with the value of the original MSB of the operand. Thus in an arithmetic shift to the right, the original sign of the number is extended. This operation is equivalent to division by 2 as long as the bit shifted out of the LSB is a zero.

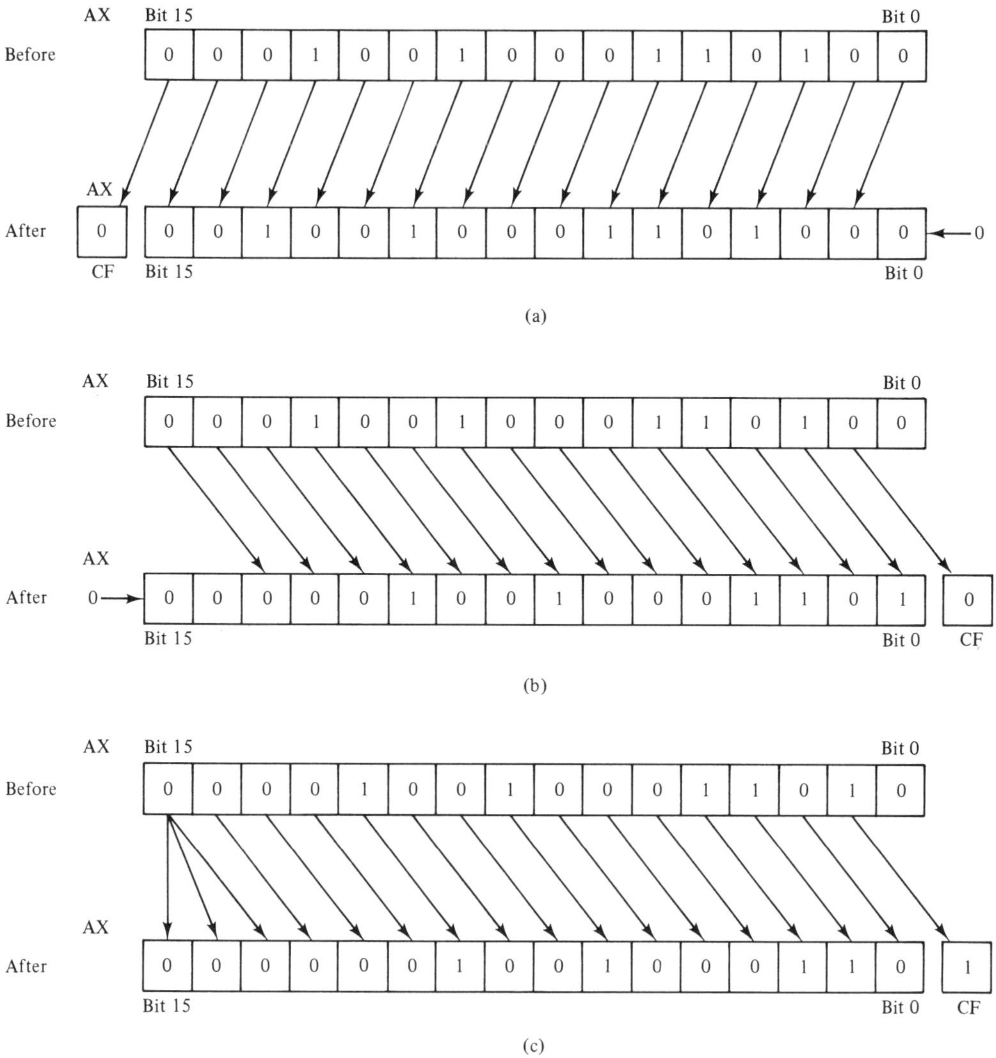

Figure 3.23(a) Results of executing SHL AX,1; **(b)** results of executing SHR AX,CL; **(c)** results of executing SAR AX,CL.

Example 3.12

Assume that CL contains 02_{16} and AX contains $091A_{16}$. Determine the new contents of AX and the carry flag after the instruction

SAR AX,CL

is executed.

Solution. Figure 3.23(c) shows the effect of executing the instruction. Here we see that since CL contains 02_{16}, a shift right by two bit locations takes place and the original sign bit, which is logic 0, is extended to the two vacated bit positions. Moreover, the last bit shifted out from the LSB location is placed in CF. This makes CF 1. Therefore, the results produced by execution of the instruction are

$$(AX) = 0246_{16}$$

and

$$(CF) = 1_2$$

Example 3.13

Write a program to implement the following expression using shift instructions to perform the arithmetic.

$$3(AX) + 7(BX) \longrightarrow (DX)$$

Solution. Shifting left by 1 bit position causes a multiplication by 2. To perform multiplication by an odd number, we can use a shift instruction to multiply to the nearest multiple of 2 and then add or subtract the appropriate value to get the desired result.

The algorithm for performing the arithmetic operations in the expression starts by shifting (AX) left by 1 bit. This gives 2 times (AX). Then adding the original (AX) gives multiplication by 3. Next, the contents of BX are shifted left by 3 bits to give 8 times its value and subtracting the original (BX) once gives multiplication by 7. Expressing this with instructions, we get

```
MOV   SI,AX     ; COPY (AX) INTO SI
SAL   SI,1      ; 2(AX)
ADD   SI,AX     ; 3(AX)
MOV   DX,BX     ; COPY (BX) INTO DX
MOV   CL,03H    ; LOAD SHIFT COUNT
SAL   DX,CL     ; 8(BX)
SUB   DX,BX     ; 7(BX)
ADD   DX,SI     ; RESULT
```

It is important to note that we have assumed that to obtain any of the intermediate results and the final result, overflow does not occur. For instance, if 8(BX) cannot be accommodated in the 16 bits of BX, an overflow condition would occur and the result produced by executing the program may be incorrect.

3.10 ROTATE INSTRUCTIONS

Another group of instructions, known as the *rotate instructions*, are similar to the shift instructions we just introduced. This group, as shown in Fig. 3.24(a), includes the *rotate left* (ROL), *rotate right* (ROR), *rotate left through carry* (RCL), and *rotate right through carry* (RCR) instructions.

Mnemonic	Meaning	Format	Operation	Flags Affected
ROL	Rotate left	ROL D,Count	Rotate the (D) left by the number of bit positions equal to Count. Each bit shifted out from the leftmost bit goes back into the rightmost bit position.	OF, CF
ROR	Rotate right	ROR D,Count	Rotate the (D) right by the number of bit positions equal to Count. Each bit shifted out from the rightmost bit goes into the leftmost bit position.	OF, CF
RCL	Rotate left through carry	RCL D,Count	Same as ROL except carry is attached to (D) for rotation.	OF, CF
RCR	Rotate right through carry	RCR D,Count	Same as ROR except carry is attached to (D) for rotation.	OF, CF

(a)

Destination	Count
Register	1
Register	CL
Memory	1
Memory	CL

(b)

Figure 3.24(a) Rotate instructions; **(b)** allowed operands.

As shown in Fig. 3.24(b), the rotate instructions are similar to the shift instructions in several ways. They have the ability to shift the contents of either an internal register or storage location in memory. Also, the shift that takes place can be from 1 to 256 bit positions to the left or to the right. Moreover, in the case of a multibit shift, the number of bit positions to be shifted is again specified by the contents of CL. Their difference from the shift instructions lies in the fact that the bits moved out at either the MSB or LSB end are not lost; instead, they are reloaded at the other end.

As an example, let us look at the operation of the ROL instruction. Execution of ROL causes the contents of the selected operand to be rotated left the specified number of bit positions. Each bit shifted out at the MSB end is reloaded at the LSB end. Moreover, the contents of CF reflects the state of the last bit that was shifted out. For instance, the instruction

ROL AX,1

causes a 1-bit rotate to the left. Figure 3.25(a) shows the result produced by executing this instruction. Notice that the original value of bit 15 is 0. This value has been rotated into CF and bit 0 of AX. All other bits have been rotated one bit position to the left.

The ROR instruction operates the same way as ROL except that it causes data to be rotated to the right instead of to the left. For example, execution of

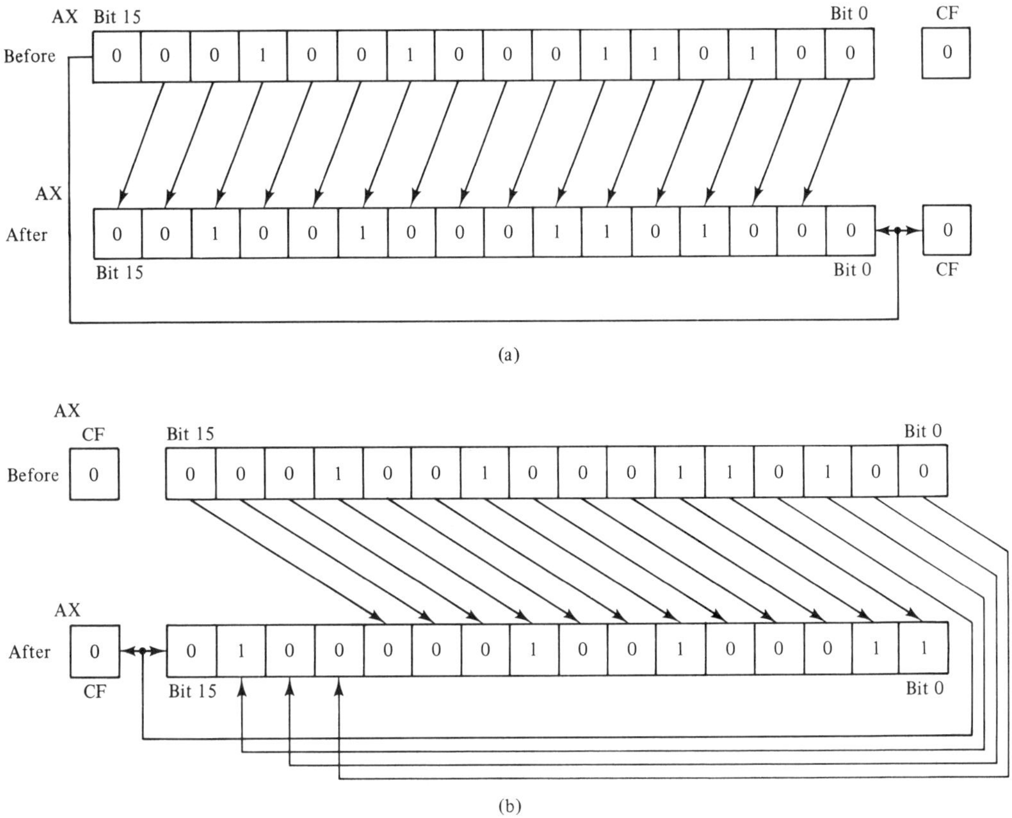

Figure 3.25(a) Result of executing ROL AX,1; **(b)** result of executing ROR AX,CL.

ROR AX,CL

causes the contents of AX to be rotated right by the number of bit positions specified in CL. The result for CL equal to 4 is illustrated in Fig. 3.25(b).

The other two rotate instructions, RCL and RCR, differ from ROL and ROR in that the bits are rotated through the carry flag. Figure 3.26 illustrates the rotation that takes place due to execution of the RCL instruction. Notice that the bit returned to bit 0 is the prior contents of CF and not bit 15. The bit shifted out of bit 15 goes into the carry flag. Thus the bits rotate through carry.

Example 3.14

What is the result in BX and CF after execution of the following instruction

RCB BX,CL?

Assume that prior to execution of the instruction (CL) = 04_{16}, (BX) = 1234_{16}, and (CF) = 0.

Solution. The original contents of BX are

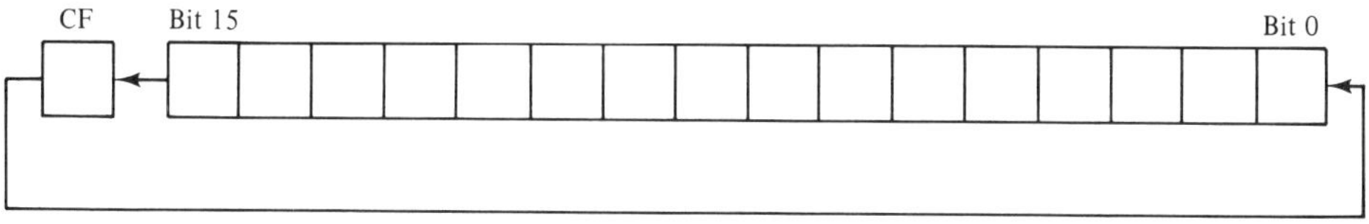

Figure 3.26 Rotation caused by execution of the RCL instruction.

$$(BX) = 0001001000110100_2 = 1234_{16}$$

Execution of the ROR instruction causes a 4-bit rotate right through carry to take place on the data in BX. Therefore, the original content of bit 3, which is 0, resides in carry; CF = 0 and 1000 has been reloaded from bit 15. The resulting contents of BX are

$$(BX) = 1000000100100011_2 = 8123_{16}$$

ASSIGNMENT

Section 3.2

1. Can the 8086 directly store a word of data starting at an odd address?
2. What type of information is contained in the software model of the 8086?
3. Which registers of the 8086 are used in memory segmentation?
4. Categorize each flag bit of the 8086 as either a control flag or a flag to monitor the effect of instruction execution.

Section 3.3

5. Identify the three parts of an assembly language instruction in each of the following statements:

```
AGAIN:  ADD   AX,CX   ;ADD THE REGISTERS
        MOV   BX,AX   ;SAVE RESULT
```

6. Identify the source and destination operands for each of the statements in problem 5.

Section 3.4

7. Make a list of the addressing modes available on the 8086.
8. Identify the addressing modes for both the source and destination operands in the instructions that follow.
   (a) MOV AL,BL
   (b) MOV AX,0FFH
   (c) MOV [SI],AX
   (d) MOV SI,[DI]
   (e) MOV [BX].XYZ,CX
   (f) MOV XYZ[SI],AH
   (e) MOV [BX].XYZ[DI],AL
9. Compute the memory address, the specified register, or the immediate value for the source operand and destination operand in each of the instructions in problem 8.

10. Write an instruction that loads AL from memory address $A000_{16}$ using three different addressing modes. Specify all assumptions made.

Section 3.6

11. Describe the operation performed by each of the following instructions.

    (a) MOV SI,ABCDH

    (b) MOV [SI],0ABCDH

12. Write an instruction sequence using MOV instructions that are equivalent to

    XCHG AX,BX

13. Assuming that (AL) = 0010_{16}, (BX) = 0100_{16}, and DS = 1000_{16}, what happens if the XLAT instruction is executed?
14. Two code conversion tables starting with offsets TABL1 and TABL2 in the data segment starting at $A000_{16}$ are to be accessed. Write a routine that initializes the needed registers and then replaces the contents of memory locations MEM1 and MEM2 (offsets in the current data segment) by the equivalent converted codes from the code conversion tables.
15. Write a single instruction to load AX from address $A000_{16}$ and DS from address $A002_{16}$.

Section 3.7

16. Two word-wide unsigned integers are stored at the memory addresses $A000_{16}$ and $B000_{16}$, respectively. Write an instruction sequence that computes and stores their sum, difference, product, and quotient. Store these results at consecutive memory locations starting at address $C000_{16}$ in memory. To obtain the difference, subtract the integer at $B000_{16}$ from the integer at $A000_{16}$. For the division, divide the integer at $A000_{16}$ by the integer at $B000_{16}$. Use register indirect relative addressing mode to store the various results.
17. Assuming that (AX) = 1000_{16} and (BL) = 10_{16}, what will be the new contents of AX after executing the instruction DIV BL?
18. Two word-long BCD integers are stored at the symbolic addresses NUM1 and NUM2, respectively. Write an instruction sequence to generate their difference and store it at NUM3. The difference is to be formed by subtracting the value at NUM1 from that at NUM2.

Section 3.8

19. Specify the relation between the old and new contents of AX after executing the following instructions.

    NOT AX

    ADD AX,01H

20. Write an instruction sequence that generates a byte-size integer in the memory location identified by label RESULT. The value of the byte integer is to be calculated as follows:

    $$\text{RESULT} = \text{AL} \bullet \text{NUM1} + (\overline{\text{NUM2}} \bullet \text{AL} + \text{BL})$$

    Assume that all parameters are byte size.

Section 3.9

21. Identify the condition under which the contents of AX would remain unchanged after executing the instructions that follow.

```
MOV  CL,04H
SHL  AX,CL
SHR  AX,CL
```

22. Implement the following operation using shift and arithmetic instructions.

$$7(AX) - 5(BX) - \frac{1}{8}(BX) \rightarrow (AX)$$

Assume that all parameters are word size.

Section 3.10

23. Write a program that saves the content of bit 5 in AL in BX as a word.

4

8086 Microprocessor Programming 2

4.1 INTRODUCTION

In Chapter 3 we discussed many of the instructions that can be executed by the 8086 microprocessor. Furthermore, we used these instructions to write simple programs. In this chapter we introduce the rest of the instruction set and at the same time cover some more complicated programming techniques. The following topics are discussed in this chapter:

1. Flag control instructions
2. Compare instruction
3. Jump instructions
4. Program examples employing loops
5. Subroutines and subroutine handling instructions
6. Example programs employing subroutines
7. Loop instructions
8. String instructions

4.2 FLAG CONTROL INSTRUCTIONS

The 8086 microprocessor has a set of flags which either monitor the status of executing instructions or control options available in its operation. These flags were described in detail in Chapter 2. The instruction set includes a group of instructions which when executed directly affect the setting of the flags. These instructions, shown in Fig. 4.1, are: *load AH from flags* (LAHF), *store AH into flags* (SAHF), *clear carry* (CLC), *set carry* (STC), *complement carry* (CMC), *clear interrupt* (CLI), and *set interrupt* (STI). A few more instructions exist that can directly affect the flags; however, we will not cover them until later in the chapter when we introduce the subroutine and string instructions.

Looking at Fig. 4.1, we see that the first two instructions, LAHF and SAHF, can be used either to read the flags or to change them, respectively. Notice that the data transfer that takes place is always between the AH register and the flag register. For instance, we may want to start an operation with certain flags set or reset. Assume that we want to preset all flags to logic 1. To do this, we can first load AH with FF_{16} and then execute the SAHF instruction.

Example 4.1

Write an instruction sequence to save the current contents of the 8086's flags in memory location MEM1 and then reload the flags with the contents of memory location MEM2.

Solution. To save the current flags, we must first load them into the AH register and then move them to the location MEM1. The instructions that do this are

```
LAHF
MOV     MEM1,AH
```

Similarly, to load the flags with the contents of MEM2, we must first copy the contents of MEM2 into AH and then store the contents of AH into the flags. The instructions for this are

```
MOV     AH,MEM2
SAHF
```

Thus the entire instruction sequence is

```
LAHF
MOV     MEM1, AH
MOV     AH, MEM2
SAHF
```

Mnemonic	Meaning	Operation	Flags Affected
LAHF	Load AH from flags	(AH) ← (Flags)	None
SAHF	Store AH into flags	(Flags) ← (AH)	SF, ZF, AF, PF, CF
CLC	Clear carry flag	(CF) ← 0	CF
STC	Set carry flag	(CF) ← 1	CF
CMC	Complement carry flag	(CF) ← $(\overline{CF})$	CF
CLI	Clear interrupt flag	(IF) ← 0	IF
STI	Set interrupt flag	(IF) ← 1	IF

Figure 4.1 Flag control instructions.

The next three instructions, CLC, STC, and CMC, are used to manipulate the carry flag. They permit CF to be cleared, set, or complemented to its inverse logic level, respectively. For example, if CF is 1 and the CMC instruction is executed, it becomes 0.

The last two instructions are used to manipulate the interrupt flag. Executing the clear interrupt (CLI) instruction sets IF to logic 0 and disables the interrupt interface. On the other hand, executing the STI instruction sets IF to 1 and the microprocessor starts accepting interrupts from that point on.

Example 4.2

Of the three carry flag instructions CLC, STC, and CMC only one is really an independent instruction. That is, the operation that it provides cannot be performed by a series of the other two instructions. Determine which one of the carry instructions is the independent instruction.

Solution. Let us begin with the CLC instruction. The clear carry operation can be performed by an STC instruction followed by a CMC instruction. Therefore, CLC is not an independent instruction. Moreover, the operation of the set carry (STC) instruction is equivalent to the operation performed by a CLC instruction followed by a CMC instruction. Thus STC is also not an independent instruction. On the other hand, the operation performed by the last instruction, complement carry (CMC), cannot be expressed in terms of the CLR and STC instructions. Therefore, it is the independent instruction.

4.3 COMPARE INSTRUCTION

There is an instruction included in the instruction set of the 8086 which can be used to compare two 8-bit or 16-bit numbers. It is the *compare* (CMP) instruction of Fig. 4.2(a). Figure 4.2(b) shows that the operands can reside in a storage location in memory, a register within the MPU, or as part of the instruction. For instance, a

Mnemonic	Meaning	Format	Operation	Flags Affected
CMP	Compare	CMP D,S	(D) − (S) is used in setting or resetting the flags	CF, AF, OF, PF, SF, ZF

(a)

Destination	Source
Register	Register
Register	Memory
Memory	Register
Register	Immediate
Memory	Immediate
Accumulator	Immediate

(b)

Figure 4.2 (a) Compare instruction; **(b)** allowed operands.

byte-wide number in a register such as BL can be compared to a second byte-wide number that is supplied as immediate data.

The result of the comparison is reflected by changes in six of the status flags of the 8086. Notice in Fig. 4.2(a) that it affects the overflow flag, sign flag, zero flag, auxiliary carry flag, parity flag, and carry flag. The logic state of these flags can be referenced by instructions in order to make a decision whether or not to alter the sequence in which the program executes.

The process of comparison performed by the CMP instruction is basically a subtraction operation. The source operand is subtracted from the destination operand. However, the result of this subtraction is not saved. Instead, based on the result the appropriate flags are set or reset.

The subtraction is done using 2's-complement arithmetic. For example, let us assume that the destination operand equals $10011001_2 = -103_{10}$ and that the source operand equals $00011011_2 = +27_{10}$. Subtracting the source from the destination, we get

$$\begin{array}{rcl} 10011001_2 & = & -103_{10} \\ -\ 00011011_2 & = & -\ (+27_{10}) \\ \hline \end{array}$$

Replacing the destination operand with its 2's-complement and adding yields

$$\begin{array}{rcl} 10011001_2 & = & -103_{10} \\ +\ 11100101_2 & = & -\ \ 27_{10} \\ \hline 01111110_2 & = & +126_{10} \end{array}$$

In the process of obtaining this result, we set the status that follows:

1. No carry is generated from bit 3 to bit 4; therefore, the auxiliary carry flag AF is at logic 0.
2. There is a carry out from bit 7. Thus carry flag CF is set.
3. Even through a carry out of bit 7 is generated, there is no carry from bit 6 to bit 7. This is an overflow condition and the OF flag is set.
4. There are an even number of 1s; therefore, this makes parity flag PF equal to 1.
5. Bit 7 is zero and therefore sign flag SF is at logic 0.
6. The result that is produced is nonzero, which makes zero flag ZF logic 0.

Notice that the result produced by the subtraction of the two 8-bit numbers is not correct. This condition was indicated by setting the overflow flag.

Example 4.3

Describe what happens to the status flags as the sequence of instructions that follow is executed.

```
MOV  AX,01234H
MOV  BX,0ABCDH
CMP  AX,BX
```

Assume that flags ZF, SF, CF, AF, OF, and PF are all initially reset.

Solution. The first instruction loads AX with 1234_{16}. No status flags are affected by the execution of a MOV instruction. The second instruction puts $ABCD_{16}$ into the BX register. Again status is not affected. Thus, after execution of these two move instructions, the contents of AX and BX are

$$(AX) = 1234_{16} = 0001001000110100_2$$

and

$$(BX) = ABCD_{16} = 1010101111001101_2$$

The third instruction is a 16-bit comparison with AX representing the destination and BX the source. Therefore, the contents of BX are subtracted from that of AX.

$$(AX) - (BX) = 0001001000110100_2 - 1010101111001101_2$$

Replacing (BX) with its 2's complement and adding, we get

$$(AX) + \text{2's complement } (BX) = 0001001000110100_2 + 0101010000110010_2 + 1_2$$
$$= 0110011001100111_2$$

The flags are either set or reset based on the result of this subtraction. Notice that the result is nonzero and positive. This makes ZF and SF equal to zero. Moreover, the carry, auxiliary carry, and no overflow conditions have occurred. Therefore, CF and AF are at logic 1 while OF is at logic 0.

Finally, the result has odd parity; therefore, PF is set to 0. These results are summarized in Fig. 4.3.

Instruction	ZF	SF	CF	AF	OF	PF
Initial state	0	0	0	0	0	0
MOV AX, 01234H	0	0	0	0	0	0
MOV BX,0ABCDH	0	0	0	0	0	0
CMP AX,BX	0	0	1	1	0	0

Figure 4.3 Affect on flags of executing instructions.

4.4 JUMP INSTRUCTIONS

The purpose of a *jump* instruction is to alter the execution path of instructions in the program. In the 8086 microprocessor, the code segment register and instruction pointer keep track of the next instruction to be executed. Thus a jump instruction involves altering the contents of these registers. In this way, execution continues at an address other than that of the next sequential instruction. That is, a jump occurs to another part of the program. Typically, program execution is not intended to return to the next sequential instruction after the jump instruction. Therefore, no return linkage is saved when the jump takes place.

The Unconditional and Conditional Jump

The 8086 microprocessor allows two different types of jump instructions. They are the *unconditional jump* and the *conditional jump*. In an unconditional jump, no status requirements are imposed for the jump to occur. That is, as the instruction is executed, the jump always takes place to change the execution sequence.

This concept is illustrated in Fig. 4.4(a). Notice that when the instruction JMP AA in part I is executed, program control is passed to a point in part III identified by the label AA. Execution resumes with the instruction corresponding to AA. In this way, the instructions in part II of the program have been bypassed. That is, they have been jumped over.

On the other hand, for a conditional jump instruction, status conditions that exist at the moment the jump instruction is executed decide whether or not the jump will occur. If this condition or conditions are met, the jump takes place; otherwise,

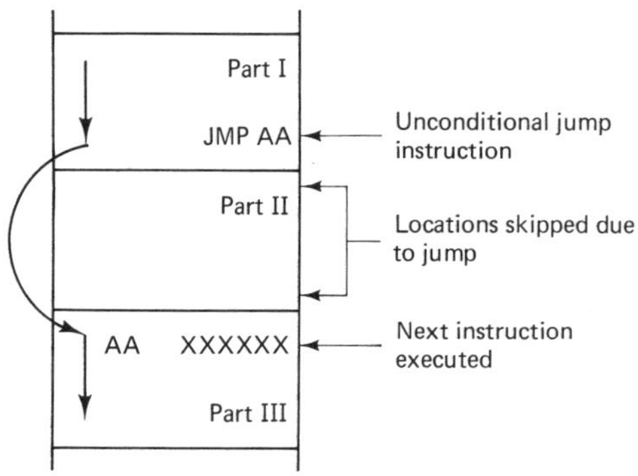

(a)

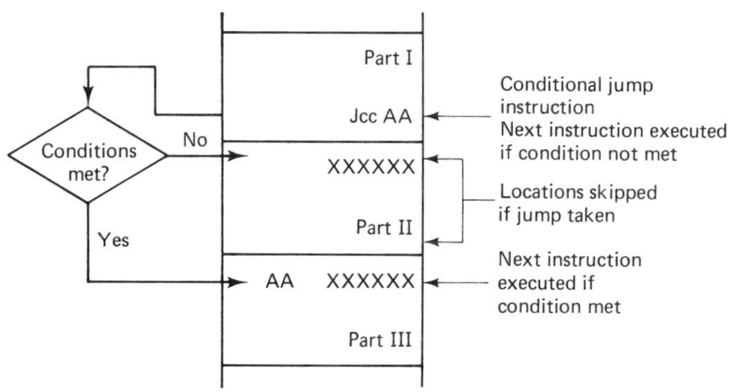

(b)

Figure 4.4 **(a)** Unconditional jump program sequence; **(b)** conditional jump program sequence.

execution continues with the next sequential instruction of the program. The conditions that can be referenced by a conditional jump instruction are status flags such as carry (CF), parity (PF), and overflow (OF).

Looking at Fig. 4.4(b), we see that execution of the conditional jump instruction in part I causes a test to be initiated. If the conditions of the test are not met, the NO path is taken and execution continues with the next sequential instruction. This corresponds to the first instruction in part II. However, if the result of the conditional test is YES, a jump is initiated to the segment of the program identified as part III and the instructions in part II are bypassed.

Unconditional Jump Instruction

The unconditional jump instruction of the 8086 is shown in Fig. 4.5(a) together with its valid operand combinations in Fig. 4.5(b). There are two basic kinds of unconditional jumps. The first, called an *intrasegment jump*, is limited to addresses within the current code segment. This type of jump is achieved by just modifying the value in IP. The other kind of jump, the *intersegment jump*, permits jumps from one code segment to another. Implementation of this type of jump requires modification of the contents of both CS and IP.

Jump instructions specified with a *Short-label, Near-label, Memptr16*, or *Regptr16 operand* represent intrasegment jumps. The Short-label and Near-label operands specify the jump relative to the address of the jump instruction itself. For example, in a Short-label jump instruction an 8-bit number is coded as an immediate operand to specify the *signed displacement* of the next instruction to be executed from the location of the jump instruction. When the jump instruction is executed, IP is reloaded with a new value equal to the updated value in IP, which is (IP) + 2, plus the signed displacement. The new value of IP and current value in CS give the ad-

Mnemonic	Meaning	Format	Operation	Flags Affected
JMP	Unconditional jump	JMP Operand	Jump is initiated to the address specified by Operand	None

(a)

Operand
Short-label
Near-label
Far-label
Memptr16
Regptr16
Memptr32

(b)

Figure 4.5 **(a)** Unconditional jump instruction; **(b)** allowed operands.

dress of the next instruction to be fetched and executed. With an 8-bit displacement, the Short-label operand can only be used to initiate a jump in the range −126 to +129 bytes from the location of the jump instruction.

On the other hand, Near-label operands specify the displacement with a 16-bit immediate operand. This corresponds to a range equal to 32K bytes forward or backward from the jump instruction. The displacement is automatically calculated by the 8086's assembler during program assembly. Thus a programmer can use symbolic labels as operands.

An example is the instruction

JMP LABEL

This means to jump to the point in the program corresponding to the tag LABEL. The programmer does not have to worry about counting the number of bytes from the jump instruction to the location to which control is to be passed. Moreover, the fact that it is coded as a Short- or Near-label displacement is also determined by the assembler.

The jump to address can also be specified indirectly by the contents of a memory location or the contents of a register. These two types correspond to the Memptr16 and Regptr16 operands, respectively. Just as for the Near-label operand, they both permit a jump of + or − 32K bytes from the address of the jump instruction.

For example,

JMP BX

uses the contents of register BX for the displacement. That is, the value in BX is copied into IP. Then the physical address of the next instruction is obtained by using the current contents of CS and this new value in IP.

To specify an operand to be used as a pointer, the various addressing modes available with the 8086 can be used. For instance,

JMP [BX]

uses the contents of BX as the address of the memory location that contains the offset address. This offset is loaded into IP, where it is used together with the current contents of CS to compute the "jump to" address.

The intersegment unconditional jump instructions correspond to the *Far-label* and *Memptr32 operands* that are shown in Fig. 4.5(b). Far-label uses a 32-bit immediate operand to specify the jump to address. The first 16 bits of this 32-bit pointer are loaded into IP and are an offset address relative to the contents of the code segment register. The next 16 bits are loaded into the CS register and define the new 64K-byte code segment.

An indirect way to specify the offset and code segment address for an intersegment jump is by using the Memptr32 operand. This time four consecutive memory bytes starting at the specified address contain the offset address and the new code segment address, respectively. Just like the Memptr16 operand, and Memptr32 operand may be specified using any one of the various addressing modes of the 8086.

An example is the instruction

JMP FARSEG[DI]

It uses the contents of DS and DI to calculate the address of the memory location that contains the first word of the pointer that identifies the location to which the jump will take place. The two-word pointer starting at this address is read into IP and CS to pass control to the new point in the program.

Conditional Jump Instruction

The second type of jump instructions are those which perform conditional jump operations. Figure 4.6(a) shows a general form of this instruction and Fig. 4.6(b) is a list of each of the conditional jump instructions in the 8086's instruction set. Notice that each of these instructions tests for the presence or absence of certain conditions.

For instance, the *jump on carry* (JC) instruction makes a test to determine if carry flag (CF) is set. Depending on the result of the test, the jump to the location specified by its operand either takes place or does not. If CF equals 0, the test fails and execution continues with the instruction at the address following the JC instruc-

Mnemonic	Meaning	Format	Operation	Flags Affected
Jcc	Conditional jump	Jcc Operand	If the specific condition cc is true, the jump to the address specified by the Operand is initiated; otherwise, the next instruction is executed	None

(a)

Mnemonic	Meaning
JA/JNBE	Jump if above/jump if not below or equal
JAE/JNB	Jump if above or equal/jump if not below
JB/JNAE	Jump if below/jump if not above or equal
JBE/JNA	Jump if below or equal/jump if not above
JC	Jump if carry
JCXZ	Jump if CX is zero
JE/JZ	Jump if equal/jump if zero
JG/JNLE	Jump if greater/jump if not less or equal
JGE/JNL	Jump if greater or equal/jump if not less
JLE/JNG	Jump if less or equal/jump if not greater
JNC	Jump if not carry
JNE/JNZ	Jump if not equal/jump if not zero
JNO	Jump if not overflow
JNP/JPO	Jump if not parity/jump if parity odd
JNS	Jump if not sign
JO	Jump if overflow
JP/JPE	Jump if parity/jump if parity even
JS	Jump if sign

(b)

Figure 4.6 **(a)** Conditional jump instruction; **(b)** types of conditional jump instructions.

tion. On the other hand, if CF is set to 1, the test condition is satisfied and the jump is performed.

Notice that for some of the instructions in Fig. 4.6(b) two different mnemonics can be used. This feature can be used to improve program readability. That is, for each occurrence of the instruction in the program, it can be identified with the mnemonic that best describes its function.

For instance, the instruction *jump on parity* (JP)/*jump on parity even* (JPE) can be used to test parity flag PF for logic 1. Since PF is set to 1 if the result from a computation has even parity, this instruction can initiate a jump based on the occurrence of even parity. The reverse instruction JNP/JNPE is also provided. It can be used to initiate a jump based on the occurrence of a result with odd parity instead of even parity.

In a similar manner, the instructions *jump if equal* (JE) and *jump if zero* (JZ) have the same function. Either notation can be used in a program to determine if the result of a computation was zero.

All other conditional jump instructions work in a similar way except that they test different conditions to decide whether or not the jump is to take place. Examples of these conditions are that the contents of CX are zero, an overflow has occurred, or the result is negative.

To distinguish between comparisons of signed and unsigned numbers by jump instructions, two different names, which seem to be the same, have been devised. They are above and below for comparison of unsigned numbers and less and greater for comparison of signed numbers. For instance, the number $ABCD_{16}$ is above the number 1234_{16} if considered as an unsigned number. On the other hand, if they are considered as signed numbers, $ABCD_{16}$ is negative and 1234_{16} is positive. Therefore, $ABCD_{16}$ is less than 1234_{16}.

Example 4.4

Write a program to move a block of N bytes of data starting at offset address BLK1ADDR to another block starting at offset address BLK2ADDR. Assume that both blocks are in the same data segment, whose starting point is defined by the data segment address DATASEGADDR.

Solution. The steps to be implemented to solve this problem are outlined in the flowchart in Fig. 4.7(a). It has four basic operations. The first operation is initialization. Initialization involves establishing the initial address of the data segment. This is done by loading the DS register with the value DATASEGADDR. Furthermore, source index register SI and destination index register DI are initialized with addresses BLK1ADDR and BLK2ADDR, respectively. In this way, they point to the beginning of the source block and the beginning of the destination block, respectively. To keep track of the count, register CX is initialized with N, the number of points to be moved. This leads us to the following assembly language statements.

```
MOV    AX,DATASEGADDR
MOV    DS,AX
MOV    SI,BLK1ADDR
MOV    DI,BLK2ADDR
```

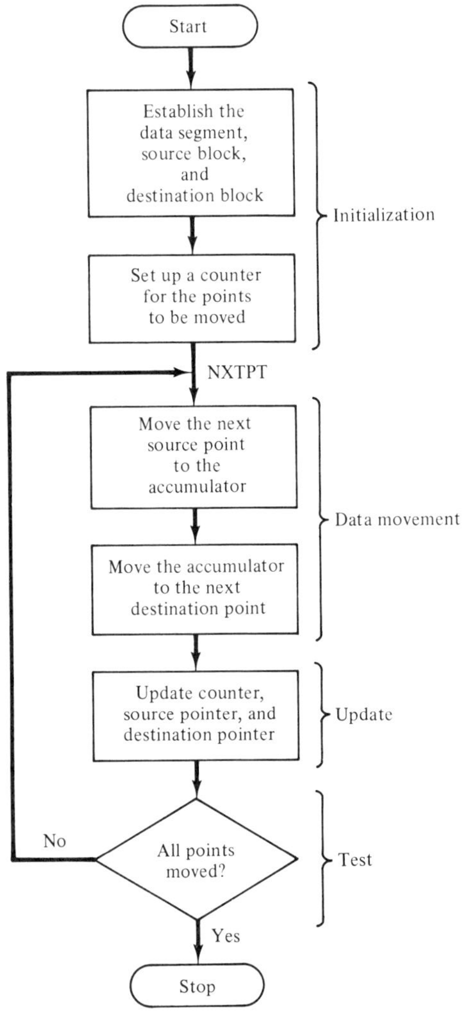

(a)

```
        MOV     AX, DATASEGADDR
        MOV     DS, AX
        MOV     SI, BLK1ADDR
        MOV     DI, BLK2ADDR
        MOV     CX, N
NXTPT:  MOV     AH, [SI]
        MOV     [DI], AH
        INC     SI
        INC     DI
        DEC     CX
        JNZ     NXTPT
        HLT
```

(b)

Figure 4.7 **(a)** Block transfer flowchart; **(b)** program.

```
MOV CX,N
```

Notice that DS cannot be directly loaded by immediate data with a MOV instruction. Therefore, the address was first loaded into AX and then moved to DS. SI, DI, and CX can be loaded directly with immediate data.

The next operation that must be performed is the actual movement of data from the source block of memory to the destination block. The offset addresses are already loaded into SI and DI; therefore, move instructions that employ indirect addressing can be used to accomplish the data transfer operation. Remember that the 8086 does not allow direct memory-to-memory moves. For this reason, AX will be used as an intermediate storage location for data. The source byte is moved into AX with one instruction and then another instruction is needed to move it from AX to the destination location. Thus the data move is accomplished by the following instructions:

```
NXTPT:  MOV  AH,[SI]
        MOV  [DI],AH
```

Notice that for a byte move only the higher 8 bits of AX are used. Therefore, the operand is specified as AH instead of AX.

The next operation is to update the pointers in SI and DI so that they are ready for the next byte move. Also, the counter must be decremented so that it corresponds to the number of bytes that remain to be moved. These updates can be done by the following sequence of instructions:

```
INC  SI
INC  DI
DEC  CX
```

The test operation involves determining whether or not all the data points have been moved. The contents of CX represents this condition. When its value is nonzero, there still are points to be moved; whereas a value of zero indicates that the block move is complete. This zero condition is reflected by 1 in ZF. The instruction needed to perform this test is

```
JNZ NXTPT
```

Here NXTPT is a label that corresponds to the first instruction in the data move operation. The last instruction in the program can be a *halt* (HLT) instruction to indicate the end of the block move operation. The entire program is shown in Fig. 4.7(b).

Example 4.5

It is required to determine the average of a set of data points stored in a buffer. The number of points in the buffer, the offset address of the beginning of the buffer, and the data segment address are stored in a table called a parameter table. Figure 4.8(a) shows the parameters needed for the average program. Notice that the beginning address of this table is $ABCD0_{16}$. This first address holds the number that indicates how many data points are in the buffer. Since a byte is used to specify the number of data points, the size of the buffer is limited to 256 bytes. The offset address of the beginning of the buffer is stored at table locations $ABCD1_{16}$ and $ABCD2_{16}$. This buffer table offset address is with respect to the data segment defined by the address in locations

Address	Contents	Meaning
$ABCD0_{16}$	FF	Number of points in buffer
$ABCD1_{16}$	10	Offset address for the beginning of the buffer
$ABCD2_{16}$	00	
$ABCD3_{16}$	00	Data segment address
$ABCD4_{16}$	A0	

(a)

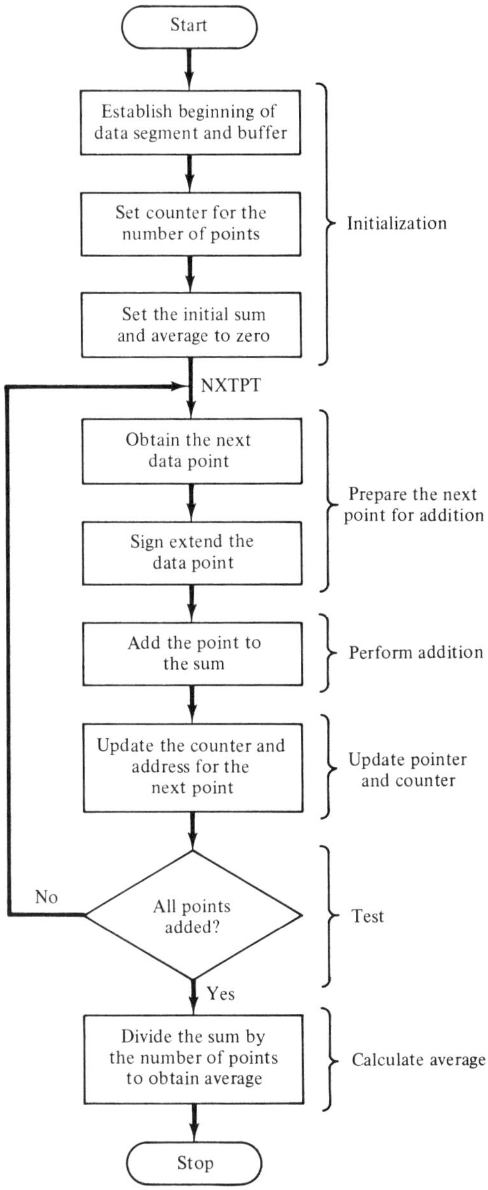

(b)

```
        MOV     AX, 0A000H
        MOV     DS, AX
        MOV     DI, 0BCD0H
        MOV     CL, [DI]
        MOV     BL, CL
        LDS     SI, [DI + 1]
        MOV     DX, 0000H
NXTPT:  MOV     AL, [SI]
        CBW
        ADD     DX, AX
        INC     SI
        DEC     CL
        JNZ     NXTPT
        MOV     AX, DX
        IDIV    BL
        HLT
```

(c).

Figure 4.8 **(a)** Parameter table; **(b)** flowchart for the average calculation program; **(c)** program.

$ABCD3_{16}$ and $ABCD4_{16}$. Assuming that the data points are signed 8-bit binary numbers, write a program to find their average.

Solution. The average can be found by adding all the signed numbers and then dividing their sum by the number of points that were added. Even though 8-bit data points are being added, the sum that results can be more than 8 bits. Therefore, we will consider a 16-bit result for the sum and it will be held in register DX. The average that is obtained turns out to be just 8 bits long. It will be available in AL at the completion of the program.

Our plan for the program that will solve this problem is shown in Fig. 4.8(b). This flowchart can be divided into six basic operations, which are: initialization, preparing the next point for addition, performing the addition, updating the counter and pointer, testing for the end of the summation, and computing the average.

Initialization involves establishing the data segment and data buffer addresses and loading the data point counter. This is achieved by loading the appropriate registers within the 8086 with parameters from the parameter table. The instructions that perform this initialization are:

```
MOV  AX,0A000H
MOV  DS,AX
MOV  DI,0BCD0H
MOV  CL,[DI]
MOV  BL,CL
LDS  SI,[DI+1]
```

The first two instructions define the data segment in which the parameter table resides. This is achieved by first loading AX with the immediate operand $A000_{16}$ of a MOV instruction and then copying it into DS. Then another MOV instruction establishes a pointer to the parameter table in register DI. This is done by loading DI with immediate operand $BCD0_{16}$. The instruction that follows this uses DI as a pointer to load CL from the first address in the parameter table. This address is $ABCD0_{16}$ and contains the number of points to be used in forming the average. Looking at Fig. 4.8(a), we see that this value is FF_{16}. The next instruction copies the number in CL into BL for later use. The LDS instruction is used to define the buffer together with the data segment in which it resides. This instruction first loads SI with the offset address of the beginning of the buffer from table locations $ABCD1_{16}$ and $ABCD2_{16}$ and then DS with the address of the data segment in which the data table lies from table locations $ABCD3_{16}$ and $ABCD4_{16}$. The sum must start with zero; therefore, register DX, which is to hold the sum, is loaded with zeros by the instruction.

```
MOV DX,0000H
```

The next operation involves obtaining a byte of data from the buffer, making it into a 16-bit number by sign extension, and adding it to the contents of the DX register. This is accomplished by the following sequence of instructions:

```
NXTPT:  MOV  AL,[SI]
        CBW
        ADD  DX,AX
```

The first instruction loads AL with the element in the buffer that is pointed to by the address in SI. The CBW instruction converts the signed byte in AL to a signed word in AX by extending its sign. Next the 16-bit signed number in AX is added to the sum in DX. Notice that the label NXTPT (next point) has been used on the first instruction.

To prepare for the next addition, we must increment the value in SI such that it points to the next element in the buffer and decrement the count in CL. To do this, we use the following instructions:

```
INC   SI
DEC   CL
```

If the contents of CL at this point are nonzero, we should go back to obtain and add the next element from the buffer; otherwise, we just proceed with the next instruction in the program. To do this, we execute the following instruction:

```
JNZ NXTPT
```

Execution of this instruction tests the value in ZF that results from the DEC CL instruction. If this flag is not set to 1, a jump is initiated to the instruction corresponding to the label NXTPT. Remember that NXTPT is placed at the instruction used to move a byte into AL for addition to the sum. In this way, we see that this part of the program will be repeated until all data points have been added. After this is complete, the sum resides in DX.

The average is obtained by dividing the accumulated sum in DX by the number of data points. The count of data points was saved earlier in BL. However, the contents of DX cannot be divided directly. It must first be moved into AX. Once there, the signed divide instruction can be used to do the division. This gives the following instructions:

```
MOV    AX,DX
IDIV   BL
```

The result of the division, which is the average, is now in AL. The entire average calculation program is shown in Fig. 4.8(c).

Example 4.6

It is required to sort an array of 16-bit signed binary numbers such that they are arranged in ascending order. For instance, if the original array is

$$5,\ 1,\ 29,\ 15,\ 38,\ 3,\ -8,\ -32$$

after sorting, the array that results would be

$$-32,\ -8,\ 1,\ 3,\ 5,\ 15,\ 29,\ 38$$

Assume that the array of numbers is stored at consecutive memory locations from addresses $A0400_{16}$ through $A04FE_{16}$ in memory. Write a sort program.

Solution. First we will develop an algorithm that can be used to sort an array of elements A(0), A(1), A(2), through A(N) into ascending order. One way of doing this is to take the first number in the array, which is A(0), and compare it to the second number A(1). If A(0) is greater than A(1), the two numbers are swapped; otherwise, they are left alone. Next A(0) is compared to A(2) and based on the result of this comparison they are either swapped or left alone. This sequence is repeated until A(0) has been compared with all numbers up through A(N). When this is complete, the smallest number will be in the A(0) position.

Now A(1) must be compared to A(2) through A(N) in the same way. After this is done, the second smallest number is in the A(1) position. Up to this point, just two of the N numbers have been put in ascending order. Therefore, the procedure must be continued for A(2) through A(N – 1) to complete the sort.

Figure 4.9(a) illustrates the use of this algorithm for an array with just four numbers. The numbers are A(0) = 5, A(1) = 1, A(2) = 29, and A(3) = – 8. During the sort sequence, A(0) = 5 is first compared to A(1) = 1. Since 5 is greater than 1, A(0) and A(1) are swapped. Now A(0) = 1 is compared to A(2) = 29. This time 1 is less than 29; therefore, the numbers are not swapped and A(0) remains equal to 1. Next, A(0) = 1 is compared with A(3) = – 8. A(0) is greater than A(3). Thus A(0) and A(3) are swapped and A(0) becomes equal to –8. Notice in Fig. 4.9(a) that the lowest of the four numbers now resides in A(0).

The sort sequence in Fig. 4.9(a) continues with A(1) = 5 being compared first to A(2) = 29 and then to A(3) = 1. In the first comparison, A(1) is less than A(2). For this reason, their values are not swapped. But in the second comparison, A(1) is greater than A(3); therefore, the two values are swapped. In this way, the second lowest number, which is 1, is sorted into A(1).

It just remains to sort A(2) and A(3). Comparing these two values, we see that 29 is greater than 5. This causes the two values to be swapped such that A(2) = 5 and A(3) = 29. As shown in Fig. 4.9(a), the sorting of the array is now complete.

Now we will implement the algorithm on the 8086 microprocessor. The flowchart for its implementation is shown in Fig. 4.9(b). The first block in the flowchart represents the initialization of data segment register DS and pointers $PNTR_1$ and $PNTR_3$. The DS register is initialized with $A000_{16}$ to define a data segment starting from memory address $A0000_{16}$. $PNTR_1$ points to the first element in the array. It will be register SI and will be initialized to 0400_{16}. Therefore, the first element of the array is at address $A0400_{16}$. For pointer $PNTR_3$, we will use register BX and will initialize it to $04FE_{16}$. It points to the last element in the array, which is at address $A04FE_{16}$. Next, $PNTR_2$,

I	0	1	2	3	Status
A(I)	5	1	29	−8	Original array
A(I)	1	5	29	−8	Array after comparing A(0) and A(1)
A(I)	1	5	29	−8	Array after comparing A(0) and A(2)
A(I)	−8	5	29	1	Array after comparing A(0) and A(3)
A(I)	−8	5	29	1	Array after comparing A(1) and A(2)
A(I)	−8	1	29	5	Array after comparing A(1) and A(3)
A(I)	−8	1	5	29	Array after comparing A(2) and A(3)

(a)

Figure 4.9 **(a)** Sort example; **(b)** flowchart for the sort program; **(c)** sort program.

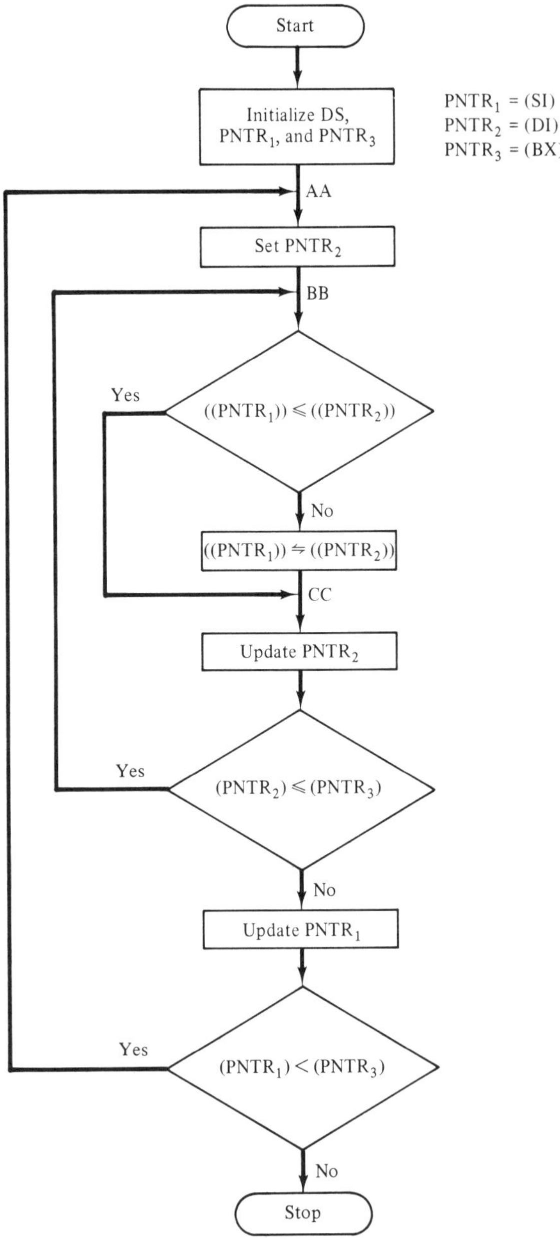

(b)

Figure 4.9 *(continued)*

```
        MOV   AX, 0A000H
        MOV   DS, AX
        MOV   SI, 0400H
        MOV   BX, 04FEH
AA:     MOV   DI, SI
        ADD   DI, 02H
BB:     MOV   AX, [SI]
        CMP   AX, [DI]
        JLE   CC
        MOV   [DX], [DI]
        MOV   [SI], DX
        MOV   [DI], AX
CC:     INC   DI
        INC   DI
        CMP   DI, BX
        JBE   BB
        INC   SI
        INC   SI
        CMP   SI, BX
        JB    AA
        HLT
```

Figure 4.9 *(continued)* (c)

the moving pointer, is initialized so that it points to the second element in the array. Register DI will be used for this pointer. This leads to the following instruction sequence for initialization:

```
        MOV  AX,0A000H
        MOV  DS,AX
        MOV  SI,0400H
        MOV  BX,04FEH
AA:     MOV  DI,SI
        ADD  DI,02H
```

Notice that DS was loaded via AX with the immediate data $A000_{16}$ to define a data segment starting at $A0000_{16}$. SI and BX, which are $PNTR_1$ and $PNTR_3$, respectively, are loaded with immediate operands 0400_{16} and $04FE_{16}$. In this way, they point to the first and last elements of the array, respectively. Finally, register DI, which is $PNTR_2$, is loaded with 0400_{16} from SI and then incremented by 2 with an ADD instruction such that it points to the second element in the array. This completes the initialization process.

Next, the array element pointed to by $PNTR_1$ is to be compared to the element pointed to by $PNTR_2$. If the element corresponding to $PNTR_1$ is arithmetically less than the element corresponding to pointer $PNTR_2$, the two elements are already in ascending order. But if this is not the case, the two elements must be interchanged. Both of these elements are in memory. However, the 8086 cannot directly compare two values in memory. For this reason, one of the two elements must be moved to a register within the 8086. We will use AX for this purpose. The resulting code is as follows:

```
BB:     MOV  AX,[SI]
        CMP  AX,[DI]
```

```
       JLE   CC
       MOV   [DX],[DI]
       MOV   [SI],DX
       MOV   [DI],AX
CC:
```

The first instruction moves the element pointed to by $PNTR_1$ into AX. The second instruction compares the value in AX with the element pointed to by $PNTR_2$. The result of this comparison is reflected in the status flags. The jump on less than or equal to instruction that follows checks if the first element is arithmetically less than or equal to the second element. If the result of this check is yes, control is transferred to CC. CC is a label to be used in the segment of program that will follow. If the check fails, the two elements must be interchanged. In this case, the instructions executed next move the element pointed to by $PNTR_2$ into the location pointed to by $PNTR_1$. Then the copy of the original value pointed to by $PNTR_1$, which is saved in AX, is moved to the location pointed to by $PNTR_2$.

To continue sorting through the rest of the elements in the array, we update $PNTR_2$ such that it points to the next element in the array. This comparison should be repeated until the first element has been compared to each of the other elements in the array. That is, $PNTR_2$ equals $PNTR_3$. This part of the program can be done with the code that follows:

```
CC:   INC   DI
      INC   DI
      CMP   DI,BX
      JBE   BB
```

The first two instructions update $PNTR_2$ such that it points to the next element. The third instruction compares $PNTR_2$ to $PNTR_3$ to determine whether or not they are equal. If they are equal to each other, the first element has been compared to the last element and we are ready to continue with the second element. Otherwise, we must repeat from the label BB. This test is done with the jump on below or equal instruction. Notice that label BB corresponds to the beginning of the part of the program that compares the elements of the array. Once we fall through the JBE instruction, we have placed the smallest number in the array into the position pointed to by $PNTR_1$. To process the rest of the elements in the array in a similar way, $PNTR_1$ must be moved over the entire range of elements and the foregoing procedure repeated. This can be done by implementing the code that follows:

```
      INC   SI
      INC   SI
      CMP   SI,BX
      JB    AA
      HLT
```

The first two instructions increment pointer $PNTR_1$ such that it points to the next element in the array. The third instruction checks if all the elements have been sorted. The fourth instruction passes control back to the sorting sequence of instructions if $PNTR_1$ does not point to the last element. However, if all elements of the array have been sorted, we come to a halt at the end of the program. The entire program appears in Fig. 4.9(c).

4.5 SUBROUTINES AND SUBROUTINE-HANDLING INSTRUCTIONS

Subroutines are procedures written separate from the main program. Whenever the main program must perform a function that is defined by a subroutine, it calls the subroutine into operation. In order to do this, control must be passed from the main program to the starting point of the subroutine. Execution continues with the subroutine and upon completion control is returned back to the main program at the instruction that follows the one that called the subroutine. Notice that the difference between the operation of a subroutine call and a jump is that a call to a subroutine not only produces a jump to an appropriate address in program storage memory, but it also has a mechanism for saving information such as IP and CS, which is needed to return back to the main program.

CALL and RET Instructions

There are two basic instructions in the instruction set of the 8086 for subroutine handling. They are the *call* (CALL) and *return* (RET) instructions. Together they provide the mechanism for calling a subroutine into operation and returning control back to the main program at its completion. We will first discuss these two instructions and later introduce other instructions which can be used in conjunction with subroutines.

Just like the JMP instruction, CALL allows implementation of two types of operations, the *intrasegment call* and the *intersegment call.* The CALL instruction is shown in Fig. 4.10(a) and its allowed operand variations are shown in Fig. 4.10(b).

It is the operand that initiates either ran intersegment or an intrasegment call. The operands Near-proc, Memptr16, and Regptr16 all specify intrasegment calls to a subroutine. In all three cases, execution of the instruction causes the contents of IP to be saved on the stack. Then the stack pointer (SP) is decremented by 2. The saved values of IP is the address of the instruction that follows the CALL instruction. After saving the return address, a new 16-bit value, which corresponds to the storage location of the first instruction in the subroutine, is loaded into IP.

The three types of intrasegment operands represent different ways of specifying this new value of IP. In a Near-proc operand, the displacement of the first instruction of the subroutine from the current value of IP is supplied directly by the instruction. An example is

CALL NEAR PROC

Here the label NEAR determines the 16-bit displacement and is coded as an immediate operand following the opcode for the call instruction. Call is actually a relative addressing mode instruction; that is, the offset address is calculated relative to the address of the call instruction itself. With 16 bits, the displacement is limited to + or − 32K bytes.

Mnemonic	Meaning	Format	Operation	Flags Affected
CALL	Subroutine call	CALL operand	Execution continues from the address of the subroutine specified by the operand. Information required to return back to the main program such as IP and CS are saved on the stack.	None

(a)

Operand
Near-proc Far-proc Memptr16 Regptr16 Memptr32

(b)

Figure 4.10 **(a)** Subroutine call instruction; **(b)** allowed operands.

The Memptr16 and Regptr16 operands provide indirect subroutine addressing by specifying a memory location or an internal register, respectively, as the source of a new value for IP. The value specified in this way is not a displacement. It is the actual offset that is to be loaded into IP. An example of the Regptr16 operand is

CALL BX

When this instruction is executed, the contents of BX are loaded into IP and execution continues with the subroutine starting at a physical address derived from CS and IP.

By using one of the various addressing modes of the 8086, an internal register can be used as a pointer to an operand that resides in memory. This represents a Memptr16 type of operand. In this case, the value of the physical address of the offset is obtained from the current contents of the data segment register DS and the address or addresses held in the specified registers. For instance, the instruction

CALL [BX]

has its subroutine offset address at the memory location whose physical address is derived from the contents of DS and BX. The value stored at this memory location is loaded into IP. Again the current contents of CS and the new value in IP point to the first instruction of the subroutine.

Notice that in both intrasegment call examples the subroutine was located within the same code segment as the call instruction. The other type of CALL instruction, the intersegment call, permits the subroutine to reside in another code segment. It corresponds to the Far-proc and Memptr32 operands. These operands specify both a new offset address for IP and a new segment address for CS. In both cases, execution of the call instruction causes the contents of the CS and IP registers to be saved on the stack and then new values are loaded into IP and CS. The saved values of CS and IP permit return to the main program from a different code segment.

Far-proc represents a 32-bit immediate operand that is stored in the four bytes that follow the opcode of the call instruction in program memory. These two words are loaded directly from code segment memory into IP and CS with execution of the CALL instruction. An example is the instruction

CALL FAR PROC

On the other hand, when the operand is Memptr32, the pointer for the subroutine is stored as four bytes in data memory. The location of the first byte of the pointer can be specified indirectly by one of the 8086's registers. An example is

CALL FAR [DI]

Here the physical address of the first byte of the four-byte pointer in memory is derived from the contents of DS and DI.

Every subroutine must end by executing an instruction that returns control to the main program. This is the return (RET) instruction. It is described in Fig. 4.11(a) and (b). Notice that its execution causes the value of IP or both the values of IP and CS that were saved on the stack to be returned back to their corresponding registers. In general, an intrasegment return results from an intrasegment call and an intersegment return results from an intersegment call.

There is an additional option with the return instruction. It is that a two-byte code following the return instruction can be included. This code gets added to the stack pointer after restoring the return address into IP or IP and CS for Far-proc calls. The purpose of this stack pointer displacement is to provide a simple means by which the *parameters* that were saved on the stack before the call to the subroutine was initiated, can be discarded.

Mnemonic	Meaning	Format	Operation	Flags Affected
RET	Return	RET or RET Operand	Return to the main program by restoring IP (and CS for fat-proc). If Operand is present, it is added to the contents of SP.	None

(a)

Operand
None Disp16

(b)

Figure 4.11 **(a)** Return instruction; **(b)** allowed operands.

PUSH and POP Instructions

After the context switch to a subroutine, we find that it is usually necessary to save the contents of certain registers or some other main program parameters. These values are saved by pushing them onto the stack. Typically, these data correspond to registers and memory locations that are used by the subroutine. In this way, their original contents are kept intact in the stack segment of memory during the execution of the subroutine. Before a return to the main program takes place, the saved registers and main program parameters are restored. This is done by poping the saved values from the stack back into their original locations. Thus a typical structure of a subroutine is that shown in Fig. 4.12.

```
To save registers        { PUSH XX
and parameters           { PUSH YY
on the stack             { PUSH ZZ

                         {   .
                         {   .
Main body of the         {   .
subroutine               {   .
                         {   .
                         {   .

To restore registers     { POP  ZZ
and parameters           { POP  YY
from the stack           { POP  XX
return to main           { RET
program
```

Figure 4.12 Structure of a subroutine.

The instruction that is used to save parameters on the stack is the *push* (PUSH) instruction and that used to retrieve them back is the *pop* (POP) instruction. Notice in Fig. 4.13(a) that the standard PUSH and POP instructions can be written with a general-purpose register, a segment register (excluding CS), or a storage location in memory as their operand.

Execution of a PUSH instruction causes the data corresponding to the operand to be pushed onto the top of the stack. For instance, if the instruction is

PUSH AX

the result is as follows:

$$((SP) - 1) \leftarrow (AH)$$
$$((SP) - 2) \leftarrow (AL)$$
$$(SP) \leftarrow (SP) - 2$$

This shows that the two bytes of AX are saved in the stack part of memory and the stack pointer is decremented by 2 such that it points to the new top of the stack.

On the other hand, if the instruction is

POP AX

its execution results in

$$(AL) \leftarrow ((SP))$$

Mnemonic	Meaning	Format	Operation	Flags Affected
PUSH	Push word onto stack	PUSH S	((SP)) ← (S)	None
POP	Pop word off stack	POP D	(D) ← ((SP))	None

(a)

Operand (S or D)
Register Seg-reg (CS illegal) Memory

(b)

Figure 4.13 **(a)** Push and pop instructions; **(b)** allowed operands.

$$(AH) \longleftarrow ((SP) + 1)$$
$$(SP) \longleftarrow (SP) + 2$$

In this manner, the saved contents of AX are restored back into the register.

At times, we also want to save the contents of the flag register and if saved we will later have to restore them. These operations can be accomplished with the *push flags* (PUSHF) and *pop flags* (POPF) instructions, respectively. These instructions are shown in Fig. 4.14. Notice that PUSHF saves the contents of the flag register on the top of the stack. On the other hand, POPF returns the flags from the top of the stack to the flag register.

Example 4.7

Write a program to generate the first 20 elements of a Fibonacci series. In this series, the first and second elements are 0 and 1, respectively. Each element that follows is obtained by adding the previous two elements. Use a subroutine to generate the next element from the previous two elements. Store the elements of the series starting at address FIBSER.

Solution. Our plan for the solution of this problem is shown in Fig. 4.15(a). This flowchart shows the use of a subroutine to generate an element of the series, store it in memory, and prepare for generation of the next element.

The first step in the solution is initialization. It involves setting up a data segment, generating the first two numbers of the series, and storing them at memory locations with offset addresses FIBSER and FIBSER + 1. Then a pointer must be established

Mnemonic	Meaning	Operation	Flags Affected
PUSHF	Push flags onto stack	((SP)) ← (Flags)	None
POPF	Pop flags from stack	(Flags) ← ((SP))	OF, DF, IF, TF, SF, ZF, AF, PF, CF

Figure 4.14 Push flags and pop flags instructions.

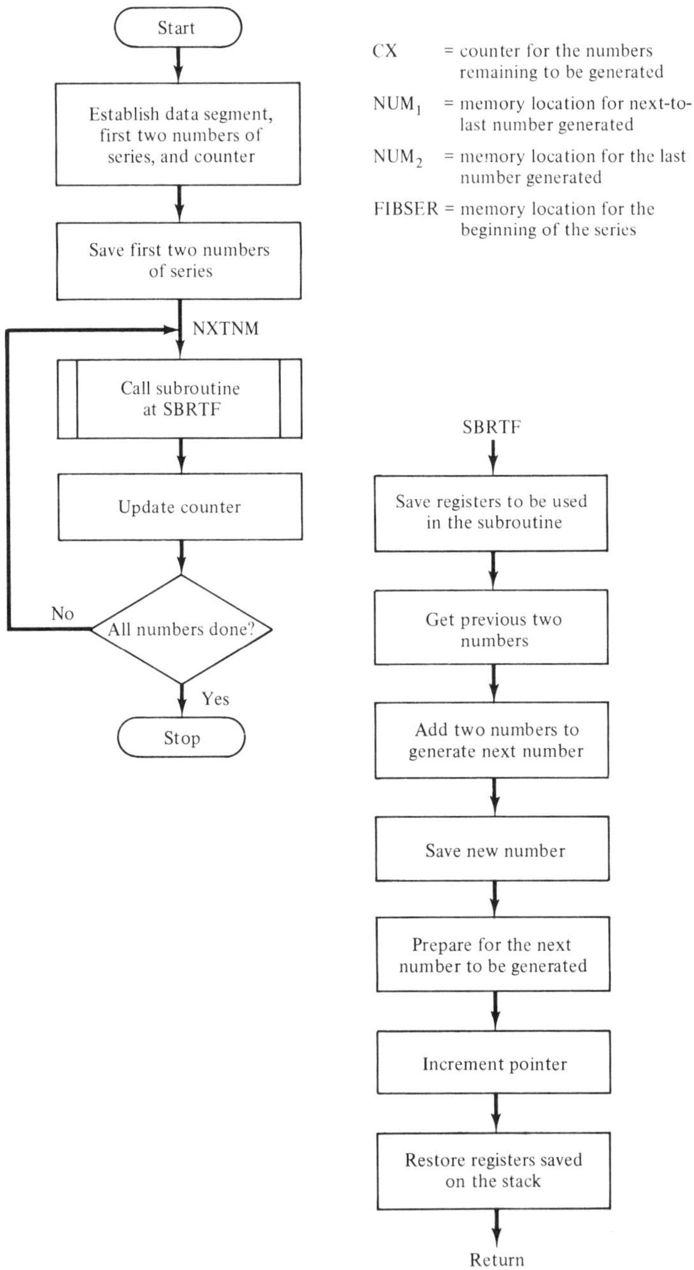

(a)

Figure 4.15 **(a)** Flowchart for generation of a Fibonacci series; **(b)** program.

```
         MOV    AX, DATASEGSTART
         MOV    DS, AX
         MOV    NUM1, 0H
         MOV    NUM2, 01H
         MOV    FIBSER, 0H
         MOV    FIBSER+1, 01H
         LEA    DI, FIBSER+2
         MOV    CX, 012H
NXTNM:   CALL   SBRTF
         DEC    CX
         JNZ    NXTNM
         HLT
SBRTF:   PUSH   AX
         PUSH   BX
         MOV    AX, NUM1
         MOV    BX, NUM2
         ADD    AX, BX
         MOV    [DI], AX
         MOV    NUM1, BX
         MOV    NUM2, AX
         INC    DI
         POP    BX
         POP    AX
         RET
```

Figure 4.15 *(continued)* (b)

to address the locations for other terms of the series. This address will be held in the DI register. Finally, a counter with initial value equal 18 can be set up in CX to keep track of how many numbers remain to be generated. The instructions needed for initialization are:

```
MOV   AX,DATASEGSTART
MOV   DS,AX
MOV   NUM1,0H
MOV   NUM2,01H
MOV   FIBSER,0H
MOV   FIBSER + 1,01H
LEA   DI,FIBSER + 2
MOV   CX,012H
```

Notice that the data segment address which is defined by variable DATASEGSTART is first moved into AX and then DS is loaded from AX with another MOV operation. Next the memory locations assigned to NUM_1 and NUM_2 are loaded with immediate data 0000_{16} and 0001_{16}, respectively. These same values are then copied into the storage locations for the first two series elements, FIBSER and FIBSER + 1. Now DI is loaded with the address of FIBSER + 2, which is a pointer to the storage location of the third element of the series. Finally, CX is loaded with 12_{16}, which is the hexadecimal equivalent of 18_{10}.

To generate the next term in the series we call a subroutine. This subroutine generates and stores the elements. Before returning to the main program, it also updates memory locations $NUM_1$and NUM_2 with the values of the immediate past two elements. After this, the counter in CX is decremented to record that a series element has been generated and stored. This process must be repeated until the counter becomes equal to zero. This leads to the following assembly language code:

```
NXTNM:  CALL  SBRTF
        DEC   CX
        JNZ   NXTNM
        HLT
```

The call is to the subroutine labeled SBRTF. After the subroutine runs to completion, program control returns to the DEC CX statement. This statement causes the count in CX to be decremented by 1. Next, a conditional jump instruction tests the zero flag to determine if the result after decrementing CX is zero. If CX is not zero, control is returned to the CALL instruction at NXTNM. If it is zero, the program is complete and execution halts.

The subroutine itself is given next.

```
SBRTF:  PUSH  AX
        PUSH  BX
        MOV   AX,NUM1
        MOV   BX,NUM2
        ADD   AX,BX
        MOV   [DI],AX
        MOV   NUM1,BX
        MOV   NUM2,AX
        INC   DI
        POP   BX
        POP   AX
        RET
```

First we save the contents of AX and BX on the stack. Then NUM_1 and NUM_2 are copied into AX and BX, respectively. They are then added together to form the next element. The resulting sum is produced in AX. Now the new element is stored in memory indirectly through DI. Remember that DI holds a pointer to the storage location of the next element of the series in memory. Then the second element, which is held in BX, becomes the new first element by copying it into NUM_1. The sum, which is in AX, becomes the new second term by copying it into NUM_2. Finally, DI is incremented by 1 such that it points to the next element of the series. The registers saved on the stack are restored and then we return back to the main program.

Notice that both the subroutine call and its return have Near-proc operands. The entire program is presented in Fig. 4.15(b).

4.6 LOOP INSTRUCTIONS

The 8086 microprocessor has three instructions specifically designed for implementing *loop operations*. These instructions can be used in place of certain conditional jump instructions and give the programmer a simpler way of writing loop sequences. The loop instructions are listed in Fig. 4.16.

The first instruction, *loop* (LOOP), works with respect to the contents of the CX register. CX must be preloaded with a count representing the number of times the loop is to be repeated. Whenever LOOP is executed, the contents of CX are first decremented by 1 and then checked to determine if they are equal to zero. If equal to zero, the loop is complete and the instruction following LOOP is executed; otherwise, control is returned to the instruction at the label specified in the loop instruction. In this way, we see that LOOP is a single instruction that functions the same as a decrement CX instruction followed by a JNZ instruction.

For example, the LOOP instruction sequence shown in Fig. 4.17 will cause the part of the program from the label NEXT through the instruction LOOP to be repeated a number of times equal to the value of count stored in CX. For example, if CX contains $000A_{16}$, the sequence of instructions included in the loop is executed 10 times.

The other two instructions in Fig. 4.16 operate in a similar way except that they check for two conditions. For instance, the instruction *loop while equal* (LOOPE)/*loop while zero* (LOOPZ) checks the contents of both CX and the ZF flag. Each time the loop instruction is executed, CX decrements by 1 without affecting the flags, its contents are checked for zero, and the state of ZF that results from execution of the previous instruction is tested for 1. If CX equals 0 and ZF equals 1, a jump is initiated to the location specified with the Short-label operand and the

Mnemonic	Meaning	Format	Operation
LOOP	Loop	LOOP Short-label	$(CX) \leftarrow (CX) - 1$ Jump is initiated to location defined by short-label if $(CX) \neq 0$; otherwise, execute next sequential instruction
LOOPE/LOOPZ	Loop while equal/ loop while zero	LOOPE/LOOPZ Short-label	$(CX) \leftarrow (CX) - 1$ Jump to location defined by short-label if $(CX) \neq 0$ and $(ZF) \neq 0$; otherwise, execute next sequential instruction
LOOPNE/ LOOPNZ	Loop while not equal/ loop while not zero	LOOPNE/LOOPNZ Short-label	$(CX) \leftarrow (CX) - 1$ Jump to location defined by short-label if $(CX) \neq 0$ and $(ZF) = 0$; otherwise, execute next sequential instruction

Figure 4.16 Loop instructions.

```
        MOV CX,COUNT     Load count for the number of repeats
NEXT:        .         ⎫
             .         ⎪
             .         ⎪
             .         ⎬— Body of routine that is repeated
             .         ⎪
             .         ⎪
             .         ⎭
        LOOP NEXT        Loop back to label NEXT if count not zero
```

Figure 4.17 Typical loop routine structure.

loop continues. If either CX is not 0 or ZF is not 1, the loop is complete and the instruction following the loop instruction is executed.

Instruction *loop while not equal* (LOOPNE)/*loop while not zero* (LOOPNZ) works in a similar way to the LOOPE/LOOPZ instruction. The difference is that it checks ZF and CX looking for ZF equal to 0 together with CX not equal to 0. If these conditions are met, the jump back to the location specified with the Short-label operand is performed and the loop continues.

Example 4.8

Given the following sequence of instructions:

```
        MOV    DL,05H
        MOV    DS,0H
        MOV    SI,0A000H
        MOV    CX,0FH
AGAIN:  INC    SI
        CMP    [SI],DL
        LOOPNE
NEXT:
```

explain what happens as they are executed.

Solution. The first four instructions are for initializing internal registers. Data register DL is loaded with the 05_{16}; data segment register DS is cleared; source index register SI is loaded with $A000_{16}$; and count register CX is loaded with $0F_{16}$ (15_{10}). After initialization, a data segment is set up at address 00000_{16} and SI points to the memory location at address $A000_{16}$ in this data segment. Moreover, DL contains the data 5_{10} and the CX register contains the loop count 15_{10}.

The part of the program that starts at the label AGAIN and ends with the LOOPNE instruction is a software loop. The first instruction in the loop increments SI by one. Therefore, the first time through the loop SI contains $A001_{16}$. The next instruction compares the contents of this memory location with the contents of DL, which is 5_{10}. If the data held at $A001_{16}$ is 5_{10}, the zero flag is set; otherwise, it is left at logic 0. The LOOPNE instruction then decrements CX (making it E_{16}) and then checks for CX = 0 or ZF = 1. If neither of these two conditions are satisfied, program control is returned to the instruction with the label AGAIN. This causes the comparison to be repeated for the examination of the contents of the next byte in memory. On the other hand, if either condition is satisfied, the loop is terminated and execution continues with the instruction identified by the label NEXT. In this way, we see that the loop is repeated until either a number 5_{16} is found or all locations in the address range $A001_{16}$ through $A00F_{16}$ have been tested and are all found to not contain 5_{16}.

4.7 STRING INSTRUCTIONS

The 8086 microprocessor is equipped with special instructions to handle *string operations*. By "string" we mean a series of data words or bytes that reside in consecutive memory locations. The string instructions of the 8086 permit a programmer to implement operations such as to move data from one block of memory to a block elsewhere in memory. A second type of operation that is easily performed is to scan a string of data elements stored in memory looking for a specific value. Other examples are to compare the elements of two strings together in order to determine whether they are the same or different, and to initialize a set of consecutive memory locations. Complex operations such as these typically require several nonstring instructions to be implemented.

There are five basic string instructions in the instruction set of the 8086. These instructions, as listed in Fig. 4.18, are *move byte* or *word string* (MOVS, MOVSB/MOVSW), *compare strings* (CMPS), *scan string* (SCAS), *load string* (LODS), and *store string* (STOS). They are called the *basic string instructions* be-

Mnemonic	Meaning	Format	Operation	Flags Affected
MOVS	Move string	MOVS Operand	((ES)0 + (DI)) ← ((DS)0 + (SI)) (SI) ← (SI) ± 1 or 2 (DI) ← (DI) ± 1 or 2	None
MOVSB	Move string byte	MOVSB	((ES)0 + (DI)) ← ((DS)0 + (SI)) (SI) ← (SI) ± 1 (DI) ← (DI) ± 1	None
MOVSW	Move string word	MOVSW	((ES)0 + (DI)) ← ((DS)0 + (SI)) ((ES)0 + (DI) + 1) ← ((DS)0 + (SI) + 1) (SI) ← (SI) ± 2 (DI) ← (DI) ± 2	None
CMPS	Compare string	CMPS Operand	Set flags as per ((DS)0 + (SI)) − ((ES)0 + (DI)) (SI) ← (SI) ± 1 or 2 (DI) ← (DI) ± 1 or 2	CF, PF, AF, ZF, SF, OF
SCAS	Scan string	SCAS Operand	Set flags as per (AL or AX) − ((ES)0 + (DI)) (DI) ← (DI) ± 1 or 2	CF, PF, AF, ZF, SF, OF
LODS	Load string	LODS Operand	(AL or AX) ← ((DS)0 + (SI)) (SI) ← (SI) ± 1 or 2	None
STOS	Store string	STOS Operand	((ES)0 + (DI)) ← (AL or AX) ± 1 or 2 (DI) ← (DI) ± 1 or 2	None

Figure 4.18 Basic string instructions.

cause each defines an operation for one element of a string. Thus these operations must be repeated to handle a string of more than one element. Let us first look at the basic operations performed by these instructions.

Move String—MOVS, MOVSB/MOVSW

The instructions MOVS, MOVSB, and MOVSW all perform the same basic operation. An element of the string specified by the source index (SI) register with respect to the current data segment (DS) register is moved to the location specified by the destination index (DI) register with respect to the current extra segment (ES) register. The move can be performed on a byte or a word of data. After the move is complete, the contents of both SI and DI are automatically incremented or decremented by 1 for a byte move and by 2 for a word move. Remember the fact that the address pointers in SI and DI increment or decrement depends on how the direction flag DF is set. The instruction MOVS requires that an operand be specified, whereas MOVSB and MOVSW have no operands. This operand is simply either WORD or BYTE. For example, one way of writing a MOVS instruction is

MOVS BYTE

This instruction could also be written simply as

MOVSB

Compare Strings and Scan Strings—CMPS and SCAS

The CMPS instruction can be used to compare two elements in the same or different strings. It subtracts the destination operand from the source operand and adjusts flags CF, PF, AF, ZF, SF, and OF accordingly. The result of subtraction is not saved; therefore, the operation does not affect the operands in any way.

An example of a compare strings instruction for bytes of data is

CMPS BYTE

Again, the source element is pointed to by the address in SI with respect to the current value in DS and the destination element is specified by the contents of DI relative to the contents of ES. Moreover, both SI and DI are updated such that they point to the next elements in their respective strings.

The scan string (SCAS) instruction is similar to CMPS; however, it compares the byte or word element of the destination string at the physical address derived from DI and ES to the contents of AL or AX, respectively. The flags are adjusted based on this result and DI incremented or decremented.

Load and Store Strings—LODS and STOS

The last two instructions in Fig. 4.18, load string (LODS) and store string (STOS), are specifically provided to move string elements between the accumulator and memory. LODS loads either a byte or a word from a string in memory into AL or

AX, respectively. The address in SI is used relative to DS to determine the address of the memory location of the string element. For instance, the instruction

LODS WORD

indicates that the word string element at the physical address derived from DS and SI is to be loaded into AX. Then the index in SI is automatically incremented by 2.

On the other hand, STOS stores a byte from AL or a word from AX into a string location in memory. This time the contents of ES and DI are used to form the address of the storage location in memory.

Repeat String—REP

In most applications, the basic string operations must be repeated in order to process arrays of data. This is done by inserting a repeat prefix before the instruction that is to be repeated. The *repeat prefixes* of the 8086 are shown in Fig. 4.19.

The first prefix, REP, causes the basic string operation to be repeated until the contents of register CX become equal to zero. Each time the instruction is executed, it causes CX to be tested for zero. If CX is found to be nonzero, it is decremented by 1 and the basic string operation is repeated. On the other hand, if it is 0, the repeat string operation is done and the next instruction in the program is executed. The repeat count must be loaded into CX prior to executing the repeat string instruction.

Example 4.9

Describe what happens as the following sequence of instructions are executed.

```
MOV      AX,DATA _ SEGMENT
MOV      DS,AX
MOV      AX,EXTRA _ SEGMENT
MOV      ES,AX
MOV      CX,020H
MOV      SI,MASTER
MOV      DI,COPY
REPMOVSB
```

Prefix	Used with:	Meaning
REP	MOVS STOS	Repeat while not end of string $CX \neq 0$
REPE/REPZ	CMPS SCAS	Repeat while not end of string and strings are equal $CX \neq 0$ and $ZF = 1$
REPNE/REPNZ	CMPS SCAS	Repeat while not end of string and strings are not equal $CX \neq 0$ and $ZF = 0$

Figure 4.19 Prefixes for use with the basic string operations.

Solution. The first two instructions initialize DS with the value DATA _ SEGMENT. It is followed by two instructions that load ES with the value EXTRA _ SEGMENT. Then the number of repeats, 0020_{16}, is loaded into CX. The next two instructions load SI and DI with beginning offset addresses MASTER and COPY for the source and destination strings. Now we are ready to perform the string operation. Execution of REPMOVSB moves a block of 32 consecutive bytes from the block of memory locations starting at offset address MASTER with respect to the current data segment (DS) to a block of locations starting at offset address COPY with respect to the current extra segment (ES).

The prefixes REPE and REPZ stand for the same function. They are meant for use with the CMPS and SCAS instructions. With REPE/REPZ, the basic compare or scan operation can be repeated as long as both the contents of CX are not equal to zero and the zero flag is 1. The first condition CX not equal to zero indicates that the end of the string has not yet been reached and the second condition ZF = 1 indicates that the elements that were compared are equal.

The last prefix, REPNE/REPNZ, works similarly to REPE/REPZ except that now the operation is repeated as long as CX is not equal to zero and ZF is zero. That is, the comparison or scanning is to be performed as long as the string elements are unequal and the end of the string is not yet found.

Autoindexing for String Instructions

Earlier we pointed out that during the execution of a string instruction the address indices in SI and DI are either automatically incremented or decremented. Moreover, we indicated that the decision to increment or decrement is made based on the setting of the direction flag DF. The 8086 provides two instructions, clear direction flag (CLD) and set direction flag (STD), to permit selection between *autoincrement* and *autodecrement mode* of operation. These instructions are shown in Fig. 4.20. When CLD is executed, DF is set to 0. This selects autoincrement mode and each time a string operation is performed SI and/or DI are incremented by 1 if byte data are processed and by 2 if word data are processed.

Example 4.10

Given a string of 100 EBCDIC characters stored starting at offset address EBCDIC_ CHAR. Convert them to their equivalent string of ASCII characters and store them at offset address ASCII _ CHAR. The translation may be done using an EBCDIC-to -ASCII conversion table that starts at offset memory address EBCDIC _ TO _ ASCII.

Solution. The problem to be programmed is illustrated in Fig. 4.21(a). Here we have assumed that the various data elements—the 100 given EBCDIC characters, the conversion table for EBCDIC to ASCII, and the generated ASCII characters—all reside in the same data segment. This data segment starts at the address DATA _SEGMENT.

Mnemonic	Meaning	Format	Operation	Flags Affected
CLD	Clear DF	CLD	(DF) ← 0	DF
STD	Set DF	STD	(DF) ← 1	DF

Figure 4.20 Instructions for autoincrementing and autodecrementing in string instructions.

With respect to this data segment, the offset addresses EBCDIC_CHAR, ASCII_CHAR, and EBCDIC_TO_ASCII are as shown in the diagram. Moreover, we are assuming that the string of 100 EBCDIC characters and the EBCDIC-to-ASCII table already exist at the correct locations in memory.

Our solution to the problem is flowcharted in Fig. 4.21(b). We will use the string, translate, and loop instructions to implement the solution. Moreover, we will also use autoincrement mode for the string operations.

The initialization involves setting up the data segment (DS) register to address the area in memory that stores the 100 given EBCDIC characters and conversion table. The same memory area will be used to store the converted ASCII characters; therefore, we will make the extra segment, which is needed by the string instructions, overlap the data segment by loading both DS and ES with the same address. This is the value assigned to variable DATA_SEGMENT. Then SI and DI must be loaded with addresses that point to the first characters in the EBCDIC string and the ASCII string, respectively. These addresses are equal to EBCDIC_CHAR and ASCII_CHAR, respectively. The code translation is made using a conversion table and the XLAT instruction. XLAT requires that BX hold a pointer to the beginning of the conversion table. Therefore, BX must be loaded with the address corresponding to EBCDIC_TO_ASCII. To keep track of the number of characters that are converted, CX will be loaded with 100_{10} equal to 64_{16}. Finally, the autoincrement feature is invoked by resetting the direction flag DF. This leads to the following initialization code:

```
        MOV     AX,DATA_SEGMENT
        MOV     DS,AX
        MOV     ES,AX
        MOV     SI,EBCDIC_CHAR
        MOV     DI,ASCII_CHAR
        MOV     BX,EBCDIC_TO_ASCII
        MOV     CX,064H
        CLD
```

Next, an EBCDIC character can be loaded, translated to its corresponding ASCII character, and stored in the memory area reserved for storage of ASCII characters. This gives us the instructions

```
MORE:   LODS    BYTE
        XLAT
        STOS    BYTE
```

Execution of the LODS instruction loads the first element of the EBCDIC string into AL. Notice that use of autoincrementing prepares SI to handle the next conversion. Next, the XLAT instruction uses the EBCDIC character code in AL as an offset to address the equivalent ASCII character in the table at EBCDIC_TO_ASCII. This ASCII character is transferred to AL. The translation is now complete; however, the resulting character must be stored in the table defined by the address ASCII_CHAR. This is done with the STOS instruction. During the execution of this instruction, DI is automatically incremented so that it points to the next storage location in the ASCII string.

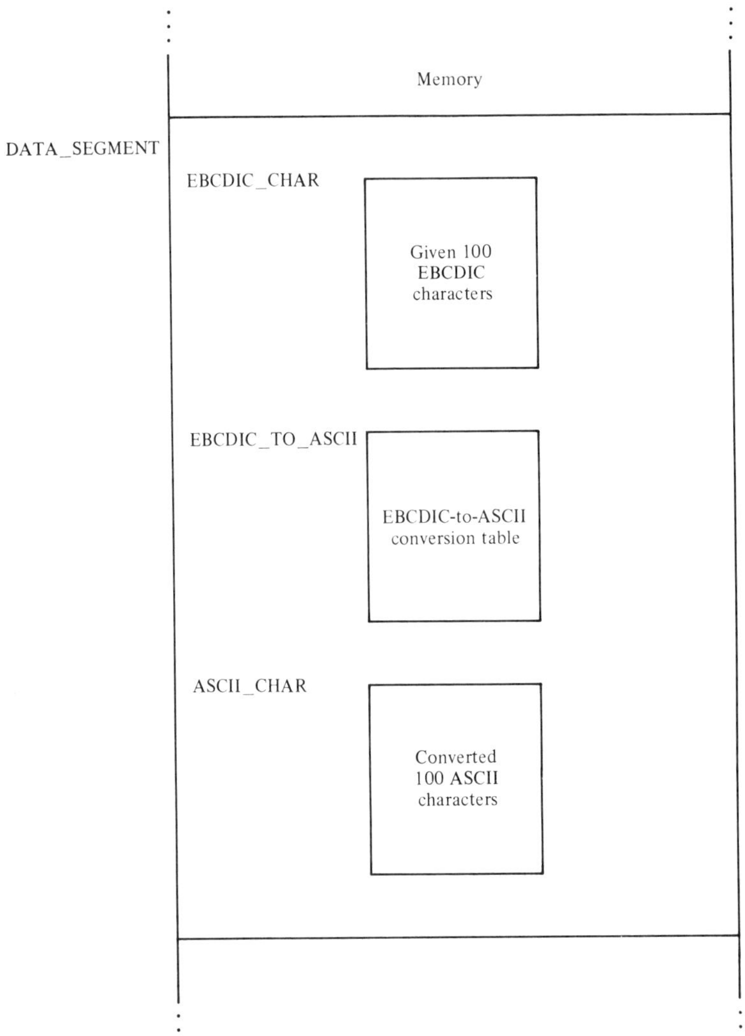

(a)

Figure 4.21 **(a)** EBCDIC-to-ASCII conversion; **(b)** flowchart; **(c)** program.

To repeat the process starting from label MORE, we can use a loop instruction that will decrement CX and jump to MORE as long as the contents of CX are not zero. This assures that translation is repeated for each of the 100 characters in the EBCDIC string. To do this, the instruction is

LOOP MORE

To end the program, the halt (HLT) instruction can be executed. The entire program is repeated in Fig. 4.21(c).

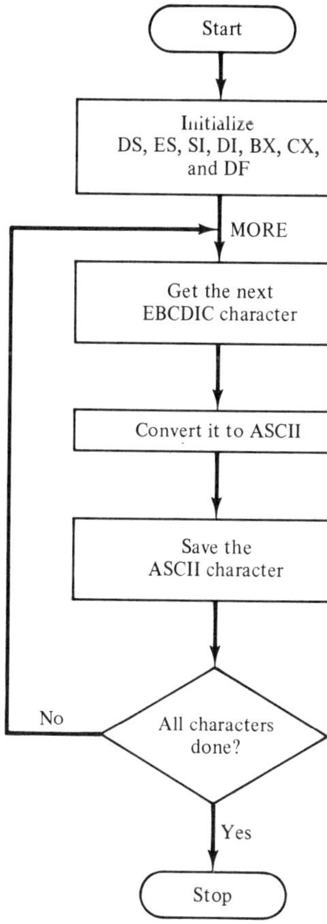

(b)

```
        MOV     AX, DATA_SEGMENT
        MOV     DS, AX
        MOV     ES, AX
        MOV     SI, EBCDIC_CHAR
        MOV     DI, ASCII_CHAR
        MOV     BX, EBCDIC_TO_ASCII
        MOV     CX, 064H
        CLD
MORE:   LODS    BYTE
        XLAT
        STOS    BYTE
        LOOP    MORE
        HLT
```

(c)

Figure 4.21 *(continued)*

ASSIGNMENT

Section 4.2

1. Write an instruction sequence to configure the 8086 as follows: interrupts not accepted; save the original contents of flags SF, ZF, AF, PF, and CF at the address $A000_{16}$; and then clear CF.

Section 4.3

2. Describe the difference in operation and effect on status flags due to the execution of the subtract words and compare words instructions.
3. What happens to the ZF and CF status flags as the following sequence of instructions is executed? Assume that they are both initially cleared.

```
MOV    BX,01111H
MOV    AX,0BBBBH
CMP    AX,BX
```

Section 4.4

4. What value must be loaded into BX such that execution of the instruction JMP BX transfers control to the memory location offset from the beginning of the current code segment by 256_{10}?
5. The program that follows implements what is known as a *delay loop*.

```
        MOV    CX,01000H
DLY:    DEC    CX
        JNZ    DLY
NXT:    ---    ---
```

   (a) How many times does the JNZ DLY instruction get executed?
   (b) Change the program so that JNZ DLY is executed just 17 times.
   (c) Change the program so that JNZ DLY is executed 2^{32} times.
6. Given a number N in the range $0 < N \leq 5$, write a program that computes its factorial and saves the result in memory location FACT.
7. Modify the program in example 4.4 so that when it is executed, N bytes of data starting at offset BLK2ADDR are moved to offset BLK1ADDR.
8. Write a program that compares the elements of two arrays, A(I) and B(I). Each array contains 100 16-bit signed numbers. The comparison is to be done by comparing the corresponding elements of the two arrays until either two elements are found to be unequal or all elements of the arrays have been compared and found to be equal. Assume that the arrays start at addresses $A000_{16}$ and $B000_{16}$, respectively. If the two arrays are found to be unequal, save the address of the first unequal element of A(I) in memory location FOUND; otherwise, write all 0s into this location.
9. Given an array A(I) of 100 16-bit signed numbers that are stored in memory starting at address $A000_{16}$ write a program to generate two arrays from the given array such that

one P(J) consists of all the positive numbers and the other N(K) contains all of the negative numbers. Store the array of positive numbers in memory starting at address $B000_{16}$ and the array of negative numbers starting at address $C000_{16}$.

10. Given a 16-bit binary number in DX, write a program that converts it to its equivalent BCD number in DX. If the result is bigger than 16 bits, place all 1s in DX.

11. Change the program in Fig. 4.9(c) so that it can be used to sort an array in descending order.

12. Given an array A(I) with 100 16-bit signed integer numbers, write a program to generate a new array B(I) as follows:

$$B(I) = A(I) \qquad \text{for } I = 1, 2, 99, \text{ and } 100$$

and

$$B(I) = \text{median value of } A(I-2), A(I-1), A(I), A(I+1), \text{ and } A(I+2) \qquad \text{for all other Is}$$

Section 4.5

13. Describe the difference between a jump and call instruction.

14. Why are intersegment and intrasegment call instructions provided in the 8086?

15. Write a subroutine that converts a given 16-bit BCD number to its equivalent binary number. The BCD number is to be passed to a subroutine through register DX and the routine returns the equivalent binary number in DX.

16. When is it required to include PUSHF and POPF instructions in a subroutine?

17. Given an array A(I) of 100 16-bit signed integer numbers, write a subroutine to generate a new array B(I) such that

$$B(I) = A(I) \qquad \text{for } I = 1 \text{ and } 100$$

and

$$B(I) = \frac{1}{4}(A(I - 1) - 5A(I) + 9A(I + 1)) \qquad \text{for all other Is}$$

The values of A(I − 1), A(I), and A(I + 1) are to be passed to the subroutine in registers AX, BX, and CX and the subroutine returns the result B(I) in register AX.

18. Write a segment of main program and show its subroutine structure to perform the following operations. The program is to check continuously the three most significant bits in register DX and depending on their setting executes one of three subroutines: SUBA, SUBB, or SUBC. The subroutines are selected as follows:

(a) If bit 15 of DX is set, initiate SUBA.

(b) If bit 14 of DX is set and bit 15 is not set, initiate SUBB.

(c) If bit 13 of DX is set and bits 14 and 15 are not set, initiate SUBC.

If the subroutine is executed, the corresponding bits of DX are to be cleared and then control returned to the main program. After returning from the subroutine, the main program is repeated.

Section 4.6

19. Using loop instructions, implement the program in problem 6.

20. Using loop instructions, implement the program in problem 8.

Section 4.7

21. Write equivalent string instruction sequences for each of the following:

(a)
```
MOV   [AX], [SI]
MOV   [DI], AX
INC   SI
INC   DI
```

(b)
```
MOV   AX, [SI]
INC   SI
INC   SI
```

(c)
```
MOV   AL, [DI]
CMP   AL, [SI]
DEC   SI
DEC   DI
```

22. Use string instructions to implement the program in problem 8.

23. Write a program to convert a table of 100 ASCII characters stored starting at offset address ASCII _CHAR into their equivalent table of EBCDIC characters and store them at offset address EBCDIC_ CHAR. The translation is to be done using an ASCII-to-EBCDIC conversion table starting at offset address ASCII_ TO_ EBCDIC. Assume that all three tables are located in different segments of memory.

5

Using the SDK-86 Microcomputer for Program Development

5.1 INTRODUCTION

In previous chapters we considered the 8086 microprocessor's instruction set and writing of assembly language programs. This chapter describes the SDK-86 microcomputer, which is an instrument that can be used to verify whether a program written for a specific application accurately implements its intended function. The topics discussed are as follows:

1. The microcomputer development system
2. Converting source programs to machine code
3. The monitor program
4. Monitor commands
5. Loading and executing a machine code program
6. Debugging a program

5.2 THE MICROCOMPUTER DEVELOPMENT SYSTEM

A *development system* is an instrument that is used to develop programs and hardware for a microprocessor-based system. Typically, the system is designed to permit development work to be done for only specific microprocessors, for instance, devices produced by a specific manufacturer. It can be a sophisticated system such as Intel's *Series IV development system,* which is shown in Fig. 5.1. This kind of system gives the microcomputer designer important capabilities, such as the ability to develop pro-

Figure 5.1 Intel's Series IV development system (*Courtesy of Intel Corporation*).

grams in either assembly language or a variety of high-level languages, powerful tools for efficient debugging of programs, facilities for connection to external hardware for circuit debugging, and the ability to integrate the user's software and hardware for testing and debugging. Use of this type of instrumentation system is essential for major microcomputer development projects. Its use results in much saved time and higher-quality hardware and software.

On the other hand, inexpensive systems such as Intel's *System Design Kit 86 (SDK-86)* are also available. The SDK-86, which is shown in Fig. 5.2, can also be considered a development system. However, compared to a Series IV development system, it offers only a limited set of capabilities to the designer. Even with its limited capabilities, the SDK-86 serves as an effective vehicle for learning the basics of microcomputer program development. This is the development system we describe in this chapter.

The SDK-86 can be used to execute and debug small programs. The programs are entered into the microcomputer using a hexadecimal keypad; therefore, assembly language instructions need to be first converted to machine code and then entered.

Keys are also provided on the SDK-86 to enter program development commands, such as display a register's contents, modify a byte or a word in memory, or start executing the program. Command execution is done with the help of an EPROM-based monitor program on the SDK-86. This program is called the *keypad monitor*. Although the SDK-86 provides another monitor, which is intended for use together with a terminal, we will limit our discussion to the keypad monitor.

Figure 5.2 Intel's system design kit for the 8086 (SDK-86) (*Courtesy of Intel Corporation*).

5.3 CONVERTING SOURCE PROGRAMS TO MACHINE CODE

To convert an assembly language program to machine code, we must convert each assembly language instruction to its equivalent machine code instruction. In general, for an instruction, the machine code specifies such things as what operation is to be performed, what operand or operands are to be used, whether the operation is performed on byte or word data, whether the operation involves operands that are located in registers or a register and a storage location in memory, and if one of the operands is in memory, how its address is to be generated. All of this information is encoded into the bits of the machine code instruction.

The machine code instructions of the 8086 vary in the number of bytes used to encode them. Some instructions can be encoded with just one byte, others in two bytes, and many require more. The maximum number of bytes that an instruction might take is six. *Single-byte instructions* generally specify a simpler operation with a register or a flag bit. For instance, complement carry (CMC) is an example of a single-byte instruction. It is specified by the machine code byte 11110101, which equals $F5_{16}$:

$$CMC = 11110101_2 = F5_{16}$$

The machine codes for instructions can be obtained by following the formats that are used in encoding the instructions of the 8086 microprocessor. Most of the *multibyte instructions* of the 8086 use the *general instruction format* shown in Fig. 5.3. Exceptions to this format will be considered separately later. For now, let us describe the functions of the various bits and fields (groups of bits) in each byte of this format.

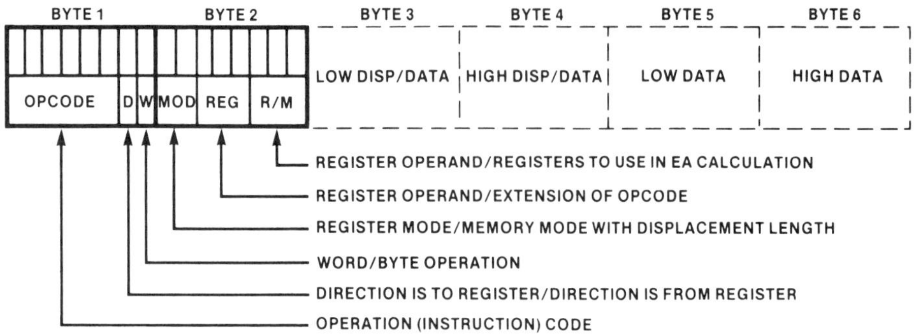

Figure 5.3 General instruction format (*Courtesy of Intel Corporation*).

Looking at Fig. 5.3, we see that byte 1 contains three kinds of information: the *operation code (opcode)*, the *register direction bit* (D), and the *data size bit* (W). Let us summarize the function of each of these pieces of information.

1. *Opcode field* (6 bits): specifies the operation, such as add, subtract, or move, that is to be performed.
2. *Register direction bit* (D bit): specifies whether the register operand that is specified in byte 2 is the source or the destination operand. A logic 1 at this bit position indicates that the register operand is a destination operand, and a logic 0 indicates that it is a source operand.
3. *Data-size bit* (W bit): specifies whether the operation will be performed on 8-bit or 16-bit data. Logic 0 selects 8 bits and 1 selects 16 bits.

For instance, if a 16-bit value is to be added to register AX, the 6 most significant bits specify the add register operation. This opcode is 000000_2. The next bit, D, will be at logic 1 to specify that a register, AX in this case, holds the destination operand. Finally, the least significant bit, W, will be logic 1 to specify a 16-bit data operation.

The second byte in Fig. 5.3 has three fields: the *mode (MOD) field,* the *register (REG) field*, and the *register/memory (R/M) field*. These fields are used to specify which register is used for the first operand and where the second operand is stored. The second operand can be in either a register or a memory location.

The 3-bit REG field is used to identify the register for the first operand. This is the operand that was defined as the source or destination by the D bit in byte 1. The encoding for each of the 8086's registers is shown in Fig. 5.4. Here we find that the 16-bit register AX and the 8-bit register AL are specified by the same binary code. Notice that the decision as to whether to use AX or AL is made based on the setting of the operation-size (W) bit in byte 1.

For instance, in our earlier example, we said that the first operand, which is the destination operand, is register AX. For this case, the REG field is set to 000.

The 2-bit MOD field and 3-bit R/M field together specify the second operand. Encoding for these two fields is shown in Fig. 5.5(a) and (b), respectively. MOD in-

REG	W=0	W=1
000	AL	AX
001	CL	CX
010	DL	DX
011	BL	BX
100	AH	SP
101	CH	BP
110	DH	SI
111	BH	DI

Figure 5.4 Register (REG) field encoding (*Courtesy of Intel Corporation*).

dicates whether the operand is in a register or memory. Notice that in the case of a second operand that is in a register, the MOD field is always 11. The R/M field together with the W bit from byte 1 selects the register.

For example, if the second operand, the source operand, in our earlier addition example is to be in BX, the MOD and R/M fields will be made MOD = 11 and R/M = 011, respectively.

Example 5.1

The instruction

MOV BL,AL

stands for move the byte contents from source register AL to destination register BL. Using the general format in Fig. 5.3, show how to encode the instruction in machine code. Assume that the 6-bit opcode for the move operation is 100010.

Solution. In byte 1 the first 6 bits specify the move operation and thus must be 100010.

$$\text{OPCODE} = 100010_2$$

The next bit, which is D, indicates whether the register that is specified by the REG part of byte 2 is a source or a destination operand. Let us say that we will encode AL in the REG field of byte 2; therefore, D is set equal to 0 for source operand.

$$D = 0$$

The last bit (W) in byte 1 must specify a byte operation. For this reason, it is also set to 0.

$$W = 0$$

This leads to

$$\text{BYTE 1} = 10001000_2 = 88_{16}$$

In byte 2 the source operand, which is specified by the REG field, is AL. The corresponding code from Fig. 5.4 is

$$\text{REG} = 000$$

Since the second operand is also a register, the MOD field is made 11. The R/M field specifies that the destination register is BL and the code from Fig. 5.5(b) is 011. This gives

$$\text{MOD} = 11$$
$$\text{R/M} = 011$$

CODE	EXPLANATION
00	Memory Mode, no displacement follows*
01	Memory Mode, 8-bit displacement follows
10	Memory Mode, 16-bit displacement follows
11	Register Mode (no displacement)

*Except when R/M = 110, then 16-bit displacement follows

(a)

MOD = 11			EFFECTIVE ADDRESS CALCULATION			
R/M	W = 0	W = 1	R/M	MOD = 00	MOD = 01	MOD = 10
000	AL	AX	000	(BX) + (SI)	(BX) + (SI) + D8	(BX) + (SI) + D16
001	CL	CX	001	(BX) + (DI)	(BX) + (DI) + D8	(BX) + (DI) + D16
010	DL	DX	010	(BP) + (SI)	(BP) + (SI) + D8	(BP) + (SI) + D16
011	BL	BX	011	(BP) + (DI)	(BP) + (DI) + D8	(BP) + (DI) + D16
100	AH	SP	100	(SI)	(SI) + D8	(SI) + D16
101	CH	BP	101	(DI)	(DI) + D8	(DI) + D16
110	DH	SI	110	DIRECT ADDRESS	(BP) + D8	(BP) + D16
111	BH	DI	111	(BX)	(BX) + D8	(BX) + D16

(b)

Figure 5.5 **(a)** Mode (MOD) field encoding; **(b)** Register/memory (R/M) field encoding (*Courtesy of Intel Corporation*).

Therefore, byte 2 is

$$\text{BYTE 2} = 11000011_2 = \text{C3}_{16}$$

The entire hexadecimal code for the instruction is

MOV BL,AL = 88C3H

On the other hand, for a second operand that is located in memory, there are a number of different ways in which its location can be specified. That is, any of the addressing modes supported by the 8086 microprocessor can be used to generate its address. The addressing mode is also selected with the MOD and R/M fields.

Notice that the addressing mode for an operand in memory is indicated by one of the other three values (00, 01, and 10) in the MOD field and an appropriate R/M code. The different ways in which the operand's address can be generated are shown in the effective address calculation part of the table in Fig. 5.5(b). These different address calculation expressions correspond to the addressing modes that we introduced in Chapter 3. For instance, if the base index register contains the memory address, this fact is encoded into the instruction by making MOD = 00 and R/M = 111.

Example 5.2

The instruction

ADD AX,[SI]

stands for add the 16-bit contents of the memory location indirectly specified by SI to AX. Encode the instruction in machine code. The opcode for add is 000000_2.

Solution. To specify a 16-bit add operation with a register as the destination, the first byte of machine code will be

$$\text{BYTE 1} = 00000011_2 = 03_{16}$$

The REG field bits in byte 2 are 000 to specify AX as the destination register. The other operand is in memory and its address is specified by the contents of SI with no displacement. From Fig. 5.5(a) and (b), we find that for indirect addressing using SI with no displacement, MOD equals 00 and R/M equals 100.

$$\text{MOD} = 00$$

$$\text{R/M} = 100$$

This gives

$$\text{BYTE 2} = 00000100_2 = 04_{16}$$

Thus the machine code for the instruction is

ADD AX,[SI] = 0304H

Some of the addressing modes of the 8086 need either data or an address displacement to be coded into the instruction. These types of information are encoded using additional bytes. For instance, looking at Fig. 5.3, we see that byte 3 is needed in the encoding of an instruction if it uses a byte-size address displacement, and both byte 3 and byte 4 are needed if the instruction uses a word-size displacement.

The size of the displacement is encoded into the MOD field. For example, if the effective address is to be generated by the expression

$$(\text{BX}) + \text{D8}$$

MOD is set to 01 to specify memory mode with an 8-bit displacement and R/M is set to 111 to select BX.

Bytes 3 and 4 are also used to encode byte-wide immediate operands, word-wide immediate operands, and direct addresses. For example, in an instruction where direct addressing is used to specify the location of an operand in memory, the MOD field must be 00 and the R/M field 110. The actual value of the operand's address is coded into the bytes that follow.

If both a 16-bit displacement and an immediate operand are used in the same instruction, the displacement is encoded into bytes 3 and 4 and the immediate operand into bytes 5 and 6.

Example 5.3

What is the machine code for the following instruction?

XOR CL,[1234H]

This instruction stands for exclusive-OR the byte of data at memory address 1234_{16} with the byte contents of CL. The opcode for exclusive-OR is 001100_2.

Solution. Using the XOR opcode 001100_2, 1 for destination operand, and 0 for byte data, we get

$$\text{BYTE 1} = 00110010_2 = 32_{16}$$

The REG field has to specify CL, which makes it equal to 001. In this case a direct address has been specified for operand 2. This requires that MOD = 00 and R/M = 110. Thus

$$\text{BYTE 2} = 00001110_2 = 0E_{16}$$

To specify the address 1234_{16}, we must use bytes 3 and 4. The least significant byte of the address is encoded first, followed by the most significant byte. This gives

$$\text{BYTE 3} = 34_{16}$$

and

$$\text{BYTE 4} = 12_{16}$$

The entire machine code form of the instruction is

XOR CL,[1234H] = 320E3412H

Example 5.4

The instruction

ADD [BX].DISP[SI],AX

means add the word contents of AX to the contents of the memory location specified by based indexed addressing mode. The opcode for the add operation is 000000_2 and assume that DISP equals 1234_{16}.

Solution. The add opcode, which is 000000_2, a 0 for source operand, and a 1 for word data gives

$$\text{BYTE 1} = 00000001_2 = 01_{16}$$

The REG field in byte 2 is 000 to specify AX as the source register. Since there is a displacement and it needs 16 bits for encoding, the MOD field obtained from Fig. 5.5(a) is 10. The R/M field, also obtained from Fig. 5.5(b), for an effective address generated by SI and BX is 000. This gives the second byte as

$$\text{BYTE 2} = 10000000_2 = 80_{16}$$

The displacement 1234_{16} is encoded in the next two bytes with the least significant byte first. Therefore, the machine code that results is

ADD [BX].DISP[SI],AX = 01803412H

As we indicated earlier, the general format in Fig. 5.3 cannot be used to encode all of the instructions that can be executed by the 8086. There are minor modifications that must be made to this general format to encode a few instructions. In some

Field	Value	Function
S	0 1	No sign extension Sign extend 8-bit immediate data to 16 bits if W=1
V	0 1	Shift/rotate count is one Shift/rotate count is specified in CL register
Z	0 1	Repeat/loop while zero flag is clear Repeat/loop while zero flag is set

Figure 5.6 Additonal one bit fields and their functions (*Courtesy of Intel Corporation*).

instructions one or more additional single-bit fields need to be added. These one-bit fields and their functions are shown in Fig. 5.6.

For instance, the general format of the repeat (REP) instruction is

REP = 1111001Z

Here bit Z is made 1 or 0 depending on whether the repeat operation is to be done when the zero flag is set or when it is reset. Similarly, the other two bits, S and V, are used to encode sign extension for arithmetic instructions and to specify the source of the count for shift or rotate instructions, respectively.

The formats for all of the instructions in the 8086's instruction set are shown in Fig. 5.7. This is the information that can be used to encode any 8086 program.

Example 5.5

The instruction

MOV [BP].DISP[DI],0ABCDH

stands for move the immediate data word $ABCD_{16}$ into the memory location specified by based indexed addressing mode. Express the instruction in machine code. Let DISP equal 1234_{16}.

Solution. Since this instruction does not involve one of the registers as an operand, it does not follow the general format that we have been using. From Fig. 5.7 we find that the format of byte 1 in an immediate data-to-memory move is

1100011W

In our case, we are moving word-size data; therefore, W equals 1. This gives

$$\text{BYTE 1} = 11000111_2 = C7_{16}$$

Again from Fig. 5.7, we find that byte 2 has the form

BYTE 2 = MOD 000 R/M

For a memory operand using a 16-bit displacement, Fig. 5.5(a) shows that MOD equals

10 and for based indexed addressing using BP and DI with a 16-bit displacement, Fig. 5.5(b) shows that R/M equals 011. This gives

$$\text{BYTE 2} = 10000011_2 = 83_{16}$$

Bytes 3 and 4 encode the displacement with its low byte first. Thus for a displacement of 1234_{16}, we get

$$\text{BYTE 3} = 34_{16}$$

and

$$\text{BYTE 4} = 12_{16}$$

Finally, bytes 5 and 6 encode the immediate data, also with the least significant byte first. For data word ABCD_{16}, we get

$$\text{BYTE 5} = \text{CD}_{16}$$

and

$$\text{BYTE 6} = \text{AB}_{16}$$

The entire instruction in machine code is

MOV [BP].DISP[DI],0ABCDH = C7833412CDABH

DATA TRANSFER

MOV = Move:	7 6 5 4 3 2 1 0	7 6 5 4 3 2 1 0	7 6 5 4 3 2 1 0	7 6 5 4 3 2 1 0	7 6 5 4 3 2 1 0	7 6 5 4 3 2 1 0
Register/memory to/from register	1 0 0 0 1 0 d w	mod reg r/m	(DISP-LO)	(DISP-HI)		
Immediate to register/memory	1 1 0 0 0 1 1 w	mod 0 0 0 r/m	(DISP-LO)	(DISP-HI)	data	data if w = 1
Immediate to register	1 0 1 1 w reg	data	data if w = 1			
Memory to accumulator	1 0 1 0 0 0 0 w	addr-lo	addr-hi			
Accumulator to memory	1 0 1 0 0 0 1 w	addr-lo	addr-hi			
Register/memory to segment register	1 0 0 0 1 1 1 0	mod 0 SR r/m	(DISP-LO)	(DISP-HI)		
Segment register to register/memory	1 0 0 0 1 1 0 0	mod 0 SR r/m	(DISP-LO)	(DISP-HI)		

PUSH = Push:				
Register/memory	1 1 1 1 1 1 1 1	mod 1 1 0 r/m	(DISP-LO)	(DISP-HI)
Register	0 1 0 1 0 reg			
Segment register	0 0 0 reg 1 1 0			

POP = Pop:				
Register/memory	1 0 0 0 1 1 1 1	mod 0 0 0 r/m	(DISP-LO)	(DISP-HI)
Register	0 1 0 1 1 reg			
Segment register	0 0 0 reg 1 1 1			

Figure 5.7 8086 instruction encoding tables (*Courtesy of Intel Corporation*).

	7 6 5 4 3 2 1 0	7 6 5 4 3 2 1 0	7 6 5 4 3 2 1 0	7 6 5 4 3 2 1 0	7 6 5 4 3 2 1 0	7 6 5 4 3 2 1 0
DATA TRANSFER (Cont'd.)						
XCHG = Exchange:						
Register/memory with register	1 0 0 0 0 1 1 w	mod reg r/m	(DISP-LO)	(DISP-HI)		
Register with accumulator	1 0 0 1 0 reg					
IN = Input from:						
Fixed port	1 1 1 0 0 1 0 w	DATA-8				
Variable port	1 1 1 0 1 1 0 w					
OUT = Output to:						
Fixed port	1 1 1 0 0 1 1 w	DATA-8				
Variable port	1 1 1 0 1 1 1 w					
XLAT = Translate byte to AL	1 1 0 1 0 1 1 1					
LEA = Load EA to register	1 0 0 0 1 1 0 1	mod reg r/m	(DISP-LO)	(DISP-HI)		
LDS = Load pointer to DS	1 1 0 0 0 1 0 1	mod reg r/m	(DISP-LO)	(DISP-HI)		
LES = Load pointer to ES	1 1 0 0 0 1 0 0	mod reg r/m	(DISP-LO)	(DISP-HI)		
LAHF = Load AH with flags	1 0 0 1 1 1 1 1					
SAHF = Store AH into flags	1 0 0 1 1 1 1 0					
PUSHF = Push flags	1 0 0 1 1 1 0 0					
POPF = Pop flags	1 0 0 1 1 1 0 1					
ARITHMETIC						
ADD = Add:						
Reg/memory with register to either	0 0 0 0 0 0 d w	mod reg r/m	(DISP-LO)	(DISP-HI)		
Immediate to register/memory	1 0 0 0 0 0 s w	mod 0 0 0 r/m	(DISP-LO)	(DISP-HI)	data	data if s: w=01
Immediate to accumulator	0 0 0 0 0 1 0 w	data	data if w=1			
ADC = Add with carry:						
Reg/memory with register to either	0 0 0 1 0 0 d w	mod reg r/m	(DISP-LO)	(DISP-HI)		
Immediate to register/memory	1 0 0 0 0 0 s w	mod 0 1 0 r/m	(DISP-LO)	(DISP-HI)	data	data if s: w=01
Immediate to accumulator	0 0 0 1 0 1 0 w	data	data if w=1			
INC = Increment:						
Register/memory	1 1 1 1 1 1 1 w	mod 0 0 0 r/m	(DISP-LO)	(DISP-HI)		
Register	0 1 0 0 0 reg					
AAA = ASCII adjust for add	0 0 1 1 0 1 1 1					
DAA = Decimal adjust for add	0 0 1 0 0 1 1 1					

Figure 5.7 *(continued)*

ARITHMETIC (Cont'd.)

	7 6 5 4 3 2 1 0	7 6 5 4 3 2 1 0	7 6 5 4 3 2 1 0	7 6 5 4 3 2 1 0	7 6 5 4 3 2 1 0	7 6 5 4 3 2 1 0
SUB = Subtract:						
Reg/memory and register to either	0 0 1 0 1 0 d w	mod reg r/m	(DISP-LO)	(DISP-HI)		
Immediate from register/memory	1 0 0 0 0 0 s w	mod 1 0 1 r/m	(DISP-LO)	(DISP-HI)	data	data if s: w=01
Immediate from accumulator	0 0 1 0 1 1 0 w	data	data if w=1			
SBB = Subtract with borrow:						
Reg/memory and register to either	0 0 0 1 1 0 d w	mod reg r/m	(DISP-LO)	(DISP-HI)		
Immediate from register/memory	1 0 0 0 0 0 s w	mod 0 1 1 r/m	(DISP-LO)	(DISP-HI)	data	data if s: w=01
Immediate from accumulator	0 0 0 1 1 1 0 w	data	data if w=1			
DEC Decrement:						
Register/memory	1 1 1 1 1 1 1 w	mod 0 0 1 r/m	(DISP-LO)	(DISP-HI)		
Register	0 1 0 0 1 reg					
NEG Change sign	1 1 1 1 0 1 1 w	mod 0 1 1 r/m	(DISP-LO)	(DISP-HI)		
CMP = Compare:						
Register/memory and register	0 0 1 1 1 0 d w	mod reg r/m	(DISP-LO)	(DISP-HI)		
Immediate with register/memory	1 0 0 0 0 0 s w	mod 1 1 1 r/m	(DISP-LO)	(DISP-HI)	data	data if s: w=1
Immediate with accumulator	0 0 1 1 1 1 0 w	data				
AAS ASCII adjust for subtract	0 0 1 1 1 1 1 1					
DAS Decimal adjust for subtract	0 0 1 0 1 1 1 1					
MUL Multiply (unsigned)	1 1 1 1 0 1 1 w	mod 1 0 0 r/m	(DISP-LO)	(DISP-HI)		
IMUL Integer multiply (signed)	1 1 1 1 0 1 1 w	mod 1 0 1 r/m	(DISP-LO)	(DISP-HI)		
AAM ASCII adjust for multiply	1 1 0 1 0 1 0 0	0 0 0 0 1 0 1 0	(DISP-LO)	(DISP-HI)		
DIV Divide (unsigned)	1 1 1 1 0 1 1 w	mod 1 1 0 r/m	(DISP-LO)	(DISP-HI)		
IDIV Integer divide (signed)	1 1 1 1 0 1 1 w	mod 1 1 1 r/m	(DISP-LO)	(DISP-HI)		
AAD ASCII adjust for divide	1 1 0 1 0 1 0 1	0 0 0 0 1 0 1 0	(DISP-LO)	(DISP-HI)		
CBW Convert byte to word	1 0 0 1 1 0 0 0					
CWD Convert word to double word	1 0 0 1 1 0 0 1					
LOGIC						
NOT Invert	1 1 1 1 0 1 1 w	mod 0 1 0 r/m	(DISP-LO)	(DISP-HI)		
SHL/SAL Shift logical/arithmetic left	1 1 0 1 0 0 v w	mod 1 0 0 r/m	(DISP-LO)	(DISP-HI)		
SHR Shift logical right	1 1 0 1 0 0 v w	mod 1 0 1 r/m	(DISP-LO)	(DISP-HI)		
SAR Shift arithmetic right	1 1 0 1 0 0 v w	mod 1 1 1 r/m	(DISP-LO)	(DISP-HI)		
ROL Rotate left	1 1 0 1 0 0 v w	mod 0 0 0 r/m	(DISP-LO)	(DISP-HI)		

Figure 5.7 *(continued)*

LOGIC (Cont'd.)	7 6 5 4 3 2 1 0	7 6 5 4 3 2 1 0	7 6 5 4 3 2 1 0	7 6 5 4 3 2 1 0	7 6 5 4 3 2 1 0	7 6 5 4 3 2 1 0
ROR Rotate right	1 1 0 1 0 0 v w	mod 0 0 1 r/m	(DISP-LO)	(DISP-HI)		
RCL Rotate through carry flag left	1 1 0 1 0 0 v w	mod 0 1 0 r/m	(DISP-LO)	(DISP-HI)		
RCR Rotate through carry right	1 1 0 1 0 0 v w	mod 0 1 1 r/m	(DISP-LO)	(DISP-HI)		
AND = And:						
Reg/memory with register to either	0 0 1 0 0 0 d w	mod reg r/m	(DISP-LO)	(DISP-HI)		
Immediate to register/memory	1 0 0 0 0 0 0 w	mod 1 0 0 r/m	(DISP-LO)	(DISP-HI)	data	data if w=1
Immediate to accumulator	0 0 1 0 0 1 0 w	data	data if w=1			
TEST = And function to flags no result:						
Register/memory and register	0 0 0 1 0 0 d w	mod reg r/m	(DISP-LO)	(DISP-HI)		
Immediate data and register/memory	1 1 1 1 0 1 1 w	mod 0 0 0 r/m	(DISP-LO)	(DISP-HI)	data	data if w=1
Immediate data and accumulator	1 0 1 0 1 0 0 w	data				
OR = Or:						
Reg/memory and register to either	0 0 0 0 1 0 d w	mod reg r/m	(DISP-LO)	(DISP-HI)		
Immediate to register/memory	1 0 0 0 0 0 0 w	mod 0 0 1 r/m	(DISP-LO)	(DISP-HI)	data	data if w=1
Immediate to accumulator	0 0 0 0 1 1 0 w	data	data if w=1			
XOR = Exclusive or:						
Reg/memory and register to either	0 0 1 1 0 0 d w	mod reg r/m	(DISP-LO)	(DISP-HI)		
Immediate to register/memory	0 0 1 1 0 1 0 w	data	(DISP-LO)	(DISP-HI)	data	data if w=1
Immediate to accumulator	0 0 1 1 0 1 0 w	data	data if w=1			

STRING MANIPULATION	
REP = Repeat	1 1 1 1 0 0 1 z
MOVS = Move byte/word	1 0 1 0 0 1 0 w
CMPS = Compare byte/word	1 0 1 0 0 1 1 w
SCAS = Scan byte/word	1 0 1 0 1 1 1 w
LODS = Load byte/wd to AL/AX	1 0 1 0 1 1 0 w
STDS = Stor byte/wd from AL/A	1 0 1 0 1 0 1 w

Figure 5.7 *(continued)*

CONTROL TRANSFER

CALL = Call:	7 6 5 4 3 2 1 0	7 6 5 4 3 2 1 0	7 6 5 4 3 2 1 0	7 6 5 4 3 2 1 0	7 6 5 4 3 2 1 0	7 6 5 4 3 2 1 0
Direct within segment	1 1 1 0 1 0 0 0	IP-INC-LO	IP-INC-HI			
Indirect within segment	1 1 1 1 1 1 1 1	mod 0 1 0 r/m	(DISP-LO)	(DISP-HI)		
Direct intersegment	1 0 0 1 1 0 1 0	IP-lo	IP-hi			
		CS-lo	CS-hi			
Indirect intersegment	1 1 1 1 1 1 1 1	mod 0 1 1 r/m	(DISP-LO)	(DISP-HI)		

JMP = Unconditional Jump:				
Direct within segment	1 1 1 0 1 0 0 1	IP-INC-LO	IP-INC-HI	
Direct within segment-short	1 1 1 0 1 0 1 1	IP-INC8		
Indirect within segment	1 1 1 1 1 1 1 1	mod 1 0 0 r/m	(DISP-LO)	(DISP-HI)
Direct intersegment	1 1 1 0 1 0 1 0	IP-lo	IP-hi	
		CS-lo	CS-hi	
Indirect intersegment	1 1 1 1 1 1 1 1	mod 1 0 1 r/m	(DISP-LO)	(DISP-HI)

RET = Return from CALL:			
Within segment	1 1 0 0 0 0 1 1		
Within seg adding immed to SP	1 1 0 0 0 0 1 0	data-lo	data-hi
Intersegment	1 1 0 0 1 0 1 1		
Intersegment adding immediate to SP	1 1 0 0 1 0 1 0	data-lo	data-hi
JE/JZ = Jump on equal/zero	0 1 1 1 0 1 0 0	IP-INC8	
JL/JNGE = Jump on less/not greater or equal	0 1 1 1 1 1 0 0	IP-INC8	
JLE/JNG = Jump on less or equal/not greater	0 1 1 1 1 1 1 0	IP-INC8	
JB/JNAE = Jump on below/not above or equal	0 1 1 1 0 0 1 0	IP-INC8	
JBE/JNA = Jump on below or equal/not above	0 1 1 1 0 1 1 0	IP-INC8	
JP/JPE = Jump on parity/parity even	0 1 1 1 1 0 1 0	IP-INC8	
JO = Jump on overflow	0 1 1 1 0 0 0 0	IP-INC8	
JS = Jump on sign	0 1 1 1 1 0 0 0	IP-INC8	
JNE/JNZ = Jump on not equal/not zer0	0 1 1 1 0 1 0 1	IP-INC8	
JNL/JGE = Jump on not less/greater or equal	0 1 1 1 1 1 0 1	IP-INC8	
JNLE/JG = Jump on not less or equal/greater	0 1 1 1 1 1 1 1	IP-INC8	
JNB/JAE = Jump on not below/above or equal	0 1 1 1 0 0 1 1	IP-INC8	
JNBE/JA = Jump on not below or equal/above	0 1 1 1 0 1 1 1	IP-INC8	
JNP/JPO = Jump on not par/par odd	0 1 1 1 1 0 1 1	IP-INC8	
JNO = Jump on not overflow	0 1 1 1 0 0 0 1	IP-INC8	

Figure 5.7 *(continued)*

CONTROL TRANSFER (Cont'd.)

RET = Return from CALL:	7 6 5 4 3 2 1 0	7 6 5 4 3 2 1 0	7 6 5 4 3 2 1 0	7 6 5 4 3 2 1 0	7 6 5 4 3 2 1 0	7 6 5 4 3 2 1 0
JNS = Jump on not sign	0 1 1 1 1 0 0 1	IP-INC8				
LOOP = Loop CX times	1 1 1 0 0 0 1 0	IP-INC8				
LOOPZ/LOOPE = Loop while zero/equal	1 1 1 0 0 0 0 1	IP-INC8				
LOOPNZ/LOOPNE = Loop while not zero/equal	1 1 1 0 0 0 0 0	IP-INC8				
JCXZ = Jump on CX zero	1 1 1 0 0 0 1 1	IP-INC8				
INT = Interrupt:						
Type specified	1 1 0 0 1 1 0 1	DATA-8				
Type 3	1 1 0 0 1 1 0 0					
INTO = Interrupt on overflow	1 1 0 0 1 1 1 0					
IRET = Interrupt return	1 1 0 0 1 1 1 1					
PROCESSOR CONTROL						
CLC = Clear carry	1 1 1 1 1 0 0 0					
CMC = Complement carry	1 1 1 1 0 1 0 1					
STC = Set carry	1 1 1 1 1 0 0 1					
CLD = Clear direction	1 1 1 1 1 1 0 0					
STD = Set direction	1 1 1 1 1 1 0 1					
CLI = Clear interrupt	1 1 1 1 1 0 1 0					
STI = Set interrupt	1 1 1 1 1 0 1 1					
HLT = Halt	1 1 1 1 0 1 0 0					
WAIT = Wait	1 0 0 1 1 0 1 1					
ESC = Escape (to external device)	1 1 0 1 1 x x x	m o d y y y r / m	(DISP-LO)	(DISP-HI)		
LOCK = Bus lock prefix	1 1 1 1 0 0 0 0					
SEGMENT = Override prefix	0 0 1 reg 1 1 0					

Figure 5.7 *(continued)*

Instructions that involve a segment register need a 2-bit field, to encode which register is to be affected. This field is called the *SR field*. The four segment registers ES, CS, SS, and DS are encoded according to the table in Fig. 5.8.

Example 5.6

The instruction

MOV [BP].DISP[DI],DS

stands for move the contents of the data segment register to the memory location specified by based indexed addressing mode. Express the instruction in machine code. Let DISP equal 1234_{16}.

Register	SR
ES	00
CS	01
SS	10
DS	11

Figure 5.8 Segment register codes.

Solution. From Fig. 5.7 we see that this instruction is encoded as

10001100 MOD 0 SR R/M DISP

The MOD and R/M fields are the same as in Example 5.5. That is,

MOD = 10

R/M = 011

Moreover, the value of DISP is given as 1234_{16}. Finally, from Fig. 5.8 we find that for DS the SR field is

SR = 11

Therefore, the instruction is coded as

$$10001100100110110011010000010010_2 = 8C9B3412_{16}$$

Encoding a Complete 8086 Program

To encode a complete assembly language program in machine code, we must individually encode each of its instructions. This can be done by using the instruction formats shown in Fig. 5.7 and the information in the tables of Figs. 5.4, 5.5, 5.6, and 5.8. We first identify the general machine code format for the instruction in Fig. 5.7. After determining the format, the bit fields can be evaluated using the tables of Figs. 5.4, 5.5, 5.6, and 5.8. Finally, the binary-coded instruction can be expressed in hexadecimal form.

In order to have the SDK-86 microcomputer execute a program, we must first store the machine code of the program in the code segment of memory. The bytes of machine code are stored in sequentially addressed locations in memory. The first byte of the program is stored at the lowest-value address and it is followed by the other bytes in the order in which they are encoded. That is, the address is incremented by one after storing each byte of machine code in memory.

Example 5.7

Encode the "block move" program shown in Fig. 5.9(a) and show how it would be stored in memory starting at address 200_{16}.

Solution. To encode this program to its equivalent machine code, we will use the instruction set table in Fig. 5.7. The first instruction,

MOV AX,0020H

is a move immediate data to register instruction. In Fig. 5.7, we find that it has the form

1011 W REG DATA DATA IF W = 1

Since the move is to register AX, Fig. 5.4 shows that the W bit is 1 and REG is 000. The immediate data 0020H follow this byte, with the least significant byte coded first. This gives the machine code for the instruction as

$$101110000010000000000000_2 = B82000_{16}$$

The second instruction,

MOV DS,AX

(a)

```
        MOV AX,020H     ;LOAD AX REGISTER
        MOV DS,AX       ;LOAD DATA SEGMENT ADDRESS
        MOV SI,0100H    ;LOAD SOURCE BLOCK POINTER
        MOV DI,0120H    ;LOAD DESTINATION BLOCK POINTER
        MOV CX,010H     ;LOAD REPEAT COUNTER
NXTPT:  MOV AH,[SI]     ;MOVE SOURCE BLOCK ELEMENT TO AX
        MOV [DI],AH     ;MOVE ELEMENT FROM AX TO DESTINATION BLOCK
        INC SI          ;INCREMENT SOURCE BLOCK POINTER
        INC DI          ;INCREMENT DESTINATION BLOCK POINTER
        DEC CX          ;DECREMENT REPEAT COUNTER
        JNZ NXTPT       ;JUMP TO NXTPT IF CX NOT EQUAL TO ZERO
        HLT             ;HALT
```

(b)

Instruction	Type of Instruction	Machine Code
MOV AX,020H	Move immediate data to register	$101110000010000000000000_2 = B82000_{16}$
MOV DS,AX	Move register to segment register	$1000111011011000_2 = 8ED8_{16}$
MOV SI,0100H	Move immediate data to register	$101111100000000000000001_2 = BE0001_{16}$
MOV DI,0120H	Move immediate data to register	$101111110010000000000001_2 = BF2001_{16}$
MOV CX,010H	Move immediate data to register	$101110010001000000000000_2 = B91000_{16}$
MOV AH,[SI]	Move memory data to register	$1000101000100100_2 = 8A24_{16}$
MOV [DI],AH	Move register data to memory	$1000100000100101_2 = 8825_{16}$
INC SI	Increment register	$01000110_2 = 46_{16}$
INC DI	Increment register	$01000111_2 = 47_{16}$
DEC CX	Decrement register	$01001001_2 = 49_{16}$
JNZ NXTPT	Jump on not equal to zero	$0111010111111000_2 = 75F8_{16}$
HLT	Halt	$11110100_2 = F4_{16}$

Figure 5.9 **(a)** Block move program; **(b)** machine coding of the block move program; **(c)** storing the machine code in memory.

Memory address	Contents	Instruction
200H	B8H	MOV AX,020H
201H	20H	
202H	00H	
203H	8EH	MOV DS,AX
204H	D8H	
205H	BEH	MOV SI,0100H
206H	00H	
207H	01H	
208H	BFH	MOV DI,0120H
209H	20H	
20AH	01H	
20BH	B9H	MOV CX,010H
20CH	10H	
20DH	00H	
20EH	8AH	MOV AH,[SI]
20FH	24H	
210H	88H	MOV [DI],AH
211H	25H	
212H	46H	INC SI
213H	47H	INC DI
214H	49H	DEC CX
215H	75H	JNZ $-9
216H	F7H	
217H	F4H	HLT

(c)

Figure 5.9 *(continued)*

represents a move register to segment register operation. This instruction has the general format

10001110 MOD 0 SR R/M

From Fig. 5.5(a) and (b), we find that for this instruction MOD = 11 and R/M is 000 for AX. Furthermore, from Fig. 5.8, we find that SR = 11 for the data segment. This results in the code

$$1000111011011000_2 = 8ED8_{16}$$

for the second instruction.

The next three instructions have the same format as the first instruction. In the third instruction, REG is 110 for SI and the data are encoded as 0100H. This gives

$$101111100000000000000001_2 = BE0001_{16}$$

The fourth instruction has REG coded as 111 (DI) and the data as 0120H. This results in

$$101111110010000000000001_2 = BF2001_{16}$$

In the fifth instruction REG is 001 for CX, with 10_{16} as the data. This gives

$$101110010001000000000000_2 = B91000_{16}$$

The sixth instruction changes. It is a move of byte data from memory to a register. From Fig. 5.7 we find that its general format is

100010 D W MOD REG R/M

Since AH is the destination and the instruction operates on bytes of data, the D and W bits are 1 and 0, respectively, and the REG field is 100. The contents of SI are used as a pointer to the source operand; therefore, MOD is 00 and R/M is 100. This gives

$$1000101000100100_2 = 8A24_{16}$$

The last MOV instruction has the same form. However, in this case, AH is the destination and DI is the address pointer. This makes D equal 0 and R/M equal 101. Therefore, we get

$$1000100000100101_2 = 8825_{16}$$

The next two instructions increment a register and have the general form

01000 REG

For the first one, register SI is incremented. Therefore, REG equals 110. This results in

$$01000110_2 = 46_{16}$$

In the second, DI (REG = 111) is incremented and this gives

$$01000111_2 = 47_{16}$$

The two INC instructions are followed by a DEC instruction. Its general form is

01001 REG

To decrement CX (REG = 001), we get

$$01001001_2 = 49_{16}$$

The next instruction is a jump to the location NXTPT. Its form is

01110101 IP-INC8

We will not yet complete this instruction because it will be easier to determine the number of bytes to be jumped after the data have been coded for storage in memory. The final instruction is HLT and it is coded as

$$11110100_2 = F4_{16}$$

The entire machine code program is shown in Fig. 5.9(b).

As shown in Fig. 5.9(c), our encoded program will be stored in memory starting from memory address 200H. The choice of program beginning address establishes the address for the NXTPT label. Notice that the MOV AH,[SI] instruction, which has this label, starts at address $20E_{16}$. This is nine bytes back from the JNZ instruction. Therefore, the displacement (IP-INC8) in the JNZ instruction is -9 and it is encoded as

$$0111010111110001_2 = 75F7_{16}$$

5.4 THE SDK-86 MICROCOMPUTER AND ITS MONITOR PROGRAM

Now that we know how to convert an assembly language program to machine code and how this machine code is to be stored in memory, we are ready to enter the program into the memory of the SDK-86 microcomputer, execute it, examine the results that it produces, and if necessary debug any error. It is the keypad monitor program that permits us to initiate these types of operations from the keypad of the SDK-86 microcomputer.

The keypad monitor is the program that implements the *user interface* to the SDK-86 microcomputer. It is a simple monitor that provides for program entry, execution, and display of information. The monitor program consists of a number of subroutines that are written to perform the various operations that are to be performed by the microcomputer. For instance, the monitor must read inputs from the keypad, analyze the input key sequences, initiate the appropriate operations, and display the required information. The monitor is stored in EPROM on the microcomputer's printed circuit board.

Initially, the microcomputer is reset. When in this state, it repeatedly scans the keypad looking for user entries. The user can issue *commands* to the microcomputer from the keypad. When a command entry sequence is complete, the key entry and decoding part of the monitor causes control to be passed to the subroutine that performs the operation specified by the command. At the completion of the operation, the results are displayed by the display driver part of the monitor and keypad scanning is resumed. The microcomputer remains in this state until new entries are made from the keypad.

The keys of the keypad are shown in Fig. 5.10. This keypad is the input unit of the microcomputer and permits the user to enter data such as the machine code of a program and commands such as "single-step execute the program." Notice that the keys are arranged into two separate sections called the *function keys* and the *hexadecimal keys*.

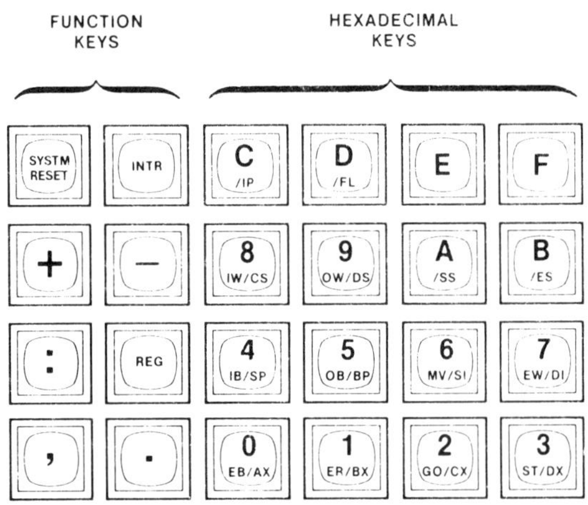

Figure 5.10 Keypad of the SDK-86 microcomputer (*Courtesy of Intel Corporation*).

Each key in the group of function keys has a single function. These functions are summarized in Fig. 5.11. For example, the key labeled "SYSTM RESET," when depressed, initiates a hardware reset of the microcomputer. Typically, this is the first thing done when the microcomputer is powered on. On the other hand, keys such as "," and "." have different types of functions. They are used to separate the elements in a command and to terminate entry of a command, respectively.

The keys in the hexadecimal key section have multiple functions. First, they serve as the keys for entry of hexadecimal numbers 0 through F. However, as shown in Fig. 5.12, most of these keys also have a command function and a register function. For instance, the 0 key serves two other functions: the EB label stands for the "*examine byte*" *monitor command* and its AX label stands for "*accumulator register*." The monitor has the ability to determine which of these three functions is to be performed by the sequence in which the keypad entries have been made.

An example of the key sequence needed to load the AX register with the data word $00FF_{16}$ is

ER AX 0 0 F F

The output device in the SDK-86 microcomputer is the display. It gives visual feedback to the user of the microcomputer. As shown in Fig. 5.13, the eight digits of the display are organized into two four-digit groups: the *address field* on the left and the *data field* on the right. When keying in entries to the microcomputer, address information, register identifiers, and messages are always displayed in the address field. Figure 5.14 shows what is displayed in the address field to identify each of the 8086's internal registers.

The data field is used to display the contents of registers or memory locations when they are examined. Moreover, it echos back hexadecimal data as they are entered from the keypad. The seven-segment display format for numbers 0 through F, shown in Fig. 5.15, is used to display the hexadecimal data.

5.5 THE KEYPAD MONITOR COMMANDS

In Section 5.4 we introduced the SDK-86 microcomputer, its monitor program, keypad, and display. Here we will discuss the actual commands that can be issued to the microcomputer through the monitor.

There are three basic types of information that are typically entered in order to initiate a command: a *command keyword*, an *address or a register name*, and *data*. The entire *command set* of the SDK-86 microcomputer is shown in Fig. 5.16. This table gives the name for each command, briefly describes its function, and illustrates its *syntax*. By syntax, we mean the order in which key entries must be made to initiate the command.

Let us now look at the syntax for one of the commands in more detail. Notice that the syntax for the "*examine byte*" *command* is

Function Key	Operation
SYSTM RESET	The **SYSTM RESET** key allows you to terminate any present activity and to return your SDK-86 to an initialized state. When pressed, the 8086 sign-on message appears in the display and the monitor is ready for command entry.
INTR	The **INTR** (interrupt) key is used to generate an immediate, non-maskable type 2 interrupt (NMI). The NMI interrupt vector is initialized on power up or system reset to point to a routine within the monitor which causes all of the 8086's registers to be saved. Control is returned to the monitor for subsequent command entry.
+	The **+** (plus) key allows you to add two hexadecimal values. This function simplifies relative addressing by allowing you to readily calculate an address location relative to a base address.
–	The **–** (minus) key allows you to subtract one hexadecimal value from another.
:	The **:** (colon) key is used to separate an address to be entered into two parts; a segment value and an offset value.
REG	The **REG** (register) key allows you to use the contents of any of the 8086's registers as an address or data entry.
,	The **,** (comma) key is used to separate keypad entries and to increment the address field to the next consecutive memory location.
.	The **.** (period) key is the command terminator. When pressed, the current command is executed. Note that when using the Go command, the 8086 begins program execution at the address specified when the key is pressed.

Figure 5.11 Uses of the function keys (*Courtesy of Intel Corporation*).

Hexadecimal Key	Command		Register	
	Acronym	Name	Acronym	Name
0 EB/AX	EB	Examine Byte	AX	Accumulator
1 ER/BX	ER	Examine Register	BX	Base
2 GO/CX	GO	Go	CX	Count
3 ST/DX	ST	(Single) Step	DX	Data
4 IB/SP	IB	Input Byte	SP	Stack Pointer
5 OB/BP	OB	Output Byte	BP	Base Pointer
6 MV/SI	MV	Move	SI	Source Index
7 EW/DI	EW	Examine Word	DI	Destination Index
8 IW/CS	IW	Input Word	CS	Code Segment
9 OW/DS	OW	Output Word	DS	Data Segment
A /SS	none	N/A	SS	Stack Segment
B /ES	none	N/A	ES	Extra Segment
C /IP	none	N/A	IP	Instruction Pointer
D /FL	none	N/A	FL	Flag
E	none	N/A	none	N/A
F	none	N/A	none	N/A

Figure 5.12 Uses of the hexadecimal keys (*Courtesy of Intel Corporation*).

Figure 5.13 Display of the SDK-86 microcomputer.

Register Name	Keypad Acronym	Display Abbreviation
Accumulator	AX	A
Base	BX	b
Count	CX	C
Data	DX	d
Stack Pointer	SP	SP
Base Pointer	BP	bP
Source Index	SI	SI
Destination Index	DI	dI
Code Segment	CS	CS
Data Segment	DS	dS
Stack Segment	SS	SS
Extra Segment	ES	ES
Instruction Pointer	IP	IP
Flag	FL	FL

Figure 5.14 Display abbreviations for the 8086's registers (*Courtesy of Intel Corporation*).

EB<addr>,[[<data>],]*.

Here the command keyword is EB and it is entered into the microcomputer by depressing the EB key of the keypad. When the monitor recognizes that this key has been depressed, it considers up to the next four entries from the hexadecimal part of the keypad as the address of the byte location in memory that is to be accessed. This part of the command is identified as <addr> in the syntax diagram and the value of the address is a compulsory entry. The comma that follows the address is used to separate terms in the command. In this case it indicates to the monitor that the complete address has been entered. The element that follows the address in the syntax diagram is enclosed in square brackets. Anything that is enclosed in this type of bracket is optional and may or may not be entered as part of the command. The notation [<data>] represents hexadecimal data. When data are entered, they replace the current contents of the memory location that is being accessed. The data value is also terminated with a comma. The period at the end of the command terminates the command.

Actually, multiple sequential bytes of data can be entered with this command. This is indicated by an outer set of brackets to enclose the inner set and an *. The values are entered separated by commas. In this way, execution of the command causes the contents of consecutive bytes of memory to be modified.

Hexadecimal Value	Display Format
0	0
1	1
2	2
3	3
4	4
5	5
6	6
7	7
8	8
9	9
A	A
B	b
C	C
D	d
E	E
F	F

Figure 5.15 Display format for hexadecimal numbers (*Courtesy of Intel Corporation*).

For the purpose of discussion, we will divide the monitor commands in Fig. 5.16 into four groups. We will call them the *examine/enter commands,* the *input/output commands*, the *program execution control commands*, and the *block move command.*

Examine/Enter Commands

The three commands in Fig. 5.16 that we will consider as the examine/enter commands are *"examine byte" (EB), "examine word" (EW),* and *"examine register" (ER).* These commands are provided to give the programmer the ability to display or modify the contents of a storage location in memory or a register within the 8086. This capability is essential for debugging a program. For instance, the contents of a specific memory location or register can be examined prior to and after the execution of an instruction. In this way, we can determine if the instruction performed

Command	Function/Syntax
Examine Byte	Displays/modifies memory byte locations `EB` <addr>`,`[[<data>]`,`]*`.`
Examine Word	Displays/modifies memory word locations `EW` <addr>`,`[[<data>]`,`]*`.`
Examine Register	Displays/modifies 8086 register contents `ER` <reg key>[[<data>]`,`]*[`.`]
Input Byte	Displays data byte at input port `IB` <port addr>`,`[`,`]*`.`
Input Word	Displays data word at input port `IW` <port addr>`,`[`,`]*`.`
Output Byte	Outputs data byte to output port `OB` <port addr>`,`<data>[`,`<data>]*`.`
Output Word	Outputs data word to output port `OW` <port addr>`,`<data>[`,`<data>]*`.`
Go	Transfers control from monitor to user program `GO` [<addr>][`,`<breakpoint addr>]`.`
Move	Moves block of data within memory `MV` <start addr>`,`<end addr>`,`<destination addr>`.`
Step	Executes single user program instruction `ST` [<start addr>]`,`[[<start addr>]`,`]*`.`

Figure 5.16 Monitor commands (*Courtesy of Intel Corporation*).

the required operation. Other uses of these commands are for initialization of registers or memory, and for loading of programs into memory.

The syntax we just described is that of the EB and EW commands. For this reason, let us look at a few examples of how the commands can be used. A first example is the command

EB 25,

It is issued by first depressing the "EB" key and then the "2" key, "5" key, and "," key in that sequence. Entering this command causes the contents of memory address 25_{16} to be displayed. Let us assume that this location contains FF_{16}. Then 25 is displayed in the address field of the display and FF in the data field.

Let us now look at a couple of examples of commands that can be used to modify the contents of memory. For example, in order to change the byte contents at address 25_{16} to EF_{16}, we can use the command

EB 25, EF.

Notice that we have included both an address and data element in the command.

If the contents of sequential memory locations are to be modified, the "," key can be depressed after the data entry instead of the "." key. This causes the next address to be displayed and it will be modified by the data that are entered following the comma. For instance, to load the three bytes of memory starting at address 25_{16} with the value $0A_{16}$, $0B_{16}$, and $0C_{16}$, we issue the command

EB 25, 0A, 0B, 0C.

In each of the examples we have considered up to this point, the address that was entered with the command was used relative to the current contents of the code segment register to form the address of the location that is to be accessed in memory. It is also possible to access a location relative to one of the other segment registers. This is done by depressing the REG key followed by the key for the segment register and the colon key before entering the value of the address. For instance, the key sequence

EB REG DS: 25, EF.

changes the contents of address 25_{16} relative to the current contents of the data segment register to EF_{16}.

Example 5.8

Write a command sequence that will display the contents of the first three byte locations in the current data segment.

Solution. We will use the EB command but must modify the segment register by following it with the REG key and DS key. Moreover, since we want to look at the first three locations in the segment, the address for the first byte is 0_{16} and to examine the next two bytes we simply depress the "," key twice more. This gives

EB REG DS: 0, , , .

The "examine word" command is similar to EB except that now a word of memory is displayed or modified. For instance, the command

EW 25,

displays the contents of addresses 25_{16} and 26_{16} relative to the current code segment. The byte from address 25_{16} is displayed in the two least significant digits of the data field and the byte from address 26_{16} is displayed in the two most significant digits.

The last of the examine/enter commands, "examine register," is used to display or modify the contents of one of the 8086's internal registers. Looking at Fig. 5.16, we see that its syntax differs from that of the EB and EW commands. Instead of entering an address, the key corresponding to the register that is to be accessed is depressed. For example, to examine the contents of the accumulator register, the command is

ER AX,

The contents of the register is always displayed as a word. For instance, in the case of AX, the high byte, AH, is displayed in the two most significant digits of the data field and the low byte, AL, is displayed in the two least significant digits.

The contents of a register can also be changed with this command. For instance, to change the contents of the code segment register to $A00_{16}$, the command is

ER CS A00.

Notice that "." is entered at the end of the command to terminate it.

The contents of any number or all of the internal registers can be displayed or modified with just one "examine register" command. This is done by using a comma after the register or data entry instead of a period. The registers are accessed in the order shown in Fig. 5.14. For example, the sequence

ER CS, , , .

displays the contents of registers CS, DS, SS, and ES in that order.

Example 5.9

Write a command sequence that will initialize AX, BX, CX, and DX to the values $A000_{16}$, $B000_{16}$, $000C_{16}$, and $B000_{16}$, respectively.

Solution. The ER command must be issued to modify the contents of registers. Looking at the table of Fig. 5.14, we find that these registers can be accessed sequentially starting with AX. Therefore, they can be modified with the command sequence

ER AX A000, B000, C, B000.

Example 5.10

Write a sequence of commands that will create a data segment at address 700_{16} and initialize the first eight storage locations in the data segment to the values 1, 3, 5, 7, 9, B, D, and F, respectively.

Solution. First we will initialize the DS register to 70_{16} to create a data segment starting at address 700_{16}. This is done with the command

ER DS 70.

Now the memory locations can be initialized with the command sequence

ER REG DS: 0, 1, 3, 5, 7, 9, B, D, F.

Entries that use incorrect syntax or that attempt to modify a part of the memory implemented using PROMs are identified with an *error message (-Err)* in the display.

Input/Output Commands

There are six byte-wide I/O ports on the SDK-86 microcomputer. Figure 5.17(a) shows that these ports are produced by two parallel I/O devices called P_1 and P_2. Device P_1 implements the three byte-wide I/O ports labeled P_{1A}, P_{1B}, and P_{1C}. As shown in Fig. 5.17(a) and (b), these ports are located at addresses $FFF9_{16}$, $FFFB_{16}$, and $FFFD_{16}$, respectively, of the I/O address space.

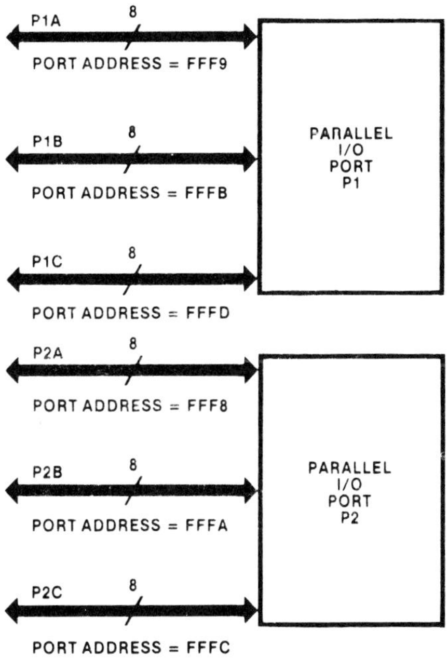

(a)

Port	Address
P2A	FFF8
P1A	FFF9
P2B	FFFA
P1B	FFFB
P2C	FFFC
P1C	FFFD

(b)

Port Number	Port Address	Data Byte or Word	
		Input	Output
P2	FFFEH	9BH	80H
P1	FFFFH	9BH	80H
P2/P1	FFFEH	9B9BH	8080H

(c)

Figure 5.17 **(a)** Byte-wide parallel I/O ports; **(b)** byte-wide I/O port address map; **(c)** control register addresses (*Courtesy of Intel Corporation*).

Parallel I/O ports P_1 and P_2 can be individually configured under software control to operate as either input ports or output ports. This is done by writing appropriate value control bytes into their control registers. The addresses of the control registers for ports P_1 and P_2 are given in Fig. 5.17(c). Here we see that the control register for P_2 is located at I/O address $FFFE_{16}$ and that for P_1 is at I/O address $FFFF_{16}$. The value loaded into the control register for P_2 determines the operation of I/O ports P_{2A}, P_{2B}, and P_{2C}. At system reset, this register is automatically initialized with $9B_{16}$ by the monitor's reset software routine. This sets all three of these byte-wide ports for input mode of operation. To reconfigure all of them as output ports, Fig. 5.17(c) says that we must write 80_{16} into P_2's control register.

Figure 5.18 shows that the I/O ports of the SDK-86 microcomputer can be accessed through software as word-wide ports instead of byte-wide ports. In this case, the I/O address used in the instruction must be that of the lower addressed port. For example, if ports P_{1A} and P_{2A} are to be read as a word-wide input port, the address of the word-wide port is $FFF8_{16}$. In this example, P_1 supplies the most significant byte of the data word and P_2 the least significant byte. Moreover, as shown in Fig. 5.17(c), the control ports of P_1 and P_2 can be written together by outputting a control word to address $FFFE_{16}$.

Looking at the table in Fig. 5.16, we see that the command used to output a byte of data is called "*output byte*." The syntax for this command shows that it is initiated by depressing the OB key on the keypad. This entry must be followed by the address of the I/O port and the value of data to be output. For instance, if we

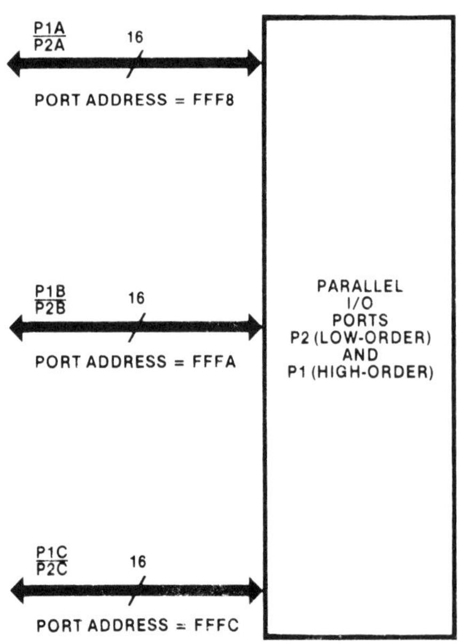

Figure 5.18 Word-wide parallel I/O ports (*Courtesy of Intel Corporation*).

want to set the ports on P_2 for output mode of operation, 80_{16} must be output to the control register at address $FFFE_{16}$. This is done with the command

OB FFFE, 80.

Once this parallel port is initialized for output mode of operation, data can be output to P_{2A}, P_{2B}, and P_{2C} with additional output byte commands. As an example, let us write commands to clear all three of these ports:

OB FFF8, 00.

OB FFFA, 00.

OB FFFC, 00.

Example 5.11

Write an output command that will load output port P_{2A} with AA_{16}.

Solution. This operation can be done with an OB command to address $FFF8_{16}$. Therefore, we get

OB FFF8, AA.

It is also possible to output the contents of a register to a port with the OB command. An example would be to output the least significant byte in DX to output port P_{2B}. The command to do this is

OB FFFA, REG DX.

To output a word of data, we use the "*output word*" *(OW)* command. This command is similar to the OB command; however, now 16 bits of data (four hexadecimal digits) are output to a 16-bit output port. Remember that to use this command on the SDK-86 microcomputer, both parallel I/O ports must be set to the output mode. Assuming that this is the case, the command needed to output the word $AAAA_{16}$ to the word-wide output port consisting of P_{1A} and P_{2A} is

OW FFF8, AAAA.

Similarly, to load this same word-wide port from the DX register, the command is

OW FFF8, REG DX.

The input commands "*input byte*" *(IB)* and "*input word*" *(IW)* permit the user of the SDK-86 microcomputer to examine the logic levels applied to input ports. From the table of Fig. 5.16, we see that the form of the input commands are similar to that of their corresponding output commands. However, in this case, no data are entered as part of the command. For instance, to input the data at P_{2B}, the command that must be issued is

IB FFFA,

Moreover, to read the contents of ports P_{1B} and P_{2B} as a word, the command is

IW FFFA,

Remember that before using either of these two commands the ports that are to be accessed must first be set to operate as input ports.

Example 5.12

Assume that port P_{2A} is configured for input mode of operation. Write an input command that will repeatedly input the byte contents from P_{2A}.

Solution. P_{2A} is a byte-wide input port; therefore, we will use the IB command with the address for P_{2A}, which is $FFF8_{16}$. We can examine the port repeatedly by depressing the "," key. This gives the command sequence

IB FFF8, , , , , ,

Program Execution Control Commands

The SDK-86 microcomputer's monitor has two commands that can be used to control the execution of a program: the *"go" (GO) command* and the *"step" (ST) command.* Let us begin with the GO command. This command gives the programmer the ability to execute a segment of program. The table in Fig. 5.16 shows that the general form of the GO command has two address elements. The first address, <addr>, is the *starting address* of the program segment that is to be executed, that is, the address of the instruction at which execution is to begin. The second address, <breakpoint addr>, is the address of the end of the program segment, that is, the address of the instruction at which execution is to stop. The *breakpoint address* that is specified must correspond to the first byte of an instruction.

An example of the GO command is

GO 10:0, A.

This command loads the code segment register with 10_{16}, thereby creating a code segment that starts at address 100_{16}. The offset that follows the value for CS is 0_{16}; therefore, the starting address is simply 100_{16}. On the other hand, the breakpoint address offset is A. This sets the breakpoint at address $10A_{16}$. As "." is entered, program execution begins at 100_{16} and proceeds through the 10 bytes of machine code up to address $10A_{16}$. When the breakpoint address is reached, program execution is terminated and control is returned to the monitor.

If CS was already loaded with 10_{16}, the same results could have been obtained by issuing the command

GO 0, A.

Sometimes we just want to execute a program without using a breakpoint. This can also be done with the GO command. For instance, to execute a program that starts at 100_{16}, we can issue the GO command without a breakpoint address. This gives

GO 10:0.

or in the case of a program where CS is already initialized with 10_{16}.

GO .

When the program is being executed, execution can be terminated at any time by depressing the *interrupt request (INTR)* key.

The GO command is typically used to execute programs that are already debugged or to aid in the process of debugging programs in the latter stages of debugging. For example, if the earlier part of a program is already operating correctly, a GO command can be issued to execute this group of instructions and then stop execution at a point in the program where additional debugging is to begin.

The other program execution control command is "step" (ST). This command provides the programmer with the ability to execute one instruction at a time. This mode of operation is also known as single stepping the program and is very useful during early phases of program debugging. This is because debugging operations such as examining the contents of registers or memory can be performed both before and after the execution of each instruction to determine if the correct operation was performed.

The general form of the command is shown in Fig. 5.16. Notice that a starting address is specified as part of the command. For instance, the command

ST 10:0,

causes the instruction at address 100_{16} to be executed. Now the debug operations can be performed. If the code segment register already contains 10_{16}, the command can be issued as

ST ,

If we want to single step through several instructions, the step command can be terminated with a comma instead of a period. In this case, depressing the "," key will cause the single-step operation to be performed. Therefore, in order to single step through five instructions that start at address 100_{16}, the command that must be issued is

ST 10:0, , , , , .

There are some restrictions on the use of the step command. They are:

1. Interrupt instructions should not be single stepped.
2. Instructions that change the stack segment (SS) or stack pointer (SP) registers should not be single stepped.
3. MOV or POP instructions that change the contents of a segment register should not be single stepped.

Block Move Command

The last command available in the SDK-86's keypad monitor is the *"move" (MV) command*. This command permits the user to move a block of data from one part of memory to another part. For instance, using this command, a 256-byte program that resides in memory from address 100_{16} to $1FF_{16}$ can be moved to the address range 200_{16} through $2FF_{16}$ with a single MV command.

Looking at the general form of the command in Fig. 5.16, we find that it is initiated by depressing the MV key. After this, we must key in three addresses. The first two addresses are the *starting address* and *ending address* of the source block of data, that is, the block of data that is to be moved. The third address is the *destination starting address*, that is, the starting address of the segment of memory to which the block is to be moved. The first address may be specified relative to a segment register; however, the second address must assume the same segment register as the first address. The third address can be specified using a segment and an offset value. The move command for our earlier example can be written as

MV 10:0, FF, 20:0.

The source block of memory can correspond to either ROM or RAM memory, but the destination block must always be in RAM. Notice that we can copy code from ROM into RAM. This means that the whole monitor program is available to the user, and segments of it can be copied into the *user's application program*. This capability is very useful for application program development.

5.6 LOADING AND EXECUTING A PROGRAM

After a machine code program has been prepared, it must be entered into the memory of the SDK-86 microcomputer. We found in Section 5.5 that the monitor program has commands that can be used to modify memory. They are the commands which are used to enter the program into the microcomputer's memory. For instance, the program can be entered byte by byte with a series of examine byte (EB) commands. Programs can also be entered word by word by using the examine word (EW) command.

Example 5.13

Show the sequence of keypad entries needed to enter the machine code program of Fig. 5.9(c) into the memory of an SDK-86 microcomputer. The program is to be loaded into memory starting at address 200_{16}.

Solution. We will use the EB command to enter the program byte by byte. The first command must set up the starting address, enter the first byte of code, and increment the address for the next byte to be entered. This command is

EB 20:0, B8,

The rest of the bytes are entered one after the other each followed by a comma. This gives the following entries:

20, 00, 8E, D8, BE, 00, 01, BF, 20, 01, B9, 10,

00, 8A, 24, 88, 25, 46, 47, 49, 75, F7, F4.

Example 5.14

Show a key sequence that can be used to examine the program entered in Example 5.13 to assure that it has been entered correctly.

Solution. The examine byte command can also be used to verify the entry of a program. In this case, the first command sets up the starting address and displays the first byte to show whether it has been loaded correctly. This command is

EB 20:0,

The rest of the bytes can be examined one after the other by simply repeatedly depressing the comma key.

Once the program has been entered into the microcomputer's memory, it is ready to be executed. The SDK-86's monitor allows us to execute the entire program with one GO command or to execute the program in several segments of instructions by using breakpoints in the GO command. On the other hand, by using the ST command, the program can be stepped through by executing one instruction at a time.

Example 5.15

What command must be issued to initiate execution of the program that was entered in Example 5.13? What will happen when the last instruction of the program is executed?

Solution. The GO command will be issued to initiate execution of the complete program. This command is

GO 20:0.

When the last instruction is reached, program execution stops. This happens because the last instruction is the "halt" instruction.

Example 5.16

Show the sequence of key entries needed to single step through the program of Example 5.13.

Solution. The first step command must set up the starting address and cause execution of the first instruction.

ST 20:0,

The rest of the instructions can be executed one after the other by repeatedly depressing the comma key.

5.7 DEBUGGING A PROGRAM

In Section 5.6 we showed how to load a program into the memory of the SDK-86 microcomputer and how to execute it. However, we did not determine if the program when executed performed the operation for which it was written. It is common to have errors in programs, and even a single error can render the program useless. For instance, if the address to which a "call" instruction passes control is wrong, the program may get hung up. Errors in a program are also referred to as bugs and the process of removing them is called *debugging*.

The two types of errors that can be made by a programmer are the *syntax error* and the *execution error*. A syntax error is an error caused by not following the rules for coding or entering an instruction. These types of errors are typically identified by the microcomputer and signaled to the user with an error message. For this reason, they are usually easy to find and correct.

For example, if the first EB command in Example 5.13 was entered as

EB FE00, B8,

an error condition exists. This is because an attempt was made to modify a part of the address space already implemented as read-only memories. The address entered as part of an EB command that is to modify memory must always correspond to a storage location in data memory. This incorrect entry is signaled by the warning "-Err" in the display.

An execution error is an error in the logic behind the development of the program. That is, the program is correctly coded and entered, but still it does not perform the operation for which it was planned. This type of error can be identified by entering the program into the microcomputer and executing it. Even when an execution error problem has been identified, it is usually not easy to find the exact cause of the problem.

Our ability to debug execution errors in a program is aided by the commands of the monitor program. For instance, the ST command allows us to step through the program by executing just one instruction at a time. In this way, we can use the register examine and memory examine commands to determine the state of the microcomputer prior to execution of the instruction and after its execution. This information will tell us whether the instruction has performed the operation planned for it. If an error is found, its cause can be determined and corrected.

To illustrate the process of debugging a program, let us once again consider the program in Fig. 5.9(a). Its machine code is given in Fig. 5.9(c) and we showed how to enter the program into the memory of the SDK-86 microcomputer in Example 5.13. The program resides in memory starting at address 200_{16}. This program implements a block data transfer operation. The block of data to be moved starts at memory address 300_{16} and is 10_{16} bytes in length. It is to be moved to another block location starting at address 320_{16}.

Before executing the program, let us issue commands to initialize the block of memory locations from address 300_{16} through $30F_{16}$ to FF_{16}. This is done with the command sequence

EB 30:0, FF, FF, FF, FF, FF, FF, FF, FF,

FF, FF, FF, FF, FF, FF, FF, FF, .

Moreover, the bytes in the block starting at 320_{16} can be initialized to 00_{16}. To do this, we issue the command sequence

EB 32:0, 0, 0, 0, 0, 0, 0, 0, 0, 0, 0, 0, 0, 0, 0, 0, 0, .

The first two instructions of the program in Fig. 5.9(a) are

MOV AX,020H

and

MOV DS,AX

These two instructions when executed load the data segment register and define a data segment starting at address 200_{16}. Let us show how to execute these instructions and then determine if they perform the correct function. The two instructions are executed with the command

ST 20:0, , .

This command sequence establishes the code segment starting at 200_{16} by executing the first two instructions.

To determine if these two instructions performed the correct operation, we need to look at the contents of the DS register. This is done with the "examine register" command

ER DS.

When this command is issued to the microcomputer, dS will be displayed in the address field and 0020 in the data field.

Now we are ready to execute the next three instructions, which are used to load the SI, DI, and CX registers with 100_{16}, 120_{16}, and 10_{16}, respectively. Again the ST command can be used to execute the instructions. This gives

ST , , , .

and their operation is checked by examining the registers with the commands

ER SI.

ER DI.

ER CX.

The next two instructions copy the contents of memory location 300_{16} into the storage location at address 320_{16}. Let us first check the contents of the destination address with the command

EB 32:0,

This should show that the original contents of this location are 00_{16}. After terminating the EB command with a ".", the instructions are executed with the command

ST , , .

and the contents of address 320_{16} are checked once again with the command

EB 320:0.

This time, FF should be displayed, showing that the first element of the source block was correctly moved to the location of the first element of the destination block. Therefore, both address 300_{16} and address 320_{16} now contain the same data.

The next two instructions are used to increment SI and DI, respectively. To execute them we issue the command

ST , , .

and to verify their operation, we issue the commands

ER SI.

"." should be entered only after the displayed contents of SI are noted.

ER DI.

The new values found in SI and DI should be 101_{16} and 121_{16}, respectively.

The next instruction decrements the block count in CX. It is executed and the contents of CX are displayed with the command sequence

ST,

ER CX

The contents of CX should now be $000F_{16}$.

The jump instruction transfers control to the instruction 8 bytes back. It is executed with the command

ST,

As the result of executing this instruction, the address field of the display should read E. This corresponds to the location of the instruction

MOV AH,[SI]

Control has been returned to the part of the program that performs the move operation.

The move operation performed by this part of the program was already checked; however, we must still determine if it runs to completion when the count in CX decrements to zero. Therefore, we will execute the complete loop with a GO command. This command is

GO 20:E, 15.

where 15 specifies the breakpoint address 215H (the address of the jump instruction). Correct operation can be verified by determining if CX has been decremented. This is done with the command

ER CX.

Now we are at address 215H. To execute the instruction at this location, we can use the step command

ST,

Now the previous three commands can be repeated until the complete block is moved and CX equals 0_{16}. At which point a ST command should step the program control to the HLT instruction.

The overall operation of the program can be verified by examining the contents of the destination block with the command sequence

EB 32:0, , , , , , , , , , , , , , , , .

FF_{16} should be displayed as the data held in each storage location.

The entire debugging command sequence and the corresponding information displayed are shown in Fig. 5.19.

Command sequence	Display	
	Address field	Data field
EB 30:0,FF	0	ΓΓ.
,FF	1	FF.
,FF	2	FF.
.	.	.
.	.	.
.	.	.
,FF	F	FF.
.	—	
EB 32:0,0	0	00.
,0	1	00.
,0	2	00.
.	.	.
.	.	.
.	.	.
,0	F	00.
.	—	
ST 20:0,	3.	8E
,	5.	bE
.	—	
ER DS	dS	0020.
.	—	
ST,	8.	bF
,	b.	b9
,	E.	8A
.	—	
ER SI	SI	0100.
.	—	
ER DI	dI	0120.
.	—	
ER CX	C	0010.
.	—	
EB 32:0,	0.	00.
.	—	
ST,	10.	88
,	12.	46
,	13.	47
EB 32:0,	0	FF.
.	—	
ST,	14.	49
,	15.	75
.	—	

Figure 5.19 Example command and display sequences.

Command sequence	Display	
	Address field	Data field
ER SI	SI	0101.
.	—	
ER DI	dI	0121.
.	—	
ST,	E.	8A
.	—	
ER CX	C	000F.
ST,	10.	88
.	—	
GO 20:E, 15	—	br
.	—	
ER CX	C	000E.
.	—	
ST,	E.	8A
.	—	
GO 20:E,15	—	br
.	—	
ER CX	C	000d.
.	—	
.	.	.
.	.	.
.	.	.
GO 20:E,15	—	br
.	—	
ER CX	C	0000.
.	—	
ST,	17.	F4
.	—	
EB 32:0,	0	00.
,	1	00.
,	2	00.
.	.	.
.	.	.
.	.	.
,	F	00.
.	—	

Figure 5.19 *(continued)*

ASSIGNMENT

Section 5.3

1. Encode the following instruction using the information in Figs. 5.3, 5.4, and 5.5.

   ADD AX,DX

   The opcode for ADD is 000000_2.

2. Encode the following instructions using the information in Figs. 5.3, 5.4, and 5.5.

   (a) MOV [DI],DX

   (b) MOV [1234H],01234H

   (c) MOV [BX].[SI],BX

   (d) MOV DL,DISP[BX] where DISP = 10_{16}

3. Encode the instructions that follow using the tables in Figs. 5.6, 5.7, and 5.8.

   (a) PUSH DS

   (b) ROL BL,CL

   (c) XCHG CX

Section 5.4

4. Describe the difference between the function keys and the hexadecimal keys.
5. Draw a simple flowchart that overviews how the SDK-86 monitor goes through the sequence of accepting entry of a command and initiating execution for it.

Section 5.5

6. Write a command sequence that will load the first 16 locations of the current data segment with FF_{16}.
7. Write a series of commands that will configure the memory segments of the SDK-86 microcomputer as follows: code segment starts at 100_{16}, data segment starts at 200_{16}, extra segment starts at 300_{16}, and the stack segment starts at 400_{16}.
8. Write commands that will first configure all P_1 ports as inputs and all P_2 ports as outputs and then display the byte contents of input port P_{1B} and output AB_{16} to output port P_{2B}.
9. The CS register contents are 20_{16}. A program segment starting at address 250_{16} and ending at $2FF_{16}$ is to be executed. Write the appropriate command or commands to do this.
10. Write a "move" (MV) command that will fill memory locations 300_{16} to $3FF_{16}$ with the number contained in location 300_{16}.

Section 5.6

11. Describe the operation of the command

    GO CS:10,2A.

    Assume that CS contains 25_{16}.

Section 5.7

12. What is a syntax error?

13. How does an execution error differ from a syntax error?

14. Change the debugging command sequence shown in Fig. 5.19 so that GO commands are used instead of the ST commands. Also indicate what is displayed on the SDK-86 as these commands are executed.

6

Memory Interface of the 8086 Microprocessor

6.1 INTRODUCTION

Up to this point in the book, we have introduced the 8086 microprocessor, its signal leads, and internal architecture. Moreover, from a software point of view, we have covered its instruction set and how to write programs in assembly language. Now we will begin to examine the hardware interfaces of the 8086. This chapter is devoted to its memory interface and external memory subsystems. For this purpose, we have included the following topics in the chapter:

1. Memory interface block diagram
2. Address space and data organization
3. Dedicated and general use of memory
4. Generating a physical memory address
5. Hardware organization of the memory address space
6. Memory bus status codes and memory control signals
7. Read and write bus cycles
8. The stack and stack pointer
9. Demultiplexing the address/data bus
10. 4K-word program storage memory
11. 1K-word static RAM data storage memory
12. 128K-byte dynamic RAM subsystem

6.2 MEMORY INTERFACE BLOCK DIAGRAM

In either the minimum- or maximum-mode-system configuration, the 8086 microprocessor can address up to 1M bytes of memory. However, the interface to the memory subsystem is different for each of these two modes of operation. The circuit diagram in Fig. 6.1 is that of the minimum-system memory interface. Here we find that it consists of the *multiplexed address/data bus lines* AD_0 through AD_{15} together with *additional address lines* A_{16} through A_{19} and *bank high enable* ($\overline{BHE}$). Notice that *memory control signals* ALE, $\overline{RD}$, $\overline{WR}$, $M/\overline{IO}$, $DT/\overline{R}$, and $\overline{DEN}$ are produced by the 8086.

The maximum-mode memory interface is shown in Fig. 6.2. This circuit configuration includes an 8288 bus controller device. Notice that bus *status signals* $\overline{S}_0$ through $\overline{S}_2$ are input to this device. It decodes this 3-bit code to identify the type of bus cycle that is to be initiated. In turn, it generates *read/write signals* $\overline{MRDC}$, $\overline{MWTC}$, and $\overline{AMWC}$ as well as *control signals* ALE, $DT/\overline{R}$, and $\overline{DEN}$. In this way we see that in the maximum-mode system the bus controller instead of the 8086 generates most of the timing and control signals for the memory interface.

Address Space and Data Organization

Looking at Figs. 6.1 and 6.2, we find that the 8086 has a 20-bit address bus. This bus consists of address lines AD_0 through AD_{15} and A_{16} through A_{19}. Of these, AD_0 is the LSB of the address and A_{19} the MSB. With this 20-bit *physical address*, it can directly address up to 1,048,576 bytes (1M byte) of memory. As shown in the memory map of Fig. 6.3, these byte storage locations are assigned to consecutive addresses over the range from 00000_{16} to $FFFFF_{16}$.

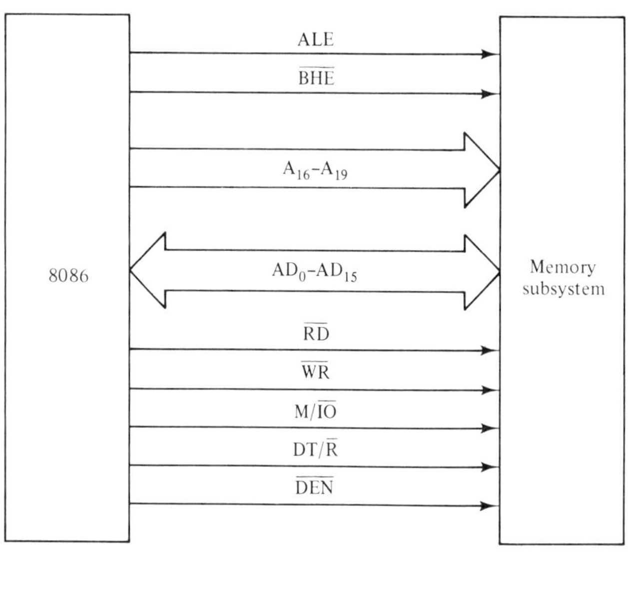

Figure 6.1 Minimum 8086 system memory interface.

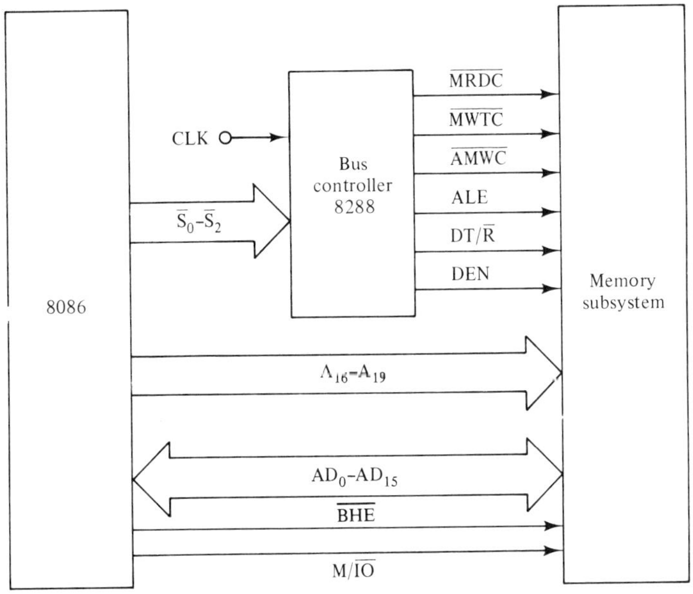

Figure 6.2 Maximum 8086 system memory interface.

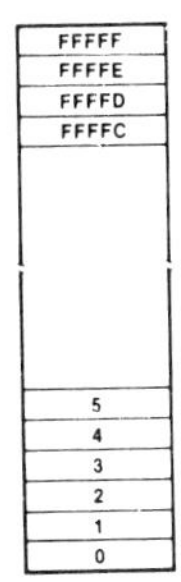

Figure 6.3 Address space of the 8086.

In this way we see that the memory subsystem in an 8086 microcomputer system is actually organized as 8-bit bytes, not as 16-bit words. However, any two consecutive bytes can be accessed as a word. The lower-addressed byte is the least significant byte of the word and the higher-addressed byte is its most significant byte.

Figure 6.4(a) demonstrates the storage of a word. Notice that the storage location at the lower address, 00724_{16}, contains the value $00000010_2 = 02_{16}$. Moreover, the contents of the next-higher-addressed storage location 00725_{16} are $01010101_2 = 55_{16}$. These two bytes represent the word $0101010100000010_2 = 5502_{16}$.

To permit efficient use of memory, words of data can be stored at even- or odd-address boundaries. The LSB A_0 of the address determines the type of *word boundary*. If this bit is 0, the word is said to be held at an *even-address boundary*.

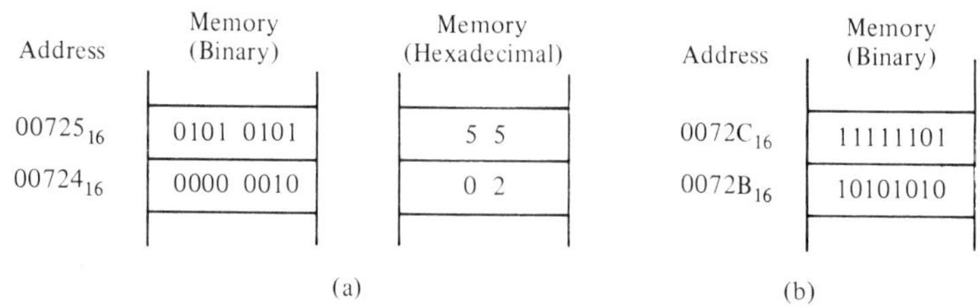

Figure 6.4 **(a)** Storage of a word at an even address boundary (*Courtesy of Intel Corporation*); **(b)** example word storage (*Courtesy of Intel Corporation*).

That is, a word at an even-address boundary corresponds to two consecutive bytes with the least significant byte located at an even address.

For example, the word in Fig. 6.4(a) has its least significant byte at address 00724_{16}. Therefore, it is stored at an even-address boundary.

Example 6.1

What is the data word shown in Fig. 6.4(b)? Express the result in hexadecimal form. Is it stored at an even- or an odd-address boundary?

Solution. The most significant byte of the word is stored at address $0072C_{16}$ and equals

$$11111101_2 = FD_{16}$$

Its least significant byte is stored at address $0072B_{16}$ and is

$$10101010_2 = AA_{16}$$

Together these two bytes give the word

$$1111110110101010_2 = FDAA_{16}$$

Expressing the address of the least significant byte in binary form gives

$$0072B_{16} = 00000000011100101011_2$$

Since bit A_0 is logic 1, the word is stored at an odd-address boundary in memory.

All data bytes and words at even-address boundaries can be accessed by the 8086 in one bus cycle. With the 5-MHz 8086, this takes 800 ns. On the other hand, accesses of words at odd-address boundaries require two bus cycles instead of one. This takes 1.6 μs when the 8086 is operating at a 5-MHz clock rate.

Data can be accessed either as bytes or words and can be stored at even- or odd-address boundaries. However, instructions are always accessed as words. For this reason they should always be stored at even-address boundaries. This minimizes the number of bus cycles needed to fetch them for execution; thereby maximizing performance.

The *double word* is another data form that can be processed in an 8086 system. A double word corresponds to two consecutive words of data stored in memory. An example of double-word data is a pointer that is used to address data or code outside the current segment. The word of the pointer that is stored at the higher address is the segment base address and the word at the lower address is the offset value.

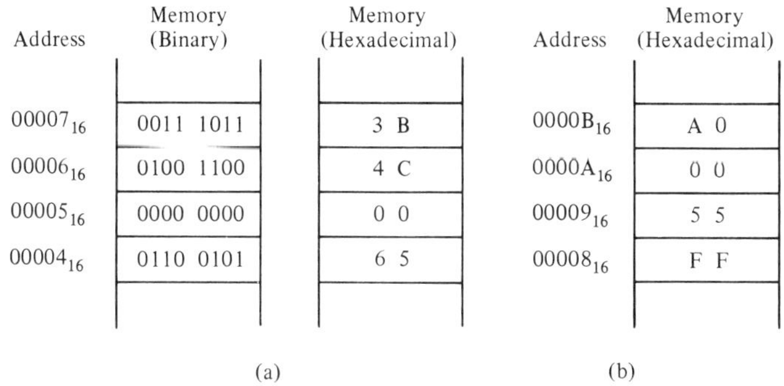

Figure 6.5 **(a)** Storage of a double word pointer (*Courtesy of Intel Corporation*); **(b)** another double word pointer (*Courtesy of Intel Corporation*).

An example showing storage of a pointer in memory is given in Fig. 6.5(a). Here we find that the higher-addressed word, which represents the segment address, is stored starting at even-address boundary 00006_{16}. The most significant byte of this word is at address 00007_{16} and equals $00111011_2 = 3B_{16}$. Its least significant byte is at address 00006_{16} and equals $01001100_2 = 4C_{16}$. Combining these two values, we get the segment base address, which equals $0011101101001100_2 = 3B4C_{16}$.

The offset part of the pointer is the lower-addressed word. Its least significant byte is stored at address 00004_{16}. This location contains $01100101_2 = 65_{16}$. The most significant byte is at address 00005_{16}, which contains $00000000_2 = 00_{16}$. The resulting offset is $0000000001100101_2 = 0065_{16}$.

Example 6.2

How should the pointer with segment base address equal to $A000_{16}$ and offset address $55FF_{16}$ be stored at an even-address boundary starting at 00008_{16}?

Solution. Storage of the two-word pointer requires four consecutive byte locations in memory starting at address 00008_{16}. The least significant byte of the offset is stored at address 00008_{16}. This value is shown as $11111111_2 = FF_{16}$ in Fig. 6.5(b). The most significant byte of the offset, which is 55_{16}, is stored at address 00009_{16}. These two bytes are followed by the least significant byte of the segment base address, 00_{16}, at address $0000A_{16}$ and its most significant byte, $A0_{16}$, at address $0000B_{16}$.

The 1M-byte address space of the 8086 is actually organized into *64K-byte segments*. These segments represent independently addressable units of memory consisting of 64K consecutive byte storage locations. Each segment is assigned a base address that identifies its lowest-addressed byte storage location.

Only four of these 64K-byte segments are active at a time. The segments that are active, as shown in Fig. 6.6(a), are identified by the values held in the four internal address segment registers: CS (code segment), SS (stack segment), DS (data segment), and ES (extra segment). This gives a logical address space of 256K bytes of active memory. Of this, 64K bytes are allocated for code (program) storage, 64K bytes for a stack, and 128K bytes for data storage.

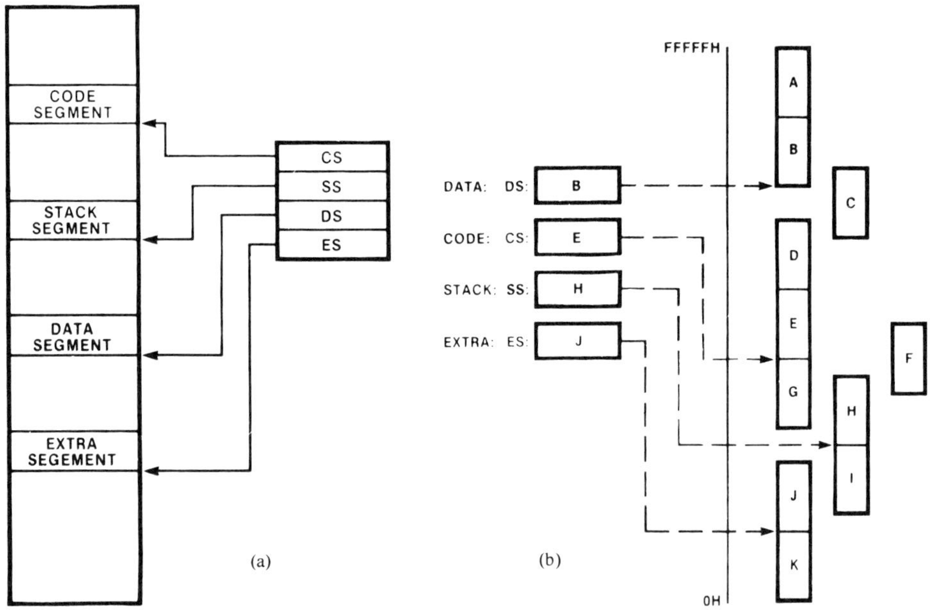

Figure 6.6 **(a)** Active nonoverlapping memory segments (*Courtesy of Intel Corporation*); **(b)** active overlapping memory segments (*Courtesy of Intel Corporation*).

Figure 6.6(b) illustrates the segmentation of system memory. In this diagram we have identified 64K-byte segments with letters such as A, B, and C. The data segment (DS) register presently contains the value B. Therefore, the 64K-byte segment of memory labeled B acts as the data storage segment. Segment E is selected for the current code segment. It is this part of memory from which the 8086 fetches instructions of the program. The stack segment (SS) register contains H, thereby selecting the 64K-byte segment labeled as H for use as a stack. Finally, the extra segment register ES is loaded with J such that segment J of memory can function as a second data storage segment.

The values in the internal segment registers can be modified through software. Therefore, for a program to gain access to another part of memory it just has to change the value of the appropriate register or registers. For instance, a new 128K-byte data space can be brought in by simply changing the values in DS and ES. This can be done with the load data segment (LDS) instruction and load extra segment (LES) instruction, respectively.

There is one restriction on the value that can be assigned to a segment as a base address: this is that it must reside on a 16-byte address boundary. Valid examples are 00000_{16}, 00010_{16}, and 00020_{16}. Other than this restriction, segments can be *contiguous, adjacent, disjointed*, or even *overlapping*. For example, in Fig. 6.6(b), segments A and B are contiguous, whereas segments B and C are overlapping.

Dedicated Memory Locations

Any part of the 1M-byte address space of the 8086 can be implemented with either ROM or RAM. However, some address locations have dedicated functions. These locations should not be used as general memory space for data or program storage.

Figure 6.7 shows the *reserved* and *general use (open) parts* of the 8086's *address space*. Notice that storage locations from address 00000_{16} to $0007F_{16}$ are dedicated. These 128 bytes of memory are reserved for storage of pointers to interrupt

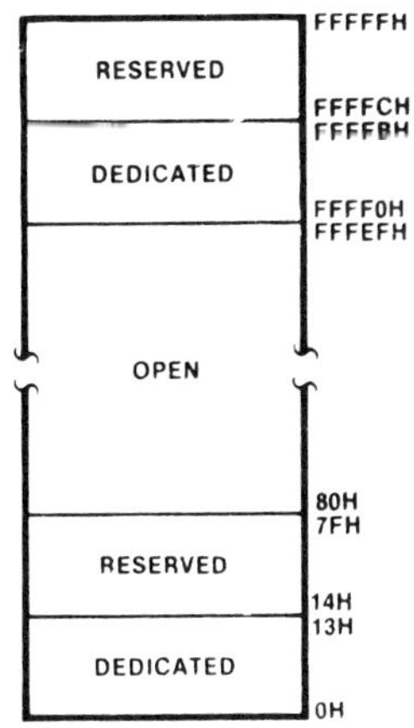

Figure 6.7 Dedicated and general use of memory (*Courtesy of Intel Corporation*).

service routines. As indicated earlier, each pointer requires four bytes of memory. Two bytes hold the 16-bit segment address and the other two hold the 16-bit offset.

At the high end of the memory address space is another pointer area. It is located from address $FFFFC_{16}$ through $FFFFF_{16}$. These four memory locations are reserved for storage of the pointer to the hardware reset function. Moreover, Intel Corporation has identified the 12 storage locations from address $FFFF0_{16}$ through $FFFFB_{16}$ as dedicated for use with future products.

Generating a Memory Address

The *logical addresses* that occur in the program of the 8086 are always 16 bits in length. This is because all registers and memory locations are 16 bits in length. However, the physical address that is placed on the address bus during a memory cycle is 20 bits. The generation of the physical address involves combining a 16-bit offset value that is located in either an index register or pointer register and a 16-bit base value that is located in a segment register. Together the base value and offset represent the logical address.

The source of the offset address depends on which type of memory reference is taking place. It can be the base pointer (BP) register, base (BX) register, source index (SI) register, destination index (DI) register, or instruction pointer (IP). On the other hand, the base value always resides in one of the segment registers: CS, DS, SS, or ES.

For instance, when an instruction acquisition takes place, the source of the base address is always the code segment (CS) register and the source of the offset is always the instruction pointer (IP).

Moreover, if the value of a variable is being written to memory during the execution of an instruction, typically, the base segment address will be in the data segment (DS) register and the offset will be in the destination index (DI) register. Segment override prefixes can be used to change the segment from which the variable is accessed.

Another example is the stack address that is needed when pushing words onto the stack. This address is formed from the contents of the stack segment (SS) register and stack pointer (SP).

Remember that the base segment address represents the starting location of the 64K-byte segment in memory: that is, the lowest-addressed byte in the segment. The offset identifies the distance in bytes that the storage location of interest resides from this starting address. Therefore, the lowest-addressed byte in a segment has an offset of 0000_{16} and the highest-addressed byte has an offset of $FFFF_{16}$.

Figure 6.8 shows how a segment address and offset value are combined to give a physical address. What happens is that the value in the segment register is shifted left by 4 bits with its LSBs being filled with 0s. Then the offset value is added to the 16 LSBs of the shifted segment address. The result of this addition is the 20-bit physical address.

The example in Fig. 6.8 represents a base segment address of 1234_{16} and an offset address of 0022_{16}. First let us express the base address in binary form. This gives

$$1234_{16} = 0001001000110100_2$$

Shifting left four times and filling with zeros results in

$$00010010001101000000_2 = 12340_{16}$$

The offset in binary form is

$$0022_{16} = 0000000000100010_2$$

Adding the shifted address and offset, we get

$$00010010001101000000_2 + 0000000000100010_2 = 00010010001101100010_2$$
$$= 12362_{16}$$

The bus interface unit does this address calculation each time a memory access is initiated.

Example 6.3

What would be the offset required to map to address location $002C3_{16}$ if the segment base address is $002A_{16}$?

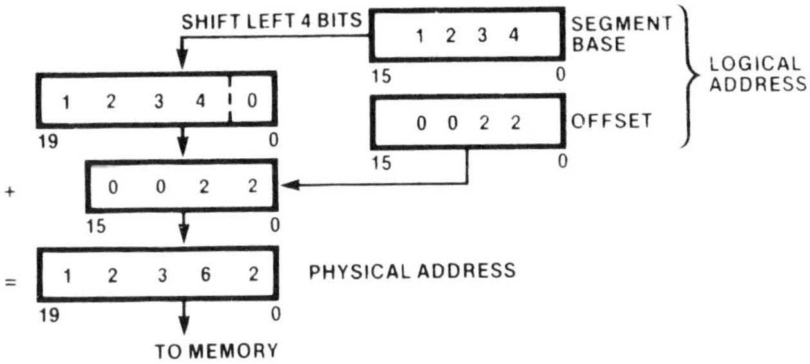

Figure 6.8 Generating a physical address (*Courtesy of Intel Corporation*).

Solution. The offset value can be obtained by shifting the segment base address left 4 bits and then subtracting it from the physical address. Shifting left gives

$$002A0_{16}$$

Now subtracting, we get the value of the offset:

$$002C3_{16} - 002A0_{16} = 0023_{16}$$

Actually, many different logical addresses can be mapped to the same physical address location in memory. This is done by simply changing the values of the base address in the segment register and its corresponding offset. The diagram in Fig. 6.9

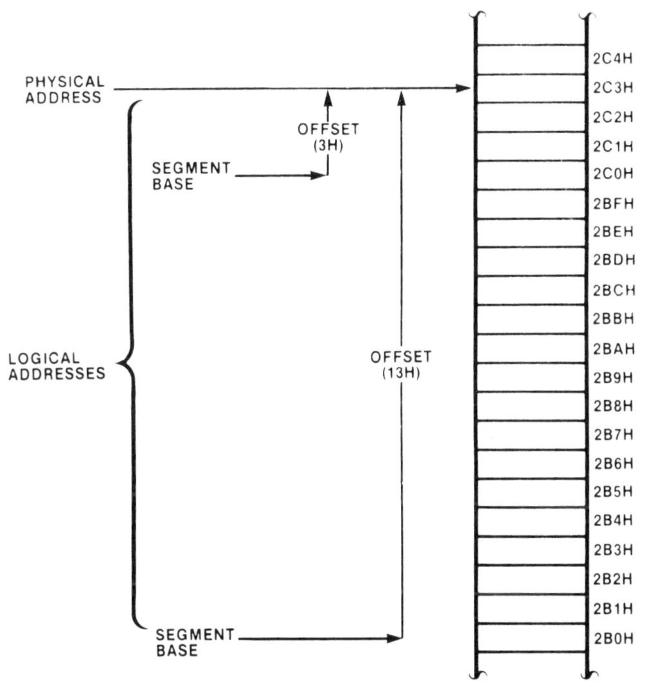

Figure 6.9 Relationship between logical segment address and offset and physical memory address (*Courtesy of Intel Corporation*).

demonstrates this idea. Notice that base $002B_{16}$ with offset 0013_{16} maps to physical address $002C3_{16}$ in memory. However, if the segment base address is changed to $002C_{16}$ with a new offset of 0003_{16}, the physical address is still $002C3_{16}$.

Example 6.4

Show the sequence of instructions that are needed to initialize the code segment to address 00000_{16} and the stack, data, and extra segments such that they are all at address 10000_{16}.

Solution. Since memory addresses are formed by the 16-bit contents of a segment register augmented by four zeros in the least significant bit locations, we must load CS with 0000_{16} and SS, DS, and ES with 1000_{16}. CS is loaded with the instruction sequence

```
MOV    AX, 0H
MOV    CS, AX
```

Then the other three registers are loaded by the instructions

```
MOV    AX,1000H
MOV    SS, AX
MOV    DS, AX
MOV    EX, AX
```

6.3 HARDWARE ORGANIZATION OF THE MEMORY ADDRESS SPACE

From a hardware point of view, the memory address space of the 8086 is implemented as two independent 512K-byte banks. They are called the *low (even) bank* and the *high (odd) bank*. Data bytes associated with an even address (00000_{16}, 00002_{16}, etc.) reside in the low bank and those with odd addresses (00001_{16}, 00003_{16}, etc.) reside in the high bank.

Looking at the circuit diagram in Fig. 6.10, we see that address bits A_1 through A_{19} select the storage location that is to be accessed. Therefore, they are applied to both banks in parallel. A_0 and bank high enable ($\overline{BHE}$) are used as bank select signals. Logic 0 at A_0 identifies an even-addressed byte of data and causes the low bank of memory to be enabled. On the other hand, $\overline{BHE}$ equal to 0 enables the high bank for access of an odd-addressed byte of data. Each of the memory banks provides

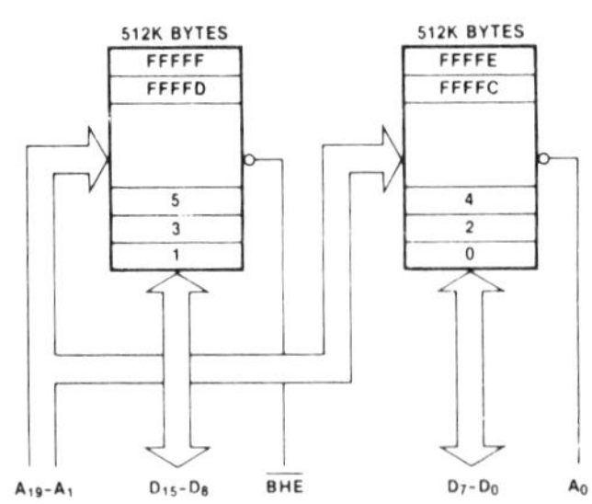

Figure 6.10 High and low memory banks (*Courtesy of Intel Corporation*).

half of the 8086's 16-bit data bus. Notice that the lower bank transfers bytes of data over data lines D_0 through D_7, while data transfers for the high bank use D_8 through D_{15}.

Figure 6.11(a) shows that when a byte memory operation is performed to address X, which is an even address, a storage location in the low bank is accessed. Therefore, A_0 is set to logic 0 to enable the low bank of memory and $\overline{BHE}$ to logic 1 to disable the high bank. As shown in the circuit diagram, data are transferred to or from the lower bank over data bus lines D_0 through D_7. D_7 carries the MSB of the byte and D_0 the LSB.

On the other hand, to access a byte of data at an odd address such as X + 1 in Fig. 6.11(b), A_0 is set to logic 1 and $\overline{BHE}$ to logic 0. This enables the high bank of memory and disables the low bank. Data are transferred between the 8086 and the high bank over bus lines D_8 through D_{15}. Here D_{15} represents the MSB and D_8 the LSB.

Whenever an even-addressed word of data is accessed, both the high and low banks are accessed at the same time. Figure 6.11(c) illustrates how a word at even address X is accessed. Notice that both A_0 and $\overline{BHE}$ equal 0; therefore, both banks are enabled. In this case, a byte of data is transferred from or to both the low and high banks at the same time. This 16-bit word is transferred over the complete data bus D_0 through D_{15}. The bytes of an even-addressed word are said to be aligned and can be transferred with a memory operation that takes just one bus cycle.

A word at an odd-addressed boundary is different. It is said to be unaligned. That is, the least significant byte is at the lower address location in the high memory bank. This is demonstrated in Fig. 6.11(d). Here we see that the odd byte of the word is located at address X + 1 and the even byte at address X + 2.

Two bus cycles are required to access this word. During the first bus cycle, the odd byte of the word, which is located at address X + 1 in the high bank, is accessed. This is accompanied by select signals $A_0 = 1$ and $\overline{BHE} = 0$ and a data transfer over D_8 through D_{15}.

Next the 8086 automatically increments the address such that $A_0 = 0$. This represents the next address in memory which is even. Then a second memory bus cycle is initiated. During this second cycle, the even byte located at X + 2 in the low bank is accessed. The data transfer takes place over bus lines D_0 through D_7. This transfer is accompanied by $A_0 = 0$ and $\overline{BHE} = 1$.

6.4 MEMORY BUS STATUS CODES

Whenever a memory bus cycle is in progress, an address bus status code S_3S_4 is output on the multiplexed address lines A_{16} and A_{17}. This two-bit code is output at the same time the data are carried over the other bus lines.

Bits S_3 and S_4 together form a 2-bit binary code that identifies which one of the four segment registers was used to generate the physical address that was output during the address period in the bus cycle. The four *address bus status codes* are listed

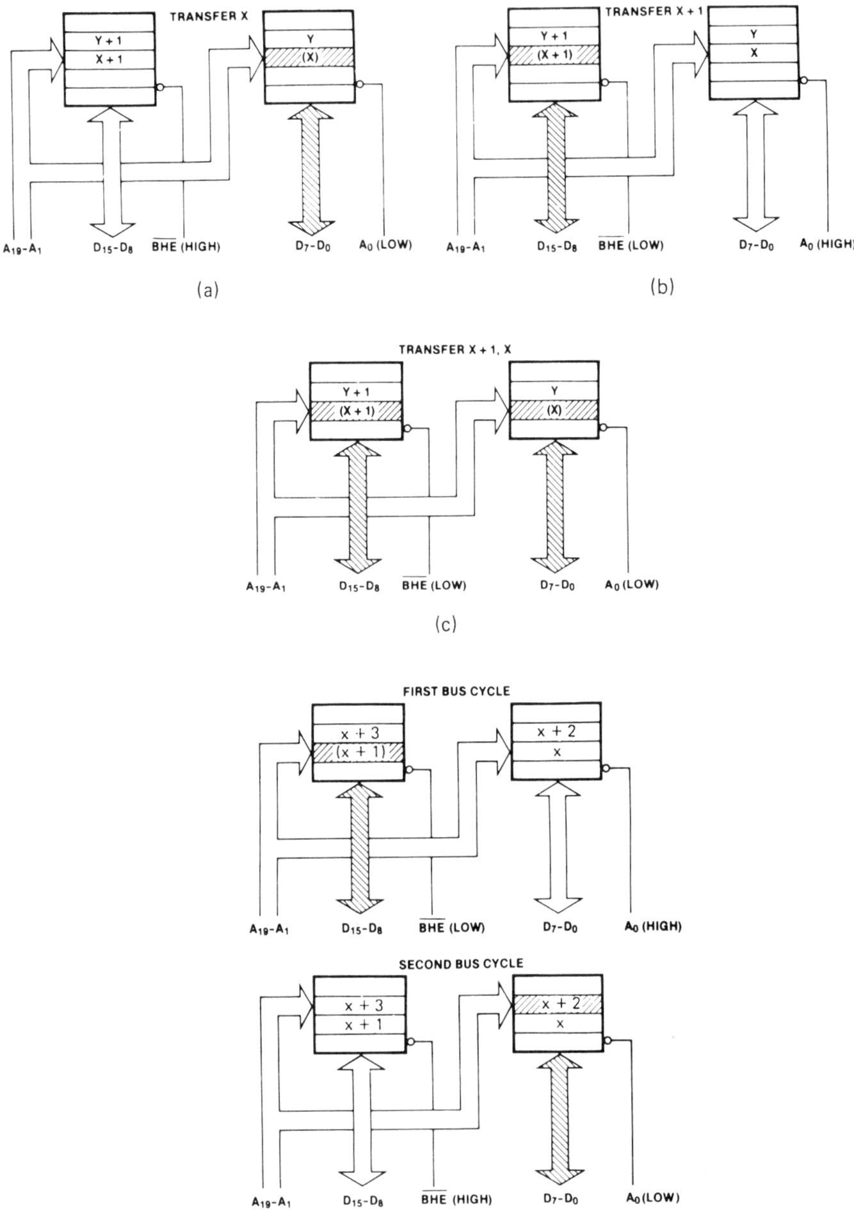

Figure 6.11 **(a)** Even addressed byte transfer (*Courtesy of Intel Corporation*); **(b)** odd addressed byte transfer (*Courtesy of Intel Corporation*); **(c)** even addressed word transfer (*Courtesy of Intel Corporation*); **(d)** odd addressed word transfer (*Courtesy of Intel Corporation*).

S_3	S_4	Address Status
0	0	Alternate (relative to the ES segment)
1	0	Stack (relative to the SS segment)
0	1	Code/None (relative to the CS segment or a default of zero)
1	1	Data (relative to the DS segment)

Figure 6.12 Address bus status code (*Courtesy of Intel Corporation*).

in Fig. 6.12. Here we find that code S_3S_4 = 00 identifies the extra segment register, 10 identifies the stack segment register, 01 identifies the code segment register, and 11 identifies the data segment register.

These status codes are output in both the minimum and the maximum system modes. They can be decoded with external circuitry to enable separate 1M-byte address spaces for ES, SS, CS, and DS. In this way, the memory address reach of the 8086 can be expanded to 4M bytes.

6.5 MEMORY CONTROL SIGNALS

Earlier in the chapter we saw that similar control signals are produced in the maximum- and minimum-mode systems. Moreover, we found that in the minimum system mode, the 8086 produces all of the control signals. But in the maximum system mode, they are produced by the 8288 bus controller. Here we will look more closely at each of these signals and their function.

Minimum-System Memory Control Signals

In the 8086 microcomputer system of Fig. 6.1, which is configured for the minimum system mode of operation, we found that the control signals provided to support the interface to the memory subsystem are: ALE, $\overline{BHE}$, M/$\overline{IO}$, DT/$\overline{R}$, $\overline{RD}$, $\overline{WR}$, and $\overline{DEN}$. These control signals are required to tell the memory subsystem when the bus is carrying a valid address, in which direction data are to be transferred over the bus, when valid write data are on the bus, and when to put read data on the bus.

For example, *address latch enable* (ALE) signals external circuitry that a valid address is on the bus. It is a pulse to the 1 logic level and is used to latch the address in external circuitry. Another important control signal involved in the memory interface is bank high enable ($\overline{BHE}$). Logic 0 is output on this line during the address part of the bus cycle whenever the high-bank part of the memory subsystem must be enabled.

The *memory/input-output* (M/$\overline{IO}$) and *data transmit/receive* (DT/$\overline{R}$) lines signal external circuitry whether a memory or I/O bus cycle is in progress and whether the 8086 will transmit or receive data over the bus. During all memory bus cycles, M/$\overline{IO}$ is held at the 1 logic level. Moreover, when the 8086 switches DT/$\overline{R}$ to logic 1 during the data transfer part of the bus cycle, the bus is in the transmit mode and data are written into memory. On the other hand, it sets DT/$\overline{R}$ to logic 0 to signal that the bus is in the receive mode. This corresponds to reading of memory.

The signals *read* ($\overline{RD}$) and *write* ($\overline{WR}$), respectively, identify that a read or write bus cycle is in progress. The 8086 switches $\overline{WR}$ to logic 0 to signal memory that a write cycle is taking place over the bus. On the other hand, $\overline{RD}$ is switched to logic 0 whenever a read cycle is in progress. During all memory operations, the 8086 produces one other control signal. It is *data enable* ($\overline{DEN}$). Logic 0 at this output is used to enable the data bus.

Maximum-System Memory Control Signals

When the 8086 is configured to work in the maximum mode, it does not directly provide all the control signals to support the memory interface. Instead, an external *bus controller*, the 8288, provides memory commands and control signals that are compatible with the *Multibus*. Figure 6.2 shows an 8086 connected in this way.

Specifically, the $\overline{WR}$, $M/\overline{IO}$, $DT/\overline{R}$, $\overline{DEN}$, ALE, and $\overline{INTA}$ signal lines on the 8086 are changed. They are replaced with *multiprocessor lock* signal ($\overline{LOCK}$), a *bus status code* ($\overline{S}_2$ through $\overline{S}_0$), and a *queue status code* (QS_1QS_0). The 8086 still does produce signals $\overline{BHE}$ and $\overline{RD}$. Moreover, these two signals provide the same functions as they did in minimum system mode.

The 3-bit bus status code $\overline{S}_2\overline{S}_1\overline{S}_0$ is output prior to the initiation of each bus cycle. It identifies which type of bus cycle is to follow. This code is input to the 8288 bus controller. Here it is decoded to identify which type of bus cycle command signals must be generated.

Figure 6.13 shows the relationship between the bus status codes and the types of 8086 bus cycle produced. Also shown in this chart are the names of the corresponding command signals that are generated at the outputs of the 8288. For instance, the input code $\overline{S}_2\overline{S}_1\overline{S}_0$ equal 100 indicates that an instruction fetch cycle is to take place. This memory read makes the $\overline{MRDC}$ command output switch to logic 0.

Another bus command that is provided for the memory subsystem is $\overline{S}_2\overline{S}_1\overline{S}_0$ equal to 110. This represents a memory write cycle and it causes both the *memory write command* ($\overline{MWTC}$) and *advanced memory write command* ($\overline{AMWC}$) outputs to switch to the 0 logic level.

Status Inputs			CPU Cycle	8288 Command
$\overline{S}_2$	$\overline{S}_1$	$\overline{S}_0$		
0	0	0	Interrupt acknowledge	$\overline{INTA}$
0	0	1	Read I/O port	$\overline{IORC}$
0	1	0	Write I/O port	$\overline{IOWC}$, $\overline{AIOWC}$
0	1	1	Halt	None
1	0	0	Instruction fetch	$\overline{MRDC}$
1	0	1	Read memory	$\overline{MRDC}$
1	1	0	Write memory	$\overline{MWTC}$, $\overline{AMWC}$
1	1	1	Passive	None

Figure 6.13 Memory bus cycle status codes (*Courtesy of Intel Corporation*).

The control outputs produced by the 8288 are DEN, DT/$\overline{R}$, and ALE. These signals provide the same functions as those produced by the corresponding pins on the 8086 in the minimum system mode.

The other two status signals, QS_0 and QS_1, form an instruction queue code. This code tells external circuitry what type of information was removed from the queue during the previous clock cycle. Figure 6.14 shows the four different queue statuses. Notice that QS_1QS_0 = 01 indicates that the first byte of an instruction was taken from the queue. The next byte of the instruction that is fetched is identified by queue status code 11. Whenever the queue is reset, for instance due to a transfer of control, the reinitialization code 10 is output. Moreover, if no queue operation occured, status code 00 is output.

QS_1	QS_0	Queue Status
0 (low)	0	No Operation. During the last clock cycle, nothing was taken from the queue.
0	1	First Byte. The byte taken from the queue was the first byte of the instruction.
1 (high)	0	Queue Empty. The queue has been reinitialized as a result of the execution of a transfer instruction.
1	1	Subsequent Byte. The byte taken from the queue was a subsequent byte of the instruction.

Figure 6.14 Queue status code (*Courtesy of Intel Corporation*).

The last signal is bus priority lock ($\overline{\text{LOCK}}$). This signal is to be used as an input to the 8289 bus arbiter together with bus status code $\overline{S}_0$ through $\overline{S}_2$, and CLK. They are used to lock other processors off the system bus during execution of an instruction. In this way the processor can be assured of uninterrupted access to common system resources such as *global memory*.

The *bus arbitration* signals produced by the 8289 are: *bus clock* ($\overline{\text{BCLK}}$), *bus request* ($\overline{\text{BREQ}}$), *bus priority in* ($\overline{\text{BPRN}}$), *bus priority out* ($\overline{\text{BPRO}}$), and *I/O busy* ($\overline{\text{BUSY}}$). These are the bus exchange signals of the Multibus. It is this bus arbiter that permits multiple processors to reside on the system bus by implementing the Multibus arbitration protocol in the 8086 microcomputer system.

6.6 READ AND WRITE BUS CYCLES

In the preceding section we introduced the status and control signals associated with the memory interface. Here we continue by studying the sequence in which they occur during the read and write bus cycles of memory.

Read Cycle

The memory interface signals of a minimum-mode 8086 system are shown in Fig. 6.15. Here their occurrence is illustrated relative to the four *time states* T_1, T_2, T_3, and T_4 of the 8086's bus cycle. Let us trace through the events that occur as data or instructions are read from memory.

The *read bus cycle* begins with state T_1. During this period, the 8086 outputs the 20-bit address of the memory location to be accessed on its multiplexed address/data bus AD_0 through AD_{15} and A_{16} through A_{19}. $\overline{BHE}$ is also output during this time. Notice that a pulse is also produced at ALE. The trailing edge of this pulse should be used to latch the address and $\overline{BHE}$ in external circuitry.

Also we see that at the start of T_1, signals $M/\overline{IO}$ and $DT/\overline{R}$ are set to the 1 and 0 logic levels, respectively. This indicates to circuitry in the memory subsystem that a memory cycle is in progress and that the 8086 is going to receive data from the bus. Notice that both of these signals are maintained at these logic levels throughout all four periods of the bus cycle.

Beginning with state T_2, status bits S_3 through S_6 are output on the upper four bus lines A_{16} through A_{19}. Remember that bits S_3 and S_4 identify to external circuitry which segment register was used to generate the address just output. This status information is maintained through periods T_3 and T_4. The rest of the address/data bus lines, AD_0 through AD_{15}, are put in the high-Z state during T_2.

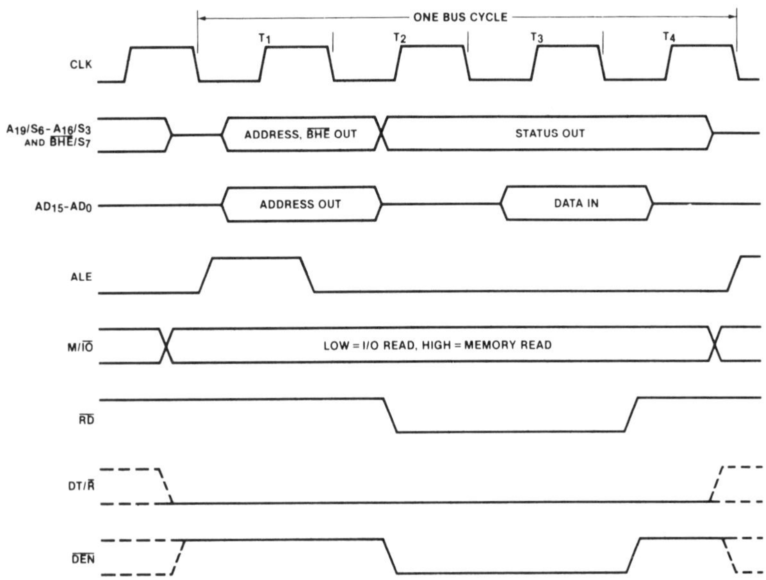

Figure 6.15 Memory read bus cycle (*Courtesy of Intel Corporation*).

Late in period T_2, $\overline{RD}$ is switched to logic 0. This indicates to the memory subsystem that a read cycle is in progress. Then $\overline{DEN}$ is switched to logic 0 to tell external circuitry to put the data that are to be read from memory onto the bus.

As shown in the waveforms, input data are read by the 8086 during T_3, after which, as shown in T_4, the 8086 returns $\overline{RD}$ and $\overline{DEN}$ to the 1 logic level. The read cycle is now complete.

Write Cycle

The *write bus cycle* timing, shown in Fig. 6.16, is similar to that given for a read cycle in Fig. 6.15. Looking at the write cycle waveforms, we find that during T_1 the address and $\overline{BHE}$ are output and latched with the ALE pulse. This is identical to the read cycle. Moreover, $M/\overline{IO}$ is set to logic 1 to indicate that a memory cycle is in progress. However, this time $DT/\overline{R}$ is also switched to logic 1. This signals external circuits that the 8086 is going to transfer data over the bus.

As T_2 starts, the 8086 switches $\overline{WR}$ to logic 0. This tells the memory subsystem that a write operation is to follow over the bus. The 8086 puts the data on the bus late in T_2 and maintains the data valid through T_4. The write of data into memory should be initiated as $\overline{WR}$ returns from 0 to 1 early in T_4. This completes the write cycle.

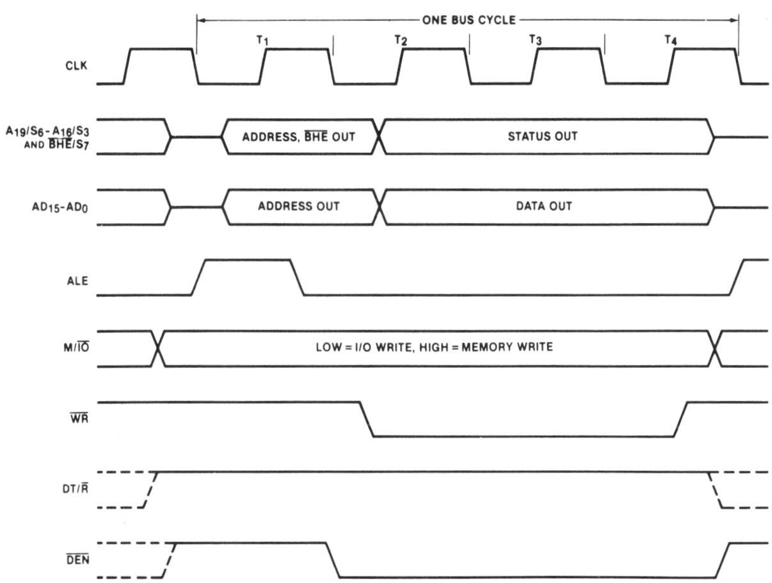

Figure 6.16 Memory write bus cycle (*Courtesy of Intel Corporation*).

Wait States in the Memory Bus Cycle

Wait states can be inserted to lengthen the memory bus cycles of the 8086. This is done with the *ready input* signal. Upon request from an event in hardware, for instance slow memory, the READY input is switched to logic 0. This signals the 8086 that the current bus cycle should not be completed. Instead, it is extended by inserting wait states with duration t_w equal 125 ns (for 8-MHz clock operation) between periods T_3 and T_4. The data that were on the bus during T_3 are maintained throughout the wait-state period. In this way, the bus cycle is not completed until READY is returned back to logic 1.

In the 8086 microcomputer system, the READY input of the 8086 is supplied by the READY output of the 8284 clock generator circuit.

Example 6.5

What is the duration of the bus cycle in the 8086-based microcomputer if the clock is 8 MHz and two wait states are inserted through wait state logic?

Solution. The duration of the bus cycle in an 8 MHz system is given in general by the expression

$$t_{cyc} = 500 \text{ ns} + N\,(125 \text{ ns})$$

In this expression N stands for the number of wait states. For a bus cycle with two wait states, we get

$$t_{cyc} = 500 \text{ ns} + 2(125 \text{ ns}) = 500 \text{ ns} + 250 \text{ ns}$$
$$= 750 \text{ ns}$$

6.7 THE STACK, STACK SEGMENT REGISTER, AND STACK POINTER

During interrupt and subroutine call types of operations, the contents of specific internal registers of the 8086 are pushed to a section of memory known as the *stack*. Here they are maintained temporarily. At the completion of the service routine or subroutine, these values are popped off the stack and put back into the same internal register where they originally resided.

For instance, when an interrupt occurs, the 8086 automatically pushes the current flags, the value in CS, and the value in IP to the stack. As part of the service routine for the interrupt, the contents of other registers can be pushed onto the stack by executing PUSH instructions. An example is the instruction PUSH SI. It causes the contents of the source index register to be pushed onto the stack.

At the end of the service routine, POP instructions can be included to pop values from the stack back into their corresponding internal registers. For example, POP SI causes the value at the top of the stack to be popped back into the source index register.

As indicated earlier, stack is implemented in the memory of the 8086 microcomputer system. It is 64K bytes long and is organized as 32K words. The lowest addressed byte in the current stack is pointed to by the address in the stack segment (SS) register.

Any number of stacks may exist in an 8086 microcomputer system. A new stack can be brought in by simply changing the value in the SS register through software. For instance, executing the instruction MOV SS,DX loads a new value from DX into SS. Even though many stacks can exist, only one can be active at a time.

Another register, the stack pointer (SP) contains an offset from the value in SS. The address obtained from the contents of SS and SP is the physical address of the last storage location in the stack to which data were pushed. This is known as the *top of the stack*. The value in the stack pointer starts at $FFFF_{16}$ upon initialization of the 8086. Combining this value with the current value in SS gives the highest-addressed location in the stack: that is, the *bottom of the stack*.

Since the data transfers to and from stack are always 16-bit words, it is important to configure the system such that all stack locations are at even word boundaries. This minimizes the number of memory cycles required to push or pop data for the stack and minimizes the amount of time required to perform a switch in program context.

The 8086 pushes data and addresses to the stack one word at a time. Each time a register value is to be pushed onto the top of the stack, the value in the stack pointer is first decremented by 2 and then the contents of the register are written into memory. In this way, we see that the stack grows down in memory from the bottom of the stack, which corresponds to the physical address derived from SS and $FFFF_{16}$, toward the end of the stack, which corresponds to the physical address obtained from SS and offset 0000_{16}.

When a value is popped from the top of the stack, the reverse of this sequence occurs. The physical address defined by SS and SP always points to the location of the last value pushed onto the stack. Its contents are first popped off the stack and put into the specified register within the 8086; then SP is incremented by 2. The top of the stack now corresponds to the previous value pushed onto the stack.

An example that shows how the contents of a register are pushed onto the stack is shown in Fig. 6.17(a). Here we find the state of the stack prior to execution of the PUSH instruction. Notice that the stack segment register contains 105_{16}. As indicated, the bottom of the stack resides at the physical address derived from SS with offset $FFFF_{16}$. This gives the bottom of stack address A_{BOS}

$$\begin{aligned} A_{BOS} &= 1050_{16} + FFFF_{16} \\ &= 1104F_{16} \end{aligned}$$

Furthermore, the stack pointer, which represents the offset from the bottom of the stack to the top of the stack, equals 0008_{16}. Therefore, the current top of the stack is at physical address A_{TOS} equals

$$\begin{aligned} A_{TOS} &= 1050_{16} + 0008_{16} \\ &= 1058_{16} \end{aligned}$$

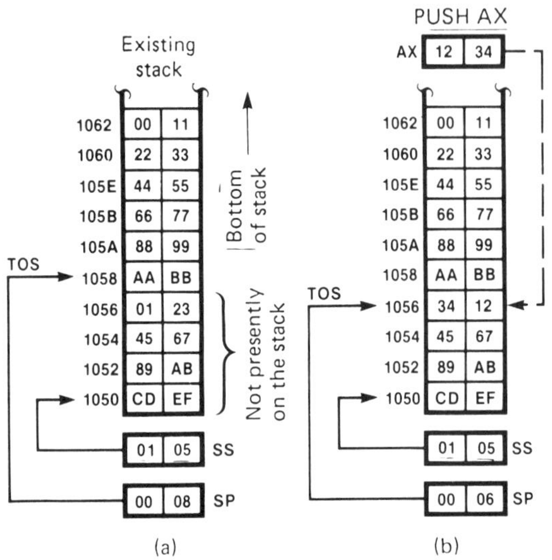

Figure 6.17 Pushing the contents of a register to the stack (*Courtesy of Intel Corporation*).

Addresses with higher values than that of the top of stack, 1058_{16}, contain valid stack data. Those with lower addresses do not yet contain valid stack data. Notice that the last value pushed to the stack in Fig. 6.17(a) was $BBAA_{16}$.

Figure 6.17(b) demonstrates what happens when the PUSH AX instruction is executed. Here we see that AX contains the value 1234_{16}. Notice that execution of the PUSH instruction causes the stack pointer to be decremented by 2 but does not affect the contents of the stack segment register. Therefore, the next location to be accessed in the stack corresponds to address 1056_{16}. It is to this location that the value in AX is pushed. Notice that the most significant byte of AX, which equals 12_{16} now resides in the least significant byte of the word in stack and the least significant byte 34_{16} is held in the most significant byte.

Now let us look at an example in which stack data are popped back into the register from which they were pushed. Figure 6.18 illustrates this operation. In Fig. 6.18(a), the stack is shown to be in the state that resulted due to our prior PUSH AX example. That is, SP equals 0006_{16}, SS equals 105_{16}, the address of the top of the stack equals 1056_{16}, and the word at the top of the stack equals 1234_{16}.

Looking at Fig. 6.18(b), we see what happens when the instructions POP AX and POP BX are executed in that order. Here we see that execution of the first instruction causes the 8086 to read the value 1234_{16} from the top of the stack and put it into the AX register as 1234_{16}. Next, SP is incremented to give 0008_{16} and another read cycle is initiated from the stack. This second read corresponds to the POP BX instruction and it causes the value $BBAA_{16}$ to be loaded into the BX register. SP is incremented once more and now equals $000A_{16}$. Therefore, the new top of stack is at address $105A_{16}$.

From Fig. 6.18(b) we see that the values read out of 1056_{16} and 1058_{16} still remain at these addresses. But now they reside at locations that are considered to be above the top of the stack. Therefore, they no longer represent valid stack data.

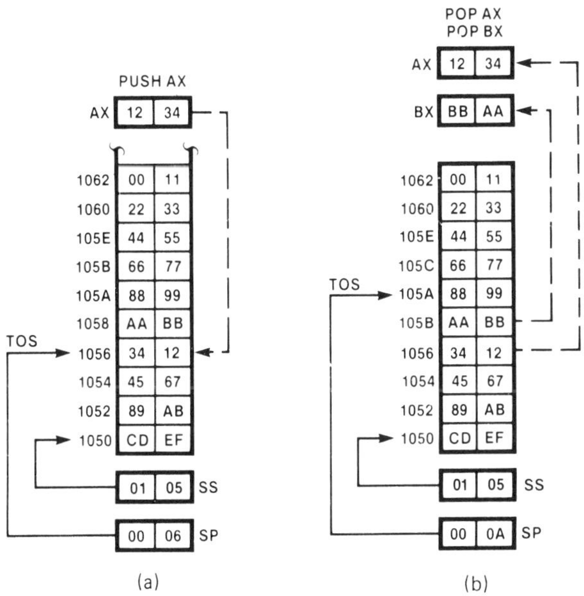

Figure 6.18 Popping the contents of a register from the stack (*Courtesy of Intel Corporation*).

6.8 DEMULTIPLEXING THE ADDRESS/DATA BUS

In an 8086 microcomputer system, memory, I/O devices, and the interrupt interface share use of the multiplexed address/data bus lines. In all three cases, a stable address is required and it must be available at the same time that data are to be transferred over the bus. For this reason, the address and data signals must be separated using external demultiplexing circuits to give a system bus. This *demultiplexed system bus* consists of the 20 address lines A_0 through A_{19}, 16 data bus lines D_0 through D_{15}, and memory control signals $\overline{BHE}$, $M/\overline{IO}$, $DT/\overline{R}$, $\overline{DEN}$, $\overline{WR}$, and $\overline{RD}$.

Several different techniques can be used to demultiplex the system bus. One approach is shown in Fig. 6.19. Here the microprocessor's bus is demultiplexed into a system bus just once at the MPU and then distributed to all other system elements. This is known as *local demultiplexing* and has the advantage of requiring minimal circuitry.

During bus cycles, a 20-bit address is output by the 8086 on AD_0 through A_{19} during period T_1 of the bus cycle. This address is accompanied by a pulse on the ALE (address latch enable) line. In this circuit, ALE tells external circuitry that a stable address is available and it should be latched.

In the circuit of Fig. 6.19 we have used three 8282 noninverting latches to demultiplex the address. These devices are octal latches. The ALE output of the 8086 is applied to the strobe (STB) input of all three latches. When pulsed at STB, the address applied to the DI_0 through DI_7 inputs of the 8282s is latched into their internal flip-flops. This happens on the 1-to-0 edge of ALE. Even though the address is latched, it is not yet available at address outputs A_0 through A_{19}. This is because

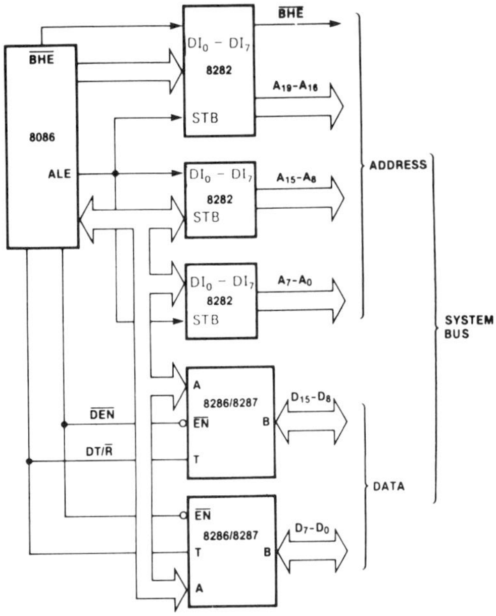

Figure 6.19 Local demultiplexing of the system bus (*Courtesy of Intel Corporation*).

the outputs of the octal latches are not yet enabled. To do this, we must switch the output enable ($\overline{OE}$) input on the 8282s to the 0 logic level. In many applications, $\overline{OE}$ can be fixed at the 0 logic level. This permanently enables the outputs of the 8282s and the address is made available at A_0 through A_{19} as soon as it is latched. Notice that signal $\overline{BHE}$ is latched together with the address. In this way, the address is latched and maintained stable throughout the bus cycle.

This circuit configuration also increases the drive capability at the system bus. The outputs of the 8282 are rated to drive up to 32 mA. However, a propagation delay of 30 ns is introduced as signals pass through it.

The data bus D_0 through D_{15} can be directly formed from the AD_0 through AD_{15} lines or buffered with bidirectional bus transceivers to increase drive capability. It is usually necessary to do this buffering because a large number of memory and peripheral devices are attached to the bus.

Two 8286 8-bit bidirectional transceiver devices can be used for this purpose. They are connected as shown in Fig. 6.19. Data can be passed in either direction between its A and B terminals. The direction of data transfer is determined by the logic level applied at the transfer (T) input. When T is logic 1, data are passed from A to B. This corresponds to the direction required for data transfers during write bus cycles. Changing the logic level of T to 0 causes data to be passed from B to A such as needed for read cycles. Moreover, logic 0 is needed at the $\overline{EN}$ input of the 8286 to enable the input and output drive circuitry selected by T. The bus side of the 8286 is able to drive up to 32 mA with propagation delays through the device equal to 30 ns.

From the circuit in Fig. 6.19, we see that the 8086 controls the direction and timing of data transfers through the 8286s with signals $DT/\overline{R}$ at the T input and $\overline{DEN}$

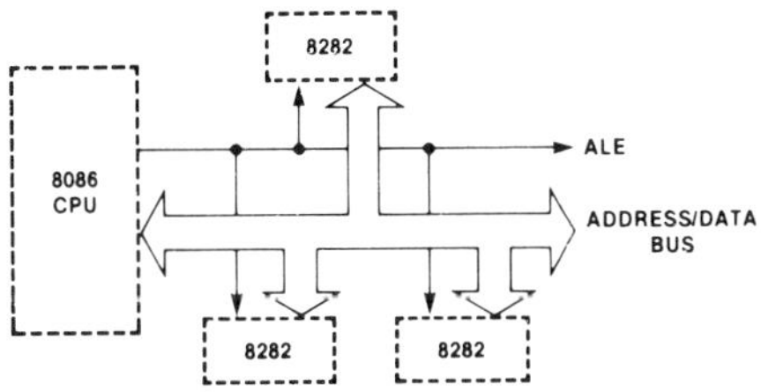

Figure 6.20 Remote demultiplexing of the system bus (*Courtesy of Intel Corporation*).

at its $\overline{EN}$ input. When DT/$\overline{R}$ is set to logic 1, the 8286s are set to pass data from MPU to memory. This sets the bus for a write operation. Switching DT/$\overline{R}$ to logic 0 changes the direction of data transfer through the 8286s such that the MPU can read data out of memory. $\overline{DEN}$ is switched to logic 0 whenever a data transfer is to take place over the bus and enables the output buffers of the 8286.

A second approach is shown in Fig. 6.20. This configuration is known as *remote demultiplexing*. In this case, the microprocessors local bus signals are distributed to each part of the system and then demultiplexed by circuits provided in the memory or I/O sections.

6.9 4K-WORD PROGRAM STORAGE MEMORY

ROM, PROM, or EPROM devices are connected to the 8086 to implement a *program storage memory*. EPROM devices such as the 2716, 2732, and 2764 are organized with a byte-wide output. For this reason, two such devices are required to store the 16-bit instruction words of the 8086.

Figure 6.21 shows how two 2732 EPROMs are connected to the demultiplexed system bus of the 8086 to provide a 4K word program storage memory. The upper of the two devices represents the high memory bank and the lower device the low memory bank. To select one of the 4K of storage locations, we need a 12-bit address. In the circuit diagram, this corresponds to A_1 through A_{12}. Notice that both EPROM devices are addressed in parallel over the bus.

The additional high-order bits of the 8086's address, which are not shown, must

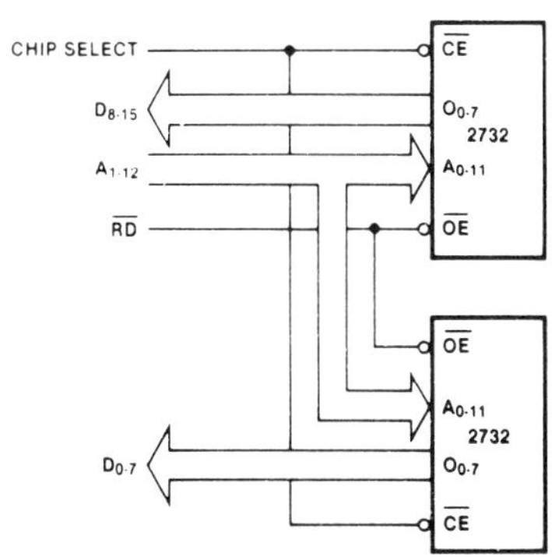

Figure 6.21 4K word program storage memory (*Courtesy of Intel Corporation*).

be decoded to produce the CHIP SELECT signal. The $\overline{CE}$ inputs of the two 2732s are connected in parallel and supplied by CHIP SELECT. Whenever the address on the system bus corresponds to program storage memory, the output of an address decoder circuit must switch this line to logic 0 to enable the EPROMs for operation.

Instructions are read as 16-bit words from the program storage memory over data bus lines D_0 through D_{15}. The upper 2732 devices provide the most significant byte of the instruction word. Looking at the circuit diagram in Fig. 6.21, we see that this byte is output on data bus lines D_8 through D_{15}. The lower 2732 outputs the least significant byte of the instruction word. This byte is carried over data bus lines D_0 through D_7. The data outputs of both devices are enabled by switching the signal $\overline{RD}$ to logic 0.

During an instruction acquisition cycle, the instruction fetch sequence of the 8086 causes a read bus cycle to be initiated. The values in CS and IP are combined in the bus interface unit to generate the address of a storage location in the address range of the program storage memory. This address is output on A_0 through A_{19} and latched in external circuitry. Bits A_1 through A_{12} are applied to both EPROMs in parallel to select the instruction word to be output. At the same time, the high-order bits of the address are decoded and switch CHIP SELECT to logic 0. Now the 2732s are enabled for operation.

When the 8086 switches read ($\overline{RD}$) to logic 0, the outputs of the two 2732s are enabled. This causes the two bytes of the instruction word to be put on data bus lines D_0 through D_{15}. The 8086 reads these two bytes simultaneously as a 16-bit word.

6.10 1K-WORD STATIC RAM DATA STORAGE MEMORY

Data are normally stored in random access read/write memory instead of read-only memory. If the amount of memory required in the microcomputer system is small, for instance, less than 16K words, the memory subsystem will usually be designed with static RAMs instead of dynamic RAMs. This is because most dynamic RAMs are organized 16K by 1 or 64K by 1. Moreover, dynamic RAMs require refresh support circuits. This additional circuitry is not warranted if storage requirements are small.

Figure 6.22 shows how a 1K-word random access read/write memory subsystem can be constructed with 2142 static RAMs. This circuit assumes that the 8086 is configured for minimum system mode. In the circuit, we find four 2142 ICs connected to form a 1K-word data storage memory. Of course, through software the 8086 can read data from the memory either as bytes, words, or double words.

Notice that the upper two 2142 devices are connected to provide the low RAM bank. The 8086 accesses the byte storage locations in this 1K by 8 section over data bus lines D_0 through D_7. They represent odd-addressed bytes of data. On the other hand, the lower two RAMs represent the high memory bank. It corresponds to even-addressed bytes of data and are accessed over bus lines D_8 through D_{15}.

Bits A_1 through A_{10} of the address are applied in parallel to the address inputs on all four 2142s. It is this part of the address that selects the storage location

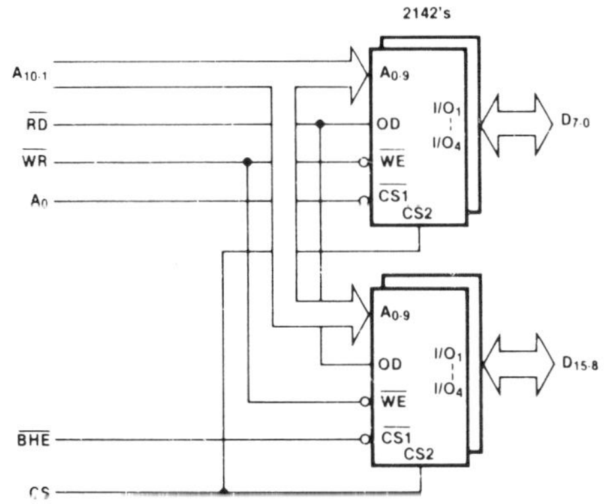

Figure 6.22 Minimum mode static RAM data storage memory (*Courtesy of Intel Corporation*).

that is to be accessed. The more significant address bits, which are not shown, are decoded to provide the CS_2 chip select signal. Addresses that correspond to locations in data storage memory must cause CS_2 to switch to logic 1. This selects the complete bank of RAMs for operation.

During word operations to an even-address boundary, the 8086 switches both address bit A_0 and bank high enable $\overline{BHE}$ to logic 0. Notice that these two signals are applied to the $\overline{CS_1}$ inputs of the RAMs in the low memory bank and high memory bank, respectively. In this way, both banks are enabled for operation and both a high byte and low byte are carried over the data bus at the same time.

$\overline{WR}$ signals the devices that valid data are on the data bus during write bus cycles. When the data put on the bus by the 8086 have stabilized (valid data), $\overline{WR}$ is switched to logic 0. It is applied to the $\overline{WE}$ input of all four 2142s in parallel and causes them to take the data off the bus and store it in the addressed location.

Also notice in Fig. 6.22 that the $\overline{RD}$ output of the 8086 supplies the OD inputs of the RAMs. This signal enables the outputs of the 2142s during read bus cycles. When the 8086 switches $\overline{RD}$ to logic 0, it tells the 2142s to put the data stored in the addressed location onto the data bus.

The read and write cycles are similar for byte data; however, the 8086 keeps either A_0 or $\overline{BHE}$ at logic 1. In this way, just the even bank or odd bank of memory is selected and a byte-wide data transfer occurs over the bus.

A maximum-mode 8086 microcomputer system with static RAM is shown in Fig. 6.23. This circuit is similar to the minimum-mode circuit we just described. The key difference is that the 8288 bus controller provides the read/write and memory control signals instead of the 8086. Notice that the advanced memory write command ($\overline{AMWC}$) output of the bus controller is used as the $\overline{WE}$ input of the 2142s. Moreover, its memory read command ($\overline{MRDC}$) output is applied to the OD inputs of the RAMs.

Finally, we find that the 8286 bus transceivers have been added to buffer the data bus. Notice that the $DT/\overline{R}$ and DEN outputs of the 8288 are applied to the T and $\overline{OE}$ inputs of the 8286, respectively. They are used to set the direction and to enable its outputs during read and write bus cycles.

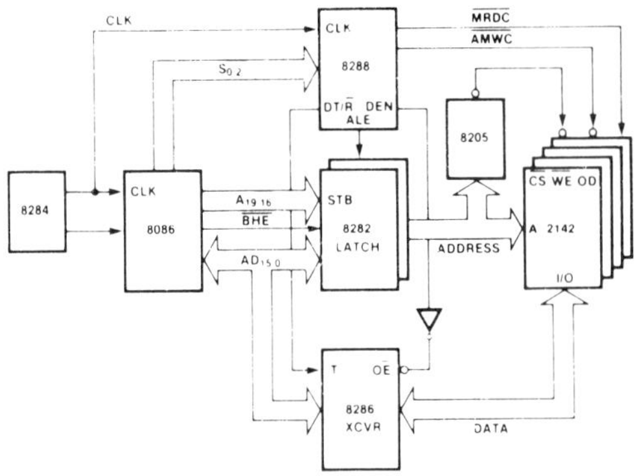

Figure 6.23 Maximum mode static RAM data storage memory (*Courtesy of Intel Corporation*).

Example 6.6

The memory in Fig. 6.22 starts at address MEM_START and ends at address MEM_STOP of the 8086's address space. Write a program that will clear this block of memory. Assume that the data segment is to be set up as the lowest addressed 64K bytes of the memory address space.

Solution. First we must load DS and SI so that they point to the memory location MEM_START. This is done with the instruction sequence

```
MOV   AX,0H
MOV   DS, AX
MOV   SI, MEM_START
```

Next CX must be loaded with the number of consecutive byte addresses that are to be cleared. This is done with the instruction

```
MOV   CX, MEM_STOP—MEM_START + 1
```

To clear the first byte location of the block, we just move zero to the address pointed to by SI. Then we must increment the address in SI by 1 so that it points to the next byte address and then loop back to the move instruction that is used to clear the memory byte. This loop is written as

```
AGAIN:  MOV    [SI], 0H
        INC    SI
        LOOP   AGAIN
        HLT
```

The complete program is repeated in Fig. 6.24.

6.11 128K-BYTE DYNAMIC RAM SUBSYSTEM

Today, microcomputer systems are being employed in more complex applications and with increased use of *high-level languages* such as BASIC, PL/M, C, and Pascal. Both of these conditions provide requirements for support of a large memory sub-

```
        MOV  AX,0H
        MOV  DS,AX
        MOV SI,MEM_START
        MOV  CX,MEM_STOP-MEM_START + 1
AGAIN:  MOV  [SI],0H
        INC  SI
        LOOP  AGAIN
        HLT
```

Figure 6.24 Memory initialization routine.

system. At the same time, dramatic decreases in the cost of semiconductor memory have made the use of large memory subsystems more practical.

If storage requirements of the 8086 microcomputer system are 16K words or larger, the memory subsystem is usually designed using dynamic RAMs instead of static RAMs. Figure 6.25 shows a dynamic RAM subsystem for a maximum mode 8086 system. The circuit employs the 16K by 1 2118 dynamic RAM and 8202 dynamic RAM refresh controller.

Looking at the circuit in Fig. 6.25, we see that the memory subsystem is formed from 64 2118 dynamic RAMs connected to produce a 128K-byte memory subsystem. The buses of the 8086 are first demultiplexed and then applied to the memory sub-

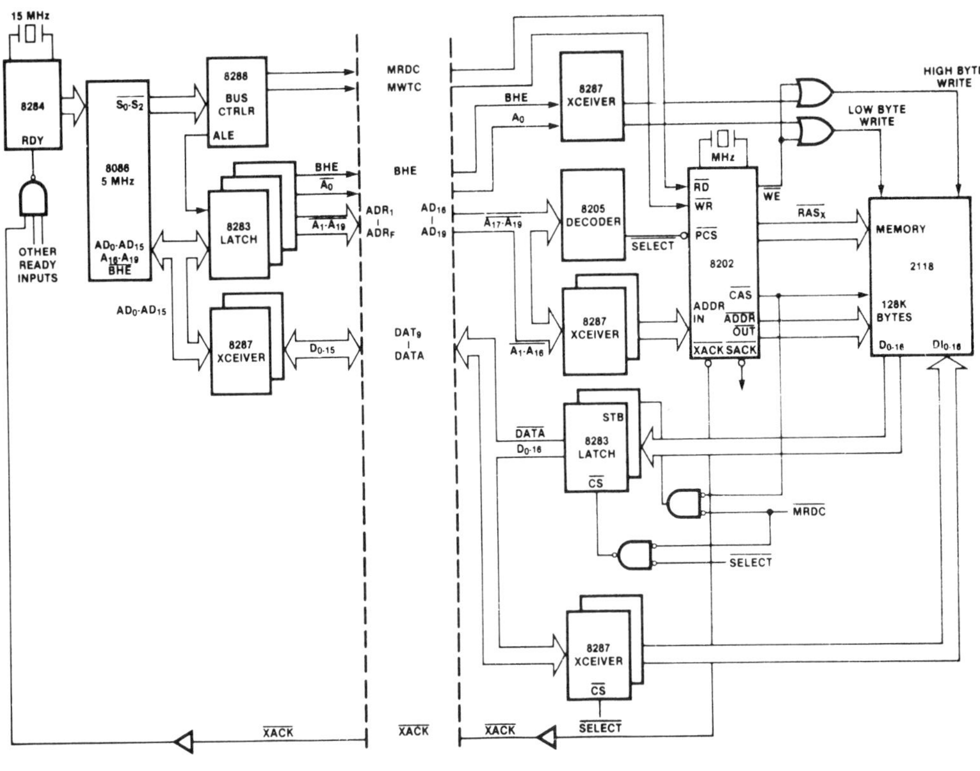

Figure 6.25 Maximum mode dynamic RAM subsystem (*Courtesy of Intel Corporation*).

system. In the memory subsystem, additional buffering is provided by 8287 bus transceivers, 8283 latches, and an 8205 decoder.

A 17-bit address, A_0 through A_{16}, is applied to the address inputs (ADDR IN) of the 8202 refresh controller. At the same time, the address bits A_{17} through A_{19} are decoded by the 8205 1-of-8 decoder to enable the refresh controller. It does this by switching the $\overline{PCS}$ input to logic 0. The refresh controller causes the 16-bit input address to be multiplexed out as an 8-bit row address and 8-bit column address at address outputs ($\overline{ADDR\ OUT}$). The appropriate $\overline{CAS}$ and $\overline{RAS}$ signals are output synchronously with the corresponding address byte. Notice that bank select signals A_0 and BHE are gated with the $\overline{WE}$ output of the 8202 to permit word or byte data transfers.

The 8288 bus controller signals whether a read or write bus cycle is in progress. In turn, it supplies the read signal MRDC and write signal MWTC to the $\overline{RD}$ and $\overline{WR}$ inputs, respectively, of the 8202. In response to these signals, the 8202 supplies the appropriate timed $\overline{WE}$, $\overline{RAS_X}$, $\overline{CAS}$, and $\overline{ADDR\ OUT}$ signals to the 128K-byte memory array.

The data outputs of the memory subsystem are interfaced to the system data bus with two 8283 latches. During memory read cycles, $\overline{SELECT}$ and $\overline{MRDC}$ are both logic 0. These signals are gated to chip select the 8283 latches. Synchronous with $\overline{CAS}$, valid read data are available at data outputs D_0 through D_{15}. The return of $\overline{CAS}$ to logic 1 completes the strobe pulse to the latches and the data output by the memory are latched on the system data bus.

During write cycles, data are input to the memory subsystem through 8287 bus transceivers. These devices are set up to just transmit data. Again the $\overline{SELECT}$ input enables the outputs of the devices such that data from the system data bus are applied to data inputs DI_0 through DI_{15} of the memory subsystem.

If the 8202 controller is busy refreshing memory, it signals this condition to the 8086 with the $\overline{XACK}$ signal. $\overline{XACK}$ is buffered and applied to the RDY input of the clock generator. In this way, wait states can be inserted into the bus cycle until the read or write cycle can be completed.

Example 6.7

Assume that the memory in Fig. 6.25 starts at address RAM_BEGIN and ends at address RAM_END. Write a program that runs a test (by writing to and reading back a rotating pattern of 01010101) to assure that the memory subsystem is operating correctly. If a bad location is found, the test is to be stopped and a subroutine named RAM_FAIL is to be called. On the other hand, if the test runs to completion, a subroutine named APP_START is to be called. Assume that DS is already set up and equals 0000_{16}.

Solution. The flowchart in Fig. 6.26(a) shows a solution for this program. Here we see that first SI, CX, and AL are initialized. SI is the pointer to the beginning of the block in memory and must contain the value of RAM_BEGIN; CX is a count of the bytes in the block and is found by the expression RAM_END − RAM_BEGIN + 1; and AL is loaded with the pattern 01010101. This is done with the sequence of instructions that follow

```
MOV    SI, RAM_START
MOV    CX, RAM_END - RAM_START + 1
MOV    AL, 055H
```

Next we will write the pattern to memory, read it back, and compare the value read back to the original pattern. To do this, we use the instructions

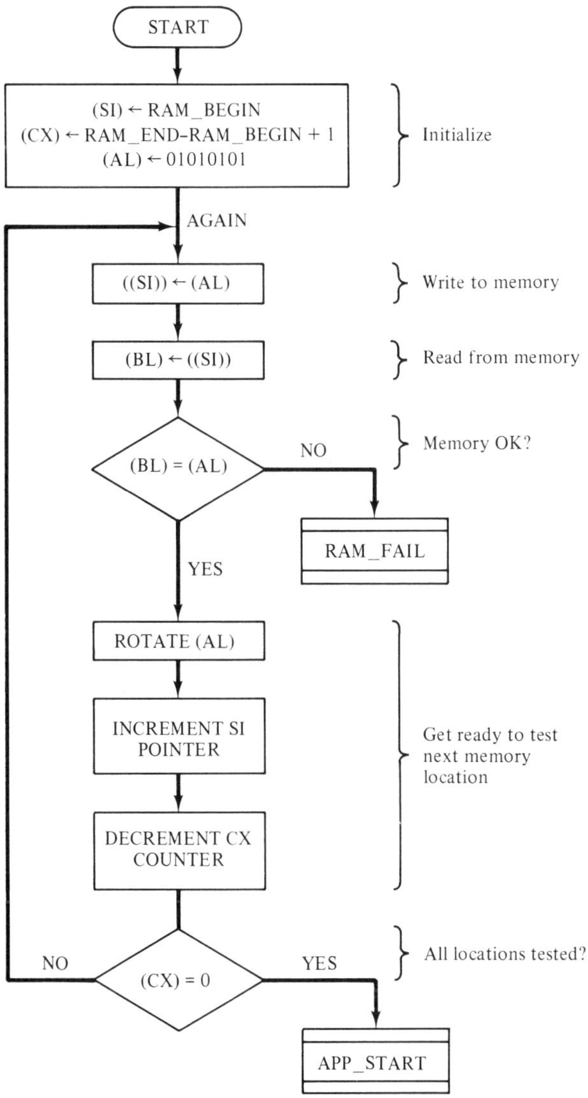

(a)

Figure 6.26 **(a)** Memory test program flowchart; **(b)** memory test program.

```
        MOV   SI,RAM_START
        MOV   CX,RAM_END-RAM_START+1
        MOV   AL,055H
AGAIN:  MOV   [SI],AL
        MOV   BL,[SI]
        CMP   BL,AL
        JNE   RAM_FAIL
        ROL   AL,1
        INC   SI
        DEC   CX
        JNZ   AGAIN
        JMP   APP_START
```

(b)

Figure 6.26 *(continued)*

```
AGAIN:  MOV   [SI], AL
        MOV   BL, [SI]
        CMP   BL, AL
```

Next the equal flag is tested. If it is not set, a memory error has been identified and control is passed to a subroutine called RAM_FAIL. This test is performed with the conditional jump instruction

```
JNE   RAM_FAIL
```

If the test passes (the equal flag is set), the jump is not taken. Instead, the pattern is rotated 1 bit position, the address pointer is incremented by 1 such that it points to the next byte address, the byte counter is decremented by 1, and if the count is not 0 control is returned to the label AGAIN. This is done as follows

```
ROL    AL, 1
INC    SI
LOOP   AGAIN
```

When the loop has run to completion, control is to be passed to the subroutine at APP_START. This is done with an unconditional jump instruction.

```
JMP   APP_START
```

Figure 6.26(b) shows the complete program.

ASSIGNMENT

Section 6.2

1. Show how the double word 12345678_{16} will be stored in memory starting at address $A001_{16}$.
2. Which range of the memory address space can be used to store instructions of the program?

3. If CS contains $A000_{16}$, what is the address range of the current code segment?
4. The data segment is to be located from address $B0000_{16}$ to $BFFFF_{16}$. What value must be loaded into DS?
5. Write a sequence of instructions that will initialize CS, DS, SS, and ES so that their corresponding segments of memory start at $A0000_{16}$, $B0000_{16}$, $C0000_{16}$, and $D0000_{16}$, respectively.

Section 6.3

6. List the memory control signals together with their active logic levels that occur when a byte of data is read from memory address $B0003_{16}$. Over which data lines is the byte of data transferred?
7. List the memory control signals together with their active logic levels that occur when a word of data is written to memory address $A0000_{16}$.

Sections 6.4 and 6.5

8. When the instruction PUSH AX is executed, what address bus status code and memory bus cycle code are output by the 8086 in a maximum-mode microcomputer system?

Section 6.6

9. Describe the bus activity that takes place as the 8086 writes a word of data into memory address $B0010_{16}$.
10. Explain why the READY input can be used to insert a wait state into the 8086's bus cycle.

Section 6.7

11. What is the function of the stack?
12. If the stack segment register contains $C000_{16}$ and the current value in SP is $FF00_{16}$, what is the address of the top of the stack?

Section 6.8

13. Explain the operation of the circuit in Fig. 6.19 as a word-wide read takes place from address $A0000_{16}$.

Section 6.9

14. Draw a circuit similar to that in Fig. 6.21 using four 2732 EPROMs to form an 8K-word program storage memory.

Section 6.10

15. Show how the circuit in Fig. 6.22 can be expanded to give a total of 2K words of read/write memory.

Section 6.11

16. Explain the need for the 8202 refresh controller in the circuit of Fig. 6.25.

7

Input/Output Interface of the 8086 Microprocessor

7.1 INTRODUCTION

In Chapter 6 we studied the memory interface of the 8086. Here we will study another important interface of the 8086 microcomputer system, the input/output interface. These are the topics in the order in which they are covered:

1. The input/output interface
2. I/O address space and data transfers
3. I/O instructions
4. The input and output bus cycles
5. Eight-byte-wide output ports
6. 8255A programmable peripheral interface
7. 8255A implementation of parallel I/O ports
8. Memory-mapped I/O
9. Serial communications interface
10. The 8251A programmable communications interface
11. Special purpose interface controllers

7.2 THE INPUT/OUTPUT INTERFACE

The *input/output interface* of the 8086 microcomputer permits it to communicate with the outside world. The way in which the 8086 deals with input/output circuitry is similar to the way in which it interfaces with memory circuitry. That is, input/output data transfers also take place over the multiplexed address/data bus. This parallel bus permits easy interface to LSI peripherals such as parallel I/O expanders and communication controllers. Through these I/O interfaces, the 8086 can input or output data in bit, byte, or word formats.

Minimum-Mode Interface

Let us begin by looking at the I/O interface for a minimum-mode 8086 system. Figure 7.1 shows the minimum-mode interface. Here we find the 8086, interface circuitry, and I/O ports for devices 0 through N. The circuits in this interface section must perform functions such as select the I/O port, latch output data, sample input data, synchronize data transfers, and translate between TTL voltage levels and those required to operate the I/O devices.

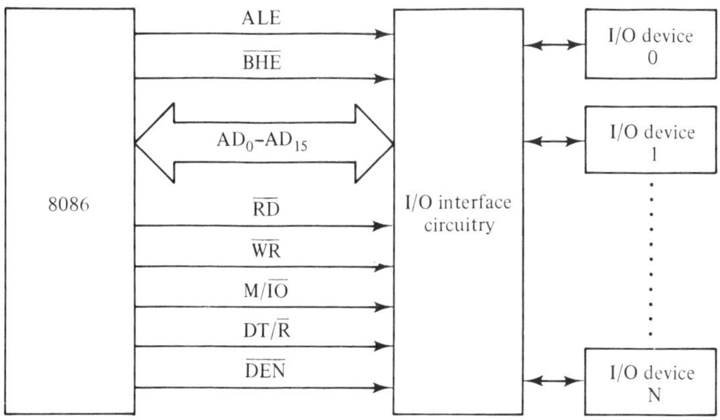

Figure 7.1 Minimum mode 8086 system I/O interface.

The data path between the 8086 and I/O interface circuits is the multiplexed address/data bus. Unlike the memory interface, this time just the 16 least significant lines of the bus, AD_0 through AD_{15}, are in use. This interface also involves the control signals that we discussed as part of the memory interface. They are: ALE, $\overline{BHE}$, $\overline{RD}$, $\overline{WR}$, $M/\overline{IO}$, $DT/\overline{R}$, and $\overline{DEN}$.

Maximum-Mode Interface

When the 8086 system is strapped to operate in the maximum mode, the interface to the I/O circuitry changes. Figure 7.2 illustrates this configuration.

As in the maximum-mode memory interface, the 8288 bus controller produces the control signals for the I/O subsystem. The 8288 decodes bus command status codes output by the 8086 at $\overline{S}_2\overline{S}_1\overline{S}_0$. These codes tell which type of bus cycle is in progress. If the code corresponds to an I/O read bus cycle, the 8288 generates the I/O *read command output* $\overline{IORC}$ and for an I/O write cycle it generates I/O *write command outputs* $\overline{IOWC}$ and $\overline{AIOWC}$. The 8288 also produces control signals ALE,

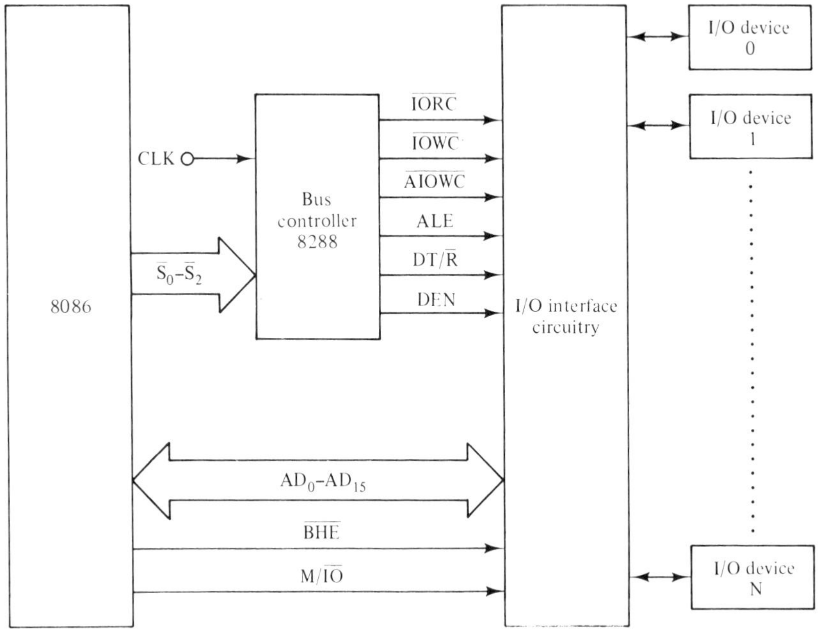

Figure 7.2 Maximum mode 8086 system I/O interface.

DT/$\overline{R}$, and DEN. Moreover, the address and data transfer path between 8086 and maximum-mode I/O interface remains address/data bus lines AD_0 through AD_{15}. In this configuration the control signals $\overline{BHE}$ and M/$\overline{IO}$ are still produced by the 8086 microprocessor.

The table in Fig. 7.3 shows the bus command status codes together with the command signals that they produce. Those for I/O bus cycles have been highlighted. The 8086 indicates that data are to be input (Read I/O port) by code $\overline{S_2}\overline{S_1}\overline{S_0}$ = 001. This input causes the bus controller to produce control output I/O read command

Status inputs			CPU cycle	8288 command
$\overline{S_2}$	$\overline{S_1}$	$\overline{S_0}$		
0	0	0	Interrupt acknowledge	$\overline{INTA}$
0	0	1	Read I/O port	$\overline{IORC}$
0	1	0	Write I/O port	$\overline{IOWC}$, $\overline{AIOWC}$
0	1	1	Halt	None
1	0	0	Instruction fetch	$\overline{MRDC}$
1	0	1	Read memory	$\overline{MRDC}$
1	1	0	Write memory	$\overline{MWTC}$, $\overline{AMWC}$
1	1	1	Passive	None

Figure 7.3 I/O bus cycle status codes *(Courtesy of Intel Corporation).*

($\overline{IORC}$). There is one other code that represents an output bus cycle. This is the Write I/O port code $\overline{S_2}\overline{S_1}\overline{S_0}$ = 010. It produces two output command signals I/O write cycle ($\overline{IOWC}$) and advanced I/O write cycle ($\overline{AIOWC}$). These command signals are used to enable data from the I/O circuitry onto the system bus and control the direction in which data are transferred.

7.3 I/O ADDRESS SPACE AND DATA TRANSFERS

Earlier we indicated that input/output ports in the 8086 microcomputer can be either byte wide or word wide. The port that is accessed for input or output of data is selected by an *I/O address*. This address is specified as part of the instruction that performs the I/O operation.

I/O addresses are 16 bits in length and are output by the 8086 to the I/O interface over bus lines AD_0 through AD_{15}. As for memory addresses, AD_0 represents the LSB and AD_{15} the MSB. The most significant bits, A_{16} through A_{19}, of the memory address are held at the 0 logic level during the address period (T_1) of all I/O bus cycles.

The 8086 signals to external circuitry that the address on the bus is for an I/O port instead of a memory location by switching the $M/\overline{IO}$ control line to the 0 logic level. This signal is held at the 0 level during the complete input or output bus cycle. For this reason, it can be used to enable the address latch or address decoder in external I/O circuitry.

Figure 7.4 shows a map of the *I/O address space* of the 8086 system. This is an independent 64K-byte address space that is dedicated for I/O devices. Notice that its address range is from 0000_{16} through $FFFF_{16}$. The part of the map from address 0000_{16} through $00FF_{16}$ is referred to as page 0. Certain I/O instructions can only perform operations to ports in this part of the address space. Other I/O instructions can input or output data for ports anywhere in the I/O address space.

Moreover, notice that the eight ports located from address $00F8_{16}$ through $00FF_{16}$ are specified as reserved. These port addresses are reserved by Intel Corporation for use in their future hardware and software products.

Data transfers between the MPU and I/O devices are performed over the data bus. Word transfers take place over the complete data bus, D_0 through D_{15}, and can require either one or two bus cycle. To assure that just one bus cycle is required for

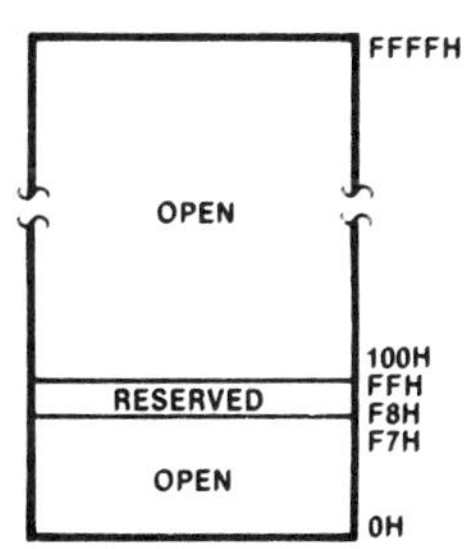

Figure 7.4 I/O address space (*Courtesy of Intel Corporation*).

the word data transfer, word-wide I/O ports should be aligned at even address boundaries.

On the other hand, data transfers to byte-wide I/O ports always require one bus cycle. Therefore, they can be located at either an even- or odd-address. Byte data transfers to a port at an even address are performed over bus lines D_0 through D_7 and those to an odd-addressed port are performed over D_8 through D_{15}.

To input or output consecutive bytes of data to an LSI peripheral device, it should be connected such that all registers reside at either even or odd addresses. In this way, all data transfers take place over the same part of the bus. For this reason, A_0 cannot be used as a register select bit when addressing peripheral devices.

7.4 INPUT/OUTPUT INSTRUCTIONS

Input/output operations are performed by the 8086 using its *in* (IN) and *out* (OUT) instructions together with the I/O port addressing mode. There are two types of IN and OUT instructions: the *direct I/O instructions* and *variable I/O instructions*. These instructions are listed in the table of Fig. 7.5. Their mnemonics and names are provided together with a brief description of their operations.

Mnemonic	Meaning	Format	Operation	
IN	Input direct	IN Acc,Port	(Acc) ← (Port)	Acc = AL or AX
	Input indirect (variable)	IN Acc,DX	(Acc) ← ((DX))	
OUT	Output direct	OUT Port,Acc	(Port) ← (Acc)	
	Output indirect (variable)	OUT DX,Acc	((DX)) ← (Acc)	

Figure 7.5 Input/output instructions.

Either of these two types of instructions can be used to transfer a byte or word of data. In the case of byte transfers, data can be input/output over the upper or lower part of the bus. This is achieved by specifying an even or odd address, for the I/O port.

All data transfers take place between I/O devices and the 8086's AL or AX register. For this reason, this method of performing I/O is known as *accumulator I/O*. Byte transfers involve the AL register and word transfers the AX register. In fact, specifying AL as the source or destination register in an I/O instruction indicates that it corresponds to a byte transfer instead of a word transfer.

In a direct I/O instruction, the address of the I/O port is specified as part of the instruction. Eight bits are provided for this direct address. For this reason, its value is limited to the address range from 0_{10} equal 0000_{16} to 255_{10} equal $00FF_{16}$. This range corresponds to page 0 in the I/O address space of Fig. 7.4. An example is the instruction

IN AL, 0FEH

Execution of this instruction causes the contents of the byte-wide I/O port at address FE_{16} of the I/O address space to be input to the AL register.

Example 7.1

Write a sequence of instructions that will output FF_{16} to a byte-wide output port at address AB_{16} of the I/O address space.

Solution. First the AL register is loaded with FF_{16} as an immediate operand in the instruction

```
MOV  AL, 0FFH
```

Now the data in AL can be output to the byte-wide output port with the instruction

```
OUT  0ABH, AL
```

The difference between the direct and variable I/O instructions lies in the way in which the address of the I/O port is specified. We just saw that for direct I/O instructions an 8-bit address is specified as part of the instruction. On the other hand, the variable I/O instructions use a 16-bit address that resides in the DX register within the 8086. The value in DX is not an offset. It is the actual address that is to be output on AD_0 through AD_{15} during the I/O bus cycle. Since this address is a full 16 bits in length, variable I/O instructions can access ports located anywhere in the 64K-byte I/O address space.

When using either type of I/O instruction, the data must be loaded into or removed from the AL or AX register before another input or output operation can be performed. Moreover, in the case of the variable I/O instructions, the DX register must be loaded with an address. This requires execution of additional instructions.

For instance, the instruction sequence

```
MOV   DX, 0A000H
IN    AL, DX
```

inputs the contents of the byte-wide input port at $A000_{16}$ of the I/O address space.

Example 7.2

Write a series of instructions that will output FF_{16} to an output port located at address $B000_{16}$ of the I/O address space.

Solution. The DX register must first be loaded with the address of the output port. This is done with the instruction

```
MOV   DX, 0B000H
```

Next the data that is to be output must be loaded into AL.

```
MOV   AL, 0FFH
```

Finally, the data are output with the instruction

```
OUT   DX, AL
```

Example 7.3

Data are to be read in from two byte-wide input ports at addresses AA_{16} and $A9_{16}$, respectively, and then output to a word-wide output port at address $B000_{16}$. Write a sequence of instructions to perform this input/output operation.

Solution. We can first read in the byte from the port at address AA_{16} into AL and move it to AH. This is done with the instructions

```
IN      AL, 0AAH
MOV     AH, AL
```

Now the other byte can be read into AL by the instruction.

```
IN      AL, 0A9H
```

To write out the word of data in AX, we can load DX with the address $B000_{16}$ and use a variable output instruction. This leads to the following

```
MOV     DX, 0B000H
OUT     DX, AX
```

7.5 INPUT AND OUTPUT BUS CYCLES

In Section 7.2 we found that the I/O interface signals for the minimum-mode 8086 system are essentially the same as those involved in the memory interface. In fact, the function, logic levels, and timing of all signals other than $M/\overline{IO}$ are identical to those already described for the memory interface in Chapter 6.

Waveforms for the *I/O input (I/O read) bus cycle* and *I/O output (I/O write) bus cycle* are shown in Figs. 7.6 and 7.7, respectively. Looking at the input and output bus cycle waveforms, we see that the timing of $M/\overline{IO}$ does not change. The 8086 switches it to logic 0 to indicate that an I/O bus cycle is in progress. It is maintained

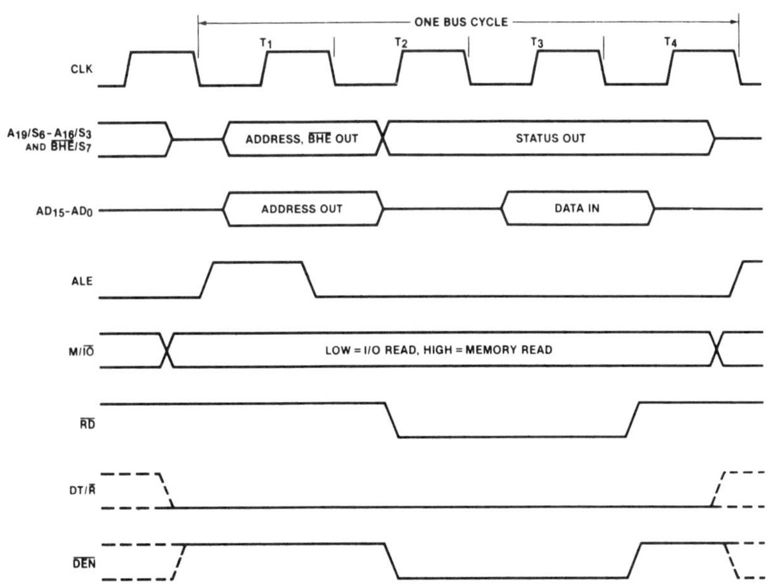

Figure 7.6 Input bus cycle (*Courtesy of Intel Corporation*).

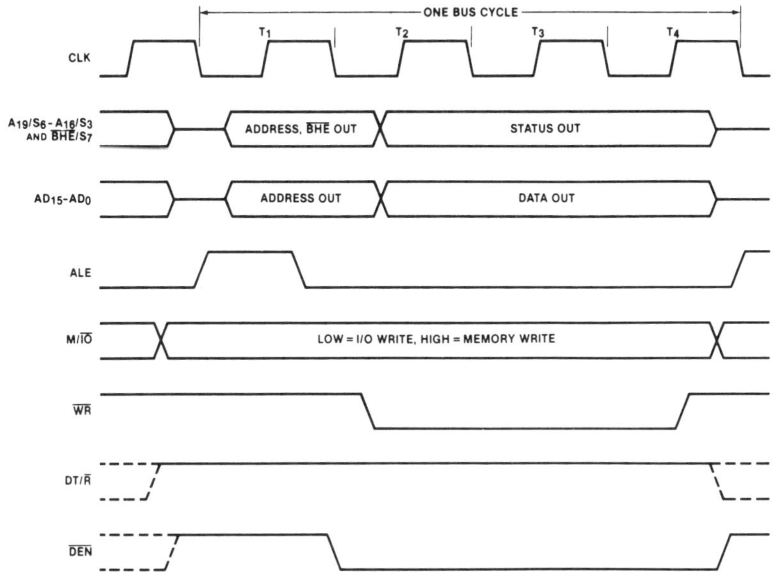

Figure 7.7 Output bus cycle (*Courtesy of Intel Corporation*).

at the 0 logic level for the duration of the I/O bus cycle. As in memory cycles, the address (ADDRESS OUT) is output together with ALE during clock period T_1. For the input bus cycle, $\overline{\text{DEN}}$ is switched to logic 0 to signal the I/O interface circuitry when to put the data onto the bus and the 8086 reads data off the bus during period T_3.

On the other hand, for the output bus cycle in Fig. 7.7, the 8086 puts write data (DATA OUT) on the bus late in T_2 and maintains it during the rest of the bus cycle. This time $\overline{\text{WR}}$ switches to logic 0 to signal the I/O section that valid data are on the bus.

The same bus cycle requirements exist for data transfers for I/O ports as were found for memory. That is, all byte transfers and word transfers to even-addressed ports require just one bus cycle. However, two bus cycles are required to perform data transfers for odd-addressed word-wide ports. Eight bits are transferred during each of these two bus cycles.

7.6 EIGHT-BYTE-WIDE OUTPUT PORTS

Up to this point in the chapter, we have introduced the I/O interface of the 8086, the I/O address space, the I/O instructions, and I/O bus cycles. Now we will show a circuit that can be used to implement parallel output ports in an 8086 system. Figure 7.8 is such a circuit. It provides eight-byte-wide output ports that are implemented with 8282 octal latches. In this circuit, the ports are labeled PORT 0 through PORT

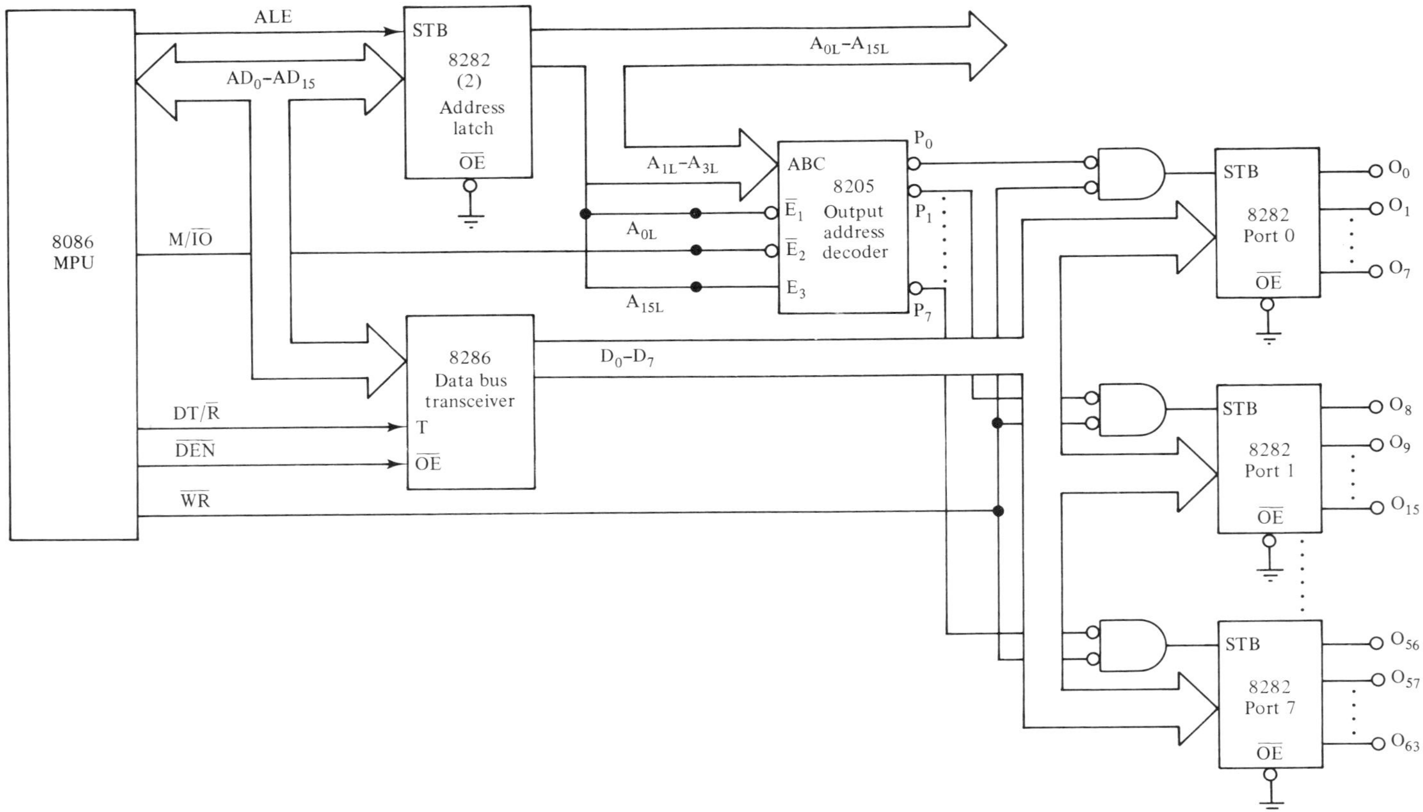

Figure 7.8 64 output circuit.

7. These eight ports give a total of 64 parallel output lines which are labeled O_0 through O_{63}.

Looking at the circuit, we see that the 8086's address/data bus is demultiplexed just as was done for the memory interface. Notice that two 8282 octal latches are used to form a 16-bit address latch. These devices latch the address A_0 through A_{15} synchronously with the ALE pulse. The latched address outputs are labeled A_{0L} through A_{15L}. Remember that address lines A_{16} through A_{19} are not involved in the I/O interface. For this reason they are not shown in the circuit diagram.

Actually, this circuit is designed such that the I/O ports reside at even byte addresses. This is the reason that only data bus lines D_0 through D_7 are shown connecting to the output latches. It is over these lines that the 8086 writes data into the output ports.

Address lines A_{0L} and A_{15L} provide two of the three enable inputs of the 8205 output address decoder. These signals are applied to enable inputs $\overline{E}_1$ and E_3, respectively. The decoder requires one more enable signal at its $\overline{E}_2$ input. It is supplied by $M/\overline{IO}$. These enable inputs must be $\overline{E}_1\overline{E}_2E_3$ equal to 001 to enable the decoder for operation. The condition $\overline{E}_1$ equal 0 corresponds to an even address and $\overline{E}_2$ equal 0 represents the fact that an I/O bus cycle is in progress. The third condition, E_3 equal 1, is an additional requirement that A_{15L} be at logic 1 during all data transfers for this section of parallel output ports.

Notice that the 3-bit code $A_{3L}A_{2L}A_{1L}$ is applied to select inputs ABC of the 8205 1-of-8 decoder. When the decoder is enabled, the P output corresponding to this select code switches to logic 0. Notice that logic 0 at this output enables the $\overline{WR}$ signal to the strobe (STB) input of the corresponding output latch. In this way, just one of the eight ports is selected for operation.

When valid output data are on D_0 through D_7, the 8086 switches $\overline{WR}$ to logic 0. This change in logic level causes the selected 8282 device to latch in the data from the bus. The outputs of the latches are permanently enabled by the 0 logic level at their $\overline{OE}$ inputs. Therefore, the data appear at the appropriate port outputs.

The 8286 in the circuit allows data to move from 8086 to the output ports. This is accomplished by enabling the 8286's T and $\overline{OE}$ pins with the $DT/\overline{R}$ and $\overline{DEN}$ signals which are at logic 1 and 0, respectively.

Example 7.4

To which output port in Fig. 7.8 are data written when the address put on the bus during an output bus cycle is 8002_{16}?

Solution. Expressing the address in binary form, we get

$$A_{15} \cdots A_0 = A_{15L} \cdots A_{0L} = 1000000000000010_{16}$$

The important address bits are:

$$A_{15L} = 1$$

$$A_{0L} = 0$$

and

$$A_{3L}A_{2L}A_{1L} = 001$$

Moreover, whenever an output bus cycle is in progress $M/\overline{IO}$ is logic 0. Therefore, the enable inputs of the 8205 decoder are

$$\overline{E}_1 = A_{0L} = 0$$
$$\overline{E}_2 = M/\overline{IO} = 0$$
$$E_3 = A_{15L} = 1$$

These inputs enable the decoder for operation. At the same time, its select inputs are supplied with the code 001. This input causes output P_1 to switch to logic 0.

$$P_1 = 0$$

The gate at the strobe input of Port 1 has as its inputs P_1 and $\overline{WR}$. When valid data are on the bus, $\overline{WR}$ switches to logic 0. Since P_1 is also 0, the STB input of the 8282 for Port 1 switches to logic 1. This causes the data on D_0 through D_7 to be latched at outputs O_8 through O_{15} of Port 1.

Example 7.5

Write a series of instructions that will output the byte contents of the memory location called DATA to output port 0 in the circuit of Fig. 7.8

Solution. To write a byte to output port 0, the address which must be output on the 8086's address bus must be

$$A_{15}A_{14} \cdots\cdots A_0 = 1XXXXXXXXXXX0000_2$$

Assuming that the don't care bits are all made logic 0, we get

$$A_{15}A_{14} \cdots\cdots A_0 = 1000000000000000_2$$
$$= 8000_{16}$$

Then the instruction sequence needed to output the contents of memory location DATA is

```
MOV   DX, 8000H
MOV   AL, DATA
OUT   DX0, AL
```

7.7 8255A PROGRAMMABLE PERIPHERAL INTERFACE (PPI)

The *8255A* is an LSI peripheral designed to permit easy implementation of *parallel I/O* in the 8086 microcomputer. It provides a flexible parallel interface which includes features such as: single-bit, 4-bit, and byte-wide input and output ports; level-sensitive inputs; latched outputs; strobed inputs or outputs; and strobed bidirectional input/outputs. These features are selected under software control.

A block diagram of the 8255A is shown in Fig. 7.9(a) and its pin layout in Fig. 7.9(b). The left side of the block represents the *microprocessor interface*. It includes an *8-bit bidirectional data bus* D_0 through D_7. Over these lines, commands, status information, and data are transferred between the 8086 and 8255A. These data are

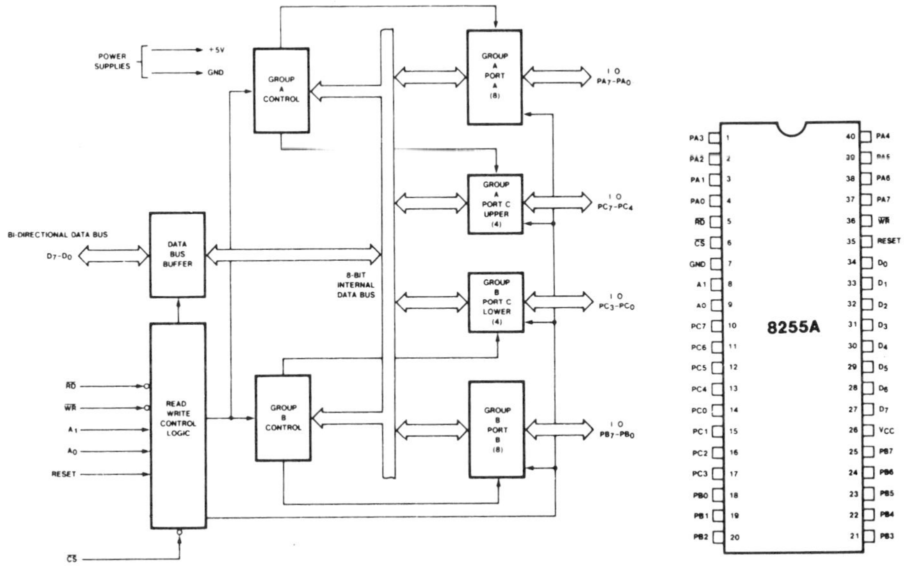

(a) (b)

Figure 7.9 **(a)** Block diagram of the 8255A (*Courtesy of Intel Corporation*); **(b)** pin layout (*Courtesy of Intel Corporation*).

transferred whenever the 8086 performs an input or output bus cycle to an address of a register within the device. Timing of the data transfers to the 8255A is controlled by the *read/write* ($\overline{RD}$ and $\overline{WR}$) *control* signals.

The source or destination register within the 8255A is selected by a 2-bit *register select code*. The 8086 must apply this code to the *register select inputs*, A_0 and A_1 of the 8255A. The *PORT A, PORT B*, and *PORT C registers* correspond to codes $A_1A_0 = 00$, $A_1A_0 = 01$, and $A_1A_0 = 10$, respectively.

Two other signals are shown on the microprocessor interface side of the block diagram. They are the *reset* (RESET) and *chip select* ($\overline{CS}$) inputs. $\overline{CS}$ must be logic 0 during all read or write operations to the 8255A. It enables the microprocessor interface circuitry for an input or output operation.

On the other hand, RESET is used to initialize the device. Switching it to logic 0 at power-up causes the internal registers of the 8255A to be cleared. *Initialization* configures all I/O ports for input mode of operation.

The other side of the block corresponds to three *byte-wide I/O ports*. They are called PORT A, PORT B, and PORT C and represent *I/O lines* PA_0 through PA_7, PB_0 through PB_7, and PC_0 through PC_7, respectively. These ports can be configured for input or output operation. This gives a total of 24 I/O lines.

We already mentioned that the operating characteristics of the 8255A can be configured under software control. It contains an 8-bit internal control register for this purpose. This register is represented by the *group A* and *group B control blocks* in Fig. 7.9(a). Logic 0 or 1 can be written to the bit positions in this register to configure the individual ports for input or output operation and to enable one of its three modes of operation. The control register is write only and its contents are modified under software control by initiating a write bus cycle to the 8255A with register select code $A_1A_0 = 11$.

The bits of the control register and their control functions are shown in Fig. 7.10. Here we see that bits D_0 through D_2 correspond to the group B control block in the diagram of Fig. 7.9(a). Bit D_0 configures the lower four lines of PORT C for input or output operation. Notice that logic 1 at D_0 selects input operation and logic 0 selects output operation. The next bit, D_1, configures PORT B as an 8-bit-wide input or output port. Again, logic 1 selects input operation and logic 0 selects output operation.

The D_2 bit is the mode select bit for PORT B and the lower 4 bits of PORT C. It permits selection of one of two different modes of operation called *MODE 0* and *MODE 1*. Logic 0 in bit D_2 selects MODE 0, while logic 1 selects MODE 1. These modes will be discussed in detail shortly.

The next 4 bits in the control register, D_3 through D_6, correspond to the group

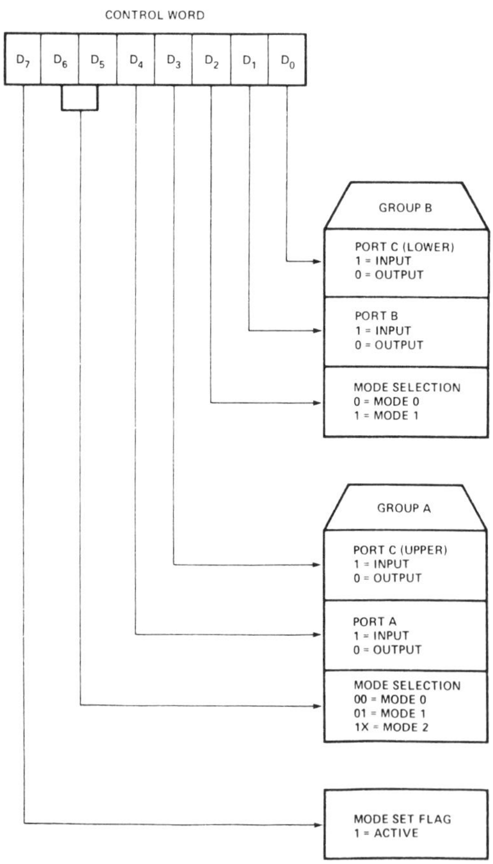

Figure 7.10 Control word bit functions (*Courtesy of Intel Corporation*).

A control block in Fig. 7.9(a). Bits D_3 and D_4 of the control register are used to configure the operation of the upper half of PORT C and all of PORT A, respectively. These bits work in the same way as D_0 and D_1 configure the lower half of PORT C and PORT B. However, there are now two mode select bits D_5 and D_6 instead of just 1. They are used to select between three modes of operation known as *MODE 0, MODE 1*, and *MODE 2.*

The last control register bit, D_7, is the *mode set flag*. It must be at logic 1 (active) whenever the mode of operation is to be changed.

MODE 0 selects what is called *simple I/O operation*. By simple I/O, we mean that the lines of the port can be configured as level-sensitive inputs or latched outputs. To set all ports for this mode of operation, load bit D_7 of the control register with logic 1, bits D_6D_5 = 00, and D_2 = 0. Logic 1 at D_7 represents an active mode set flag. Now PORT A and PORT B can be configured as 8-bit input or output ports and PORT C can be configured for operation as two independent 4-bit input or output ports. This is done by setting or resetting bits D_4, D_3, D_1, and D_0.

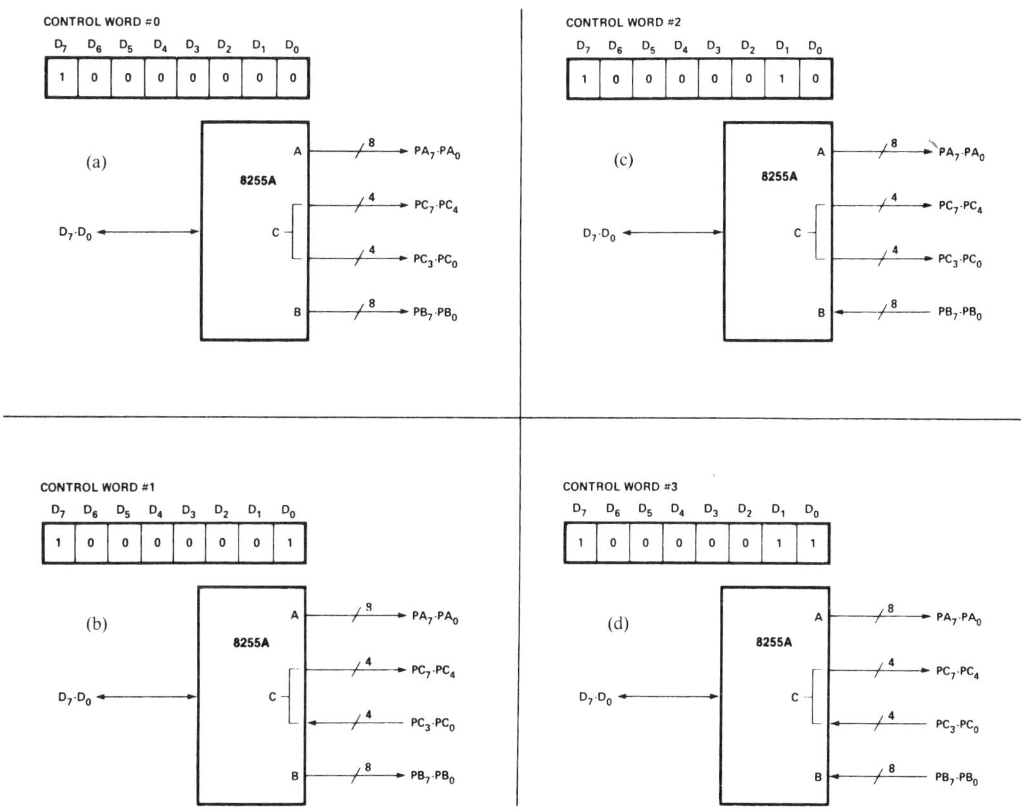

Figure 7.11 Mode 0 control words and corresponding input/output configuration *(Courtesy of Intel Corporation).*

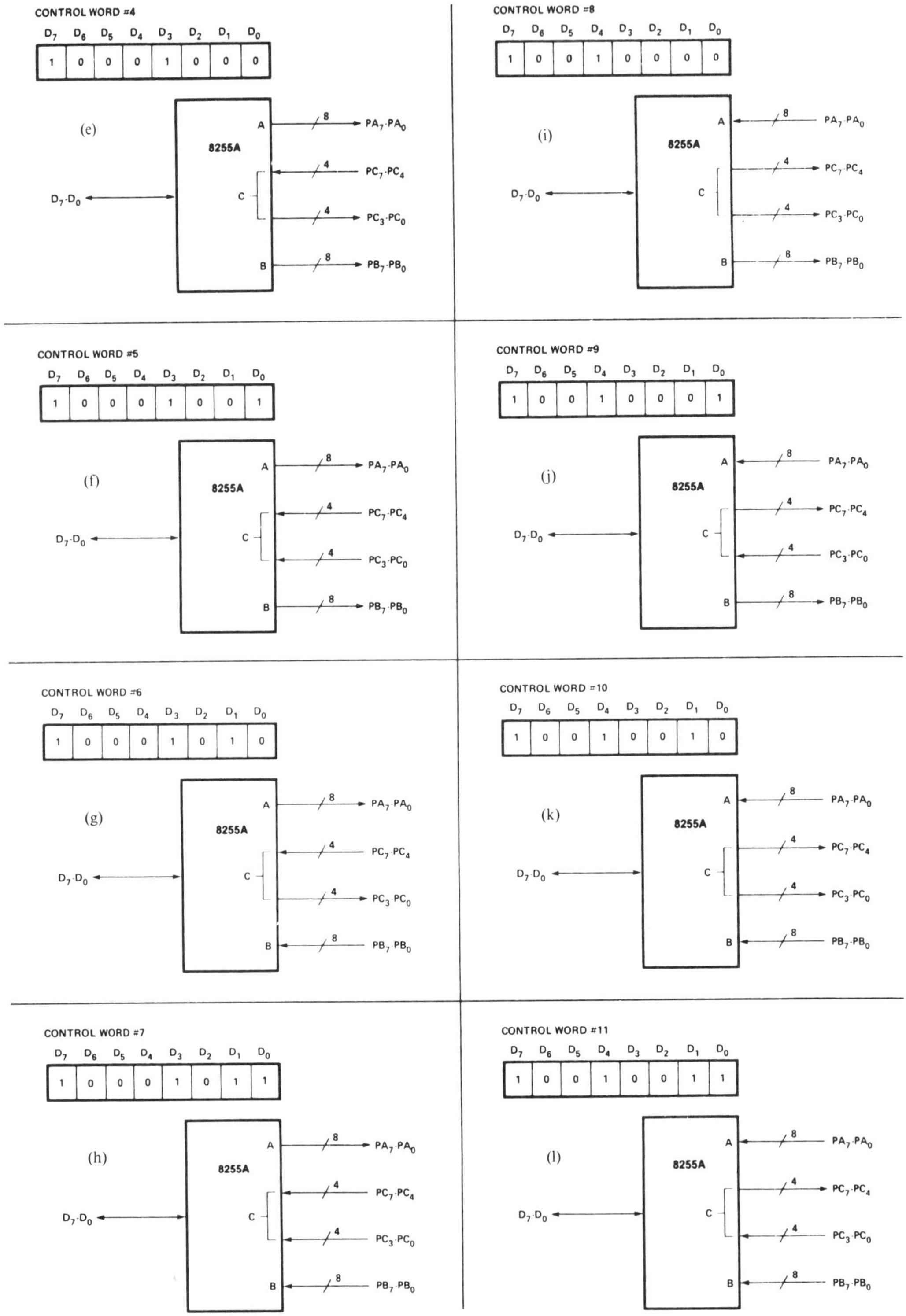

Figure 7.11 *(Continued)*

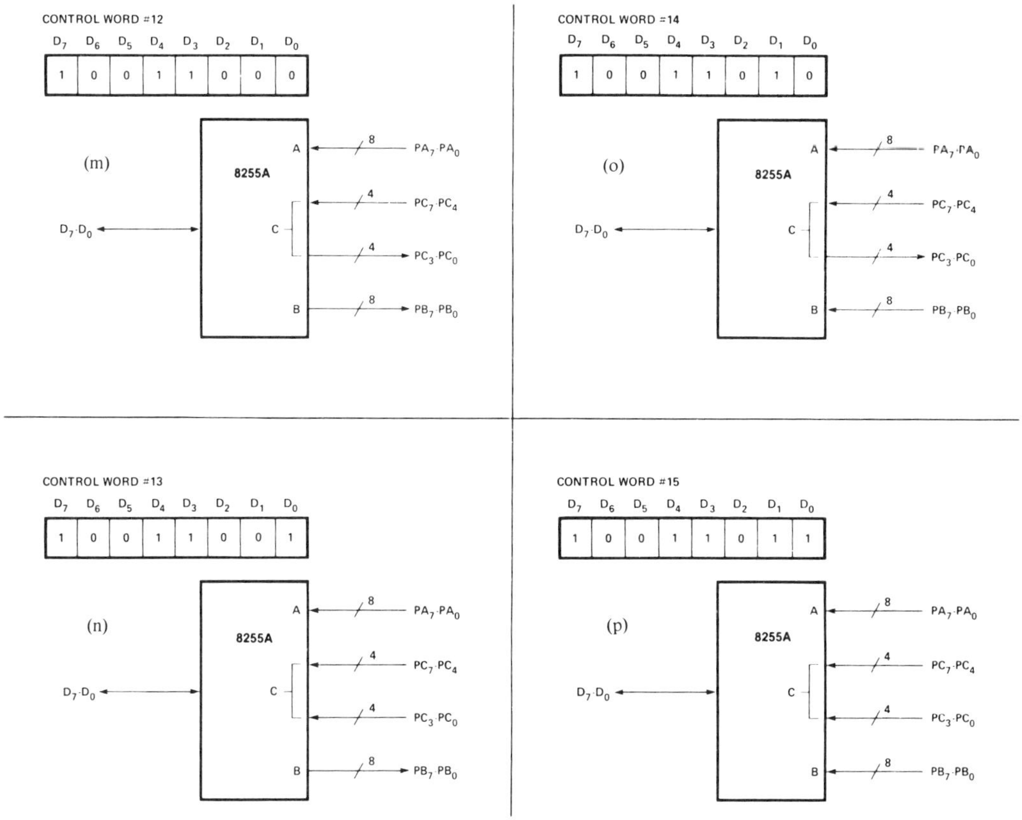

Figure 7.11 *(continued)*

For example, if $80_{16} = 10000000_2$ is written to the control register, the 1 in D_7 activates the mode set flag. MODE 0 operation is selected for all three ports because bits D_6, D_5, and D_2 are logic 0. At the same time, the 0's in D_4, D_3, D_1, and D_0 set up all port lines to work as outputs. This configuration is illustrated in Fig. 7.11(a). (See page 217.)

By writing different binary combinations into bit locations D_4, D_3, D_1, and D_0, any one of 16 different MODE 0 I/O configurations can be obtained. The control word and I/O setup for the rest of these combinations are shown in Fig. 7.11(b) through (p).

Example 7.6

What is the mode and I/O configuration for ports A, B, and C of an 8255A after its control register is loaded with 82_{16}?

Solution. Expressing the control register contents in binary form, we get

$$D_7D_6D_5D_4D_3D_2D_1D_0 = 10000010_2$$

Since D_7 is 1, the modes of operation of the ports are selected by the control word.

The 3 least significant bits of the word configure PORT B and the lower 4 bits of PORT C. They give

D_0	$= 0$	Lower 4 bits of PORT C are outputs
D_1	$= 1$	PORT B are inputs
D_2	$= 0$	MODE 0 operation for both PORT B and the lower 4 bits of PORT C

The next 4 bits configure the upper part of PORT C and PORT A.

D_3	$= 0$	Upper 4 bits of PORT C are outputs
D_4	$= 0$	PORT A are outputs
D_6D_5	$= 00$	MODE 0 operation for both PORT A and the upper part of PORT C

This MODE 0 I/O configuration is shown in Fig. 7.11(c).

MODE 1 operation represents what is known as *strobed I/O*. The ports of the 8255A are put into this mode of operation by setting $D_7 = 1$ to activate the mode set flag and setting $D_6D_5 = 01$ and $D_2 = 1$.

In this way, the A and B ports are configured as two independent *byte-wide I/O ports* each of which has a *4-bit control/data port* associated with it. The control/data ports are formed from the lower and upper nibbles of PORT C, respectively.

When configured in this way, data applied to an input port must be strobed in with a signal produced in external hardware. Moreover, an output port is provided with handshake signals that indicate when new data are available at its outputs and when an external device has read these values.

As an example, let us assume for the moment that the control register of an 8255A is loaded with $D_7D_6D_5D_4D_3D_2D_1D_0 = 10111XXX$. This configures PORT A as a MODE 1 input port. Figure 7.12(a) shows the function of the signal lines for this example. Notice that PA_7 through PA_0 form an 8-bit input port. On the other hand, the function of the upper PORT C leads are reconfigured to provide the PORT A control/data lines. The PC_4 line becomes $\overline{STB_A}$ (*strobe input*), which is used to strobe data at PA_7 through PA_0 into the input latch. Moreover, PC_5 becomes IBF_A (*input buffer full*). Logic 1 at this output indicates to external circuitry that a word has already been strobed into the latch.

The third control signal is at PC_3 and is labeled $INTR_A$ (*interrupt request*). It switches to logic 1 as long as $\overline{STB_A} = 1$, $IBF_A = 1$, and an internal signal $INTE_A$ (*interrupt enable*) equals 1. $INTE_A$ is set to logic 0 or 1 under software control by using the bit set/reset feature of the 8255A. Looking at Fig. 7.12(a) we see that logic 1 in $INTE_A$ enables the logic level of IBF_A to the $INTR_A$ output. This signal can be applied to an interrupt input of the 8086 to signal it that new data are available at the input port. The corresponding interrupt service routine can read the data and clear the interrupt request.

As another example, let us assume that the contents of the control register are changed to $D_7D_6D_5D_4D_3D_2D_1D_1 = 10101XXX$. This I/O configuration is shown

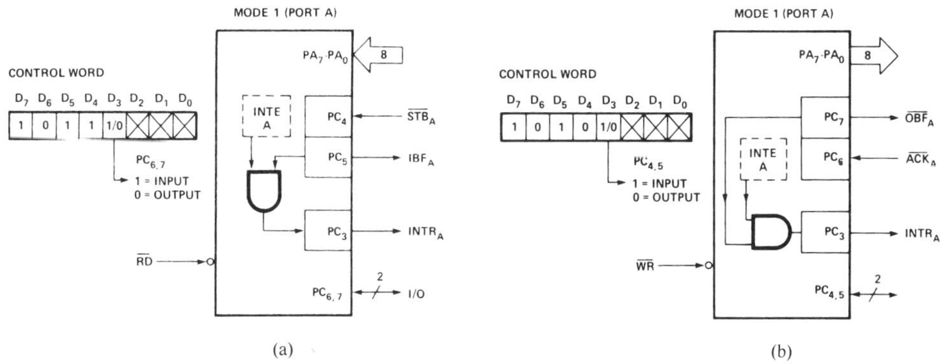

Figure 7.12 **(a)** Mode 1 port A input configuration *(Courtesy of Intel Corporation)*; **(b)** mode 1 port A output configuration (*Courtesy of Intel Corporation*).

in Fig. 7.12(b). Notice that PORT A is now configured for output operation instead of input operation. PA_7 through PA_0 are now an 8-bit output port. The control line at PC_7 is $\overline{OBF}_A$ (*output buffer full*). When data have been written into the output port, $\overline{OBF}_A$ switches to the 0 logic level. In this way, it signals external circuitry that new data are available at the port outputs.

Signal line PC_6 becomes $\overline{ACK}_A$ (*acknowledge*), which is an input. An external device can signal the 8255A that it has accepted the data provided at the output port by switching this input to logic 0. The last signal at the control port is output $INTR_A$ (*interrupt request*), which is produced at the PC_3 lead. This output is switched to logic 1 when the $\overline{ACK}_A$ input is active. It is used to signal the 8086 with an interrupt that indicates that an external device has accepted the data from the outputs. $INTR_A$ switches to the 1 level when $\overline{OBF}_A = 1$, $\overline{ACK}_A = 0$, and $INTE_A = 1$. Again the interrupt enable ($INTE_A$) bit must be set to 1 under software control.

Example 7.7

Figure 7.13(a) and (b) show how PORT B can be configured for MODE 1 operation. Describe what happens in Fig. 7.13(a) when the $\overline{STB}_B$ input is pulsed to logic 0. Assume that $INTE_B$ is already set to 1.

Solution. As $\overline{STB}_B$ is pulsed, the byte of data at PB_7 through PB_0 are latched into the PORT B register. This causes the IBF_B output to switch to 1. Since $INTE_B$ is 1, $INTR_B$ also switches to logic 1.

The last mode of operation, MODE 2, represents what is known as *strobed bidirectional I/O*. The key difference is that now the port works as either inputs or outputs and control signals are provided for both functions. Only PORT A can be configured to work in this way.

In order to set up this mode, the control register is set to $D_7D_6D_5D_4D_3D_2D_1D_0$ = 11XXXXXX. The I/O configuration that results is shown in Fig. 7.14. Here we find that PA_7 through PA_0 operate as an *8-bit bidirectional port* instead of a unidirectional port. Its control signals are: $\overline{OBF}_A$ at PC_7, $\overline{ACK}_A$

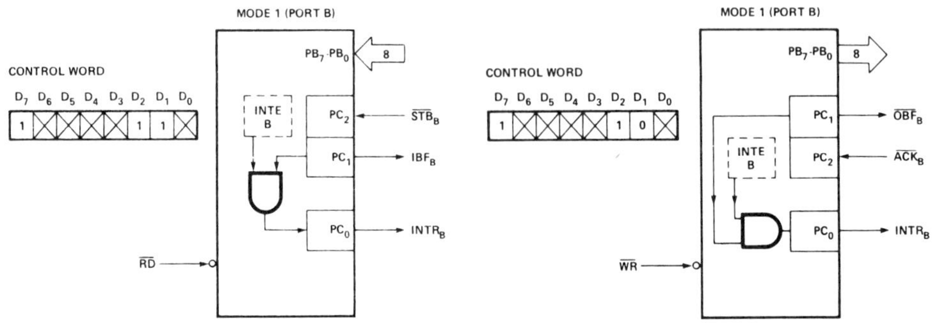

(a) (b)

Figure 7.13 **(a)** Mode 1 port B input configuration (*Courtesy of Intel Corporation*); **(b)** mode 1 port B output configuration (*Courtesy of Intel Corporation*).

at PC_6, $\overline{STB}_A$ at PC_4, IBF_A at PC_5, and $INTR_A$ at PC_3. Their functions are similar to those already discussed for MODE 1. One difference is that $INTR_A$ is produced by either gating $\overline{OBF}_A$ with $INTE_1$ or IBF_A with $INTE_2$.

In our discussion of MODE 1, we mentioned that the *bit set/reset* feature could be used to set the INTE bit to logic 0 or 1. This feature also allows the individual bits of PORT C to be set or reset. To do this, we write logic 0 to bit D_7 of the control register. This resets the bit set/reset flag. The logic level that is to be latched at a PORT C line is included as bit D_0 of the control word. This value is latched at the I/O line of PORT C, which corresponds to the 3-bit code at $D_3D_2D_1$.

The relationship between the set/reset control word and input/output lines is illustrated in Fig. 7.15. For instance, writing $D_7D_6D_5D_4D_3D_2D_1D_0 = 00001111_2$ into the control register of the 8255A selects bit 7 and sets it to 1. Therefore, output PC_7 at PORT C is switched to the 1 logic level.

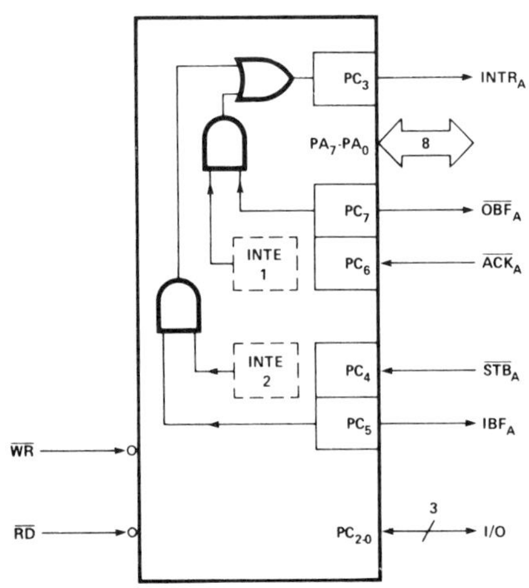

Figure 7.14 Mode 2 input/output configuration (*Courtesy of Intel Corporation*).

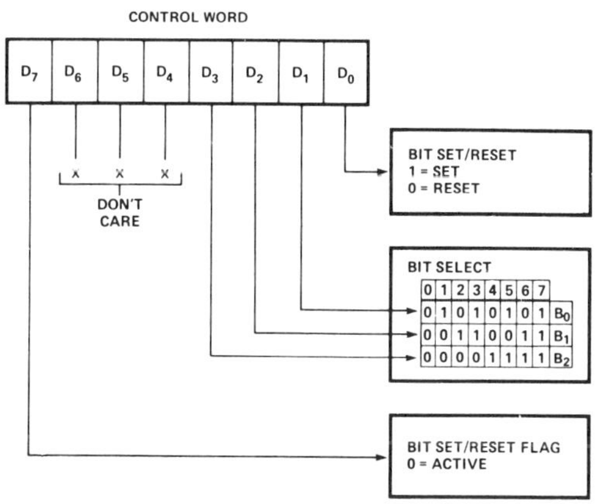

Figure 7.15 Bit set/reset format (*Courtesy of Intel Corporation*).

Example 7.8

The interrupt control flag $INTE_A$ is controlled by bit set/reset of PC_6. What command code must be written to the control register of the 8255A to set its value to logic 1?

Solution. To use the set/reset feature, D_7 must be logic 0. Moreover, $INTE_A$ is to be set to logic 1; therefore, D_0 must be logic 1. Finally, to select PC_6, the code at bits $D_3D_2D_1$ must be 110. The rest of the bits are don't-care states. This gives the control word

$$D_7D_6D_5D_4D_3D_2D_1D_0 = 0XXX1101_2$$

Replacing the don't-care states with the 0 logic level, we get

$$D_7D_6D_5D_4D_3D_2D_1D_0 = 00001101_2 = 0D_{16}$$

We have just described and given examples of each of the modes of operation that can be assigned to the ports of the 8255A. In practice, the A and B ports are frequently configured with different modes. For example, Fig. 7.16(a) shows the control word and port configuration of an 8255A set up for bidirectional MODE 2 operation of PORT A and input MODE 0 operation of PORT B.

Example 7.9

What control word must be written into the control register of the 8255A such that PORT A is configured for bidirectional operation and PORT B is set up with MODE 1 outputs?

Solution. To configure the mode of operation of the ports of the 8255A, D_7 must be 1.

$$D_7 = 1$$

PORT A is set up for bidirectional operation by making D_6 logic 1. In this case, D_5 through D_3 are don't-care states.

$$D_6 = 1$$

$$D_5D_4D_3 = XXX$$

MODE 1 is selected for PORT B by logic 1 in bit D_2 and output operation by logic 0 in D_1. Since MODE 1 operation has been selected, D_0 is a don't-care state.

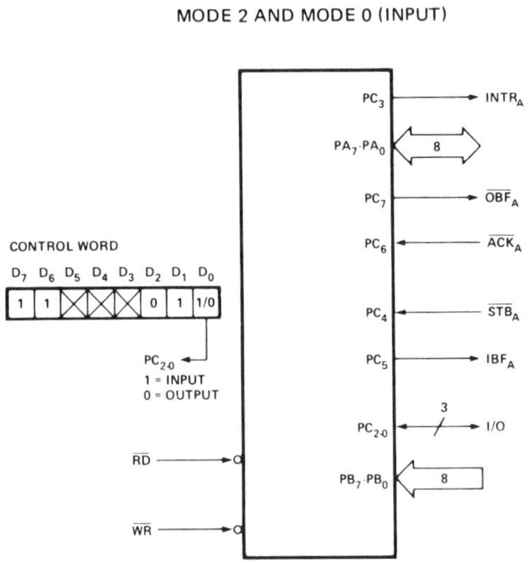

(a)

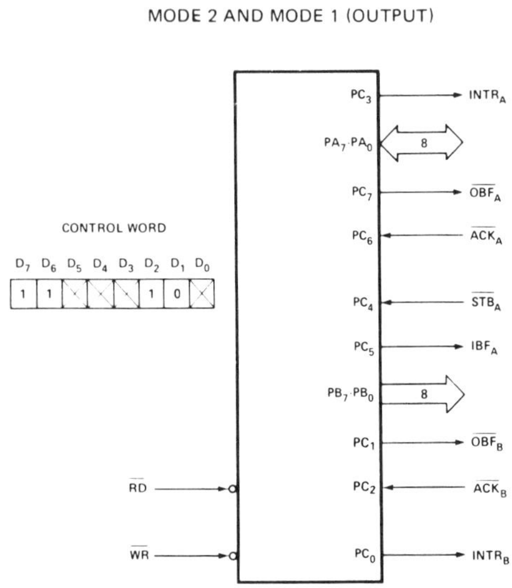

(b)

Figure 7.16 **(a)** Combined mode 2 and mode 0 (input) control word and I/O configuration (*Courtesy of Intel Corporation*); **(b)** combined mode 2 and mode 1 (output) control word and I/O configuration (*Courtesy of Intel Corporation*).

$$D_2 = 1$$
$$D_1 = 0$$
$$D_0 = X$$

This gives the control word

$$D_7D_6D_5D_4D_3D_2D_1D_0 = 11XXX10X_2$$

Assuming logic 0 for the don't-care states, we get

$$D_7D_6D_5D_4D_3D_2D_1D_0 = 11000100_2 = C4_{16}$$

This configuration is shown in Fig. 7.16(b).

Example 7.10

Write the sequence of instructions needed to load the control register of an 8255A with the control word formed in example 7.8. Assume that the 8255A resides at address $0F_{16}$ of the I/O address space.

Solution. First we must load AL with $C4_{16}$. This is the value of the control word that is to be output to the control register at address $0F_{16}$. The move instruction used to load AL is

```
MOV   AL, 0C4H
```

This data are output to the control register with the OUT instruction

```
OUT   0FH, AL
```

7.8 8255A IMPLEMENTATION OF PARALLEL I/O PORTS

The circuit in Fig. 7.17 shows how PPI devices can be connected to the bus of the 8086 to implement parallel input/output ports. This circuit configuration is for a minimum-mode 8086 microcomputer. Here we find that two groups each of up to eight 8255A devices are connected to the bus. Each group has its own 8205 address decoder. This decoder selects one of the devices at a time for input or output data transfers. The ports in the upper group are connected at odd-address boundaries and those in the lower group are at even-address boundaries. Each of these PPI devices provide up to three-byte-wide ports. In the circuit, they are labeled PORT A, PORT B, and PORT C. These ports can be individually configured as inputs or outputs through software. Therefore, each group is capable of implementing up to 192 I/O lines.

Let us look more closely at the connection of the upper port. Starting with the inputs of the 8205 address decoder, we see that its enable inputs are $\overline{E_1} = \overline{BHE}$ and $E_2 = M/\overline{IO}$. $\overline{BHE}$ is logic 0 whenever the 8086 outputs an odd address on the bus. Moreover, $M/\overline{IO}$ is switched to logic 0 whenever an I/O bus cycle is in progress. For this reason, the upper decoder is enabled for I/O bus cycles to an odd address in its part of the I/O address range.

When the 8205 decoder is enabled, the code at its A_0 through A_2 inputs causes one of the eight 8255A PPIs to get enabled for operation. Bits A_5 through A_3 of the I/O address are applied to these inputs of the decoder. It responds by switching the output corresponding to this 3-bit code to the 0 logic level. Decoder outputs O_0 through O_7 are applied to the chip select ($\overline{CS}$) inputs of the odd-addressed PPIs. For instance, $A_5A_4A_3 = 000$ switches output O_0 to logic 0. This enables the first 8255A, which is numbered 1 in Fig. 7.17.

At the same time that the PPI chip is selected, the 2-bit code A_2A_1 at inputs A_1A_0 of the 8255A selects the port for which data are input or output. For example, A_2A_1 equal 00 indicates that PORT A is to be accessed.

Since the upper group is located at odd-address boundaries, input/output data transfers take place over data bus lines D_8 through D_{15}. The timing of these read/write transfers are controlled by signals $\overline{RD}$ and $\overline{WR}$.

Example 7.11

What must be the address inputs of the even-addressed group of 8255As in Fig. 7.17 if PORT C of PPI 14 is to be accessed?

Solution. To enable PPI 14, the 8205 must be enabled for operation and its O_7 output switched to logic 0. This requires enable input $A_0 = 0$ and chip select code $A_5A_4A_3 = 111$.

$A_0 = 0$ Enables 8205

$A_5A_4A_3 = 111$ Selects PPI 14

PORT C of PPI 14 is selected with $A_1A_0 = 10$.

$A_2A_1 = 10$ Accesses PORT C

The rest of the address bits are don't-care states.

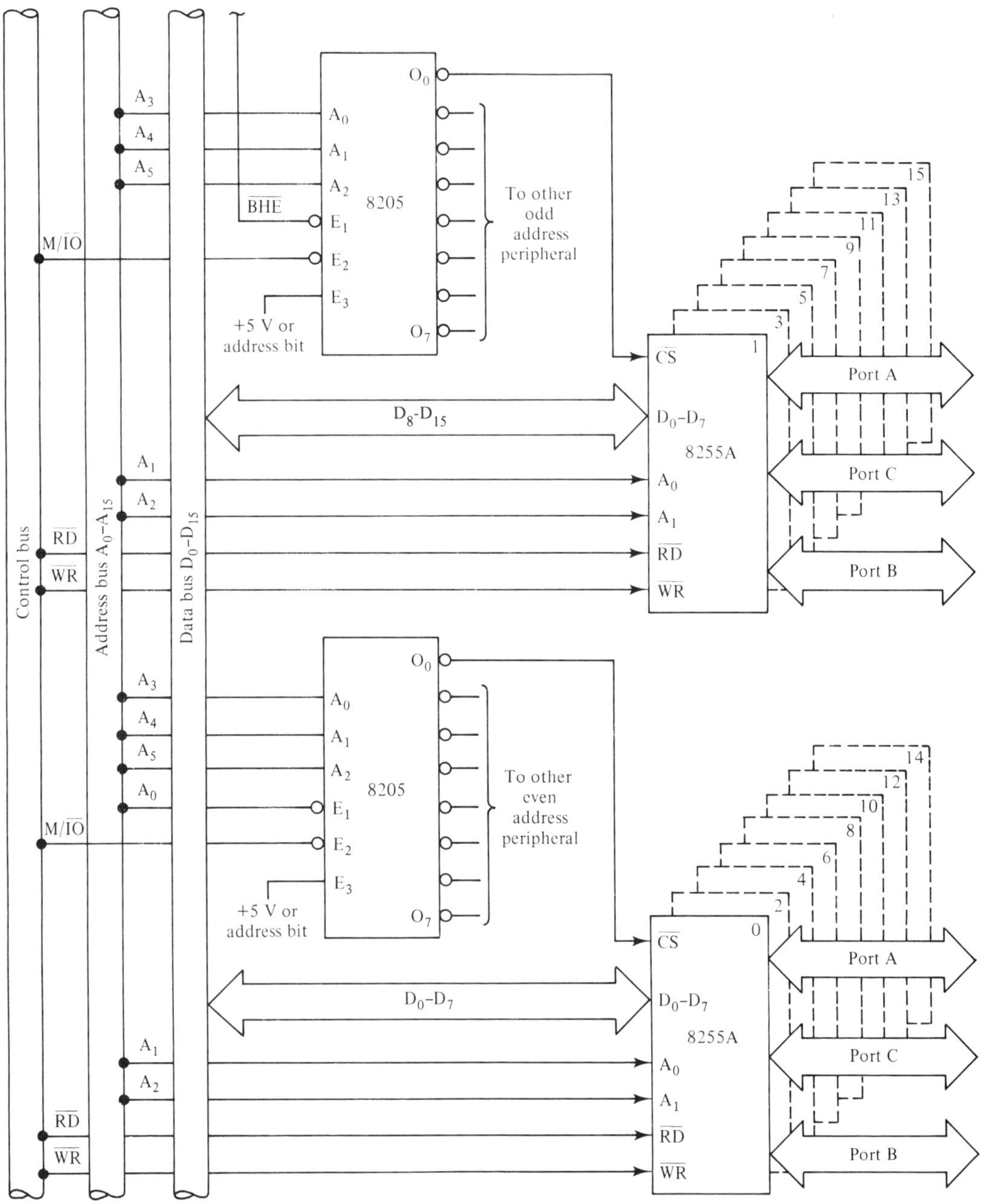

Figure 7.17 8255A parallel I/O ports at even and odd address boundaries (*Courtesy of Intel Corporation*).

Example 7.12

Assume that in Fig. 7.17 PPI 14 is configured such that port A is an output port and both port B and C are input ports and that all three ports are set up for MODE 0 operation. Write a program that will input the data at ports B and C, find the difference C–B, and output this difference to port A.

Solution. From the circuit diagram in Fig. 7.17, we find that the addresses of the three I/O ports on PPI 14 are

$$\text{PORT A} = 00111000_2 = 38_{16}$$

$$\text{PORT B} = 00111010_2 = 3A_{16}$$

$$\text{PORT C} = 00111110_2 = 3E_{16}$$

The data at ports B and C can be input with the instruction sequence

```
IN   AL, 3AH    ; READ PORT B
MOV  BL, AL     ; SAVE DATA FROM PORT B
IN   AL, 3EH    ; READ PORT C
```

Now the data from port B is subtracted from the data at port C with the instruction

```
SUB  AL, BL     ; SUBTRACT B FROM C
```

Finally, the difference is output to port A with the instruction

```
OUT  38H, AL    ; WRITE TO PORT A
```

7.9 MEMORY-MAPPED I/O

I/O devices such as the 8255A can be placed in the memory address space of the 8086 microcomputer as well as in an independent I/O address space. In this case the 8086 looks at an I/O port as though it were a memory location. For this reason, the method is known as *memory-mapped I/O*. In memory-mapped systems, some of the memory address space is dedicated to I/O ports. This permits talking to I/O ports using memory-oriented instructions such as MOV instead of the IN and OUT instructions.

The disadvantages of using this method are that part of the memory address space is lost and also the memory instructions tend to execute more slowly than those specifically designed for I/O. However, these disadvantages are frequently overcome by benefits such as that a larger number of instructions and addressing modes can be used to transfer data between the 8086 and its I/O ports. Another advantage is that data can now be located in registers other than just AL or AX.

The *memory-mapped I/O interface* of a minimum mode 8086 system is essentially the same as that employed in the accumulator I/O circuit of Fig. 7.17. Figure 7.18 shows the equivalent memory-mapped circuit. Ports are still selected by an address on the address bus and byte or word data are transferred between the 8086 and I/O

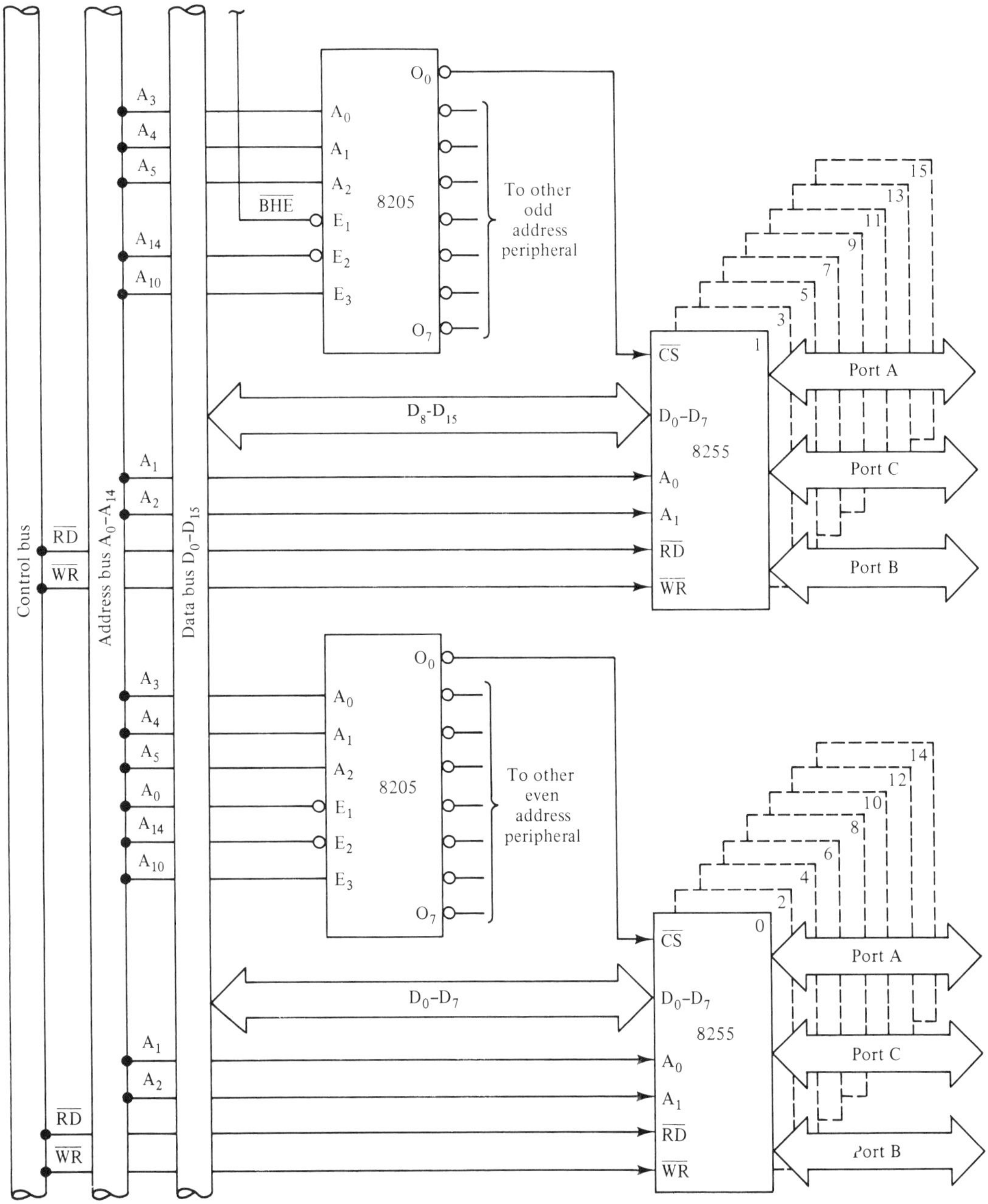

Figure 7.18 Memory mapped 8255A I/O ports (*Courtesy of Intel Corporation*).

device over the data bus. One difference is that now the full 20-bit address is available for addressing I/O. Therefore, memory-mapped I/O devices can reside anywhere in the 1M address space of the 8086.

Another difference is that during I/O operations memory read and write bus cycles are initiated instead of I/O bus cycles. This is because we are using memory instructions, not input/output instructions, to perform the data transfers. Furthermore, $M/\overline{IO}$ stays at the 1 logic level throughout the bus cycle. This indicates that a memory operation is in progress instead of an I/O operation.

The key difference between the circuits in Fig. 7.17 and 7.18 is that $M/\overline{IO}$ is no longer used as an enable input to the 8205. Instead, it is replaced by address bits A_{14} at enable input $\overline{E}_2$ and A_{10} at E_3. The I/O circuits are accessed whenever A_{14} is equal to logic 0 and A_{10} is equal to logic 1.

Example 7.13

Which I/O port in Fig. 7.18 is selected for operation when the memory address output on the bus is 0402_{16}?

Solution. We begin by converting the address to binary form. This gives

$$A_{15} \cdots A_1A_0 = 0000010000000010_2$$

In this address, bits $A_{14} = 0$, $A_{10} = 1$, and $A_0 = 0$. Therefore, the lower 8205 address decoder is enabled.

$$A_{14} = 0 \quad \text{Enables lower 8205 decoder}$$
$$A_{10} = 1$$
$$A_0 = 0$$

A memory-mapped I/O operation takes place to the port selected by $A_5A_4A_3 = 000$. This input code switches decoder output O_0 to logic 0 and chip selects PPI 0 for operation.

$$A_5A_4A_3 = 000 \quad \text{Selects PPI 0}$$
$$O_0 = 0$$

The port select inputs of the PPI are $A_2A_1 = 01$. These inputs cause PORT B to be accessed.

$$A_2A_1 = 01 \quad \text{PORT B accessed}$$

Thus the address 0402_{16} selects PORT B on PPI 0.

Example 7.14

Write the sequence of instructions needed to initialize the control register of PPI 0 in the circuit of Fig. 7.18 such that port A is an output port, ports B and C are input ports, and all three ports are configured for mode 0 operation.

Solution. Referring to Fig. 7.10, we find that the control byte required to provide this configuration is

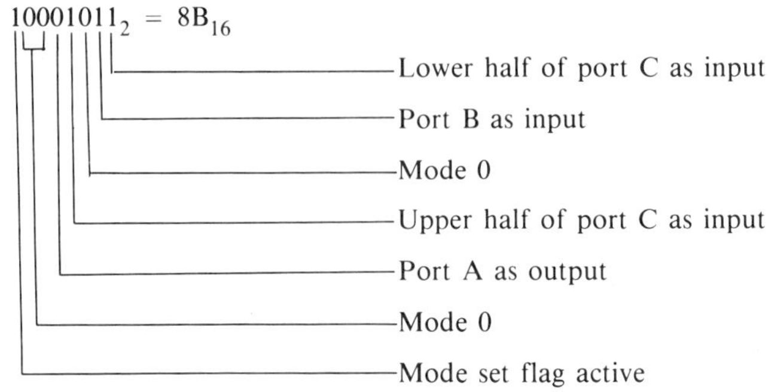

From the circuit diagram, the memory address of the control register for PPI 0 is found to be

$$\text{CONTROL REGISTER} = 00000000010000000110_2 = 00406_{16}$$

Since PPI 0 is memory-mapped, move instructions can be used to initialize the control register.

MOV DS, 0H ; CREATE DATA SEGMENT AT 00000_{16}
MOV AL, 08BH ; LOAD AL WITH CONTROL BYTE
MOV 406H, AL ; WRITE CONTROL BYTE TO PPI 0

Example 7.15

Assume that PPI 0 in Fig. 7.18 is configured as described in example 7.13. Write a program that will input the contents of ports B and C, AND them together, and output the results to port A.

Solution. From the circuit diagram, we find that the addresses of the three I/O ports on PPI 0 are

$$\text{PORT A} = 00400_{16}$$
$$\text{PORT B} = 00402_{16}$$
$$\text{PORT C} = 00404_{16}$$

Now we set up a data segment at 00000_{16} and input the data from ports B and C.

MOV DS, 0H ; CREATE DATA SEGMENT AT 00000_{16}
MOV BL, 402H ; READ PORT B
MOV AL, 404H ; READ PORT C

Next the contents of AL and BL must be ANDed and the result output to port A.

AND AL, BL ; AND DATA AT PORTS B AND C
MOV 400H, AL ; WRITE TO PORT A

7.10 SERIAL COMMUNICATIONS INTERFACE

Another type of I/O interface that is widely used in microcomputer systems is known as a *serial communications port*. This is the type of interface that is used to connect peripheral units, such as CRT terminals and printers, to a microcomputer. It permits data to be transferred between the various units of the system. For instance, data input at the keyboard of a terminal are passed to the MPU part of the microcomputer through this type of interface. Let us now look into the different types of serial interfaces that are implemented in microcomputer systems.

Synchronous and Asynchronous Data Communications

Two types of *serial data communications* are widely used in microcomputer systems. They are called *asynchronous communications* and *synchronous communications*. By synchronous, we mean that the receiver and transmitter sections of the two pieces of equipment that are communicating with each other must run synchronously. For this reason, as shown in Fig. 7.19(a), the interface includes a CLOCK line as well as TRANSMIT DATA, RECEIVE DATA, and SIGNAL COMMON lines. It is the clock signal that synchronizes both the transmission and reception of data.

The format used for synchronous communication of data is shown in Fig. 7.19(b). To initiate synchronous transmission, the transmitter first sends out synchronization characters to the receiver. The receiver reads the synchronization bit pattern and compares it to a known sync pattern. Once they are identified as being the same, the receiver begins to read character data off the communications line.

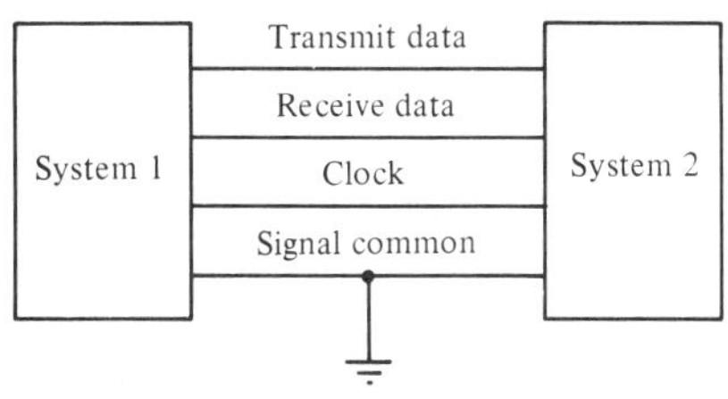

(a)

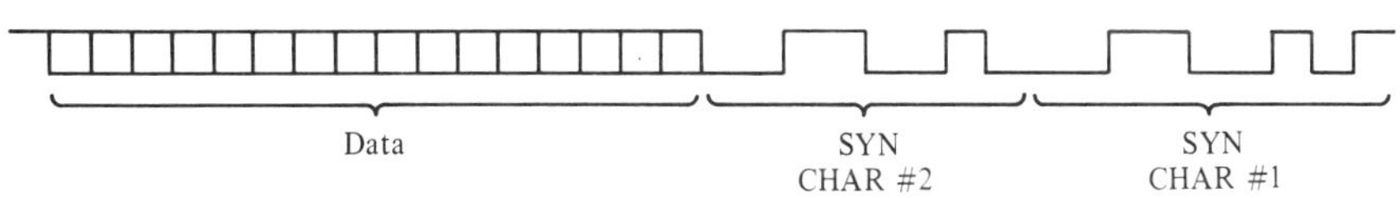

(b)

Figure 7.19 **(a)** Synchronous communications interface; **(b)** synchronous data transmission format.

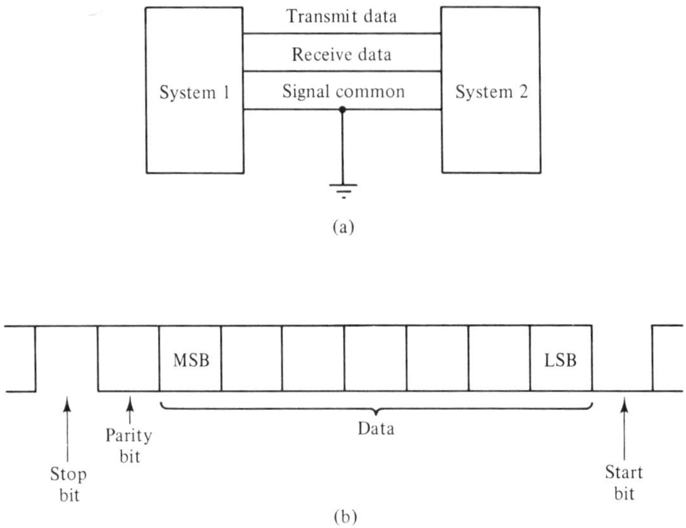

Figure 7.20 **(a)** Asynchronous communications interface; **(b)** asynchronous data transmission format.

Transfer of data continues until the complete block of data is received or synchronization is lost between the receiver and transmitter. If large blocks of data are being sent, the synchronization characters may be periodically resent to assure that synchronization is maintained. The synchronous type of communications is typically used in applications where high-speed data transfer is required.

The asynchronous method of communications eliminates the need for the CLOCK signal. As shown in Fig. 7.20(a), the simplest form of an asynchronous communication interface could consist of a RECEIVE DATA, TRANSMIT DATA, and SIGNAL COMMON communication lines. In this case, the data to be transmitted are sent out one character at a time and at the receiver end of the communication line synchronization is performed by examining synchronization bits that are included at the beginning and end of each character.

The format of a typical asynchronous character is shown in Fig. 7.20(b). Here we see that the synchronization bit at the beginning of the character is called the *START bit* and that at the end of the character the *STOP bit*. Depending on the communications scheme, 1, $1\frac{1}{2}$, or 2 STOP bits can be used. The bits of the character are embedded between the START and STOP bits. Notice that the START bit is either input or output first. It is followed in the serial bit stream by the LSB of the character, the other 6 bits of the character, a parity bit, and the STOP bits. For instance, 7-bit ASCII can be used and parity added as an eighth bit for higher reliability in transmission. The duration of each bit in the format is called a *bit time*.

The fact that an 0 or 1 logic level is being transferred over the communication line is identified by whether the voltage level on the line corresponds to that of a *MARK* or a *SPACE*. The START bit is always to the MARK level. It synchronizes the receiver to the transmitter and signals that the unit receiving data should start assembling the character. STOP bits are to the SPACE level. This assures that the receiving unit sees a transition of logic level at the START bit of the next character.

The USART and UART

Because serial communication interfaces are so widely used in modern electronic equipment, special LSI peripheral devices have been developed to permit easy implementation of these types of interfaces. Some of the names that these devices go by are *UART* (*universal asynchronous receiver/transmitter*) and *USART* (*universal synchronous/asynchronous receiver/transmitter*).

Both UARTs and USARTs have the ability to perform the parellel-to-serial conversions needed in the transmission of data and the serial-to-parallel conversions needed in the reception of data. For data that are transmitted asynchronously, they also have the ability to frame the character automatically with a START bit, PARITY bit, and the appropriate STOP bits.

Moreover, for reception of data, UARTs and USARTs typically have the ability to check characters automatically as they are received for correct parity, and for two other errors, known as *framing error* and *overrun error*. A framing error means that after the detection of the beginning of a character with a START bit the appropriate number of STOP bits were not detected. This means that the character that was transmitted was not received correctly and should be resent. An overrun error means that the prior character that was received was not read out of the USARTs receive data register by the microprocessor before another character was received. Therefore, the first character was lost and should be retransmitted.

A block diagram of a UART is shown in Fig. 7.21. Here we see that it has four key signal interfaces: the microprocessor interface, the transmitter interface, the receiver interface, and the handshake control interface. Let us now look at each of these interfaces in more detail.

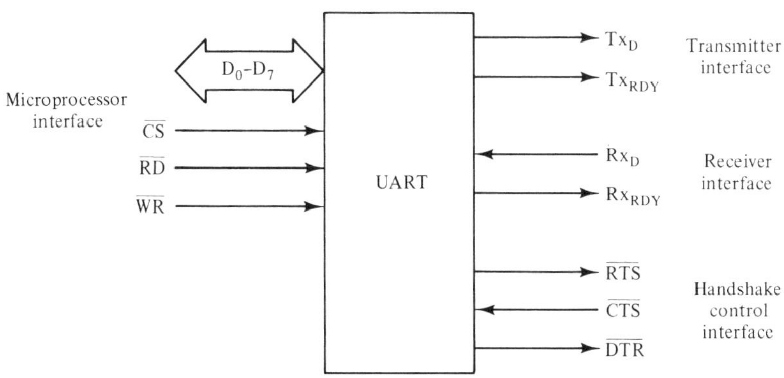

Figure 7.21 Block diagram of a UART.

LSI USARTs and UARTs cannot stand alone in a communication system. Their operation must be controlled by a general-purpose processor such as a microprocessor. The *microprocessor interface* is the interface that is used to connect the UART to an MPU. Looking at Fig. 7.21, we see that this interface consists of an 8-bit bidirectional data bus (D_0–D_7) and three control lines, $\overline{CS}$, $\overline{RD}$, and $\overline{WR}$.

All data transfers between the UART and MPU take place over the 8-bit data bus. Two uses of this bus are for the input of character data from the receiver of the UART and for the output of character data to its transmitter. Other types of information are also passed between the MPU and UART. Examples are mode control instructions, operation command instructions, and status.

LSI UARTs, just like the 8255A LSI peripheral we discussed earlier in the chapter, can be configured for various modes of operation through software. Mode control instructions are what must be issued to a UART to initialize its control registers for the desired mode of operation. For example, the format of the data frame used for transmitted or received data can be configured through software. Typical options are character length equal to from 5 to 8 bits; even, odd, or no parity; and 1, $1\frac{1}{2}$, or 2 STOP bits.

Earlier we pointed out that a UART cannot perform the communication function on its own. Instead, the sequence of events that is needed to initiate transmission and reception is controlled by commands issued to the UART by the MPU. For instance, the MPU can initiate a request for transmission of data to another unit by writing a command to the UART that forces its $\overline{RTS}$ control output to its active 0 logic level. The logic 0 at $\overline{RTS}$ signals the system at the other end of the communication line to prepare to receive data. At the receiver end of the communication line, the MPU can acknowledge that it is ready to receive data by sending a command to its UART that forces the $\overline{DTR}$ control output to logic 0.

Most UARTs have a *status register* that contains information related to its current state. For example, it may contain flag bits that represent the current logic state of signal lines such as $\overline{RTS}$ and $\overline{DTR}$. This permits the MPU to examine the logic state of these lines through software.

Besides information about the logic level of control lines, the status register typically contains flag bits for error conditions such as parity error, overrun error, and framing error. After reception of a character, the MPU can first read these bits to assure that a valid character has been received, and if the bits are at their inactive levels, the character should be read from the receive data register within the UART.

At the other side of the block in Fig. 7.21, we find the *transmitter* and *receiver interfaces*. The transmitter interface has two signal lines: transmit data (Tx_D) and transmitter ready (Tx_{RDY}). Tx_D is the line over which the transmitter section of the UART outputs serial character data. As shown in Fig. 7.22, this output line is connected to the receive data (Rx_D) input of the receiver section in the system at the other end of the communication line.

Usually, the transmitter section of an LSI UART can hold only one character at a time. This character datum is held in the *transmit data register* within the UART.

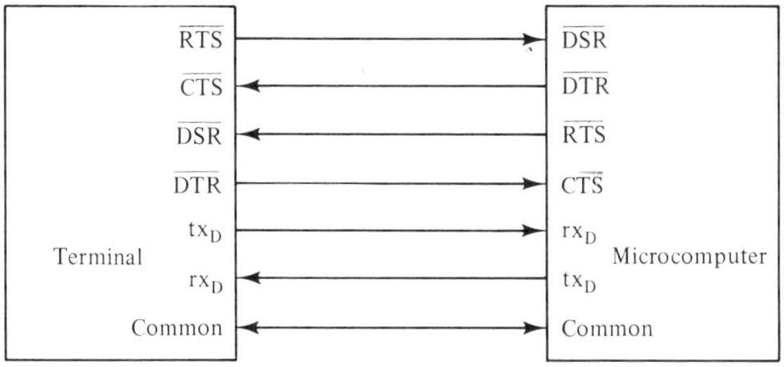

Figure 7.22 Simple asynchronous communications interface between a microcomputer and terminal.

Since only one character can be held within the UART, it must signal the MPU when it has completed transmission of this character. The Tx_{RDY} line is provided for this purpose. As soon as transmission of the character is complete, the transmitter switches Tx_{RDY} to its active logic level. This signal should be returned to an interrupt input of the MPU. In this way, its occurrence can cause program control to be passed quickly to a service routine that will output another character to the transmitter data register and then reinitiate transmission.

The receiver section is similar to the transmitter we just described. However, here the receive data (Rx_D) line is the input that accepts bit-serial character data that are transmitted from the other system's transmitter. Moreover, the receiver ready (Rx_{RDY}) output is again used as an interrupt to the MPU. But this time it signals the MPU that a character has been received. The service routine that is initiated must first determine whether or not the character is valid, and if it is, it must read the character out of the UART's *receive data register*.

Using the handshake control signals $\overline{RTS}$, $\overline{DSR}$, $\overline{DTR}$, and $\overline{CTS}$, different types of *asynchronous communication protocols* can be implemented through the serial I/O interface. By protocol we mean a handshake sequence by which two systems signal each other that they are ready to communicate.

A simple asynchronous communication interface that uses these control lines is shown in Fig. 7.22. In this example, a protocol can be set up such that when the terminal wants to send data to the microcomputer it will issue a request at its request to send ($\overline{RTS}$) output. To do this, the MPU of the terminal must issue a command to the UART that causes it to set the $\overline{RTS}$ line to its active 0 logic level. $\overline{RTS}$ of the terminal is applied to the data terminal ready ($\overline{DTR}$) input of the microcomputer. In this way, it tells the microcomputer that the terminal wants to transmit data to it.

When the microcomputer is ready to receive data, it acknowledges this fact to the terminal by activating the data set ready ($\overline{DSR}$) output of its UART. The MPU in the microcomputer does this by issuing a command to the UART that switches $\overline{DSR}$ to its active 0 logic level. This signal is returned to the clear to send ($\overline{CTS}$) input of the terminal's UART and tells the UART in the terminal to start outputting data on Tx_D. At the same time, the receiver section in the UART within the microcomputer begins to read data from its Rx_D input.

Baud Rate and the Baud Rate Generator

The rate at which data transfers take place over the receive and transmit lines is known as the *baud rate*. By baud rate we mean the number of bits of data that are transferred per second of time. For instance, some of the common data transfer rates are 300 baud, 1200 baud, and 9600 baud. They correspond to 300 bits/second (bps), 1200 bps, and 9600 bps, respectively.

The baud rate at which data are transferred determines the *bit time*. That is, the amount of time each bit of data is on the communication line. At 300 baud, the bit time is found to be

$$t_{BT} = 1/300 \text{ bps} = 3.33 \text{ ms}$$

Baud rate is set by a part of the serial communication interface called the *baud rate generator*. This part of the interface generates the clock signal that is used to drive the receiver and transmitter parts of the UART. Some LSI UARTs have a built-in baud rate generator; others need an external circuit to provide this function.

The RS-232C Interface

The *RS-232C interface* is a standard hardware interface for implementing asynchronous serial data communication ports on devices such as printers, CRT terminals, keyboards, and modems. The pin definitions and electrical characteristics of this interface are defined by the *Electronic Industries Association* (EIA). The aim behind publishing standards such as the RS-232C is to assure compatibility between equipment made by different manufacturers.

Peripherals that connect to a microcomputer can be located anywhere from several feet to many feet from the system. For instance, in large systems it is common to have the microcomputer part of the system in a separate room from the terminals and printers. This leads us to the main advantage of using a serial interface to connect peripherals to a microcomputer, which is that as few as three signal lines can be used to connect the peripheral to the MPU: a RECEIVE DATA line, a TRANSMIT DATA line, and a COMMON GROUND. This results in a large savings in wiring costs and the small number of lines that need to be put in place also leads to higher reliability.

The RS-232C standard defines a 25-pin interface. Figure 7.23 lists each pin and its function. Note that the three signals that we mentioned earlier, TRANSMIT DATA, RECEIVE DATA, and SIGNAL COMMON, are located at pins 2, 3, and 7, respectively. Pins are also provided for additional control functions. For instance, pins 4 and 5 are the REQUEST TO SEND and CLEAR TO SEND control signals. These two signals are also frequently used when implementing an asynchronous communication interface.

The RS-232C interface is specified to operate correctly over a maximum distance of 100 feet. To satisfy this distance specification, a bus driver is used to buffer the transmit line to provide the appropriate drive current and a bus receiver is used at the receive line. RS-232C drivers and receivers are available as standard ICs. These

Pin	Signal
1	Protective Ground
2	Transmitted Data
3	Received Data
4	Request to Send
5	Clear to Send
6	Data Set Ready
7	Signal Ground (Common Return)
8	Received Line Signal Detector
9	Reserved for Data Set Testing
10	Reserved for Data Set Testing
11	Unassigned
12	Secondary Received Line Signal Detector
13	Secondary Clear to Send
14	Secondary Transmitted Data
15	Transmission Signal Element Timing
16	Secondary Received Data
17	Receiver Signal Element Timing
18	Unassigned
19	Secondary Request to Send
20	Data Terminal Ready
21	Signal Quality Detector
22	Ring Indicator
23	Data Signal Rate Selector
24	Transmit Signal Element Timing
25	Unassigned

Figure 7.23 RS-232C interface pins and functions.

buffers do both the voltage-level translation needed to convert the TTL-compatible outputs of the USART to the MARK and SPACE voltage levels defined for the RS-232C interface. The voltage levels that are normally transmitted for a MARK and a SPACE are +12 V dc and −12 V dc, respectively. For the RS-232C interface, all voltages below −3 V dc are equal to a MARK and all voltages above +3 V dc are considered a SPACE.

The RS-232C interface is specified to support baud rates of up to 20,000 bps. In general, the receive and transmit baud rates do not have to be the same; however, in most simpler systems they are set to the same value. For instance, a baud rate that is widely used in communication between an MPU and a printer is 1200 bps. This corresponds to a bit time equal to .833 ms.

Simplex, Half-Duplex, and Full-Duplex Communication Links

Applications require different types of asynchronous links to be implemented. For instance, the *communication link* needed to connect a printer to a microcomputer just needs to support communications in one direction. That is, the printer is an output-only device; therefore, the MPU only needs to transmit data to the printer. Data are not transmitted back. In this case, as shown in Fig. 7.24(a), a single unidirectional communication line can be used to connect the printer and microcomputer together. This type of connection is known as a *simplex communication link*.

Other devices, such as the CRT terminal with keyboard shown in Fig. 7.24(b), need to both transmit data to and receive data from the MPU. That is, they must both input and output data. This requirement can also be satisfied with a single communication line by setting up a *half-duplex communication link*. In a half-duplex link, data are transmitted and received over the same line; therefore, transmission and reception of data cannot take place at the same time.

If higher-performance communication is required, separate transmit and receive lines can be used to connect the peripheral and microcomputer. When this is done, data can be transferred in both directions at the same time. This type of link is illustrated in Fig. 7.24(c). It is called a *full-duplex communication link*.

7.11 THE 8251A PROGRAMMABLE COMMUNICATION INTERFACE

The *8251A programmable communication interface* is another important LSI peripheral for the 8086 microcomputer system. It permits simple implementation of a serial data communications interface. For instance, it can be used to implement an RS-232C port. This is the type of interface that is used to connect a CRT terminal or printer

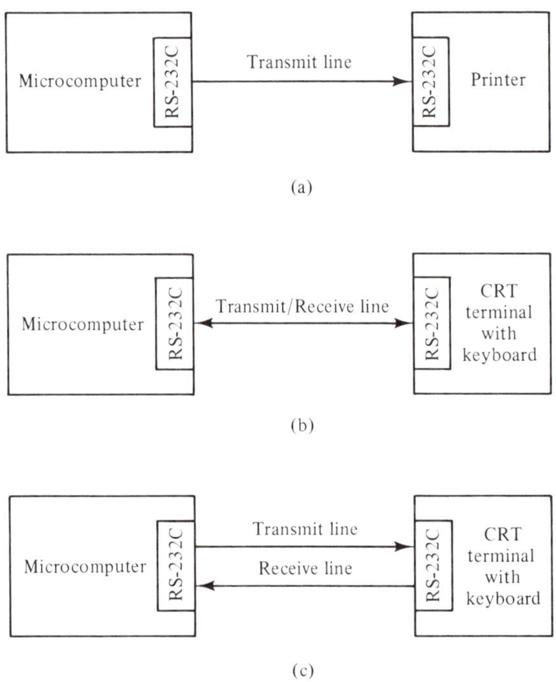

Figure 7.24 **(a)** Simplex communications link; **(b)** half-duplex communications link; **(c)** full-duplex communications link.

to a microcomputer. To support connection of these two peripheral devices, the microcomputer would need two independent RS-232C I/O ports. The 8251A is one of the most widely used USART ICs. As its name implies, the 8251A is capable of implementing either an asynchronous or synchronous communication interface. Here we will concentrate on its use as an asynchronous communication controller.

The programmability of the 8251A provides for a very flexible asynchronous communication interface. It contains a full-duplex receiver and transmitter, which can be configured through software for communication of data using formats with character lengths between five and eight characters, with even or odd parity, and with 1, $1\frac{1}{2}$, or 2 STOP bits. Moreover, it has the ability to detect automatically the occurrence of parity, framing, and overrun errors during data reception.

Internal Architecture of the 8251A

A block diagram showing the internal architecture of the 8251A is shown in Fig. 7.25(a) and its pin layout in Fig. 7.25(b). From this diagram we find that it includes four key sections: the *bus interface section*, which consists of the data bus buffer and read/write control logic blocks; the *transmit section*, which consists of the transmit buffer and transmit control blocks; the *receive section*, which consists of the receive buffer and receive control blocks; and the *modem control section*. Let us now look at each of these sections in more detail.

The bus interface section is used to connect the 8251A to a microprocessor such as the 8086. Notice that the interface includes an 8-bit bidirectional data bus D_0 through D_7 that is driven by the data bus buffer. It is over these lines that the microprocessor transfers commands to the 8251A, reads its status register, and inputs or outputs character data.

Data transfers over the bus are controlled by the signals $C/\overline{D}$ (control/data), $\overline{RD}$ (read), $\overline{WR}$ (write), and $\overline{CS}$ (chip select), which are all inputs to the read/write control logic section. Typically, the 8251A is located at a specific address in the microcomputer's I/O or memory address space. When the microprocessor is to access registers within the 8251A, it puts this address on the address bus. The address is decoded by external circuitry and must produce logic 0 at the $\overline{CS}$ input. This input must be logic 0 for a read or write bus cycle to take place to the 8251A.

The other three control signals, $C/\overline{D}$, $\overline{RD}$, and $\overline{WR}$, tell the 8251A what type of data transfer is to take place over the bus. Figure 7.26 shows the various types of read/write operations that can occur. For example, the first state in the table, $C/\overline{D} = 0$, $\overline{RD} = 0$, and $\overline{WR} = 1$, corresponds to a character data transfer from the 8251A to the microprocessor. Notice that in general, $\overline{RD} = 0$ signals that the microprocessor is reading data from the 8251A, $\overline{WR} = 0$ indicates that data are being written into the 8251A, and the logic level of $C/\overline{D}$ indicates whether character data, control information, or status information is on the data bus.

Example 7.15

What type of data transfer is taking place over the bus if the control signals are at $\overline{CS} = 0$, $C/\overline{D} = 1$, $\overline{RD} = 0$, and $\overline{WR} = 1$?

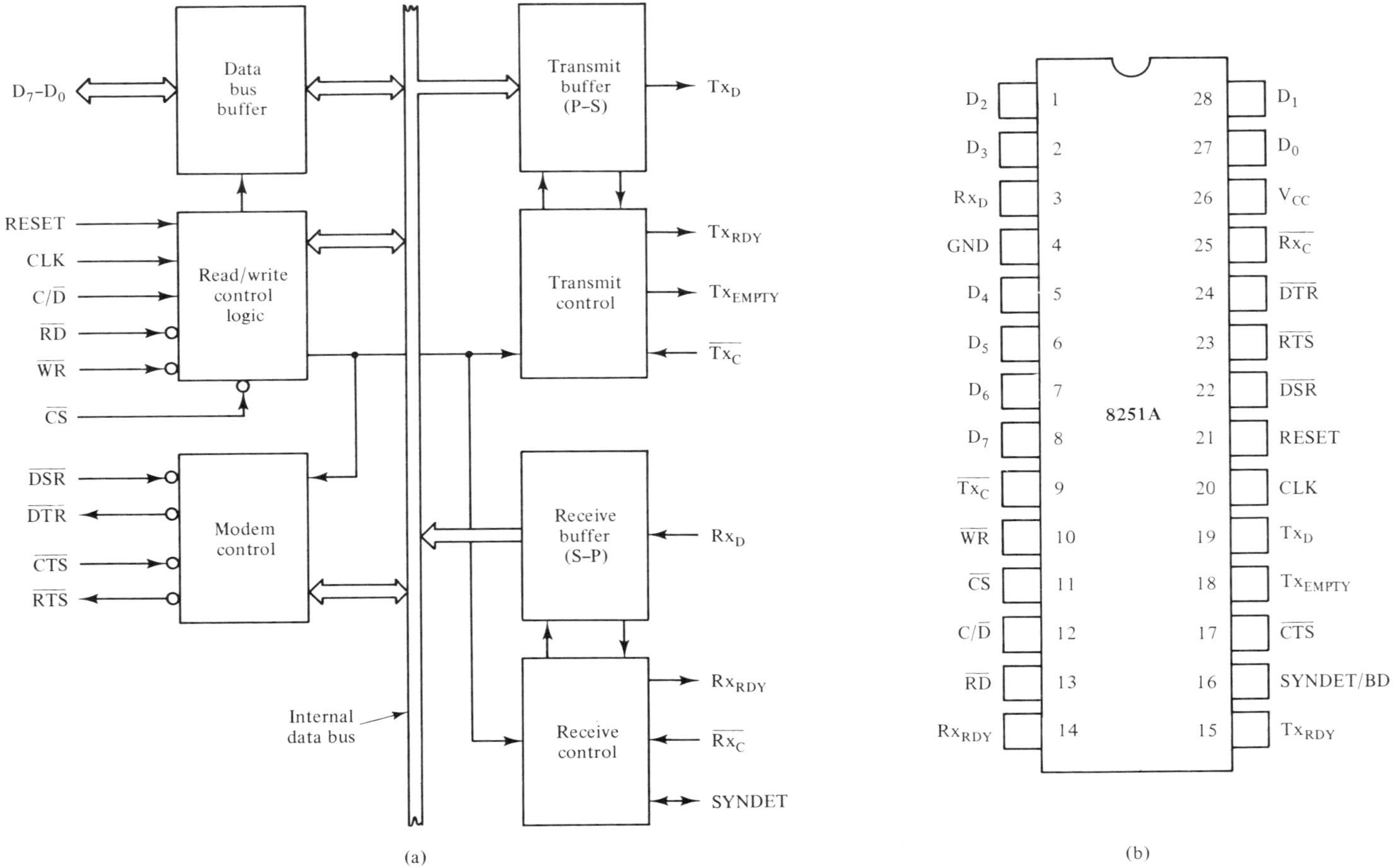

Figure 7.25 **(a)** Block diagram of the 8215A *(Courtesy of Intel Corporation);* **(b)** pin layout *(Courtesy of Intel Corporation).*

$C/\overline{D}$	$\overline{RD}$	$\overline{WR}$	$\overline{CS}$	Operation
0	0	1	0	8251A Data → Data bus
0	1	0	0	Data bus → 8251A Data
1	0	1	0	Status → Data bus
1	1	0	0	Data bus → Control
X	1	1	0	Data bus → 3-State
X	X	X	1	Data bus → 3-State

Figure 7.26 Read/write operations (*Courtesy of Intel Corporation*).

Solution. Looking at the table in Fig. 7.26, we see that $\overline{CS} = 0$ means that the 8251A's data bus has been enabled for operation. Since $C/\overline{D}$ is 1 and $\overline{RD}$ is 0, status information is read from within the 8251A.

The receiver section is responsible for reading the serial bit stream of data at the Rx_D (receive data) input and converting it to parallel form. When a MARK voltage level is detected on this line, the receiver enables a counter. As the counter increments to a value equal to one-half a bit time, the logic level at the Rx_D line is sampled again. If it is still at the MARK level, a valid START pulse has been detected. Then Rx_D is examined every time the counter increments through another bit time. This continues until a complete character is assembled and the STOP bit is read. After this, the complete character is transferred into the receive data register.

During reception of a character, the receiver automatically checks the character data for parity, framing, or overrun errors. If one of these conditions occurs, it is flagged by setting a bit in the status register. Then the Rx_{RDY} (receiver ready) output is switched to the 1 logic level. This signal is sent to the microprocessor to tell it that a character is available and should be read from the receive data register. Rx_{RDY} is automatically reset to logic 0 when the MPU reads the contents of the receive data register.

The 8251A does not have a built-in baud rate generator. For this reason, the clock signal that is used to set the baud rate must be externally generated and applied to the Rx_C input of the receiver. Through software the 8251A can be set up to internally divide the clock signal input at Rx_C by 1, 16, or 64.

The transmitter does the opposite of the receiver section. It receives parallel character data from the MPU over the data bus. The character is then automatically framed with the START bit, appropriate parity bit, and the correct number of STOP bits and put into the transmit data buffer register. Finally, it is shifted out of this register to produce a bit-serial output on the Tx_D line. When the transmit data buffer register is empty, the Tx_{RDY} output switches to logic 1. This signal is to be returned to the MPU to tell it that another character should be output to the transmitter section. When the MPU writes another character out to the transmitter buffer register, the Tx_{RDY} output resets.

Data are output on the transmit line at the baud rate set by the external transmitter clock signal that is input at Tx_C. In most applications, the transmitter and receiver operate at the same baud rate. Therefore, both Rx_C and Tx_C are supplied by the

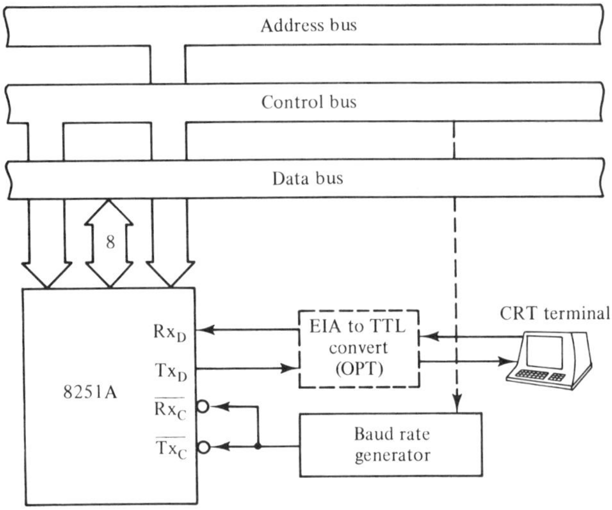

Figure 7.27 Receiver and transmitter driven at the same baud rate (*Courtesy of Intel Corporation*).

same baud rate generator. The circuit in Fig. 7.27 shows this type of system configuration.

The operation of the 8251A is controlled through the setting of bits in three internal control registers: the *mode control register*, *command register*, and the *status register*. For instance, the way in which the 8251A's receiver and transmitter operate is determined by the contents of the mode control register. Figure 7.28 shows the organization of the mode control register and the function of each of its bits. Note that the two least significant bits B_1 and B_2 determine whether the device operates as an asynchronous or synchronous communication controller and how the external baud rate input is divided within the 8251A. For example, if these two bits are 11, it is set for asynchronous operation with divide by 64 for the baud rate input. The two bits that follow these, L_1 and L_2, set the length of the character. For instance, when information is being transmitted and received as 7-bit ASCII characters, these bits should be loaded with 10.

The next two bits, PEN and EP, determine whether parity is in use and if so, whether it is even parity or odd parity. Looking at Fig. 7.28, we see that PEN enables or disables parity. To enable parity, it is set. Furthermore, when parity is enabled, logic 0 in EP selects odd parity and logic 1 in this position selects even parity. To disable parity, all we need to do is reset PEN.

We will assume that the 8251A is working in the asynchronous mode; therefore, bits S_1 and S_2 determine the number of STOP bits. Note that if 11 is loaded into these bit positions, the character is transmitted with 2 STOP bits.

Example 7.16

What value is to be written into the mode control register in order to configure the 8251A such that it works as an asynchronous communications controller with the baud rate internally divided by 16? Character size is to be 8 bits for EBCDIC, and odd parity and one STOP bit are also to be selected.

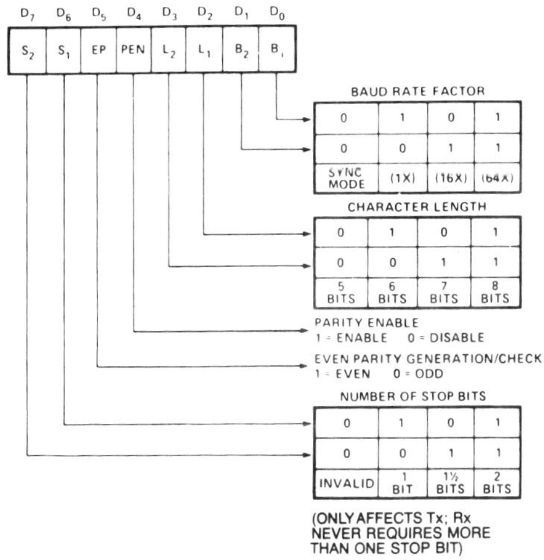

Figure 7.28 Mode instruction format (*Courtesy of Intel Corporation*).

Solution. From Fig. 7.28, we find that B_2B_1 must be set to 10 in order to select asynchronous operation with divide by 16 for the external baud rate input.

$$B_2B_1 = 10$$

To select a character length of 8 bits, the next two bits are both made logic 1. This gives

$$L_2L_1 = 11$$

To set up odd parity, EP and PEN must be made equal to 0 and 1, respectively.

$$(EP)\ (PEN) = 01$$

Finally, S_2S_1 are set to 01 for one STOP bit.

$$S_2S_1 = 01$$

Therefore, the complete control word is

$$D_7D_6 \ldots\ldots D_0 = 01011110_2$$
$$= 5E_{16}$$

Once the configuration for asynchronous communications has been set up in the mode control register, the operation of the serial interface can be controlled by the microprocessor by issuing commands to the command register within the 8251A. The format of the *command instruction byte* and the function of each of its bits is shown in Fig. 7.29. Let us look at the function of just a few of its bits.

Tx_{EN} and Rx_{EN} are enable bits for the transmitter and receiver. Since both the receiver and transmitter can operate simultaneously, these two bits can both be set. Rx_{EN} is actually an enable signal to the Rx_{RDY} signal. It does not turn the receiver section on and off. The receiver runs at all times, but if Rx_{EN} is set to 0, the 8251A does not signal the MPU that a character has been received by switching Rx_{RDY} to logic 1. The same is true for Tx_{EN}. It enables the Tx_{RDY} signal.

The ER bit of the command register can be used to reset the error bits of the

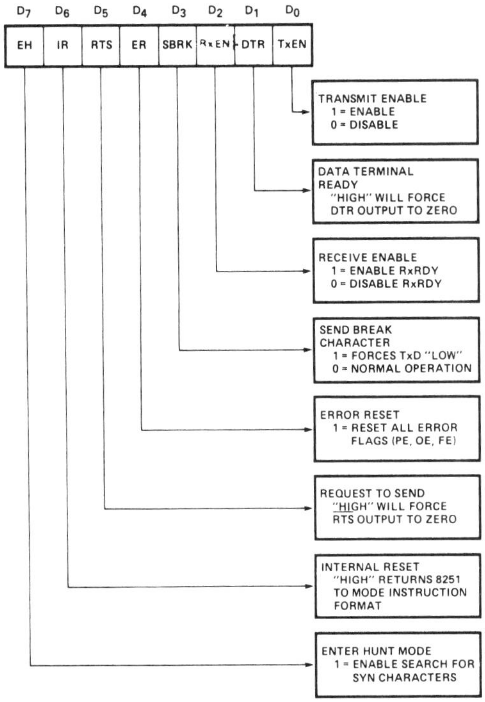

Figure 7.29 Command instruction format (*Courtesy of Intel Corporation*).

status register. The status register of the 8251A is shown in Fig. 7.30. Notice that bits PE, OE, and FE are error flags for the receiver. If the incoming character is found to have a parity error, the PE (parity error) bit gets set. On the other hand, if an overrun or framing error condition occurs, the OE (overrun error) or FE (framing error) flag is set, respectively. The MPU should always examine these error bits before reading a character from the receive data register. If an error has occurred, a command should be issued to the command register to write a 1 into the ER bit. This causes all three of the error flags in the status register to be reset. Then a software routine can be initiated to cause the character to be retransmitted.

Let us look at just one more bit of the command register. The IR bit, which stands for *internal reset,* allows the 8251A to be initialized under software control. To initialize the device, the MPU simply writes a 1 into the IR bit.

Example 7.17

What are the meanings of the Tx_{RDY}, Rx_{RDY}, and Tx_{EN} bits of the status register?

Solution. Looking at Fig. 7.30, we find that these three bits of the status register always reflect the logic levels of the Tx_{RDY} , Rx_{RDY}, and Tx_{EN} signal lines. Reading of the status register permits the MPU to determine the logic level of these signals through software.

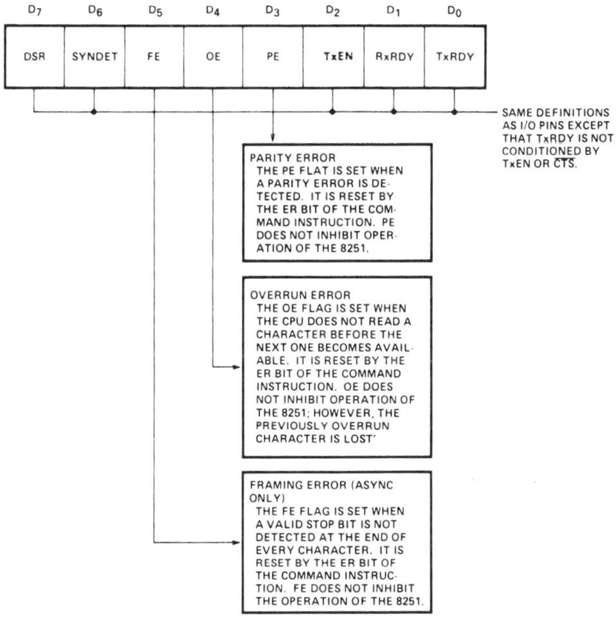

Figure 7.30 Status register (*Courtesy of Intel Corporation*).

Initializing the 8251A

Before the 8251A can be used to receive or transmit characters, its mode control and command registers must be initialized. The flowchart in Fig. 7.31 shows the sequence that must be followed when initializing the device. Let us just briefly trace through the sequence of events needed to set up the controller for asynchronous operation.

As the microcomputer powers up, it should issue a hardware reset to the 8251A. This is done by switching its RESET input to logic 1. After this, a load mode instruction must be issued to write the new configuration byte into the mode control register. Assuming that the 8251A is in the I/O address space of the 8086, the command byte formed in Example 7.16 can be written to the command register with the instruction sequence

```
MOV AL,05EH
OUT MODE
```

where MODE is a variable assigned to the address of the 8251A.

Since bits B_2B_1 of this register are not 00, asynchronous mode of operation is selected. Therefore, we go down the branch in the flowchart to the load command instruction. Execution of another OUT instruction can load the command register with its initial value. For instance, this command could enable the transmitter and receiver by setting the Tx_{EN} and Rx_{EN} bits, respectively. Next, the reset bit of the command register is tested and since we did not set it, the USART is ready to transfer data.

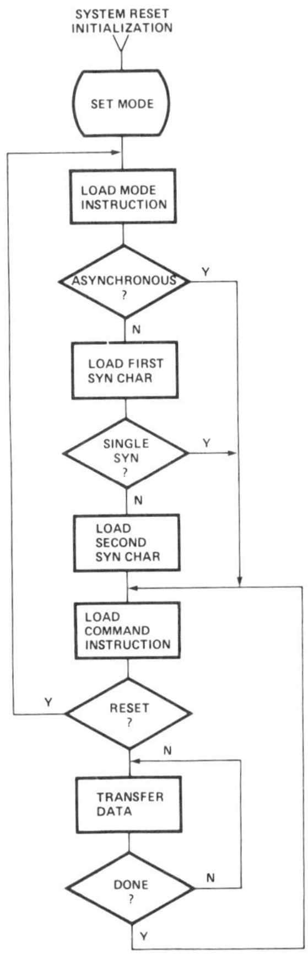

Figure 7.31 8251A initialization flowchart *(Courtesy of Intel Corporation).*

7.12 SPECIAL-PURPOSE INTERFACE CONTROLLERS

Up to this point in the chapter, we have introduced LSI controllers for two of the most widely used I/O interfaces. They are the 8255A, which is used to implement parallel input/output ports, and the 8251A, which is used to implement asynchronous and synchronous communication ports. A large number of other LSI devices are available to simplify the implementation of other complex I/O interfaces. Some examples are keyboard/display controllers, CRT controllers, floppy disk controllers, Winchester disk controllers, and IEEE-488 bus controllers. Here we will introduce just one of these devices, the *8279 programmable keyboard/display interface.* However, before starting the 8279, let us just briefly examine how the keyboard and display are typically serviced in a microcomputer system.

The Keyboard and Display Interfaces

A keyboard and display are important input and output devices in many digital electronic systems. For instance, all calculators and hand-held computers have both a keyboard and display.

The circuit diagram in Fig. 7.32 shows how a keyboard is most frequently interfaced to a microcomputer. Note that the switches in the keyboard are arranged in an *array*. The size of the array is described in terms of the number of rows and the number of columns. In our example, the keyboard array has four rows, which are labeled R_0 through R_3, and four columns, which are labeled C_0 through C_3. The location of the switch for any key in the array is uniquely defined by a row and a column. For instance, the 0 key is located at the junction of R_0 and C_0, while the 1 key is located at R_0 and C_1.

Now that we know how the keys of the keyboard are arranged, let us look at how the microcomputer services them. In most applications, the microcomputer scans the keyboard array. That is, it strobes one row of the keyboard after the other by sending out a short-duration pulse, to the 0 logic level, on the row line. During each row strobe, all column lines are examined by reading them in parallel. Typically, the column lines are pulled up to the 1 logic level; therefore, if a switch is closed, a logic 0 will be read on the corresponding column line. If no switches are closed, all 1s will be read when the column lines are examined.

For instance, if the 2 key is depressed when the microcomputer is scanning R_0, the column code read back will be $C_3C_2C_1C_0 = 1011$. Since the microcomputer knows which row it is scanning (R_0) and which column the stobe was returned on (C_2), it can determine that the number 2 key was depressed. The microcomputer does not necessarily store the row and column codes in the form that we have shown. It is more common to just maintain the binary equivalent of the row or column. In our example, the microcomputer would internally store the row number as $R_0 = 00_2$ and the column number as $C_2 = 10_2$. This is a more compact representation of the row and column information.

Several other issues arise when designing keyboards for microcomputer systems. One is that when a key in the keyboard is depressed, its contacts bounce for a short period of time. Depending on the keyboard sampling method, this could result in incorrect reading of the keyboard input. This problem is overcome by a technique known as *keyboard debouncing*. Debouncing is achieved by resampling the column lines a second time, about 10 ms later, to assure that the same column line is at the 0 logic level. If so, it is then accepted as a valid input. This technique can be implemented either in hardware or software.

Another problem occurs in keyboard sampling when more than one key is depressed at a time. In this case, the column code read by the microcomputer would have more than 1 bit that is logic 0. For instance, if the 0 and 2 keys were depressed, the column code read back during the scan of R_0 would be $C_3C_2C_1C_0 = 1010$. Typically, two keys are not actually depressed at the same time. It is more common

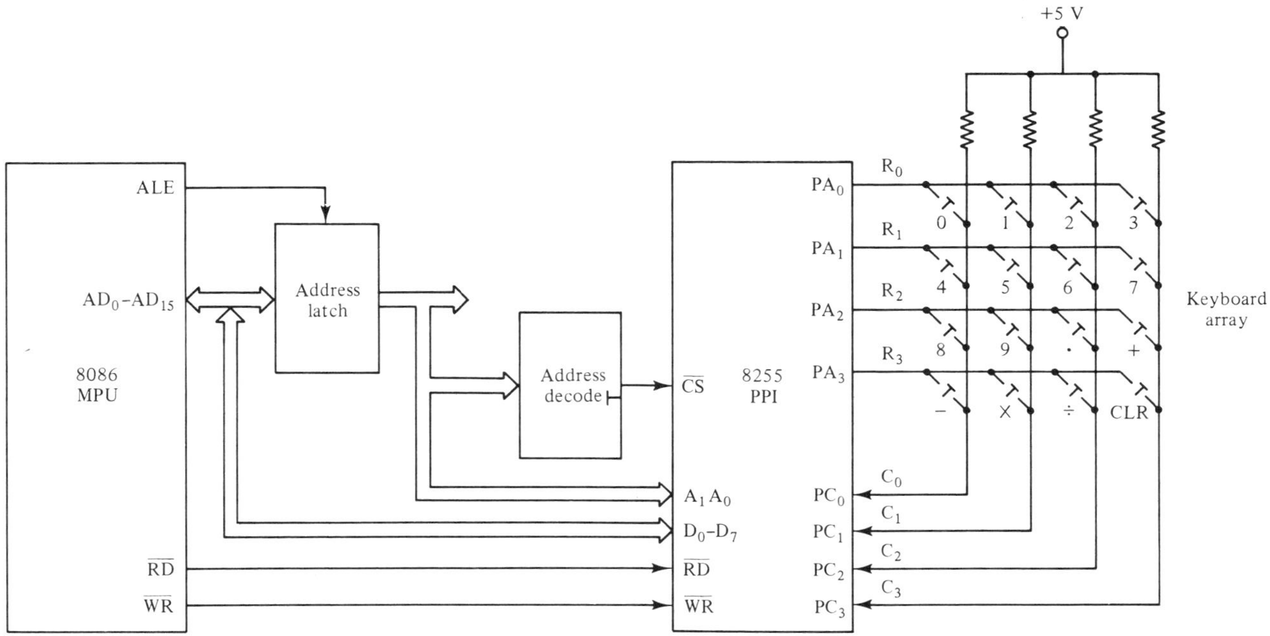

Figure 7.32 Keyboard interfaced to a microcomputer.

that the second key is depressed while the first one is still being held down and that the column code showing two key closures would show up in the second test which is made for debouncing.

Several different techniques are used to overcome this problem. One is called *two-key lockout.* With this method, the occurrence of a second key during the debounce scan causes both keys to be locked out and neither is accepted by the microcomputer. If the second key that was depressed is released before the first key is released, the first key entry is accepted and the second key is ignored. On the other hand, if the first key is released before the second key, only the second key is accepted.

A second method of solving this problem is that known as *N-key rollover.* In this case, more than one key can be depressed at a time and get accepted by the microcomputer. The microcomputer keeps track of the order in which they are depressed and as long as the switch closures are still present at another keyboard scan 10 ms later, they are accepted. That is, in the case of multiple key depressions, the key entries are accepted in the order in which their switches are closed.

The display interface used in most microcomputer systems is shown in Fig. 7.33. Here we are using a four-digit seven-segment numeric display. Notice that segment lines a through g of all digits of the display are driven in parallel by outputs of the microcomputer. It is over these lines that the microcomputer outputs signals to tell the display which segments are to be lighted to form the numbers in its digits. The way in which the segments of a seven-segment display digit are labeled is shown in Fig. 7.34. For instance, to form the number 1, a code is output to light just segments b and c.

The other set of lines in the display interface correspond to the digits of the display. These lines, which are labeled D_0 through D_3, correspond to digits 0, 1, 2, and 3, respectively. It is with these signals that the microcomputer indicates to the

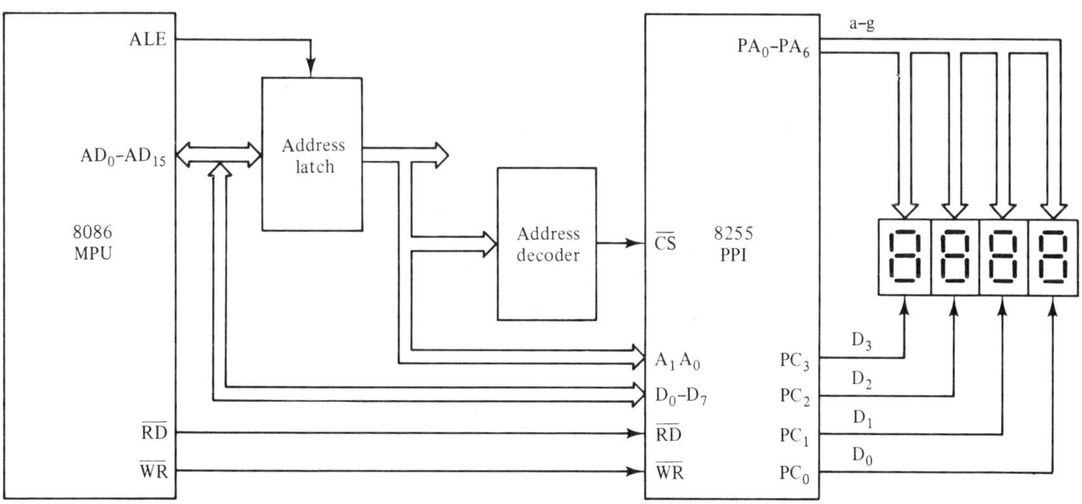

Figure 7.33 Display interfaced to a microcomputer.

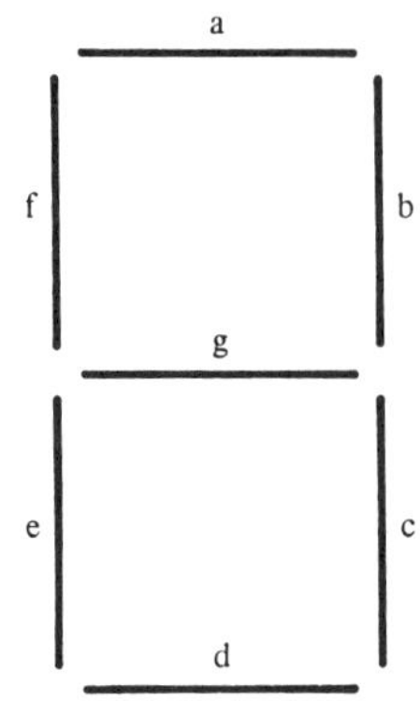

Figure 7.34 Seven segment digit labeling.

display which digit the number corresponding to the code on lines a through g should be displayed.

The way in which the display is driven by the microcomputer is said to be *multiplexed.* That is, data are not permanently displayed; instead, they are output to one digit after the other in time. This scanning sequence is repeated frequently such that the fact that the display is not permanently lighted cannot be recognized by the user.

The scanning of the digits of the display is similar to the scanning we have just described for the rows of the keyboard. A digit drive signal is output to one digit of the display after the other in time and during each digit drive pulse the seven-segment code for the number that is to be displayed in that digit is output on segment lines a through g. In fact, in most systems the digit drive signals for the display and row drive signals of the keyboard are supplied by the same set of outputs.

The 8279 Programmable Keyboard/Display Controller

The 8279 is an LSI device that is designed to make implementation of a keyboard/display interface similar to that which we have just described quite simple. This device can drive an 8 × 8 keyboard switch array and a sixteen-digit eight-segment display. Moreover, it can be configured through software to support key debouncing, two-key lockout, or N-key rollover modes of operation, and either left or right data entry to the display.

A block diagram of the device is shown in Fig. 7.35(a) and its pin layout in Fig. 7.35(b). From this diagram we see that there are four signal sections: the *MPU interface,* the *key data inputs,* the *display data outputs,* and the *scan lines* that are used by both the keyboard and display. Let us first look at the function of each of these interfaces.

The bus interface of the 8279 is similar to that found on the other peripherals that we have considered up to this point. It consists of the eight data bus lines DB_0 through DB_7. These are the lines over which the MPU outputs data to the display, inputs key codes, issues commands to the controller, and reads status information from the controller. Other signals found at the interface are the read ($\overline{RD}$), write ($\overline{WR}$), chip select ($\overline{CS}$), and address buffer (A_0) control signals. They are the signals

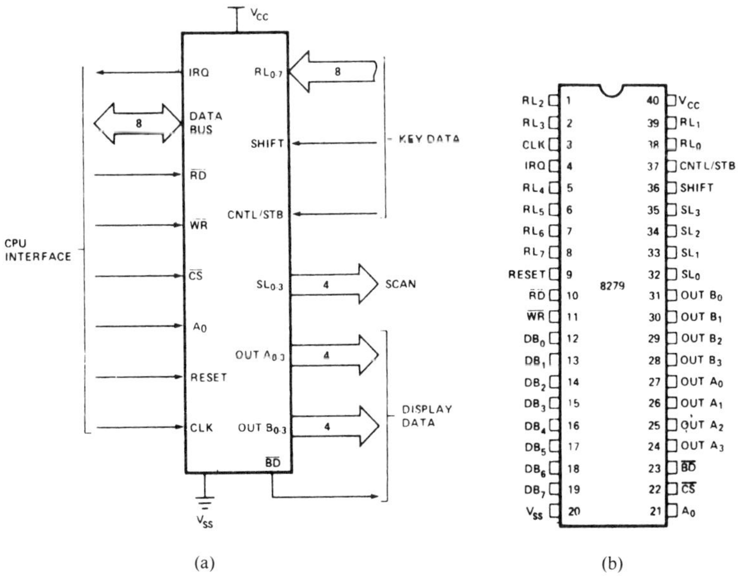

Figure 7.35 **(a)** Block diagram of the 8279 (*Courtesy of Intel Corporation*); **(b)** pin layout (*Courtesy of Intel Corporation*).

that control the data bus transfers that take place between the microprocessor and 8279.

A new signal introduced with this interface is *interrupt request (IRQ)*. This is an output that gets returned to an interrupt input of the 8086. This signal is provided so that the 8279 can tell the MPU that it contains key codes that should be read.

The scan lines are used as row drive signals for the keyboard and digit drive signals for the display. There are just four of these lines, SL_0 through SL_3. However, they can be configured for two different modes of operation through software. In applications that require a small keyboard and display (four or less rows and digits), they can be used in what is known as the *decoded mode*. Scan output waveforms for this mode of operation are shown in Fig. 7.36(a). Notice that a pulse to the 0 logic level is produced at one output after the other in time.

The second mode of operation, which is called *encoded mode,* allows use of a keyboard matrix with up to eight rows and a display with up to 16 digits. When this mode of operation is enabled through software, the binary-coded waveforms shown in Fig. 7.36(b) are output on the SL lines. These signals must be decoded with an external decoder circuit to produce the row and column drive signals.

Even though 16-digit drive signals are produced, only eight row drive signals can be used for the keyboard. This is because the key code that is stored when a key depression has been sensed has just 3 bits allocated to identify the row. Figure 7.37 shows this kind of circuit configuration.

The key data lines include the eight return lines RL_0 through RL_8. These lines

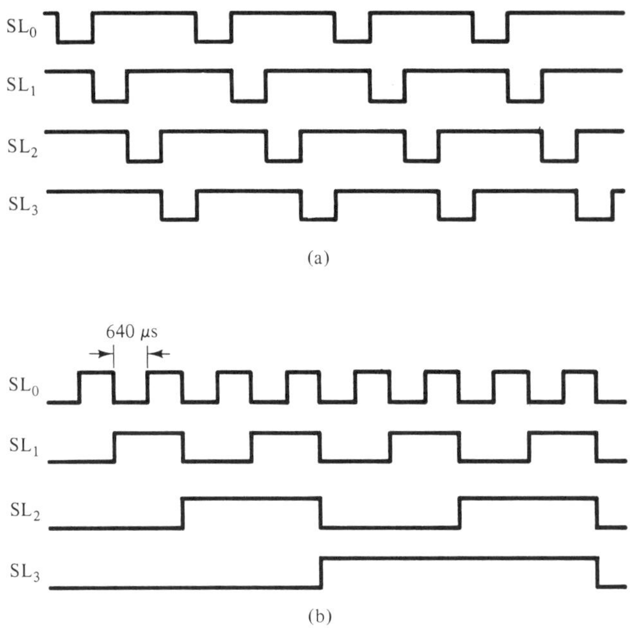

Figure 7.36 **(a)** Decoded mode scan line signals (*Courtesy of Intel Corporation*); **(b)** encoded mode scan line signals (*Courtesy of Intel Corporation*).

receive inputs from the column outputs of the keyboard array. They are not tested all at once as we described earlier. Looking at the waveforms in Fig. 7.38, we see that the RL lines are examined one after the other during each 640-μs row pulse.

If logic 0 is detected at a return line, the number of the column is coded as a 3-bit binary number and combined with the 3-bit row number to make a 6-bit key code. This key code input is first debounced and then loaded into an 8 × 8 key code FIFO within the 8279. Once the FIFO contains a key code, the IRQ output is set to logic 1. This signal can be used to tell the MPU that a keyboard input should be read from the 8279. There are two other signal inputs in this section. They are shift (SHIFT) and control/strobed (CNTL/STB). The logic levels at these two inputs are also stored as part of the key code when a switch closure is detected. The format of the complete key code byte that is stored in the FIFO is shown in Fig. 7.39.

A status register is provided within the 8279 that contains flags that indicate the status of the *key code FIFO.* The bits of the status register and their meanings are shown in Fig. 7.40. Notice that the 3 least significant bits, which are labeled NNN, identify the number of key codes that are currently held in the FIFO. The next bit, F, indicates whether or not the FIFO is full. The two bits that follow it, U and O, represent two FIFO error conditions. O, which stands for overrun, indicates that an attempt was made to enter another key code into the FIFO when it was already full. This condition could occur if the microprocessor does not respond quick enough to the IRQ signal by reading key codes out of the FIFO. The other error condition,

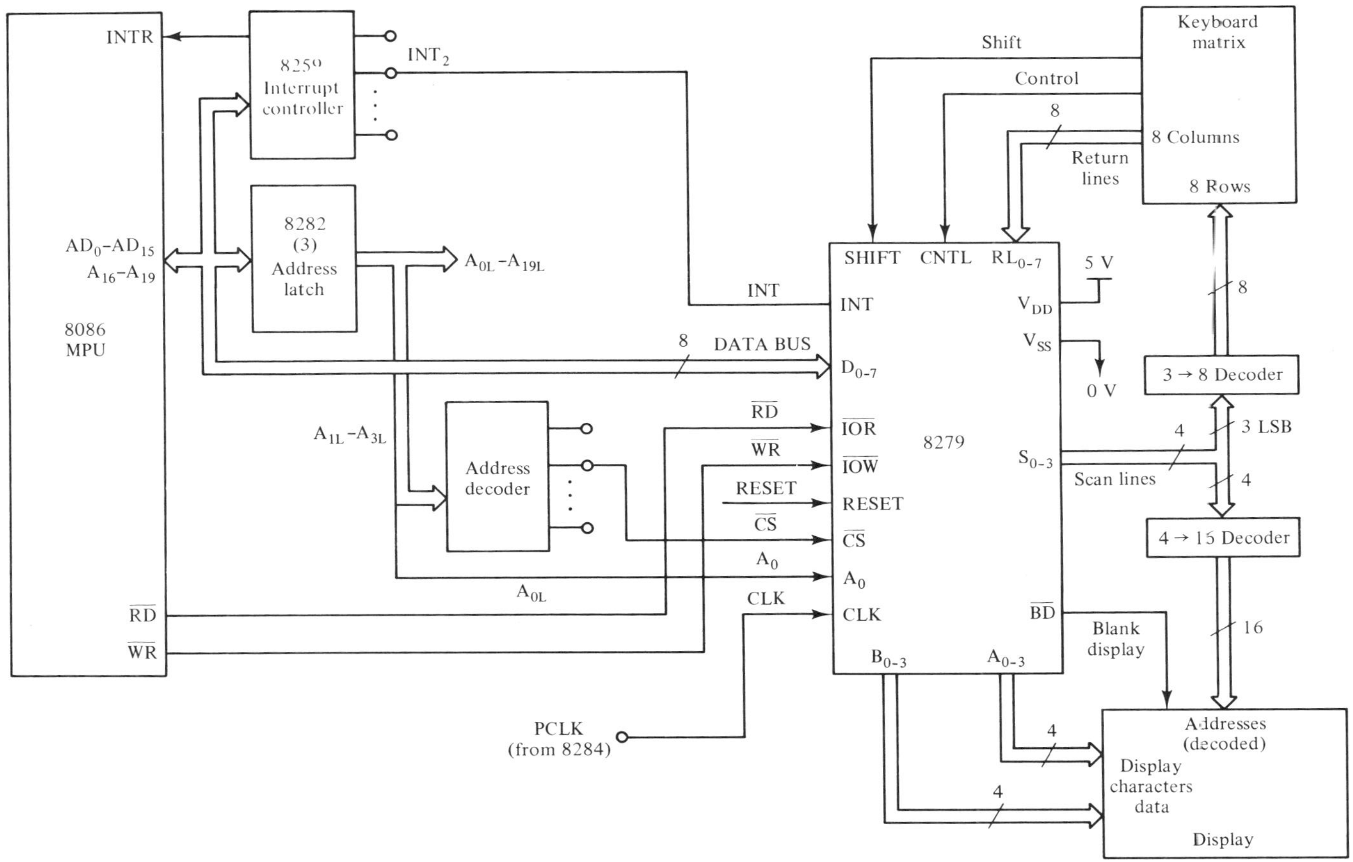

Figure 7.37 System configuration using the 8086 and 8279 (*Courtesy of Intel Corporation*).

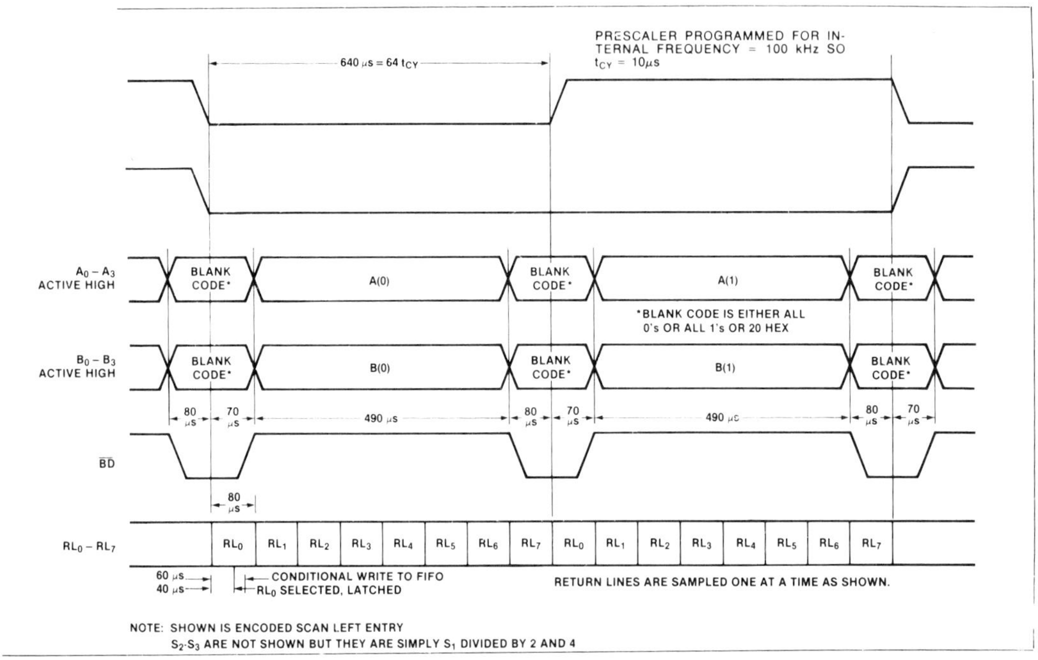

Figure 7.38 Keyboard and display signal timing (*Courtesy of Intel Corporation*).

underrun (U), means that the microprocessor attempted to read the contents of the FIFO when it was empty. The microprocessor can read the contents of this register under software control.

The display data lines include two 4-bit output ports, OUT A_0 through OUT A_3 and OUT B_0 through OUT B_3, that are used as display segment drive lines. Segment data that are output on these lines are held in a dedicated display RAM area within the 8279. This RAM is organized 16 × 8 and must be loaded with segment data by the microprocessor. In Fig. 7.38 we see that during each 640-ns scan time the segment data for one of the digits are output at the OUT A and OUT B ports.

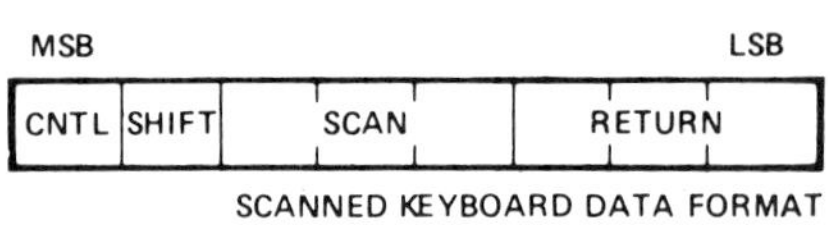

Figure 7.39 Keycode byte format (*Courtesy of Intel Corporation*).

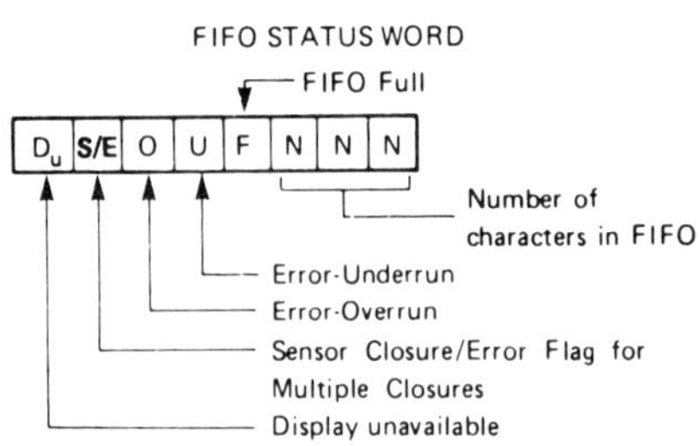

Figure 7.40 Status register (*Courtesy of Intel Corporation*).

The operation of the 8279 must be configured through software. Eight command words are provided for this purpose. These control words are loaded into the device by performing write (output) operations to the device with buffer address bit A_0 set to logic 1. Let us now look briefly at the function of each of these control words.

The first command (*command word 0*) is used to set the mode of operation for the keyboard and display. The general format of this word is shown in Fig. 7.41(a). Here we see that the three most significant bits are always reset. These three bits are a code by which the 8279 identifies which command is being issued by the microprocessor. The next two bits, which are labeled DD, are used to set the mode of operation for the display. The table in Fig. 7.41(b) shows the options that are available. After power-up reset, these bits are set to 01. From the table we see that this configures the display for 16 digits with left entry. By left entry we mean that characters are entered into the display starting from the left.

The 3 least significant bits of the command word (KKK) set the mode of operation of the display. They are used to configure the operation of the keyboard accord-

MSB							LSB
0	0	0	D	D	K	K	K

(a)

D	D	Display operation
0	0	8 8-bit character display – Left entry
0	1	16 8-bit character display – Left entry
1	0	8 8-bit character display – Right entry
1	1	16 8-bit character display – Right entry

(b)

K	K	K	Keyboard operation
0	0	0	Encoded Scan Keyboard – 2-Key Lockout
0	0	1	Decoded Scan Keyboard – 2-Key Lockout
0	1	0	Encoded Scan Keyboard – N-Key Rollover
0	1	1	Decoded Scan Keyboard – N-Key Rollover
1	0	0	Encoded Scan Sensor Matrix
1	0	1	Decoded Scan Sensor Matrix
1	1	0	Strobed Input, Encoded Display Scan
1	1	1	Strobed Input, Decoded Display Scan

(c)

Figure 7.41 **(a)** Command word 0 format (*Courtesy of Intel Corporation*); **(b)** display mode select codes (*Courtesy of Intel Corporation*); **(c)** keyboard select codes (*Courtesy of Intel Corporation*).

ing to the table in Fig. 7.41(c). The default code at power up is 000 and selects encoded scan operation with two-key lockout.

Example 7.18

What should be the value of command word 0 if the display is to be set for eight eight-segment digits with right entry and the keyboard for decoded scan with N-key rollover?

Solution. The 3 MSBs of the command word are always 0. The next two bits, DD, must be set to 10 for eight eight-segment digits with right entry. Finally, the 3 LSBs are set to 011 for decoded keyboard scan with N-key rollover. This gives

$$\text{COMMAND WORD 0} = \text{000DDKKK} = 00010011_2$$
$$= 13_{16}$$

Command word 1 is used to set the frequency of operation of the 8279. It is designed to run at 100 kHz; however, in most applications a much higher frequency signal is available to supply its CLK input. For this reason, a *5-bit programmable prescaler* is provided within the 8279 to divide down the input frequency. The format of this command word is shown in Fig. 7.42.

0	0	1	P	P	P	P	P

Figure 7.42 Command word 1 format (*Courtesy of Intel Corporation*).

For instance, in a 5-MHz 8086-based microcomputer system, the PCLK output of the 8284 clock driver IC can be used for the 8259's clock input. PCLK is one-half the frequency of the oscillator or 2.5 MHz. In this case the divider P must be

$$P = 2.5 \text{ MHz}/100 \text{ kHz} = 25$$

Twenty-five expressed as a 5-bit binary number is

$$P = 11001_2$$

Therefore, the value of command word 1 written to the 8279 is

$$\text{COMMAND WORD 1} = \text{001PPPPP} = 00111001_2$$
$$= 39_{16}$$

Let us skip now to *command word 6* because it is also used for initialization of the 8279. It can be used to initialize the complete display memory, the FIFO status, and the interrupt request output line. The format of this word is given in Fig. 7.43(a).

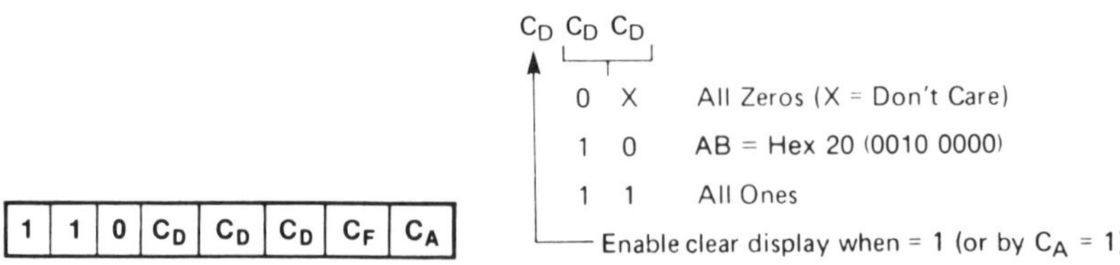

(a) (b)

Figure 7.43 **(a)** Command word 6 format *(Courtesy of Intel Corporation)*; **(b)** C_D coding (*Courtesy of Intel Corporation*).

The three C_D bits are used to control initialization of the display RAM. Figure 7.43(b) shows what values can be used in these locations. The C_F bit is provided for clearing the FIFO status and resetting the IRQ line. To perform the reset operation, a 1 must be written to C_F. The last bit, clear all (C_A), can be used to initiate both the C_D and C_F functions.

Example 7.19

What clear operations are performed if the value of command word 6 written to the 8279 is $D2_{16}$?

Solution. First we need to express the command word in binary form. This gives

$$\text{COMMAND WORD 6} = D2_{16} = 11010010_2$$

Note that the most significant C_D bit is set and the C_D bit that follows it is reset. This combination causes display memory to be cleared with all 0s. The C_F bit is also set and this causes the FIFO status and IRQ output to be reset.

As shown in Fig. 7.44, only one bit of *command word 7* is functional. This bit is labeled E and is an enable signal for what is called the special error mode. When this mode is enabled and the keyboard has N-key rollover selected, a multiple-key depression causes the S/E flag of the FIFO status register to be set. This flag can be read by the microprocessor through software.

1	1	1	E	X	X	X	X

X = Don't care.

Figure 7.44 Command word 7 format (*Courtesy of Intel Corporation*).

The rest of the command codes are related to accessing the key code FIFO and display RAM. The key code FIFO is read only. However, before the microprocessor can access it, a read FIFO command must be issued to the 8279. This is *command word 2* and has the format shown in Fig. 7.45. When the 8259 is set up for keyboard scanning, the AI and AAA bits are don't-care states. Then all that needs to be done is issue the command $01000000_2 = 40_{16}$ to the 8279 and then initiate read (input) cycles to the address of the 8279. For each read bus cycle, the key code at the top of the FIFO is read into the MPU.

0	1	0	AI	X	A	A	A

X = Don't Care

Figure 7.45 Command word 2 format (*Courtesy of Intel Corporation*).

The display RAM can be both read from or written into by the MPU. Just like for the FIFO, a command must be sent to the 8279 before reading or writing can be initiated. For instance, when the microprocessor wants to send new data to the display, it must first issue *command word 4*. This command has the format shown in Fig. 7.46. Here the AAAA in the 4 least significant bit locations is the address

1	0	0	AI	A	A	A	A

Figure 7.46 Command word 4 format (*Courtesy of Intel Corporation*).

of the first location to be accessed. For instance, if 0000_2 is put into these bits of the command, the first write operation will be to the first location in display RAM.

Moreover, if the AI bit is set in the command, autoincrement addressing is enabled. In this way, the display RAM address pointer is automatically incremented after the write operation is complete and a write cycle can be initiated to address 0001_2 of display RAM without first issuing another write command.

The MPU can also read the contents of the display RAM in a similar way. This requires that *command word 3* be issued to the 8279. Figure 7.47 shows the format of this read display RAM command.

0	1	1	AI	A	A	A	A

Figure 7.47 Command word 3 format (*Courtesy of Intel Corporation*).

ASSIGNMENT

Section 7.2

1. What is the function of the 8086's address and data bus lines relative to input/output operation?
2. In a minimum-mode 8086 system, which signal indicates to external circuitry that the current bus cycle is for the I/O interface and not the memory interface?
3. In a maximum-mode 8086 system, how does the 8086 indicate to external circuitry that an I/O operation is in progress?

Section 7.3

4. Can an I/O device be located at address $A0000_{16}$? Explain your answer.

Section 7.4

5. Describe the operation initiated by the instruction IN AX, 1AH.
6. Write an instruction sequence to perform the same operation as that of the instruction in problem 5 but this time use register DX to address the I/O port.

Section 7.5

7. Describe the sequence of events that take place at the I/O interface as the instruction of problem 5 is executed.

Section 7.6

8. Write a sequence of instructions to output the word contents of the memory location called DATA to output ports 0 and 1 in the circuit of Fig. 7.8.

Section 7.7

9. Describe the MODE 0, MODE 1, and MODE 2 I/O operations of the 8255A PPI.
10. What should be the control word if ports A, B, and C are all to be configured for MODE 0 operation? Moreover, ports A and B are to be used as inputs and C as an output.

11. Assume that the control register of an 8255A resides at memory address 0100H. Write an instruction sequence to load it with the control word formed in problem 10.

Section 7.8

12. What are the addresses of the A, B, and C ports of PPI 1 in the circuit of Fig. 7.17?
13. Assume that PPI 1 in Fig. 7.17 is configured as defined in problem 10. Write a program that will input the data at ports A and B, add these values together, and output the sum to port C.

Section 7.9

14. Distinguish between memory-mapped I/O and accumulator I/O.
15. Repeat problem 13 for the circuit in Fig. 7.18.

Section 7.10

16. Name a signal line that distinguishes an asynchronous communication interface from that of a synchronous communication interface.
17. Describe the sequence of signals that become active in Fig. 7.22 when the microcomputer transfers a character to the terminal.
18. Define a simplex, a half-duplex, and a full-duplex communication link.

Section 7.11

19. To write a byte of data to the 8251A, what logic levels must the microprocessor apply to control inputs $C/\overline{D}$, $\overline{RD}$, $\overline{WR}$, and $\overline{CS}$ of the 8251A?
20. The mode control register of an 8251A contains 11111111_2. What are the asynchronous character length, type of parity, and the number of STOP bits?
21. Write an instruction sequence to write the control word given in problem 20 to a memory-mapped 8251A that is located at address MODE.
22. Describe the difference between a mode instruction and a command instruction used in 8251A initialization.

Section 7.12

23. Referring to Fig. 7.32, what is the maximum number of keys that can be supported using all 24 I/O lines of an appropriately configured 8255A?
24. Specify the mode of operation for the keyboard and display when an 8279 is configured with command word 0 equal to $3F_{16}$.
25. Determine the clock frequency applied to the input of an 8279 if it needs command word 1 equal $1E_{16}$ to operate.
26. Summarize the function of each command word of the 8279.

8

Interrupt Interface of the 8086 Microprocessor

8.1 INTRODUCTION

In Chapter 7 we covered the input/output interface of the 8086 microcomputer system. Here we continue with a special input interface, the *interrupt interface*. The following topics are presented in this chapter:

1. Types of interrupts
2. Interrupt address pointer table
3. Interrupt instructions
4. Masking of interrupts
5. External hardware interrupt interface
6. External hardware interrupt sequence
7. The 8259A interrupt controller
8. 8259A minimum-mode-system interrupt interface
9. 8259A maximum-mode-system interrupt interface
10. Software interrupts
11. Nonmaskable interrupt
12. Reset interrupt
13. Internal interrupt functions

8.2 TYPES OF INTERRUPTS

Interrupts provide a mechanism for changing program environment. Transfer of program control is initiated by either the occurrence of an event internal to the 8086 microprocessor or an event in its external hardware. For instance, when an interrupt signal occurs indicating that an external device, such as a printer, requires service, the 8086 must suspend what it is doing in the main part of the program and pass control to a special routine that performs the function required by the device.

The section of program to which control is passed is called the *interrupt service routine*. When the 8086 terminates execution in the main program, it remembers the location where it left off and then picks up execution with the first instruction in the service routine. After this routine has run to completion, program control is returned to the point where the 8086 originally left the main body of the program.

The 8086 microcomputer is capable of implementing any combination of up to 256 interrupts. They are divided into five groups: *external hardware interrupts, software interrupts, internal interrupts*, the *nonmaskable interrupt*, and the *reset interrupt*. The function of the external hardware, software, and nonmaskable interrupts can be defined by the user. On the other hand, the internal and reset interrupts have dedicated system functions.

Hardware, software, and internal interrupts are serviced on a *priority* basis. Priority is achieved by assigning to each interrupt a *type number. Type 0* identifies the *highest-priority* interrupt and *type 255* the *lowest-priority* interrupt. Actually, a few of the type numbers are not available for use with software or hardware interrupts. This is because they are reserved for special interrupt functions of the 8086. In external hardware, a type number (priority level) is associated with an interrupt input lead.

The importance of priority lies in the fact that if an interrupt service routine has been initiated to perform a function at a specific priority level, only devices with higher priority can interrupt the active service routine. Lower-priority devices will have to wait until the routine is completed before their request for service can be acknowledged. For this reason, the user normally assigns tasks that must not be interrupted frequently to higher-priority levels and those that can be interrupted to lower-priority levels. An example of a high-priority service routine that should not be interrupted is that for a power failure.

Whenever the 8086 is executing instructions, it always makes a check during the last clock cycle of the current instruction to determine whether or not an interrupt is pending. If an interrupt is pending, it tests for the occurrence of the various groups based on the hierarchy that follows: internal interrupt, nonmaskable interrupt, software interrupt, and external hardware interrupt. Thus we see that internal interrupts are the *highest-priority group* and the external hardware interrupts are the *lowest-priority group*. However, if no interrupts are pending, the 8086 simply executes the next instruction in the program.

We just pointed out that once an interrupt service routine is initiated, it can be interrupted only by a function that corresponds to a higher-priority level. For example, if a level 50 external hardware interrupt is in progress, it can be interrupted by any software interrupt, the nonmaskable interrupt, all internal interrupts, or any external interrupt with type number less than 50. That is, external hardware interrupts with priority levels equal to 50 or greater are *masked out*.

8.3 INTERRUPT ADDRESS POINTER TABLE

An *address pointer table* is used to link the interrupt type numbers to the locations of their service routines in the program storage memory. Figure 8.1 shows a map of the pointer table in the memory of the 8086 microcomputer system. Looking at this table, we see that it contains 256 *address pointers (vectors)*. One pointer corresponds to each of the interrupt types 0 through 255. These address pointers identify the starting locations of their service routines in program memory.

Notice that the pointer table is located at the low-address end of the memory address space. It starts at address 00000_{16} and ends at $003FE_{16}$. This represents the first 1K bytes of memory.

Each of the 256 pointers requires two words (four bytes) of memory. These words are stored at even-address boundaries. The higher-addressed word of the two-word vector is called the *base address*. It identifies the program memory segment

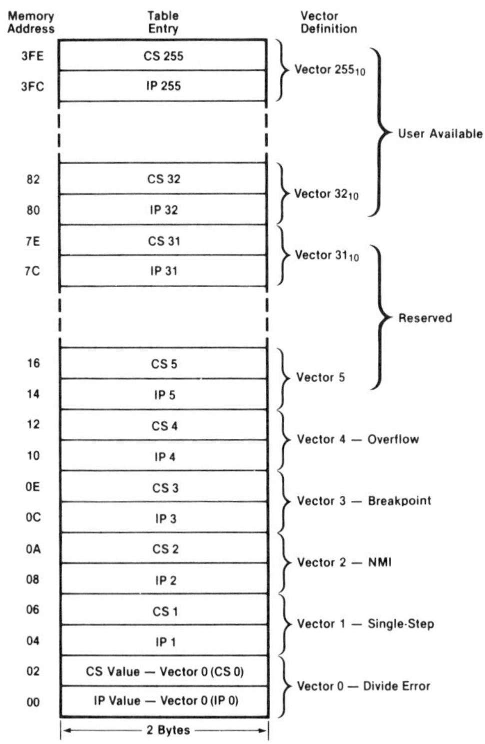

Figure 8.1 Interrupt vector table (*Courtesy of Intel Corporation*).

in which the service routine resides. For this reason, it is loaded into the code segment (CS) register within the 8086.

The lower-addressed word of the vector is the *offset* of the first instruction of the service routine from the beginning of the code segment defined by the base address loaded into CS. This offset is loaded into the instruction pointer (IP) register. For example, the vector for type number 255, IP_{255} and CS_{255}, is stored at addresses $003FC_{16}$ and $003FE_{16}$.

Looking more closely at the table in Fig. 8.1, we find that the first five pointers have *dedicated functions*. Pointers 0, 1, 3, and 4 are required for the 8086's internal interrupts: *divide error, single step, breakpoint*, and *overflow*. Pointer 2 is used to identify the starting location of the nonmaskable interrupt's service routine. The next 27 pointers, 5 through 31, represent a *reserved portion* of the pointer table. That is, these locations can be used only for storage of interrupt vectors.

The rest of the table, the 224 pointers in the address range 00080_{16} through $003FF_{16}$, are available to the user for storage of interrupt vectors. These pointers correspond to type numbers 32 through 255 and can be employed by hardware or software interrupts. This part of memory is not reserved for pointer storage. That is, if it is not in use for storage of pointers, it can be used for storage of data.

Example 8.1

At what address should vector, CS_{50} and IP_{50} be stored in memory?

Solution. Each vector requires four consecutive bytes of memory for storage. Therefore, its address can be found by multiplying the type number by 4. Since CS_{50} and IP_{50} represent the words of the type 50 interrupt pointer, we get

$$\text{Address} = 4 \times 50 = 200$$

Converting to binary form gives

$$\text{Address} = 11001000_2$$

and expressing it as a hexadecimal number results in

$$\text{Address} = C8_{16}$$

Therefore, IP_{50} is stored at $000C8_{16}$ and CS_{50} at $000CA_{16}$.

8.4 INTERRUPT INSTRUCTIONS

A number of instructions are provided in the instruction set of the 8086 for use with interrupt processing. These instructions are listed with a brief description of their functions in Fig. 8.2.

For instance, the first two instructions, which are STI and CLI, permit manipulation of the 8086's interrupt flag through software. STI stands for *set interrupt enable flag*. Execution of this instruction enables the external interrupt input (INTR) for operation. That is, it sets interrupt flag (IF). On the other hand, execution of CLI (*clear interrupt enable flag*) disables the external interrupt input. It does this by resetting IF.

Mnemonic	Meaning	Format	Operation	Flags Affected
CLI	Clear interrupt flag	CLI	$0 \rightarrow (IF)$	IF
STI	Set interrupt flag	STI	$1 \rightarrow (IF)$	IF
INT n	Type n software interrupt	INT n	$(Flags) \rightarrow ((SP) - 2)$ $0 \rightarrow TF, IF$ $(CS) \rightarrow ((SP) - 4)$ $(2 + 4 \cdot n) \rightarrow (CS)$ $(IP) \rightarrow ((SP) - 6)$ $(4 \cdot n) \rightarrow (IP)$	TF, IF
IRET	Interrupt return	IRET	$((SP)) \rightarrow (IP)$ $((SP) + 2) \rightarrow (CS)$ $((SP) + 4) \rightarrow (Flags)$ $(SP) + 6 \rightarrow (SP)$	All
INTO	Interrupt on overflow	INTO	INT 4 steps	TF, IF
HLT	Halt	HLT	Wait for an external interrupt or reset to occur	None
WAIT	Wait	WAIT	Wait for $\overline{TEST}$ input to go active	None

Figure 8.2 Interrupt instructions.

The next instruction listed in Fig. 8.2 is the *software interrupt* instruction INT n. It is used to initiate a software vector call of a subroutine. Executing the instruction causes transfer of program control to the subroutine pointed to by the vector for type number n specified in the instruction.

For example, execution of the instruction INT 50 initiates execution of a subroutine whose starting point is identified by vector 50 in the pointer table. That is, the 8086 reads IP_{50} and CS_{50} from addresses $000C8_{16}$ and $000CA_{16}$, respectively, in memory, generates a physical address, and starts to fetch instructions from this new location in program memory.

An *interrupt return* (IRET) instruction must be included at the end of each interrupt service routine. It is required to pass control back to the point in the program where execution was terminated due to the occurrence of the interrupt. When executed, IRET causes the three words IP, CS, and flags to be popped from the stack back into the internal registers of the 8086. This restores the original program environment.

INTO is the *interrupt on overflow* instruction. This instruction must be included after arithmetic instructions that can generate an overflow condition, such as divide. It tests the overflow flag and if the flag is found to be set, a type 4 internal interrupt is initiated. This causes program control to be passed to an overflow service routine that is located at the starting address identified by the vector IP_4 at 00010_{16} and CS_4 at 00012_{16} of the pointer table.

The last two instructions associated with the interrupt interface are *halt* (HLT) and *wait* (WAIT). They produce similar responses by the 8086 and permit the operation of the 8086 to be synchronized to an event in external hardware. For instance, when HLT is executed, the 8086 suspends operation and enters the idle state. It no longer executes instructions; instead, it remains idle waiting for the occurrence of an external hardware interrupt or reset interrupt. With the occurrence of either of these two events, the 8086 resumes execution with the corresponding service routine.

If the WAIT instruction is used instead of the HLT instruction, the 8086 checks the logic level of the $\overline{\text{TEST}}$ input prior to going into the idle state. Only if $\overline{\text{TEST}}$ is at logic 1, will the MPU go into the idle state. While in the idle state, the 8086 continues to check the logic level at $\overline{\text{TEST}}$ looking for its transition to the 0 logic level. As $\overline{\text{TEST}}$ switches back to 0, execution resumes with the next sequential instruction in the program.

8.5 MASKING OF INTERRUPTS

An interrupt enable flag bit is provided within the 8086. Earlier we found that it is identified as IF. It affects only the external hardware interrupt interface, not the software or internal interrupts. The ability to initiate an external hardware interrupt at the INTR input is enabled by setting IF or masked out by resetting it. Through software, this can be done by executing the STI instruction or the CLI instruction, respectively.

During the initiation sequence of an interrupt service routine, the 8086 automatically clears IF. This masks out the occurrence of an external hardware interrupt. If necessary, the interrupt flag bit can be set with an STI instruction at the beginning of the service routine to reenable the INTR input.

8.6 EXTERNAL HARDWARE INTERRUPT INTERFACE

Up to this point in the chapter, we have introduced the interrupts of the 8086, its pointer table, interrupt instructions, and masking of interrupts. Let us now look at the *external hardware interrupt interface* of the 8086.

Minimum-System Interrupt Interface

We will begin with an 8086 microcomputer configured for the minimum system mode. The interrupt interface for this system is illustrated in Fig. 8.3. Here we see that it includes the multiplexed address/data bus and dedicated interrupt signal lines INTR and $\overline{\text{INTA}}$. Moreover, external circuitry is required to interface the interrupt inputs to the 8086's interrupt interface. This interface circuitry must identify which of the pending active interrupts has the highest priority and then pass its type number to the 8086.

In this circuit we see that the key interrupt interface signals are *interrupt request* (INTR) and *interrupt acknowledge* ($\overline{\text{INTA}}$). The logic level input at the INTR line signals the 8086 that an external device is requesting service. The 8086 samples this input during the last clock period of each instruction execution cycle. Logic 1

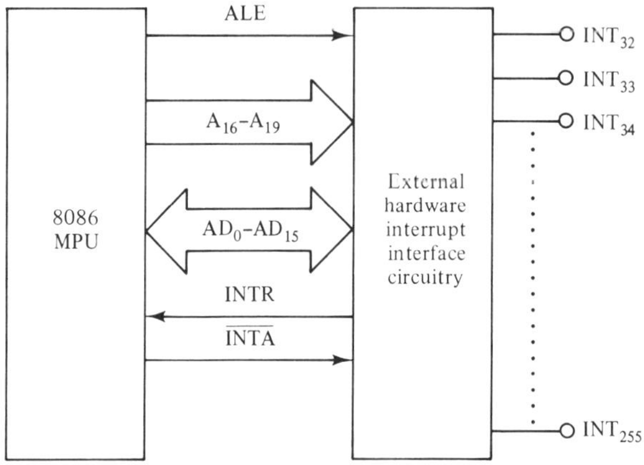

Figure 8.3 Minimum mode 8086 system external hardware interrupt interface.

represents an active interrupt request. INTR is *level triggered*; therefore, its active 1 level must be maintained until tested by the 8086. If it is not maintained, the request for service may not be recognized. Moreover, the 1 at INTR must be removed before the service routine runs to completion; otherwise, the same interrupt may be acknowledged a second time.

When an interrupt request has been recognized by the 8086, it signals this fact to external circuitry. It does this with pulses to logic 0 at its $\overline{INTA}$ output. Actually, there are just two pulses produced at $\overline{INTA}$ during the *interrupt acknowledge bus cycle*. The first pulse signals external circuitry that the interrupt request has been acknowledged and to prepare to send its type number to the 8086. The second pulse tells the external circuitry to put the type number on the data bus.

Notice that the lower 16 lines of the address/data bus, AD_0 through AD_{15}, are also part of the interrupt interface. During the second cycle in the interrupt acknowledge bus cycle, external circuitry must put an 8-bit type number on bus lines AD_0 through AD_7. The 8086 reads this number off the bus to identify which external device is requesting service. It uses the type number to generate the address of the interrupt's vector in the pointer table and to read the new values of CS and IP into the corresponding internal registers. CS and IP are transferred over the full 16-bit data bus. The old values of CS, IP, and the internal flags are automatically pushed to the stack part of memory. These word-wide transfers take place over the complete data bus.

Maximum-Mode Interrupt Interface

The maximum-mode interrupt interface of the 8086 microcomputer is shown in Fig. 8.4. The primary difference between this interrupt interface and that shown for the minimum mode in Fig. 8.3 is that the 8288 bus controller has been added. In the maximum mode system, the bus controller produces the $\overline{INTA}$ and ALE signals. Whenever the 8086 outputs an interrupt acknowledge bus status code, the 8288 generates pulses at its $\overline{INTA}$ output to signal external circuitry that the 8086 has ac-

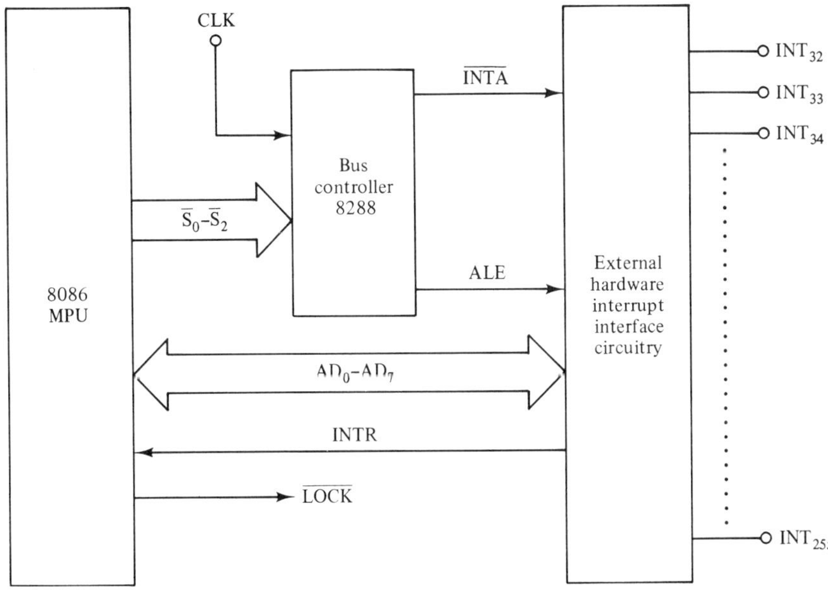

Figure 8.4 Maximum mode 8086 system external hardware interrupt interface.

Status inputs			CPU cycle	8288 command
$\overline{S_2}$	$\overline{S_1}$	$\overline{S_0}$		
0	0	0	Interrupt acknowledge	$\overline{\text{INTA}}$
0	0	1	Read I/O port	$\overline{\text{IORC}}$
0	1	0	Write I/O port	$\overline{\text{IOWC}}$, $\overline{\text{AIOWC}}$
0	1	1	Halt	None
1	0	0	Instruction fetch	$\overline{\text{MRDC}}$
1	0	1	Read memory	$\overline{\text{MRDC}}$
1	1	0	Write memory	$\overline{\text{MWTC}}$, $\overline{\text{AMWC}}$
1	1	1	Passive	None

Figure 8.5 Interrupt bus status code (*Courtesy of Intel Corporation*).

knowledged an interrupt request. This interrupt acknowledge bus status code, $\overline{S_2}\overline{S_1}\overline{S_0}$ = 000, is highlighted in Fig. 8.5.

A second change in Fig. 8.4 is that the 8086 provides a new signal for the interrupt interface. This output, which is labeled $\overline{\text{LOCK}}$, is called the *bus priority lock* signal. $\overline{\text{LOCK}}$ is applied as an input to the *bus arbiter circuit*. In response to this signal, the arbitration logic assures that no other device can take over control of the system bus until the interrupt acknowledge bus cycle is completed.

8.7 EXTERNAL HARDWARE INTERRUPT SEQUENCE

In the preceding section we showed the interrupt interfaces for the external hardware interrupts in minimum-mode and maximum-mode 8086 systems. Now we will continue by describing in detail the events that take place during the interrupt request, interrupt acknowledge bus cycle, and device service routine.

The interrupt sequence begins when an external device requests service by activating one of the interrupt inputs, INT_{32} through INT_{255} of the external interrupt interface circuit in Fig. 8.3 or Fig. 8.4. For example, the INT_{50} input could be switched to the 1 logic level. This signals that the device associated with priority level 50 wants to be serviced.

The external circuitry evaluates the priority of this input. If there is no interrupt already in progress or if this interrupt is of higher priority than that which is presently active, the external circuitry must issue a request for service to the 8086.

Let us assume that INT_{50} is the only active interrupt input. In this case, the external circuitry switches INTR to logic 1. This tells the 8086 that an interrupt is pending for service. To assure that it is recognized, the external circuitry must maintain INTR active until an interrupt acknowledge pulse is issued by the 8086.

The 8086 tests the logic level at INTR during the last clock state of the current instruction. If it is logic 1, a request for service is recognized. Before the 8086 initiates the interrupt acknowledge sequence, it checks the setting of IF. If it is logic 0, external interrupts are masked out and the request is ignored. In this case, the next sequential instruction is executed. On the other hand, if IF is at logic 1, external hardware interrupts are enabled and the service routine is to be initiated.

Let us assume that IF is set to permit interrupts to occur when INTR is tested as 1. Then the 8086 clears IF. This disables further external interrupts from requesting service. Actually, the TF flag is also cleared. This disables the single-step mode of operation if it happens to be active.

Next, the 8086 automatically pushes the contents of the flag register, CS, and IP onto the stack. This requires three write cycles to take place over the system bus. The current value of the stack pointer is decremented by 2 as each of these values is put onto the top of the stack.

The 8086 responds with two consecutive interrupt acknowledge bus cycles. These cycles are illustrated in Fig. 8.6. During T_1 of the first bus cycle, we see that a pulse is output on ALE but at the same time the address/data bus is put in the high-Z state. It stays in this state for the rest of the bus cycle. During periods T_2 and T_3, $\overline{INTA}$ is switched to logic 0. This signals external circuitry that the request for service has been granted. In response to this pulse, the logic 1 at INTR can be removed.

The signal identified as $\overline{LOCK}$ is produced only in maximum-mode systems. Notice that $\overline{LOCK}$ is switched to logic 0 during T_2 of the first INTA bus cycle and is maintained at this level until T_2 of the second INTA bus cycle. During this time, the BIU is prevented from accepting a HOLD request. Moreover, the $\overline{LOCK}$ output is used in external logic to lock other devices off the system bus, thereby assuring

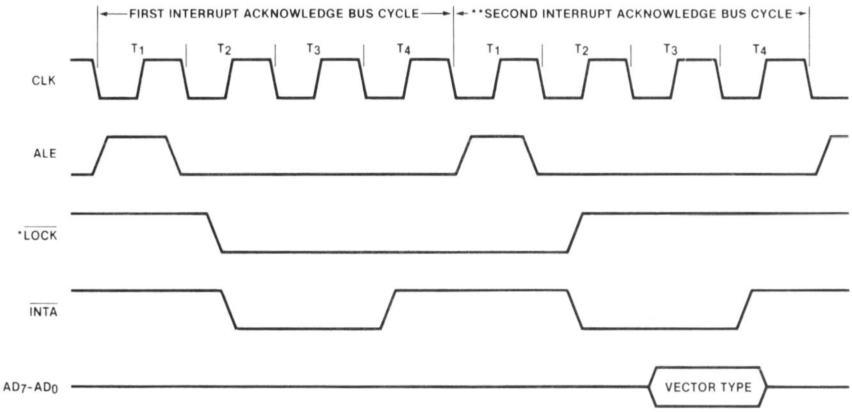

Figure 8.6 Interrupt acknowledge bus cycle (*Courtesy of Intel Corporation*).

that the interrupt acknowledge sequence continues through to completion without interruption.

During the second interrupt acknowledge bus cycle, a similar signal sequence occurs. However, this interrupt acknowledge pulse tells the external circuitry to put the type number of the active interrupt on the data bus. External circuitry gates one of the interrupt codes $32 = 20_{16}$ through $255 = FF_{16}$, onto data bus lines AD_0 through AD_7. This code must be valid during periods T_3 and T_4 of the second interrupt acknowledge bus cycle.

The 8086 sets up its bus control signals for an input data transfer to read the type number off the data bus. $DT/\overline{R}$ and $\overline{DEN}$ are set to logic 0 to enable the external data bus circuitry and set it for input of data. Also, $M/\overline{IO}$ is set to 0, indicating that data are to be input from the interrupt interface. During this input operation, the byte interrupt code is read off the data bus. For the case of INT_{50}, this code would be $00110010_2 = 32_{16}$. This completes the interrupt acknowledge part of the interrupt sequence.

Now the 8086 knows the type number associated with the external device that is requesting service. It must now fetch the vector that defines the starting point of its service routine from memory. The type number is internally multiplied by 4, and this result is used as the address of the first word of the interrupt vector in the pointer table.

Two read bus cycles are performed to read the two-word vector from memory. The first word, which is the lower-addressed word, is loaded into IP. The second, higher-addressed word, is loaded into CS. For instance, the vector for INT_{50} would be read from addresses $000C8_{16}$ and $000CA_{16}$.

The service routine is now initiated. That is, execution resumes with the first instruction of the service routine. It is located at the address generated from the new value in CS and IP. The service routine must include PUSH instructions to save the contents of those internal registers that it will use. Their contents are also saved in the stack.

At the end of the service routine, the original program environment must be restored. This is done by first popping the appropriate registers from the stack by executing POP instructions. Then the IRET instruction must be executed as the last instruction of the service routine. This instruction causes the old contents of the flags, CS, and IP to be popped from the stack back into the internal registers of the 8086. The original program environment has now been completely restored and execution resumes at the point in the program where it was interrupted.

8.8 THE 8259A PROGRAMMABLE INTERRUPT CONTROLLER

The 8259A is an LSI peripheral IC that is designed to simplify the implementation of the interrupt interface in an 8086 system. This device is known as a *programmable interrupt controller* or *PIC*. It is manufactured using the NMOS technology.

The operation of the PIC is programmable under software control and it can be configured for a wide variety of applications. Some of its programmable features are the ability to accept level-sensitive or edge-triggered inputs, the ability to be easily cascaded to expand from 8 to 64 interrupt inputs, and its ability to be configured to implement a wide variety of priority schemes.

Block Diagram of the 8259A

Let us begin our study of the PIC with its block diagram in Fig. 8.7(a). We just mentioned that the 8259A is treated as a peripheral in the 8086 microcomputer. Therefore, its operation must be initialized by the 8086 processor. The *host processor interface* is provided for this purpose. This interface consists of eight *data bus* lines D_0 through D_7 and control signals *read* ($\overline{\text{RD}}$), *write* ($\overline{\text{WR}}$), and *chip select* ($\overline{\text{CS}}$). The data bus is the path over which data are transferred between the 8086 and 8259A. These data can be command words, status information, or interrupt type numbers. Control input $\overline{\text{CS}}$ must be at logic 0 to enable the host processor interface. Moreover, $\overline{\text{WR}}$ and $\overline{\text{RD}}$ signal the 8259A whether data are to be written into or read from its internal registers. They also control the timing of these data transfers.

Two other signals are identified as part of the host processor interface. They are INT and $\overline{\text{INTA}}$. Together, these two signals provide the handshake mechanism by which the 8259A can signal the 8086 of a request for service and receive an acknowledgment that the request has been accepted. INT is the interrupt request output of the 8259A. It is applied directly to the INTR input of the 8086. Logic 1 is produced at this output whenever the 8259A receives a valid interrupt request.

On the other hand, $\overline{\text{INTA}}$ is an input of the 8259A. It is connected to the $\overline{\text{INTA}}$ output of the 8086. The 8086 pulses this input of the 8259A to logic 0 twice during the interrupt acknowledge bus cycle. Thereby, signaling the 8259A that the interrupt request has been acknowledged and that it should output the type number of the

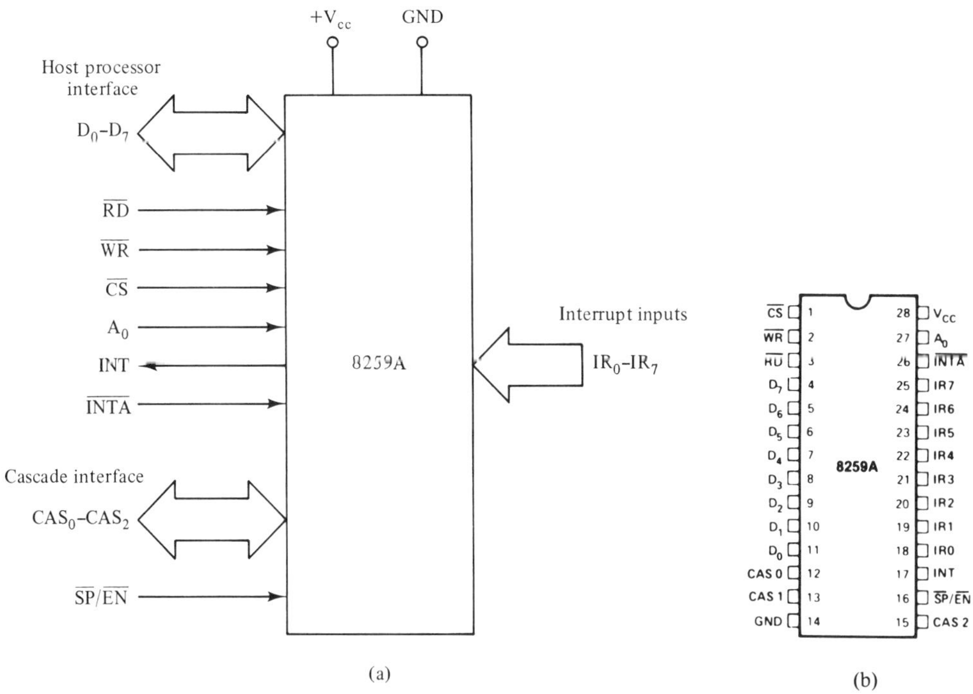

Figure 8.7 **(a)** Block diagram of the 8259A; **(b)** pin layout (*Courtesy of Intel Corporation*).

highest-priority active interrupt on data bus lines D_0 through D_7 such that it can be read by the 8086.

At the other side of the block in Fig. 8.7(a), we find the eight *interrupt inputs* of the PIC. They are labeled IR_0 through IR_7. It is through these inputs that external devices issue a request for service. One of the software options of the 8259A permits these inputs to be configured for *level-sensitive* or *edge-triggered operation*.

When configured for level-sensitive operation, logic 1 is the active level of the IR inputs. In this case, the request for service must be removed before the service routine runs to completion. Otherwise, the interrupt will be requested a second time and the service routine initiated again. Moreover, if the input returns to logic 0 before it is acknowledged by the 8086, the request for service will be missed.

Some external devices produce a short-duration pulse instead of a fixed logic level for use as an interrupt request signal. If the 8086 is busy servicing a higher-priority interrupt when the pulse is produced, the request for service could be completely missed. To overcome this problem, the edge-triggered mode of operation is used.

Inputs of the 8259A that are set up for edge-triggered operation become active on the transition from the inactive 0 logic level to the active 1 logic level. This represents what is known as a *positive edge-triggered input*. The fact that this transition has occurred at an IR line is latched internal to the 8259A. If the IR input remains at the 1 logic level even after the service routine is completed, the interrupt is not reinitiated. Instead, it is locked out. To be recognized a second time, the input must first return to the 0 logic level and then be switched back to 1. The advantage of edge-triggered operation is that if the request at the IR input is removed before the 8086 acknowledges service of the interrupt, its request is maintained latched internal to the 8259A until it can be serviced.

The last group of signals on the PIC implement what is known as the *cascade interface*. As shown in Fig. 8.7(a), it includes bidirectional *cascading bus lines* CAS_0 through CAS_2 and a multifunction control line labeled $\overline{SP}/\overline{EN}$. The primary use of these signals is in cascaded systems where a number of 8259A ICs are interconnected in a master/slave configuration to expand the number of IR inputs from 8 to as high as 64.

In a cascaded system, the CAS lines of all 8259As are connected together to provide a private bus between the master and slave devices. In response to the first $\overline{INTA}$ pulse during the interrupt acknowledge bus cycle, the master PIC outputs a 3-bit code on the CAS lines. This code identifies the highest-priority slave that is to be serviced. It is this device that is to be acknowledged for service. All slaves read this code off the *private cascading bus* and compare it to their internal ID code. A match condition tells the slave that it has the highest-priority input. In response, it puts the type number of its highest-priority active input on the data bus during the second interrupt acknowledge bus cycle.

When the PIC is configured through software for the cascaded mode, the $\overline{SP}/\overline{EN}$ line is used as an input. This corresponds to its $\overline{SP}$ (*slave program*) function. The logic level applied at $\overline{SP}$ tells the device whether it is to operate as a master or slave. Logic 1 at this input designates master mode and logic 0 designates slave mode.

If the PIC is configured for single mode instead of cascade mode, $\overline{SP}/\overline{EN}$ takes on another function. In this case, it becomes an enable output which can be used to control the direction of data transfer through the bus transceiver that buffers the data bus.

A pin layout of the 8259A is given in Fig. 8.7(b).

Internal Architecture of the 8259A

Now that we have introduced the input/output signals of the 8259A, let us look at its internal architecture. Figure 8.8 is a block diagram of the PIC's internal circuitry. Here we find eight functional parts: the *data bus buffer, read/write logic, control logic, in-service register, interrupt request register, priority resolver, interrupt mask register*, and *cascade buffer/comparator*.

We will begin with the function of the data bus buffer and read/write logic sections. It is these parts of the 8259A that let the 8086 have access to the internal registers. Moreover, it provides the path over which interrupt type numbers are passed to the 8086. The data bus buffer is an 8-bit bidirectional three-state buffer that interfaces the internal circuitry of the 8259A to the data bus of the 8086. The direction,

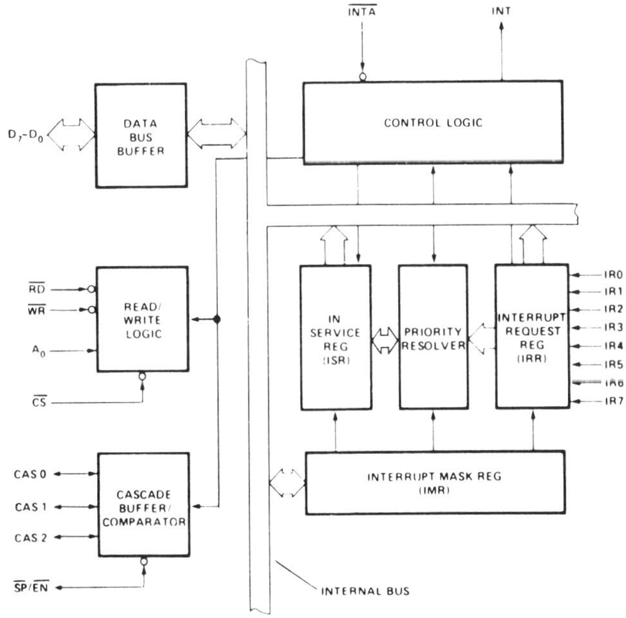

Figure 8.8 Internal architecture of the 8259A (*Courtesy of Intel Corporation*).

timing, and source or destination for data transfers through the buffer are under control of the outputs of the read/write logic block. These outputs are generated in response to control inputs $\overline{RD}$, $\overline{WR}$, A_0, and $\overline{CS}$.

The interrupt request register, in-service register, priority resolver, and interrupt mask register are the key internal blocks of the 8259A. The interrupt mask register (IMR) can be used to enable or mask out individually the interrupt request inputs. It contains 8 bits identified by M_0 through M_7. These bits correspond to interrupt inputs IR_0 through IR_7, respectively. Logic 0 in a bit position enables the corresponding interrupt input and logic 1 masks it out. This register can be read from or written into under software control.

On the other hand, the interrupt request register (IRR) stores the status of the interrupt request inputs. It also contains one bit position for each of the IR inputs. The values in these bit positions reflect whether the interrupt inputs are active or inactive.

Which of the active interrupt inputs is identified as having the highest priority is determined by the priority resolver. This section can be configured to work using a number of different priority schemes through software. Following this scheme, it identifies the highest priority of the active interrupt inputs and signals the control logic that an interrupt is active. In response, the control logic causes the INT signal to be issued to the 8086.

The in-service register differs in that it stores the interrupt level that is presently being serviced. During the first $\overline{INTA}$ pulse in an interrupt acknowledge bus cycle, the level of the highest active interrupt is strobed into ISR. Loading of ISR occurs in response to output signals of the control logic section. This register cannot be written into; however, its contents may be read as status through software.

The cascade buffer/comparator section provides the interface between master and slave 8259As. As we mentioned earlier, it is this interface that permits easy expansion of the interrupt interface using a master/slave configuration. Each slave has an *ID code* that is stored in this section.

Programming the 8259A

The way in which the 8259A operates is determined by how the device is programmed. Two types of command words are provided for this purpose. They are the *initialization command words* (ICW) and the *operational command words* (OCW). ICW commands are used to load the internal control registers of the 8259A. There are four such command words and they are identified as ICW_1, ICW_2, ICW_3, and ICW_4. On the other hand, the three OCW commands permit the 8086 to initiate variations in the basic operating modes defined by the ICW commands. These three commands are called OCW_1, OCW_2, and OCW_3.

The 8086 issues commands to the 8259A by initiating output or write cycles. This can be done by executing either the OUT or MOV instruction, respectively.

LSI peripherals such as the 8259A must be located at even-word address boundaries in the 8086's address space. The address put on the system bus during the output bus cycle must be decoded with external circuitry to chip select the peripheral. When an address assigned to the 8259A is on the bus, the output of the decoder must produce logic 0 at the $\overline{CS}$ input. This signal enables the read/write logic within the PIC and data applied at D_0 through D_7 are written into the command register within the control logic section synchronously with a write strobe at $\overline{WR}$.

The interrupt request input (INTR) of the 8086 must be disabled whenever commands are being issued to the 8259A. This can be done by clearing the interrupt enable flag by executing the CLI (clear interrupt enable flag) instruction. After completion of the command sequence, the interrupt input must be reenabled. To do this, the 8086 must execute the STI (set interrupt enable flag) instruction.

The flow diagram in Fig. 8.9 shows the sequence of events that the 8086 must perform to initialize the 8259A with ICW commands. The cycle begins with the 8086 outputting initialization command word ICW_1 to the address of the 8259A.

The moment that ICW_1 is written into the control logic section of the 8259A certain internal setup conditions automatically occur. First the internal sequence logic is set up such that the 8259A will accept the remaining ICWs as designated by ICW_1. It turns out that if the least significant bit of ICW_1 is logic 1, command word ICW_4 is required in the initialization sequence. Moreover, if the next least significant bit of ICW_1 is logic 0, the command word ICW_3 is also required.

In addition to this, writting ICW_1 to the 8259A clears ISR and IMR. Also three operation command word bits, *special mask mode* (SMM) in OCW_3, *interrupt request register* (IRR) in OCW_3, and *end of interrupt* (EOI) in OCW_2, are cleared to

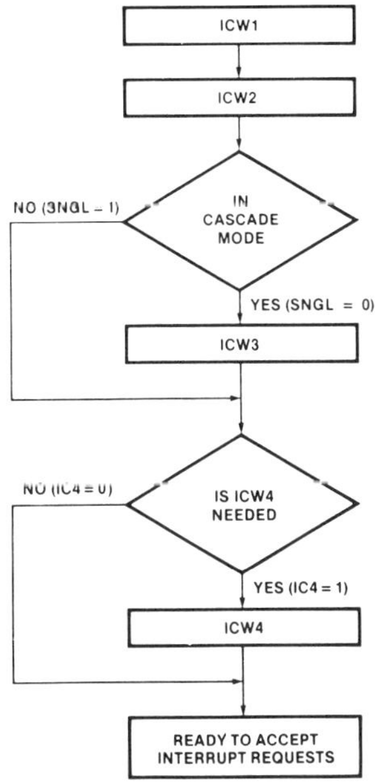

Figure 8.9 Initialization sequence of the 8259A (*Courtesy of Intel Corporation*).

logic 0. Furthermore, the *fully masked mode* of interrupt operation is entered with an initial priority assignment such that IR_0 is the highest-priority input and IR_7 the lowest-priority input. Finally, the edge-sensitive latches associated with the IR inputs are all cleared.

If the LSB of ICW_1 was initialized to logic 0, one additional event occurs. This is that all bits of the control register associated with ICW_4 are cleared.

In Fig. 8.9 we see that once the 8086 starts initialization of the 8259A by writing ICW_1 into the control register, it must continue the sequence by writing ICW_2 and then optionally ICW_3 and ICW_4 in that order. Notice that it is not possible to modify just one of the initialization command registers. Instead, all words that are required to define the device's operating mode must be output once again.

We found that all four words need not always be used to initialize the 8259A. However, for its use in the 8086 system, words ICW_1, ICW_2, and ICW_4 are always required. ICW_3 is optional and is needed only if the 8259A is to function in the cascade mode.

Initialization Command Words

Now that we have introduced the initialization sequence of the 8259A, let us look more closely at the functions controlled by each of the initialization command words. We will begin with ICW_1. Its format and bit functions are identified in Fig. 8.10(a). Notice that address bit A_0 is included as a ninth bit and it must be logic 0. This corresponds to an even address boundary.

Here we find that the logic level of the LSB D_0 of the initialization word indi-

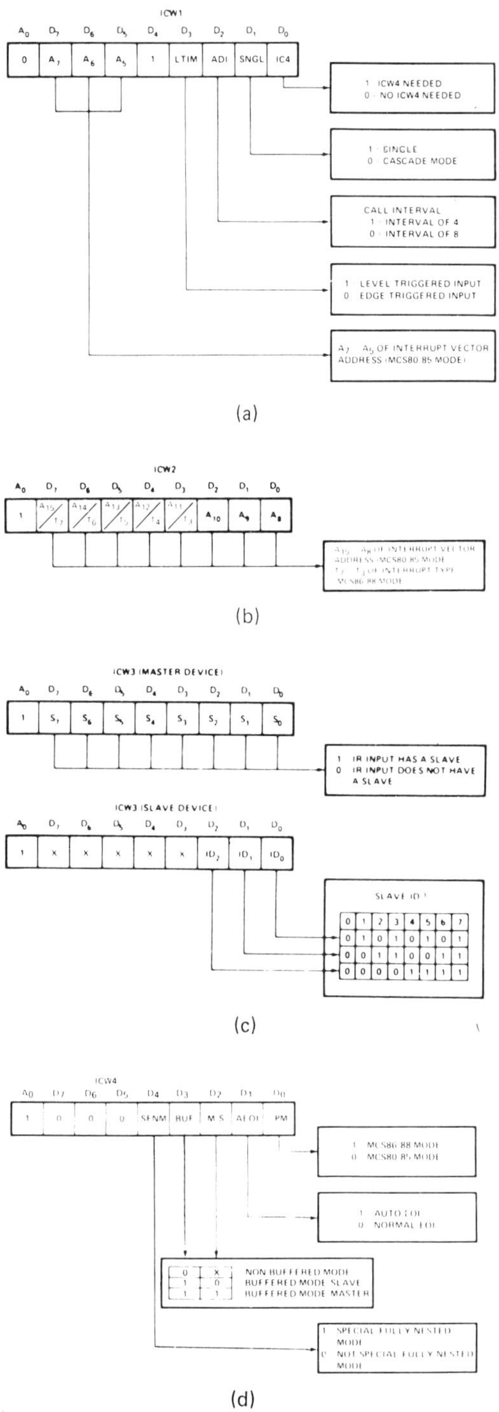

Figure 8.10 **(a)** ICW_1 format *(Courtesy of Intel Corporation)*; **(b)** ICW_2 format *(Courtesy of Intel Corporation)*; **(c)** ICW_3 format *(Courtesy of Intel Corporation)*; **(d)** ICW_4 format *(Courtesy of Intel Corporation)*.

cates to the 8259A whether or not ICW_4 will be included in the programming sequence. As we mentioned earlier, logic 1 at D_0 (IC_4) specifies that it is needed. The next bit, D_1 (SNGL), selects between *single device* or *multidevice cascaded mode* of operation. When D_1 is set to logic 0, the internal circuitry of the 8259A is configured for cascaded mode. Selecting this state also sets up the initialization sequence such that ICW_3 must be issued as part of the initialization cycle. Bit D_2 has functions specified for it in Fig. 8.10(a). However, it can be ignored when the 8259A is being connected to the 8086 and is a don't-care state. D_3, which is labeled LTIM, defines whether the eight IR inputs operate in the level-sensitive or edge-triggered mode. Logic 1 in D_3 selects level-triggered operation and logic 0 selects edge-triggered operation. Finally, bit D_4 is fixed at the 1 logic level and the three MSBs D_5 through D_7 are not required in 8086 systems.

Example 8.2

What value should be written into ICW_1 in order to configure the 8259A such that ICW_4 is needed in the initialization sequence, the system is going to use multiple 8259As, and its inputs are to be level sensitive? Assume that all unused bits are to be logic 0. Give the result in both binary and hexadecimal form.

Solution. Since ICW_4 is to be initialized, D_0 must be logic 1.

$$D_0 = 1$$

For cascaded mode of operation, D_1 must be 0

$$D_1 = 0$$

and for level-sensitive inputs D_3 must be 1.

$$D_3 = 1$$

Bits D_2 and D_5 through D_7 are don't-care states and are all made logic 0.

$$D_2 = D_5 = D_6 = D_7 = 0$$

Moreover, D_4 must be fixed at the 1 logic level.

$$D_4 = 1$$

This gives the complete command word

$$D_7D_6D_5D_4D_3D_2D_1D_0 = 00011001_2 = 19_{16}$$

The second initialization word, ICW_2, has a single function in the 8086 microcomputer. As shown in Fig. 8.10(b), its five most significant bits D_7 through D_3 define a fixed binary code T_7 through T_3 that is used as the most significant bits of its type number. Whenever the 8259A puts the 3-bit interrupt type number corresponding to its active input onto the bus, it is automatically combined with the value T_7 through T_3 to form an 8-bit type number. The three least significant bits of ICW_2 are not used. Notice that logic 1 must be output on A_0 when this command word is put on the bus.

Example 8.3

What should be programmed into register ICW_2 if the type numbers output on the bus by the device are to range from $F0_{16}$ through $F7_{16}$?

Solution. To set the 8259A up such that type numbers are in the range $F0_{16}$ through $F7_{16}$, its device code bits must be:

$$D_7D_6D_5D_4D_3 = 11110_2$$

The lower 3 bits are don't-care states and all can be 0s. This gives the command word

$$D_7D_6D_5D_4D_3D_2D_1D_0 = 11110000_2 = F0_{16}$$

The information of initialization command word ICW_3 is required by only those 8259As that are configured for the cascaded mode of operation. Figure 8.10(c) shows its bits. Notice that ICW_3 is used for different functions depending on whether the device is a master or slave. In the case of a master, bits D_0 through D_7 of the word are labeled S_0 through S_7. These bits correspond to IR inputs IR_0 through IR_7, respectively. They identify whether or not the corresponding IR input is supplied by either the INT output of a slave or directly by an external device. Logic 1 loaded in an S position indicates that the corresponding IR input is supplied by a slave.

On the other hand, ICW_3 for a slave is used to load the device with a 3-bit identification code $ID_2ID_1ID_0$. This number must correspond to the IR input of the master to which the slave's INT output is wired. The ID code is required within the slave so that it can be compared to the cascading code output by the master on CAS_0 through CAS_2.

Example 8.4

Assume that a master PIC is to be configured such that its IR_0 through IR_3 inputs are to accept inputs directly from external devices but IR_4 through IR_7 are to be supplied by the INT outputs of slaves. What code should be used for the initialization command word ICW_3?

Solution. For IR_0 through IR_3 to be configured to allow direct inputs from external devices, bits D_0 through D_3 of ICW_3 must be logic 0.

$$D_3D_2D_1D_0 = 0000_2$$

The other IR inputs of the master are to be supplied by INT outputs of slaves. Therefore, their control bits must be all 1.

$$D_7D_6D_5D_4 = 1111_2$$

This gives the complete command word

$$D_7D_6D_5D_4D_3D_2D_1D_0 = 11110000_2 = F0_{16}$$

The fourth control word, ICW_4, which is shown in Fig. 8.10(d), is used to configure the device for use with the 8086 and selects various features that are available in its operation. The LSB D_0, which is called μPM, must be set to logic 1 whenever the device is used together with the 8086. The next bit, D_1, is labeled AEOI for *automatic end of interrupt*. If this mode is enabled by writing logic 1 into the bit location, the EOI (*end of interrupt*) command does not have to be issued as part of the service routine.

Of the next two bits in ICW_4, BUF is used to specify whether or not the 8259A is to be used in a system where the data bus is buffered with a bidirectional bus transceiver. When buffered mode is selected, the $\overline{SP}/\overline{EN}$ line is configured as $\overline{EN}$. As indicated earlier, $\overline{EN}$ is a control output that can be used to control the direction of data transfer through the bus transceiver. It switches to logic 0 whenever data are transferred from the 8259A to the 8086.

If buffered mode is not selected, the $\overline{SP}/\overline{EN}$ line is configured to work as the master/slave mode select input. In this case, logic 1 at the $\overline{SP}$ input selects master mode operation and logic 0 selects slave mode.

Assume that the buffered mode was selected; then the $\overline{SR}$ input is no longer available to select between the master and slave modes of operation. Instead, the MS bit of ICW_4 defines whether the 8259A is a master or slave device.

Bit D_4 is used to enable or disable another operational option of the 8259A. This option is known as the *special fully nested mode*. This function is only used in conjunction with the cascaded mode. Moreover, it is enabled only for the master 8259A, not for the slaves. This is done by setting the SFNM bit to logic 1.

The 8259A is put into the fully nested mode of operation as command word ICW_1 is loaded. When an interrupt is initiated in a cascaded system that is configured in this way, the occurrence of another interrupt at the slave corresponding to the original interrupt is masked out even if it is of higher priority. This is because the bit in ISR of the master 8259A that corresponds to the slave is already set; therefore, the 8259A ignores all interrupts of equal or lower priority.

This problem is overcome by enabling special fully nested mode of operation at the master. In this mode, the master will respond to those interrupts that are at lower or higher priority than the active level.

The last 3 bits of ICW_4, D_5 through D_7, must always be logic 0 and the word must be written to an odd-address boundary.

Operational Command Words

Once the appropriate ICW commands have been issued to the 8259A, it is ready to operate in the fully nested mode. Three operational command words are also provided for controlling the operation of the 8259A. These commands permit further modifications to be made to the operation of the interrupt interface after it has been initialized. Unlike the initialization sequence, which requires that the ICWs be output in a special sequence after power-up, the OCWs can be issued under program control whenever needed and in any order.

The first operational command word, OCW_1, is used to access the contents of the interrupt mask register (IRR). A read operation can be performed to the register to determine its present status. Moreover, write operations can be performed to set or reset its bits. This permits selective masking of the interrupt inputs. Notice in Fig.

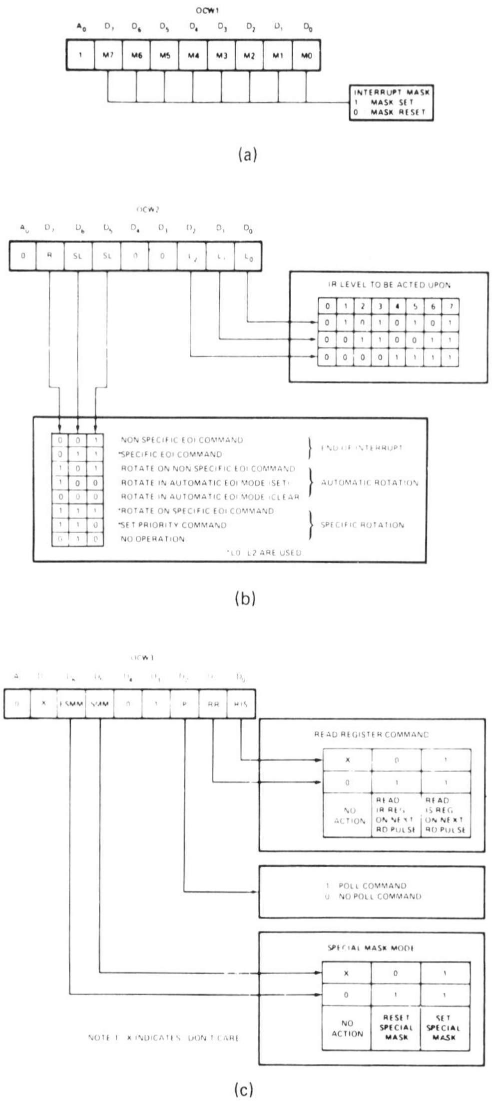

Figure 8.11 **(a)** OCW_1 format *(Courtesy of Intel Corporation);* **(b)** OCW_2 format *(Courtesy of Intel Corporation)*; **(c)** OCW_3 format *(Courtesy of Intel Corporation).*

8.11(a) that bits D_0 through D_7 of command word ICW_1 are identified as mask bits M_0 through M_7, respectively. In hardware, these bits correspond to interrupt inputs IR_0 through IR_7, respectively. Setting a bit to logic 1 masks out the associated interrupt input. On the other hand, clearing it to logic 0 enables the interrupt input.

For instance, writing $F0_{16} = 11110000_2$ into the register causes inputs IR_0 through IR_3 to be enabled and IR_4 through IR_7 to be disabled. A_0 must be logic 1 whenever the OCW_1 command is issued.

Example 8.5

What should be the OCW_1 code if interrupt inputs IR_0 through IR_3 are to be disabled and IR_4 through IR_7 enabled?

Solution. For IR_0 through IR_3 to be disabled, their corresponding bits in the mask register must be made logic 1.

$$D_3D_2D_1D_0 = 1111_2$$

On the other hand, for IR_4 through IR_7 to be enabled D_4 through D_7 must be logic 0.

$$D_7D_6D_5D_4 = 0000_2$$

Therefore, the complete word for OCW_1 is

$$D_7D_6D_5D_4D_3D_2D_1D_0 = 00001111_2 = 0F_{16}$$

The second operational command word OCW_2 selects the appropriate priority scheme and assigns an IR level for those schemes that require a specific interrupt level. The format of OCW_2 is given in Fig. 8.11(b). Here we see that the three LSBs define the interrupt level. For example, using $L_2L_1L_0 = 000_2$ in these locations specifies interrupt level 0, which corresponds to input IR_0.

The other three active bits of the word D_7, D_6, and D_5 are called *rotation* (R), *specific level* (SL), and *end of interrupt* (EOI), respectively. They are used to select a priority scheme according to the table in Fig. 8.11(b). For instance, if these bits are all logic 1, the priority scheme known as *rotate on specific EOI command* is enabled. Since this scheme requires a specific interrupt, its value must be included in $L_2L_1L_0$. A_0 must be logic 0 whenever this command is issued to the 8259A.

Example 8.6

What ICW_2 must be issued to the 8259A if the priority scheme rotate on nonspecific EOI command is to be selected?

Solution. To enable the rotate on nonspecific EOI command priority scheme, bits D_7 through D_5 must be set to 101. Since a specific level does not have to be specified, the rest of the bits in the command word can be 0. This gives OCW_2 as

$$D_7D_6D_5D_4D_3D_2D_1D_0 = 10100000_2 = A0_{16}$$

The last control word OCW_3, which is shown in Fig. 8.11(c), permits reading of the contents of the ISR or IRR registers through software, issue of the poll command, and enable/disable of the special mask mode. Bit D_1, which is called *read register* (RR), is set to 1 to initiate reading of either the in-service register (ISR) or interrupt request register (IRR). At the same time, bit D_0, which is labeled RIS, selects between ISR and IRR. Logic 0 in RIS selects IRR and logic 1 selects ISR. In response to this command, the 8259A puts the contents of the selected register on the bus, where it can be read by the 8086.

If the next bit, D_2, in OCW_3 is logic 1, a *poll command* is issued to the 8259A. The result of issuing a poll command is that the next $\overline{RD}$ pulse to the 8259A is interpreted as an interrupt acknowledge. In turn, the 8259A causes the ISR register to be loaded with the value of the highest-priority active interrupt. After this, a *poll word* is automatically put on the data bus. The 8086 must read it off the bus.

Figure 8.12 illustrates the format of the poll word. Looking at this word, we see that the MSB is labeled I for interrupt. The logic level of this bit indicates to the 8086 whether or not an interrupt input was active. Logic 1 indicates that an interrupt is active. The three LSBs $W_2W_1W_0$ identify the priority level of the highest-priority active interrupt input. This poll word can be decoded through software and when an interrupt is found to be active a branch is initiated to the starting point of its service routine. The poll command represents a software method of identifying whether or not an interrupt has occurred; therefore, the INTR input of the 8086 should be disabled.

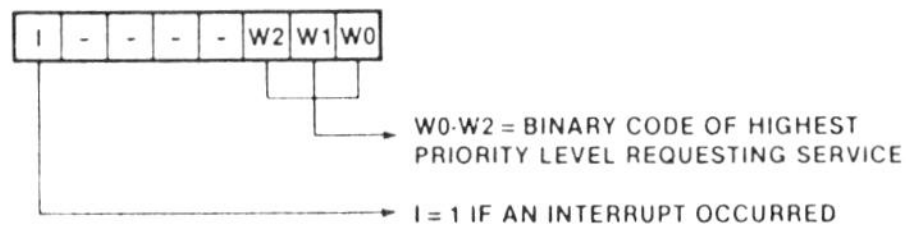

Figure 8.12 Poll word format (*Courtesy of Intel Corporation*).

D_5 and D_6 are the remaining bits of OCW_3 for which functions are defined. They are used to enable or disable the special mask mode. ESMM (*enable special mask mode*) must be logic 1 to permit changing of the status of the special mask mode with the SMM (*special mask mode*) bit. Logic 1 at SMM enables the special mask mode of operation. If the 8259A is initially configured for the fully nested mode of operation, only interrupts of higher priority are allowed to interrupt an active service routine. However, by enabling the special mask mode, interrupts of higher or lower priority are enabled, but those of equal priority remain masked out.

Example 8.7

Write a program that will initialize an 8259A with the initialization command words ICW_1, ICW_2, and ICW_3 derived in examples 8.2, 8.3, and 8.4, respectively. Moreover, ICW_4 is to be equal to $1F_{16}$. Assume that the 8259A resides at address $A000_{16}$ in the memory address space.

Solution: Since the 8259A resides in the memory address space, we can use a series of move instructions to write the initialization command words into its registers. However, before doing this, we must first disable interrupts. This is done with the instruction

```
CLI                    ; DISABLE INTERRUPTS
```

Next we will set up a data segment starting at address 00000_{16}.

```
MOV   DS,0H            ;CREATE A DATA SEGMENT AT 00000₁₆
```

Now we are ready to write the command words to the 8259A.

```
MOV   AL,019H          ; LOAD ICW 1
MOV   0A000H,AL        ; WRITE ICW 1 to 8259A
MOV   AL,0F0H          ; LOAD ICW 2
MOV   0A000H,AL        ; WRITE ICW 2 to 8259A
```

```
MOV  AL,0F0H         ; LOAD ICW 3
MOV  0A000H,AL       ; WRITE ICW 3 to 8259A
MOV  AL,01FH         ; LOAD ICW 4
MOV  0A000H,AL       ; WRITE ICW 4 to 8259A
```

Initialization is now complete and the interrupts can be enabled.

```
STI                  ; ENABLE INTERRUPTS
```

8.9 MINIMUM-MODE-SYSTEM AND MAXIMUM-MODE-SYSTEM INTERRUPT INTERFACES USING THE 8259A

Now that we have introduced the 8259A programmable interrupt controller, let us look at how it is used to implement the interrupt interface in the 8086 microcomputer system. The circuit in Fig. 8.13 shows three 8259A devices connected in a *master/slave configuration* to construct an interrupt interface for a minimum-mode 8086 microcomputer system.

Let us begin by tracing the path taken from the interrupt request inputs of the slaves to the interrupt request input of the 8086. A request for interrupt service is initiated at an input of a slave. This causes the INT output of the corresponding slave to switch to logic 1. Looking at the circuit, we see that the INT output of the slave PICs are applied to separate interrupt inputs on the master PIC. Then the INT output of the master is supplied directly to the interrupt request input of the 8086.

Notice that the demultiplexed address bus and data bus lines connect to all three 8259As in parallel. It is over these lines that the 8086 initializes the internal registers of the 8259As, reads the contents of these registers, and reads the type number of the active interrupt during the interrupt acknowledge bus cycle. Each 8259A should

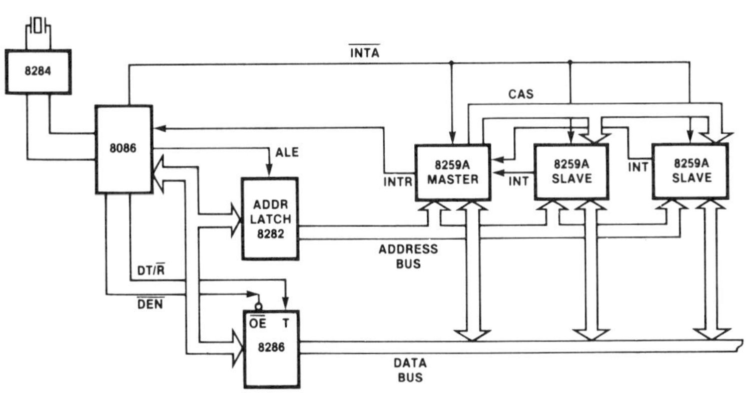

Figure 8.13 Minimum mode interrupt interface using the 8259A (*Courtesy of Intel Corporation*).

reside at a unique address. In this way, during read or write cycles to the interrupt interface, the address output on the bus can be decoded to produce an enable signal to chip-select the appropriate device.

The last group of signals in the interrupt interface are the CAS bus. Notice that these lines on all three PICs are connected in parallel. It is over these lines that the master signals the slaves whether or not the interrupt request has been acknowledged.

Whenever an interrupt input is active at the master or at a slave and the priority is higher than that of an already active interrupt, the master controller switches INTR to logic 1. This signals the 8086 that an external device needs to be serviced. As long as the interrupt flag within the 8086 is set to 1, the interrupt interface is enabled and the interrupt request will be accepted. Therefore, the interrupt acknowledge bus cycle is initiated. As the first pulse is output at interrupt acknowledge ($\overline{\text{INTA}}$), the master PIC is signaled to put the 3-bit cascade code of the device whose interrupt request is being acknowledged on the CAS bus. The slaves read this code and compare it to their internal code. In this way, the slave corresponding to the code is signaled to put the type number of its highest-priority active interrupt onto the data bus. The 8086 reads this number off the bus and then initiates a vectored transfer of control to the starting point of the corresponding service routine in program memory.

Figure 8.14 illustrates a similar interrupt interface implemented in a maximum-mode 8086 microcomputer system.

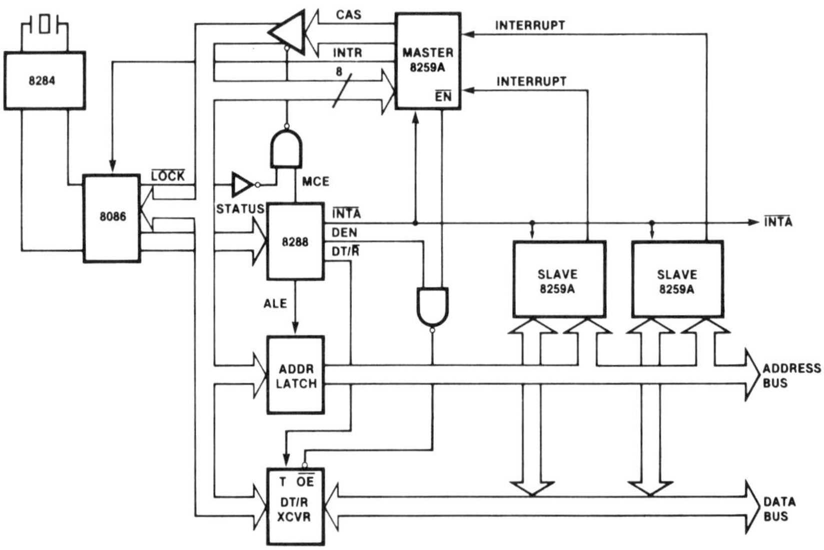

Figure 8.14 Maximum mode interrupt interface using the 8259A (*Courtesy of Intel Corporation*).

8.10 SOFTWARE INTERRUPTS

The 8086 system is capable of implementing up to 252 software interrupts. They differ from the external hardware interrupts in that their service routines are initiated in response to the execution of a software interrupt instruction, not an event in external hardware.

The INT n instruction is used to initiate a software interrupt. Earlier in this chapter we indicated that "n" represents the type number associated with the service routine. The software interrupt service routines are vectored to, using pointers from the same memory locations as the corresponding external hardware interrupts. These locations are shown in the pointer table of Fig. 8.1. Our earlier example was INT 50. It has a type number of 50 and causes a vector in program control to the service routine whose starting address is defined by the values of IP and CS stored at addresses $00C8_{16}$ through $00CB_{16}$, respectively.

The mechanism by which a software interrupt is initiated is similar to that described for the external hardware interrupts. However, no external interrupt acknowledge bus cycles are initiated. Instead, control is passed to the start of the service routine immediately upon completion of execution of the interrupt instruction. As usual, the old flags, old CS, and old IP are automatically saved on the stack and then IF and TF are cleared.

If necessary, the contents of other internal registers can be saved on the stack by including the appropriate PUSH instructions at the beginning of the service routine. Toward the end of the service routine, POP instructions must be included to restore these registers. Finally, an IRET instruction is included to restore the original program environment.

Software interrupts are of higher priority than the external interrupts and are not masked out by IF. The software interrupts are actually *vectored subroutine calls*. A common use of these software routines is as *emulation routines* for more complex functions. For instance, INT_{50} could define a *floating-point addition instruction* and INT_{51} a *floating-point subtraction instruction*. These emulation routines are written using assembly language instructions, are assembled into machine code, and then are stored in the main memory of the 8086 microcomputer system. Other examples of their use are for *supervisor calls* from an operating system and for *testing* of external hardware interrupt service routines.

8.11 NONMASKABLE INTERRUPT

The nonmaskable interrupt (NMI) is another interrupt that is initiated from external hardware. However, it differs from the other external hardware interrupts in several ways. First, it cannot be masked out with the IF flag. Second, requests for service by this interrupt are signaled to the 8086 with the 1 logic level at its NMI input, not the INTR input. Third, the NMI input is positive edge triggered. Therefore, a request for service is latched internal to the 8086.

If the contents of the NMI latch is sampled as being active for two consecutive clock cycles, it is recognized and the nonmaskable interrupt sequence initiated. Initiation of NMI causes the current flags, current CS, and current IP to be pushed onto the stack. Moreover, the interrupt enable flag is cleared to disable all external hardware interrupts and the trap flag is cleared to disable the single-step mode of operation.

As shown in Fig. 8.1, NMI has a dedicated priority level. It automatically vectors from the type 2 vector location in the pointer table. This vector is stored in memory at word addresses 0008_{16} and $000A_{16}$.

Typically, the NMI is assigned to hardware events that must be responded to immediately. Two examples are the detection of a power failure and detection of a memory read error.

8.12 RESET INTERRUPT

The RESET interrupt input of the 8086 provides a hardware means for initializing the 8086 microcomputer. This is typically done at power-up to provide an orderly startup of the system.

Figure 8.15(a) shows that the reset interface of the 8086 includes part of the 8284 clock generator device. The 8284 contains circuitry that makes it easy to implement the hardware reset function. Notice that the $\overline{RES}$ input (pin 11) of the clock generator is attached to an *RC* circuit. The signal at $\overline{RES}$ is applied to the input of a Schmitt trigger circuit. If the voltage across the capacitor is below the 1-logic-level threshold of the Schmitt trigger, the RESET output (pin 10) stays at logic 1. This output is supplied to the RESET input at pin 21 of the 8086. It can also be applied in parallel to reset inputs on LSI peripheral devices such that they are also initialized at power-on.

At power-on, $\overline{RES}$ of the 8284 is shorted to ground through the capacitor. This

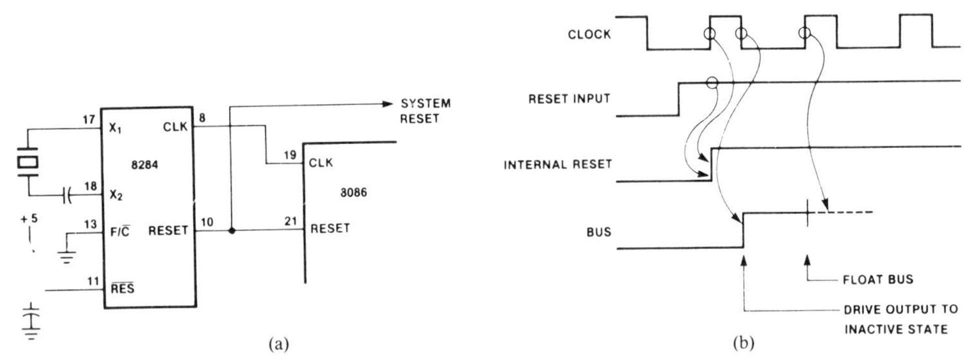

Figure 8.15 **(a)** Reset interface of the 8086 (*Courtesy of Intel Corporation*); **(b)** reset timing sequence (*Courtesy of Intel Corporation*).

represents logic 0 at the input of the Schmitt trigger and RESET switches to logic 1. At the RESET input of the 8086, this signal is synchronized to the 0-to-1 edge of CLK. This is shown in the waveforms of Fig. 8.15(b). RESET must be held at logic 1 for a minimum of four clock cycles; otherwise, it will not be recognized.

The 8086 terminates operation on the 0 to 1 edge of the internal reset signal. Its bus is put in the high-Z state and the control signals are switched to their inactive states. These signal states are summarized in Fig. 8.16. Here we see that in a minimum-mode system signals AD_0 through AD_{15}, $AD_{16}/\overline{S_3}$ through $AD_{19}/\overline{S_6}$, and $\overline{BHE}/S_7$ are immediately put in the high-Z state. On the other hand, signal lines $M/\overline{IO}$, $DT/\overline{R}$, $\overline{DEN}$, $\overline{WR}$, $\overline{RD}$, and $\overline{INTA}$ are first forced to logic 1 for one clock interval and then they are put in the high-Z state synchronously with the positive edge of the next clock pulse. Moreover, signal lines ALE and HLDA are forced to their inactive 0 logic level. The 8086 remains in this state until the RESET input is returned to logic 0.

Signals	Condition
$AD_{15\text{-}0}$	Three-State
$A_{19\text{-}16}/S_{6\text{-}3}$	Three-State
$\overline{BHE}/S_7$	Three-State
$\overline{S2}/(M/\overline{IO})$	Driven to "1" then three-state
$\overline{S1}/(DT/\overline{R})$	Driven to "1" then three-state
$\overline{S0}/\overline{DEN}$	Driven to "1" then three-state
$\overline{LOCK}/\overline{WR}$	Driven to "1" then three-state
$\overline{RD}$	Driven to "1" then three-state
$\overline{INTA}$	Driven to "1" then three-state
ALE	0
HLDA	0
$\overline{RQ}/\overline{GT0}$	1
$\overline{RQ}/\overline{GT1}$	1
QS0	0
QS1	0

Figure 8.16 Bus and control signal status during system reset (*Courtesy of Intel Corporation*).

In the maximum-mode system, the 8086 responds in a similar way. However, this time the $\overline{S_2}\overline{S_1}\overline{S_0}$ outputs, which are inputs to the 8288 bus controller, are also immediately put into the high-Z state. These inputs of the 8288 have internal pull-up resistors. Therefore, with the signal lines in the high-Z state, the input to the bus controller is $\overline{S_2}\overline{S_1}\overline{S_0} = 111$. In response, its control outputs are set to ALE = 0, DEN = 0, $DT/\overline{R} = 1$, $MCE/\overline{PDEN} = 0/1$, and all of its command outputs are switched to the 1 logic level. Moreover, outputs QS_0 and QS_1 of the 8086 are both held at logic 0 and the $\overline{RQ}/\overline{GT_0}$ and $\overline{RQ}/\overline{GT_1}$ lines are held at logic 1.

When RESET returns to logic 0, the 8086 initiates its internal initialization routine. The flags are all cleared; the instruction pointer is set to 0000_{16}; the CS register is set to $FFFF_{16}$; the DS register is set to 0000_{16}; the SS register is set to 0000_{16}; the ES register is set to 0000_{16}; and the queue is emptied. The table in Fig. 8.17 summarizes this state.

Since the flags were all cleared as part of initialization, the external hardware interrupts are disabled. Moreover, the code segment register contains $FFFF_{16}$ and the instruction pointer contains 0000_{16}. Therefore, execution begins after reset at

CPU COMPONENT	CONTENT
Flags	Clear
Instruction Pointer	0000H
CS Register	FFFFH
DS Register	0000H
SS Register	0000H
ES Register	0000H
Queue	Empty

Figure 8.17 Internal state of the 8086 after initialization (*Courtesy of Intel Corporation*).

$FFFF0_{16}$. This location can contain an instruction that will cause a jump to the start up program that is used to initialize the rest of the system's resources, such as I/O ports, the interrupt flag, and data memory. After system-level initialization is complete, another jump can be performed to the starting point of the microcomputer's application program.

8.13 INTERNAL INTERRUPT FUNCTIONS

Earlier we indicated that four of the 256 interrupts of the 8086 are dedicated to the internal functions: divide error, overflow error, single step, and breakpoint. They are assigned unique type numbers, as shown in Fig. 8.18. Notice that they are the

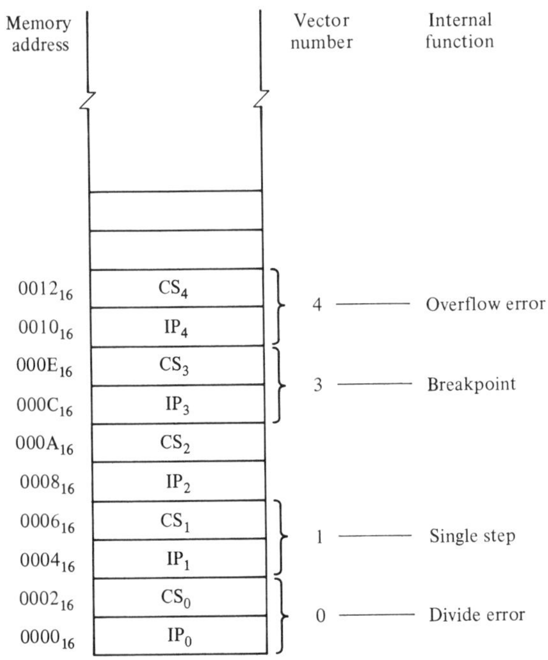

Figure 8.18 Internal interrupt vector locations.

highest-priority type numbers. Moreover, they are not masked out with the interrupt enable flag.

The occurrence of any one of these internal conditions is automatically detected by the 8086, and causes an interrupt of program execution and a vectored transfer of control to a corresponding service routine. During the control transfer sequence, no external bus cycles are produced. Let us now look at each of these internal functions in more detail.

Divide Error

The *divide error* function represents an error condition that can occur in the execution of the division instructions. If the quotient that results from a DIV (divide) instruction or an IDIV (integer divide) instruction is larger than the specified destination, a divide error has occurred. This condition causes automatic initiation of a type 0 interrupt and passes control to a service routine whose starting point is defined by the values of IP_0 and CS_0 at addresses 0000_{16} and 0002_{16}, respectively, in the pointer table.

Overflow Error

The *overflow error* is an error condition similar to that of divide error. However, it can result from the execution of any arithmetic instruction. Whenever an overflow occurs, the overflow flag gets set. In this case, the transfer of program control to a service routine is not automatic. Instead, the INTO (interrupt on overflow) instruction must be executed to test if the overflow service routine should be initiated. If the overflow flag is found to be set, a type 4 interrupt service routine is initiated. Its vector consists of IP_4 and CS_4 which are stored at 0010_{16} and 0012_{16}, respectively, in memory. The routine pointed to by this vector can be written to service the overflow condition. For instance, it could cause a message to be displayed to identify that an overflow has occurred.

Single Step

The *single-step* function relates to an operating option of the 8086. If the trap flag (TF) bit is set, the single-step mode of operation is enabled. This flag bit can be set or reset under software control.

If TF is set, the 8086 initiates a type 1 interrupt to the service routine defined by IP_1 and CS_1 at 0004_{16} and 0006_{16}, respectively, at the completion of execution of every instruction. This permits implementation of the single-step mode of operation such that the program can be executed one instruction at a time. For instance, the service routine could include a WAIT instruction. In this way, a transition to logic 0 at the $\overline{\text{TEST}}$ input of the 8086 could be used as the mechanism for stepping through a program one instruction at a time. This single-step operation can be used as a valuable software debugging tool.

Breakpoint Interrupt

The *breakpoint* function can also be used to implement a software diagnostic tool. A breakpoint interrupt is initiated by execution of the breakpoint instruction (*one-byte instruction*). This instruction can be inserted at strategic points in a program that is being debugged to cause execution to be stopped. This option can be used in a way similar to that of the single-step option. The service routine could again be put in the wait state, and resumption of execution down to the next breakpoint can be initiated by applying logic 0 to the $\overline{\text{TEST}}$ input.

ASSIGNMENT

Section 8.2

1. What are the five groups of interrupts available on the 8086 MPU?
2. What is the range of priority levels that can be assigned in an 8086 microcomputer system?

Section 8.3

3. What purpose is served by the pointer table?
4. The breakpoint service routine begins at address $AA000_{16}$ in the code segment which starts at $A0000_{16}$. Specify where and how the breakpoint vector will be stored in the pointer table.

Section 8.4

5. Explain how the CLI and STI instructions can be used to lock out external hardware interrupts during the execution of an uninterruptible subroutine.

Section 8.5

6. How can the interrupt interface be reenabled during execution of an interrupt service routine?

Section 8.6

7. Explain the function of the INTR and $\overline{\text{INTA}}$ signals in Figs. 8.3 and 8.4.

Section 8.7

8. Give an overview of the events in the order they occur during the interrupt request, interrupt acknowledge, and interrupt vector fetch cycles.

Section 8.8

9. Specify the value of ICW_1 needed to configure an 8259A as follows: ICW_4 not needed, single device interface, and edge-triggered inputs.
10. Specify the value for ICW_2 if the type numbers produced by the 8259A are to be in the range 70_{16} through 77_{16}.

11. Specify the value of ICW_4 such that the 8259A is configured for use in an 8086 system, with normal EOI, buffered mode master, and special fully nested mode disabled.
12. Write a program that will initialize an 8259A with the initialization command words derived in problems 9, 10, and 11. Assume that the 8259A resides at address $A000_{16}$ in the memory address space.
13. Write an instruction to read OCW_1 into the AL register. Assume that the 8259A has been configured by the software of problem 12.
14. What priority scheme is enabled if OCW_2 equals 67_{16}?
15. Write an instruction sequence that when executed will toggle the state of the read register bit in OCW_3. Assume that the 8259A is located at memory address $A000_{16}$.

Section 8.9

16. How many interrupt inputs can be directly accepted by the circuit in Fig. 8.13?

Section 8.10

17. Give an overview of the context switch mechanism initiated by the instruction INT 20.
18. Show the basic structure of an interrupt service routine. Assume that the routine uses the AX, BX, CX, and DI registers.

Section 8.11

19. How does NMI differ from an external hardware interrupt?

Section 8.12

20. To what address does the reset interrupt vector?
21. Write a RESET routine that initializes the block of memory locations from address $A000_{16}$ to $A100_{16}$ to zero. The initialization routine is to start at address 1000_{16}.

Section 8.13

22. What internal interrupts are serviced by the 8086?

9

The Hardware of the SDK-86 Microcomputer

9.1 INTRODUCTION

In the preceding three chapters, we presented in detail the memory, I/O, and interrupt interfaces of the 8086 microprocessor and its microcomputer system. In this chapter we examine how these interfaces are implemented in a simple microcomputer system. The microcomputer used for this purpose is that employed in Intel's 8086 microcomputer system design kit (SDK-86). The topics presented in the chapter are:

1. The microcomputer of the SDK-86
2. Clock generator and wait-state generator circuitry
3. Program storage memory
4. Data storage memory
5. Parallel I/O and interrupts
6. Serial I/O
7. The keypad and display

9.2 THE MICROCOMPUTER OF THE SDK-86

The circuitry of the SDK-86 represents the implementation of a simple 8086-based microcomputer system. A block diagram of this microcomputer system is shown in Fig. 9.1. The heart of the microcomputer, the MPU, is an 8086 microprocessor. It is this device that performs the arithmetic, logic, and control operations defined by the keypad monitor program.

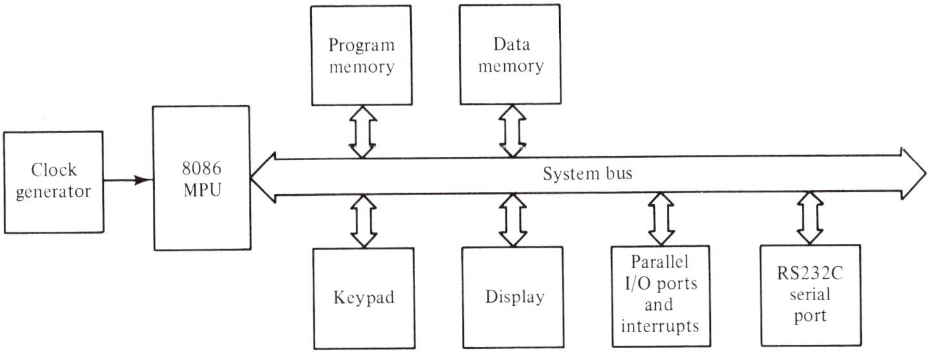

Figure 9.1 SDK-86 microcomputer block diagram.

The operations of the microprocessor and other devices in the microcomputer system are synchronized by the clock signals produced by the *clock generator section*. The 8086 in this microcomputer is set up to operate at a frequency of 4.9 MHz.

The *program memory section* stores the instructions of the monitor program. The 8086 fetches these instructions over the system's bus as it executes the program. Program memory is implemented with EPROMs and has a total storage capacity of 8K bytes. Use of EPROM makes the program storage nonvolatile. That is, the monitor program is maintained within the EPROMs even when power is removed from the system.

Data that are being processed by the microcomputer are stored in the *data memory section*. During the execution of an instruction, source or destination operands that reside in data memory are accessed over the system's bus by the 8086 microprocessor. This section of memory is implemented with 2142 static RAMs and can be as large as 4K bytes. This part of the memory subsystem is actually volatile; therefore, any information stored in it is lost when power is turned off.

When using the SDK-86 microcomputer to enter, execute, and debug 8086 machine code programs, the instructions of the program are stored and executed from data memory and not from the program memory. This permits the program to be loaded and modified by the user from the keypad. Only the monitor program resides in program storage memory.

The microcomputer in the SDK-86 also has a number of *I/O resources*. Looking at the block diagram in Fig. 9.1, we see that there is a *keypad, display, parallel I/O section,* and an *RS-232C serial communication port*. The keypad allows the user to input information to the microcomputer. For example, in Chapter 5 we showed that monitor commands such as EW or ER are issued from the keypad. Commands like these allow the programmer to enter machine code programs by modifying the contents of data memory, single-step execute programs, and implement program debug operations by giving the ability to examine register contents or memory contents.

The display unit is an output device and it provides the user with data related to the monitor commands that are entered through the keypad. For instance, as the

EB command is used to enter a byte of a program, the current contents of a memory location are first displayed and then the new value is displayed digit by digit as it is entered from the keypad. Similarly, when a command is issued to examine the contents of a register such as AX, a register descriptor and the register contents are displayed.

The keypad and display interfaces of the SDK-86 microcomputer are implemented with the 8279 LSI peripheral device. This device takes data entered at the keypad, displays the data on the display unit, and passes it to the 8086 over the system bus.

The parallel I/O section of the microcomputer provides 48 individual I/O lines. This part of the I/O interface is implemented with 8255A parallel peripheral interface devices and can be configured under software control to work as inputs or outputs and with a variety of different modes of operation.

The last I/O interface is a serial communications port that permits a terminal or a CRT to be connected to the microcomputer. When this is done, the user input/output is through the terminal instead of through the keypad and display. This serial port is implemented with an 8251A universal asynchronous receiver/transmitter (UART) IC.

Figure 9.2 is a schematic diagram that details the circuits used to implement each of the functional blocks of the microcomputer in the SDK-86.

9.3 CLOCK GENERATOR AND WAIT-STATE GENERATOR CIRCUITRY

Now that we have introduced the architecture and functions of the fundamental blocks of the SDK-86 microcomputer, let us continue by examining the circuitry used to implement these blocks. We will begin with the *clock generator* and *wait-state circuits.* Figure 9.3 shows this segment of circuitry.

Looking at the circuit in Fig. 9.3, we find that the 8284 clock generator/driver IC is used to produce the system clock. The 14.7456-MHz crystal connected between the X_1 and X_2 pins of the 8284 sets up the operating frequency. Remember that this crystal frequency is divided by 3 within the 8284 to produce the 4.9-MHz output clock at the CLK pin. Notice that this clock output is applied in parallel to both the CLK input of the 8086 and the CLK input of the 74LS164 wait-state generator circuit.

A second clock signal produced by the 8284 is peripheral clock (PCLK). PCLK is 2.45 MHz, which is one-half the frequency of CLK. From the system schematic diagram of Fig. 9.2, we find that it is supplied to the CLK inputs of the 8251A UART and 8279 keypad/display controller. In this way, their operation is synchronized to that of the MPU.

Another function supported by the 8284 is to provide the reset logic for initialization of the microcomputer system. In Fig. 9.3 we see that the SYSTM RESET key on the microcomputer's keypad connects to the $\overline{RES}$ input of the clock generator/driver. When this key is not depressed, the capacitor between $\overline{RES}$ and ground is charged to $+V_{CC}$ through the resistor. Therefore, the $\overline{RES}$ input of the 8086 is at the 1 logic level.

On the other hand, pressing the SYSTM RESET key causes $\overline{\text{RES}}$ to be short-circuited to ground. This applies logic 0 to $\overline{\text{RES}}$ and discharges the capacitor. As the key is released, the direct short to ground is broken; however, $\overline{\text{RES}}$ remains effectively short-circuited to ground through the discharged capacitor. The capacitor now begins to recharge with time toward the $+V_{CC}$ voltage level.

Remember that $\overline{\text{RES}}$ of the 8284 is a Schmitt trigger input. Therefore, as the voltage across the capacitor increases with time it remains detected as a 0 logic level as long as its value is below the logic 1 level threshhold of the Schmitt trigger. Thus we assure that $\overline{\text{RES}}$ is maintained at logic 0 for at least four clock cycles so that the reset will be detected correctly by the MPU.

Whenever $\overline{\text{RES}}$ is at the 0 logic level, the RST output of the 8284 is switched to the 1 logic level. Notice in Fig. 9.3 that this output is supplied to the RST input of the 8086, where it initiates a hardware reset of the microcomputer. The clock generator's RST output is also used to produce a peripheral reset signal called RESET OUT.

The last function performed by the circuit in Fig. 9.3 is wait-state generation. This function is implemented using several devices: the ready logic of the 8284, the 74LS164 wait-state generator, and a wait-state selection jumper. When the 8086 is running off a 4.9-MHz clock, bus cycles to memory or I/O devices take four states, or 800 ns. If slow memories or LSI peripherals are in use, wait states may have to be inserted into the bus cycle to lengthen its duration.

The circuitry in Fig. 9.3 allows for insertion of from zero to seven wait states by simply installing a jumper in positions W_{27} through W_{34}, respectively. For instance, the jumper connection, which is shown at W_{28}, causes one wait state to be inserted into the bus cycle. Therefore, it is extended from 800 ns to 1 μs.

Now that we have introduced the function of the wait-state generator circuitry, let us look at its operation in more detail. The 74LS164 is an 8-bit serial-in, parallel-out shift register. Its serial data input, which is not shown in Fig. 9.3, is fixed at the 1 logic level. The outputs are supplied through the series of jumpers to the WAIT STATE input of the OR gate. At the same time, the other input of this OR gate is supplied by a signal called ON BOARD MEMORY. This signal is generated by a three-input AND gate as follows:

$$\text{ON BOARD MEMORY} = \text{M}/\overline{\text{IO}} \bullet \overline{\text{OFF BOARD}} \bullet 1$$

When accessing either on-board memory or on-board I/O (i.e., devices directly mounted on the SDK-86 microcomputer board), $\overline{\text{OFF BOARD}}$ is always 1. Therefore, ON BOARD MEMORY will always equal M/$\overline{\text{IO}}$ and will be logic 1 during all on-board memory bus cycles. This makes the output of the OR gate, which is applied to the RDY_1 input of the 8284, immediately become logic 1 during all on-board memory bus cycles.

The logic 1 at RDY_1 causes the RDY output of the 8284 to swtich to the 1 logic level. This signal is applied to the RDY input of the MPU and signals that the current bus cycle should be completed without inserting wait states.

On the other hand, for all bus cycles to on-board I/O devices, the signal ON BOARD MEMORY is logic 0. In this case the output of the OR gate switches to logic 1 only when the output of the shift register corresponding to the inserted wait-

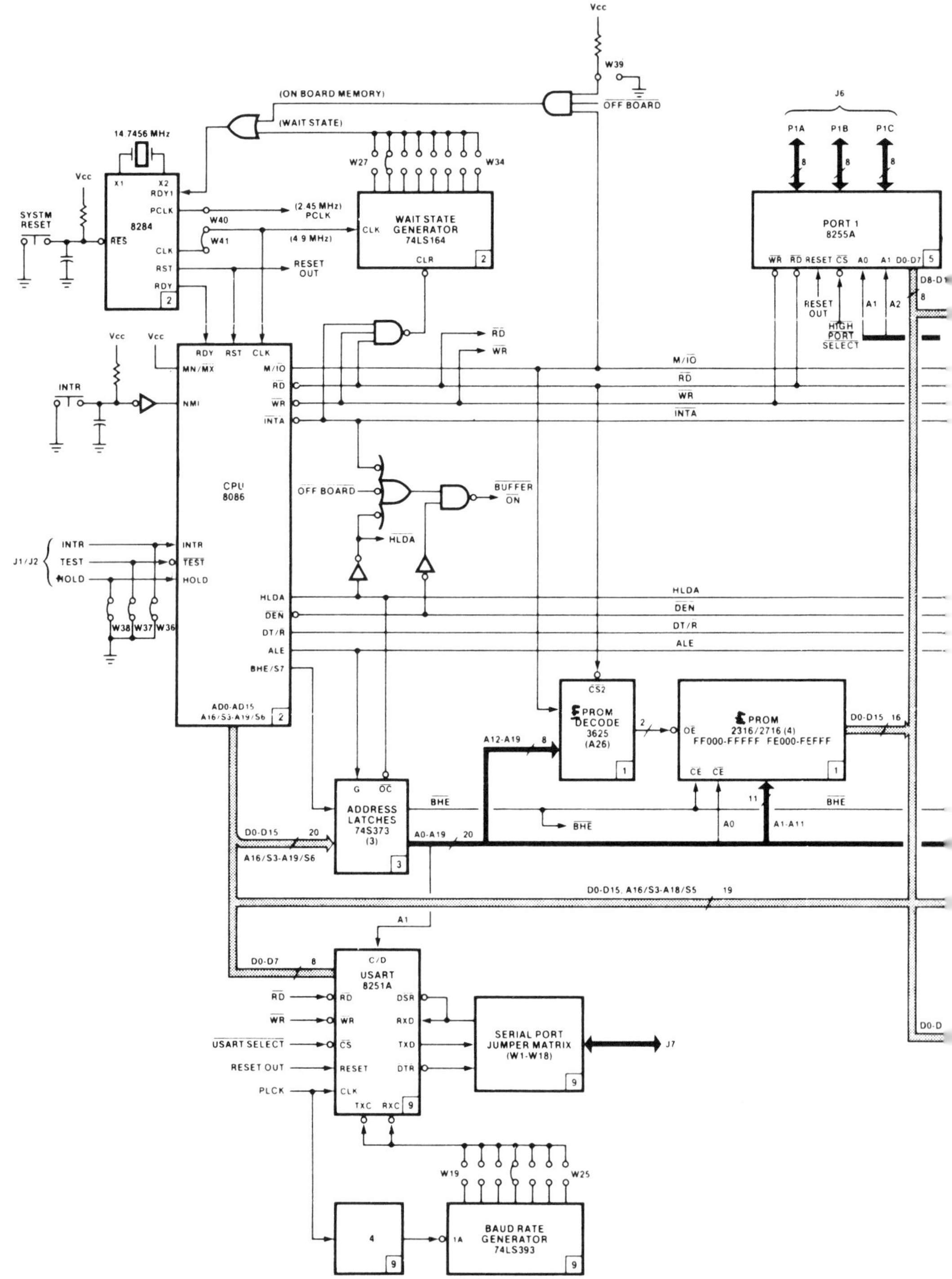

Figure 9.2 Schematic diagram of the SDK-86 microcomputer system (*Courtesy of Intel Corporation*).

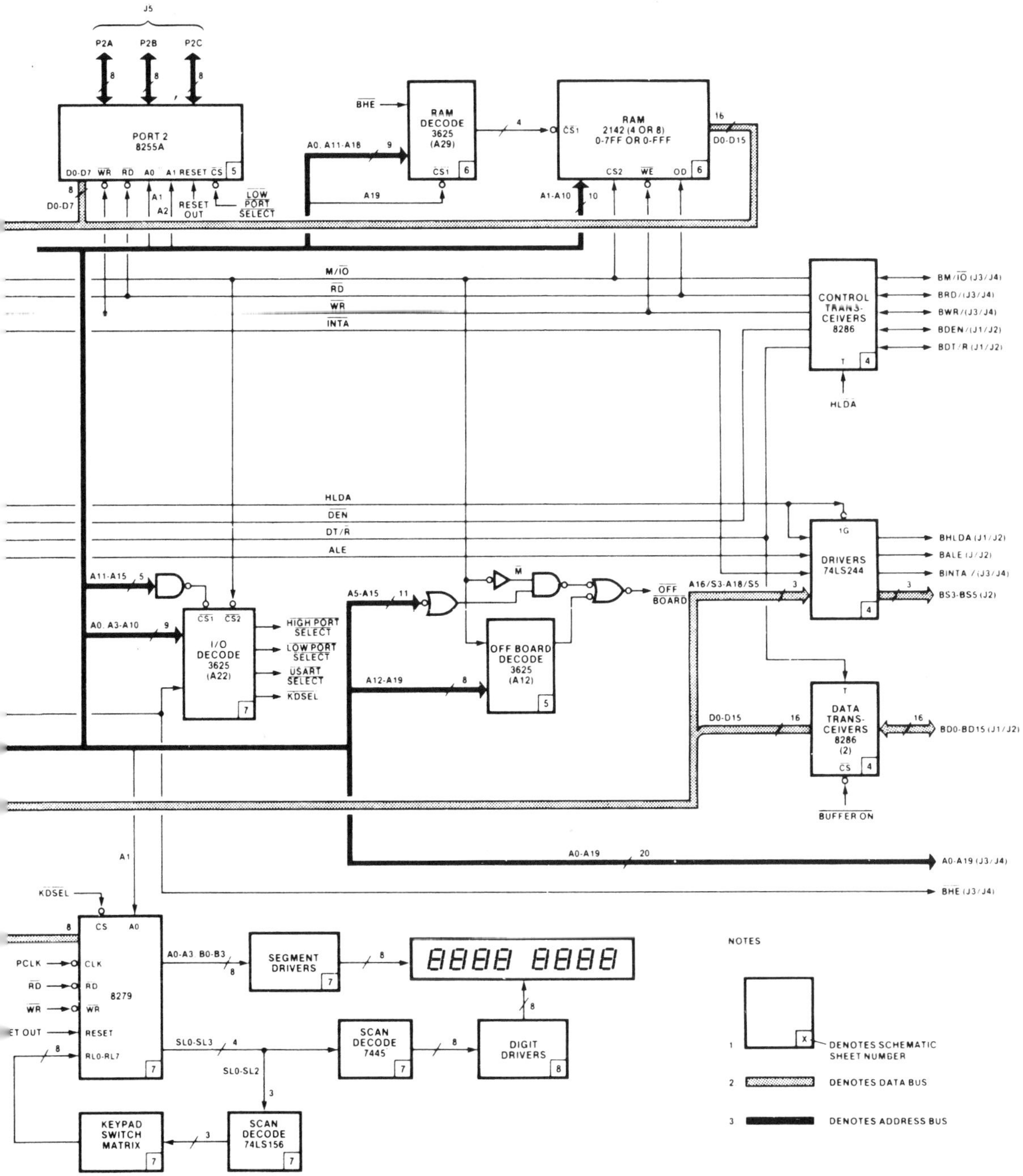

J5
P2A
P2B
P2C
PORT 2
8255A
D0-D7
WR
RD
A0
A1
RESET
CS
LOW PORT SELECT
RESET OUT
BHE
RAM DECODE
3625
(A29)
A0, A11-A18
A19
RAM
2142 (4 OR 8)
0-7FF OR 0-FFF
CS1
CS2
WE
OD
A1-A10
D0-D15
M/IO
INTA
CONTROL TRANS-CEIVERS
8286
HLDA
BM/IO (J3/J4)
BRD/(J3/J4)
BWR/(J3/J4)
BDEN/(J1/J2)
BDT/R (J1/J2)
DEN
DT/R
ALE
A11-A15
A0, A3-A10
I/O DECODE
3625
(A22)
HIGH PORT SELECT
LOW PORT SELECT
USART SELECT
KDSEL
A5-A15
A12-A19
M
OFF BOARD DECODE
3625
(A12)
OFF BOARD
A16/S3-A18/S5
DRIVERS
74LS244
BHLDA (J1/J2)
BALE (J/J2)
BINTA /(J3/J4)
BS3-BS5 (J2)
DATA TRANS-CEIVERS
8286
(2)
BD0-BD15 (J1/J2)
BUFFER ON
A0-A19
A0-A19 (J3/J4)
BHE (J3/J4)
A1
PCLK
CLK
RESET
8279
RL0-RL7
A0-A3 B0-B3
SEGMENT DRIVERS
SL0-SL3
SL0-SL2
SCAN DECODE
7445
DIGIT DRIVERS
KEYPAD SWITCH MATRIX
SCAN DECODE
74LS156
NOTES
1 DENOTES SCHEMATIC SHEET NUMBER
2 DENOTES DATA BUS
3 DENOTES ADDRESS BUS

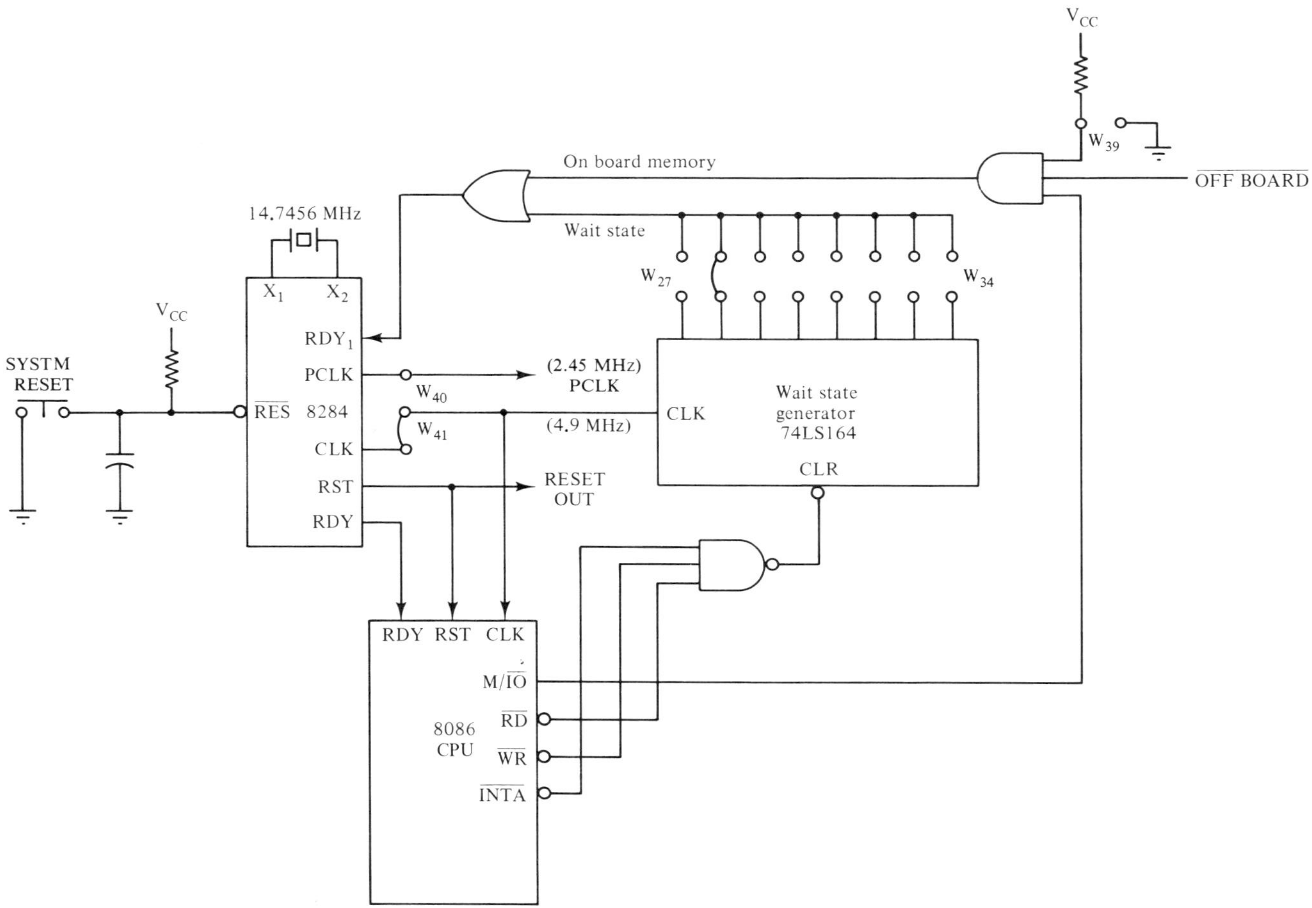

Figure 9.3 Clock generator and wait state generator circuits.

state jumper switches to logic 1. This causes the appropriate number of wait states to be inserted into the I/O bus cycle.

Even though the output of the wait-state generator is used only for input or output bus cycles, it is operating during all bus cycles. Therefore, let us now look at the general operation of this part of the circuit. Notice that control signals $\overline{RD}$, $\overline{WR}$, and $\overline{INTA}$ are gated together to drive the clear (CLR) input of the shift register. The clear signal is produced as follows:

$$CLR = \overline{\overline{RD} \bullet \overline{WR} \bullet \overline{INTA}}$$

If all of these signals are at their inactive 1 logic level, CLR is logic 0 and the shift register is held with all of its outputs at the 0 logic level. However, when any one of the signals becomes active (logic 0), CLR switches to 1 and the shift register is released for operation. This will happen whenever a bus cycle is initiated for a read of memory or I/O, write to memory or I/O, or an interrupt acknowledge.

Earlier we pointed out that the serial input of the shift register is fixed at the 1 logic level. If CLR becomes 1, at the next pulse at CLK a 1 is loaded into the first stage of the shift register. This corresponds to the W_{27} jumper output. On the next pulse, another 1 is loaded and the first 1 is shifted from the first stage of the shift register into its second stage. Now the outputs corresponding to the W_{27} and W_{28} jumpers are both logic 1. The W_{28} output is supplied to the WAIT STATE input of the OR gate and in the case of an I/O bus cycle it signals the 8284 that the bus cycle can be completed. In this way, we see that one wait state, which is equal to one CLK period (200 ns), has been inserted into the bus I/O cycle.

Example 9.1

What would be the duration of an external memory bus cycle if the jumper was accidentally connected in the W_{34} position?

Solution. With the jumper installed at W_{34}, every bus cycle to off-board memory would be performed with seven wait states. Therefore, the duration of a typical bus cycle is given in general as

$$\begin{aligned} t_D &= 800 \text{ ns} + 200 \text{ ns (number of WAIT STATES)} \\ &= 800 \text{ ns} + (200 \text{ ns})(7) \\ &= 800 \text{ ns} + 1400 \text{ ns} \\ &= 2200 \text{ ns} \\ &= 2.2\ \mu\text{s} \end{aligned}$$

Example 9.2

Assuming that the SDK-86 microcomputer system does not power-up correctly when the SYSTM RESET key is depressed, outline a procedure that could be followed to check whether the reset, clock, and wait-state circuits are operating correctly.

Solution. First, the signal at the CLK input of the 8086 can be observed to assure that the 8284 is producing the clock signal needed to drive the MPU. Next, the RST input of the 8086 should be checked while the SYSTM RESET switch is depressed. This will assure that a hardware reset is initiated at the MPU. Resetting the MPU causes it to execute the startup program from EPROM. Bus cycles to this part of memory are performed without wait states. Therefore, a last test could be to observe the RDY input of the 8086 to assure that it is logic 1. If these signals are all correct, the cause of the problem probably does not reside in the clock or reset section of circuitry.

9.4 PROGRAM AND DATA STORAGE MEMORY

In Section 9.3 we covered the clock generator and wait-state generator circuitry. At that time, we found that for on-board memory the 8086 executes bus cycles without wait states. Let us now look into the circuits used to implement the program storage and data storage parts of the memory subsystem.

Program Storage Memory

Figure 9.4 shows the 8086 MPU and the program storage part of the memory subsystem in the SDK-86 microcomputer. Notice that it involves three key elements: the *74S373 address latches,* the *3625 PROM address decoder,* and the *2716 EPROMs.* The storage array is formed from four 2716 EPROMs. These devices are organized as 2K $\times$ 8 bits and are connected to give two 2K $\times$ 16 banks of memory, for a total of 4K words of program memory. It is in this section of memory that the instructions of the monitor program are stored.

The three 74S373 address latches are common to all memory and I/O sections. They are used to latch the address in order to demultiplex the 8086's address/data bus. Notice in Fig. 9.4 that the inputs of these latches are AD_0 through AD_{15}, A_{16}/S_3 through A_{19}/S_6, and $\overline{BHE}/S_7$. Moreover, control signals HLDA and ALE are applied in parallel to the G and $\overline{OC}$ inputs, respectively, of all three 74S373s. Since the HOLD input of the 8086 is not in use, the HLDA output is always at logic 0 and the $\overline{OC}$ enable input on all three devices is at its active 0 logic level. Thus, as the 8086 puts an address on its bus and outputs a pulse at ALE, the G input becomes active and the address A_0 through A_{19} and $\overline{BHE}$ are latched and become available at the outputs. From the circuit diagram in Fig. 9.4, we see that $\overline{BHE}$ and A_0 are directly applied to $\overline{CE}$ inputs in the banks of EPROM memories. These signals are used to enable EPROMs in the high part of the bank and the low part of the bank, respectively. Furthermore, bits A_1 through A_{11} of the address are applied directly to the address inputs of all four EPROMs in parallel. Here they are used to select the storage location that is to be accessed in the enabled EPROMs.

The 7 most significant bits of the address, A_{12} through A_{19}, are supplied as inputs to a local address decoder. Here these bits are decoded to select between the two 2K $\times$ 16-bit banks of memory. Notice that two memory control signals are used to enable the decoder. They are $M/\overline{IO}$, which is logic 1 during all memory bus cycles, and $\overline{RD}$, which is logic 0 whenever an instruction is being fetched from program memory.

Let us now look more closely at the address decoding that takes place for the decoder to produce the $\overline{OE}$ signal for the EPROMs. For the higher-addressed bank

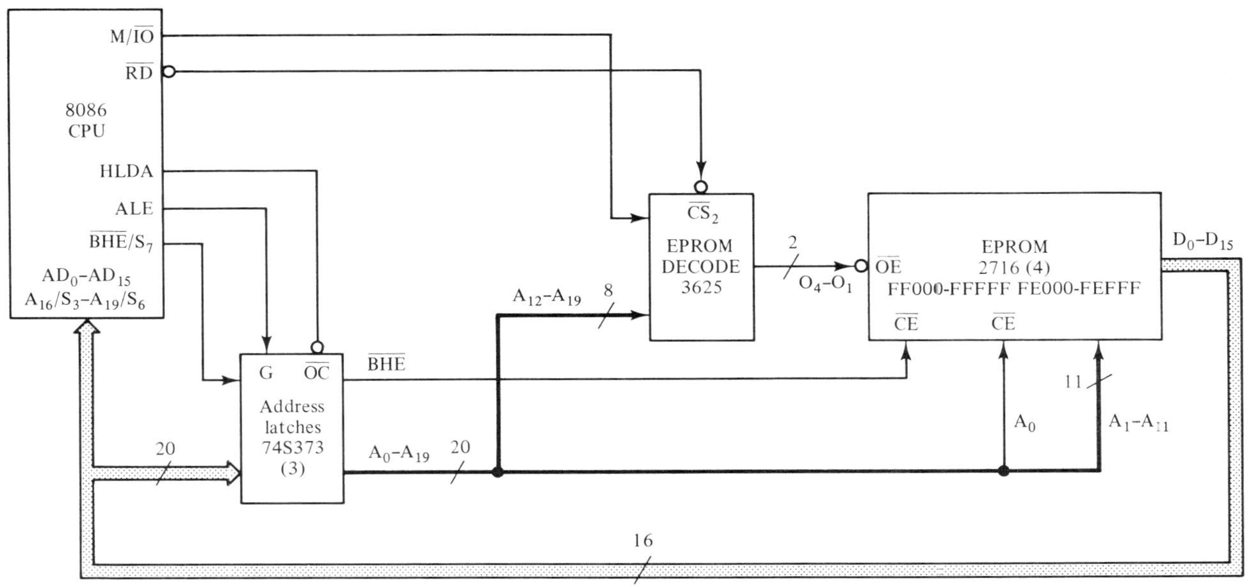

Figure 9.4 Program memory circuit diagram.

to be selected, all inputs of the local address decoder must be logic 1. That is,

$$A_{19}A_{18} \ldots\ldots A_{12} = 11111111_2$$
$$= FF_{16}$$

As shown in the address decoding table of Fig. 9.5, this input makes output O_1 of the decoder, which is applied to the $\overline{OE}$ input of the EPROM, switch to logic 0. The rest of the address bits can range from 000_{16} to FFF_{16}; therefore, one range of addresses that correspond to program memory is

$$A_{19}A_{18} \ldots\ldots A_0 = FF000_{16}$$

through

$$A_{19}A_{18} \ldots\ldots A_0 = FFFFF_{16}$$

This range is also shown in Fig. 9.5.

The second address combination that decodes to an $\overline{OE}$ signal for the bank of EPROMs is

$$A_{19}A_{18} \ldots\ldots A_{12} = 11111110_2$$
$$= FE_{16}$$

Figure 9.5 shows that this input address causes decoder output O_2 to become active. Again the lower part of the address can have any value from 000_{16} to FFF_{16}. This gives a second range for program memory as

$$A_{19}A_{18} \ldots\ldots A_0 = FE000_{16}$$

through

$$A_{19}A_{18} \ldots\ldots A_0 = FEFFF_{16}$$

PROM Inputs				PROM Outputs				EPROM Address Block Selected
$M/\overline{IO}$	A_{14}–A_{19}	A_{13}	A_{12}	O_4	O_3	O_2	O_1	
1	1	1	1	1	1	1	0	FF000H-FFFFFH
1	1	1	0	1	1	0	1	FE000H-FEFFFH
1	1	0	1	1	0	1	1	FD000H-FDFFFH ($\overline{CSX}$)
1	1	0	0	0	1	1	1	FC000H-FCFFFH ($\overline{CSY}$)
All other states				1	1	1	1	None

Figure 9.5 Program memory address decoding (*Courtesy of Intel Corporation*).

Similarly, we can determine the address locations occupied by the other two EPROMs. These are also shown in Fig. 9.5. In this way, we see that EPROMs reside at the high end of the microcomputer's address space. Data read out of the EPROMs are carried to the MPU over the complete data bus D_0 through D_{15}.

Example 9.3

The address latched into the outputs of the address latches during an instruction acquisition bus cycle is $FE330_{16}$. $\overline{BHE}$ is also latched and is at logic 0. What is the output of the EPROM address decoder, and which storage location in EPROM is accessed?

Solution. Since an instruction acquisition bus cycle is taking place,

$$M/\overline{IO} = 1$$

and

$$\overline{RD} = 0$$

These signals enable the EPROM address decoder. The high-order address bits, which are used as inputs to the address decoder, are

$$A_{19}A_{18} \ldots\ldots A_{14} = 111111_2$$
$$A_{13} = 1$$
$$A_{12} = 0$$

Looking at the table in Fig. 9.5, we see that output O_2 of the address decoder is switched to logic 0. This provides an output enable ($\overline{OE}$) signal in the bank of EPROMs at address $FE000_{16}$ through $FEFFF_{16}$. The CE inputs on these EPROMs are $\overline{BHE}$ and A_0, which are also both at their active 0 logic levels. Therefore, the word at location

$$A_{11}A_{10} \ldots\ldots A_1 = 330_{16}$$

is read out.

Data Storage Memory

The data storage memory interface of the SDK-86 microcomputer is similar to that just described for program storage memory. Looking at Fig. 9.6, we see that it again includes the *74S373 address latches*, the *3625 RAM address decoder*, and an *array of 2142 static RAMs*. The 2142 is organized 1K × 4 bits and the data RAM area can be filled with either four or eight of them to give either 1K words or 2K words, respectively. It is this part of the memory subsystem that is used to store data and programs that are keyed in for execution and debugging.

The same 74S373 address latches that we discussed relative to program storage memory are shown demultiplexing the 8086's address/data bus to give address lines A_0 through A_{19} and $\overline{BHE}$. Another 3625 PROM is used as a local address decoder to produce chip select signals for the banks of RAMs. This 3625 device is referred to as the RAM decoder. Comparing the local PROM decoder in Fig. 9.4 with the local RAM decoder in Fig. 9.6, we find that their address inputs and chip select signals are different. First we see that the address inputs of the RAM address decoder are A_0, A_{11} through A_{18}, and $\overline{BHE}$. Moreover, its chip enable input is A_{19} and this input must be logic 0 to enable the decoder for operation.

The table in Fig. 9.7 shows the relationship between input address and chip select outputs O_4, O_3, O_2, and O_1. Here we see that address bits A_{12} through A_{18} must all be logic 0. Moreover, address bit A_{11} is used to select between the two 1K word banks of RAM. When A_{11} is logic 0, data stored in the lower-addressed bank are accessed and when it is 1, data in the high-addressed bank are accessed. The next two signals, $\overline{BHE}$ and A_0, are the 8086's byte select signals. From the table in Fig.

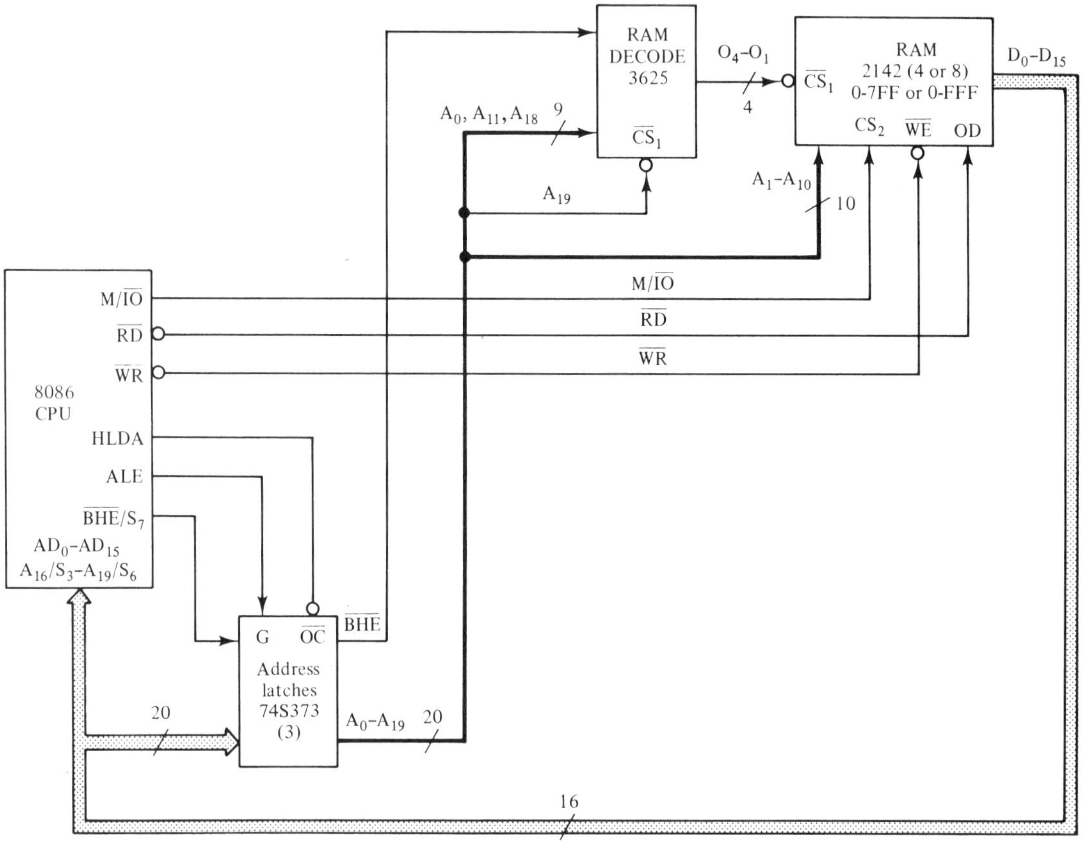

Figure 9.6 Data memory circuit diagram.

9.7, we see that a word access takes place from the selected banks of RAMs when both of these signals are at logic 0, a high byte access occurs when $\overline{BHE} = 0$ and $A_0 = 1$, and a low byte access occurs when $\overline{BHE} = 1$ and $A_0 = 0$.

The storage location that is to be accessed is selected by the part of the address that is on lines A_1 through A_{10}. It is directly applied in parallel to the address inputs of all RAMs. Since the upper 8 bits of the address are always all logic 0, RAM resides in the lower 4K of the address space, that is, the address range

$$A_{19}A_{18} \cdots\cdots A_0 = 00000_{16}$$

through

$$A_{19}A_{18} \cdots\cdots A_0 = 00FFF_{16}$$

In Fig. 9.7 we see that the lower 1K word bank is located at 00000_{16} through $003FF_{16}$ and the upper 1K word bank is located at 00400_{16} through $007FF_{16}$.

The M/$\overline{IO}$, $\overline{RD}$, and $\overline{WR}$ memory control lines are applied directly to all RAMs in parallel. From Fig. 9.6, we see that M/$\overline{IO}$ goes to the CS_2 input. During all memory

PROM Inputs				PROM Outputs				RAM address block selected
A_{12}-A_{18}	A_{11}	$\overline{BHE}$	A_0	O_4	O_3	O_2	O_1	
0	0	0	0	1	1	0	0	Both Bytes (0H-007FFH)
0	0	0	1	1	1	0	1	High Byte (0H-007FFH)
0	0	1	0	1	1	1	0	Low Byte (0H-007FFH)
0	1	0	0	0	0	1	1	Both Bytes (00800H-00FFFH)
0	1	0	1	0	1	1	1	High Byte (00800H-00FFFH)
0	1	1	0	1	0	1	1	Low Byte (00800H-00FFFH)
All other states				1	1	1	1	None

Figure 9.7 Data memory address decoding (*Courtesy of Intel Corporation*).

bus cycles, it is at logic 1 and enables the RAMs. $\overline{RD}$ is connected to output disable (OD) of the RAMs. During bus cycles when data are read from memory, $\overline{RD}$ is switched to logic 0. This enables the output buffers of the 2142 memories to put the data stored at the addressed location onto the bus. Finally, during write cycles from MPU to RAM, $\overline{WR}$ is switched to logic 0. This signal is supplied to $\overline{WE}$, where it enables the data inputs of the RAMs to accept write data from the bus.

Example 9.4

Write a program that could be used to clear all 2K word storage location of data memory in the SDK-86 microcomputer system.

Solution. The two kilobytes of RAM reside in the address range 00000_{16} to $007FF_{16}$. To clear this segment of memory, we must first load the data segment register with 0000_{16} and initialize the destination index register to 0000_{16}. This is done with the instructions

```
MOV DS,0H
MOV DI,0H
```

Now a count equal to 800_{16} is loaded into the CX register.

```
MOV CX,0800H
```

To clear the bank of memory, we need to form a loop that writes zero to the byte address formed from DS and DI, then increment the pointer in DI and decrement the counter in CX, and finally test the value of the count for zero. If the count is equal to zero, the memory clear routine is complete and the program halts; otherwise, control is returned to the beginning of the loop. This loop is implemented with the following sequence of instructions:

```
NXT: MOV [DI],0H
     INC DI
     DCR CX
     JNZ NXT
```

This program is repeated in Fig. 9.8.

```
        MOV   DS,0H          ; LOAD DATA SEGMENT REGISTER
        MOV   DI,0H          ; LOAD DESTINATION INDEX REGISTER
        MOV   CX,0800H       ; LOAD COUNT REGISTER
NXT:    MOV   [DI],0H        ; CLEAR MEMORY LOCATION
        INC   DI             ; INCREMENT DESTINATION POINTER
        DCR   CX             ; DECREMENT COUNTER
        JNZ   NXT            ; CHECK FOR BANK DONE
        HLT                  ; MEMORY INITIALIZATION COMPLETE
```

Figure 9.8 Memory bank initialization routine.

9.5 I/O INTERFACES OF THE SDK-86 MICROCOMPUTER

There are four I/O interfaces provided in the SDK-86 microcomputer. Looking at the block diagram in Fig. 9.1, we find that they are the *keypad*, the *display*, the *parallel I/O ports*, and the *RS-232C serial port*. Let us now look at how each of these interfaces are implemented in the microcomputer system.

Parallel I/O Ports

The *parallel I/O circuitry* of the SDK-86 microcomputer is shown in Fig. 9.9. Here we see that two 8255A programmable peripheral interface (PPI) ICs have been used to implement two independent I/O ports called PORT 1 and PORT 2. Each of these ports has three byte-wide groups of lines. For instance, at PORT 1 they are labeled P_{1A}, P_{1B}, and P_{1C}, respectively. This gives a total of 48 I/O lines for the two ports.

Input or output data transfers between the 8086 and the A, B, and C ports are performed by reading from or writing to a corresponding data register within the 8255A. Figure 9.9(a) lists the addresses of these registers in the SDK-86 microcomputer's I/O address space. For example, the P_{1A} I/O lines at PORT 1 are accessed through the data register at address $FFF9_{16}$.

Remember that the I/O lines on an 8255A can be configured for several different modes of operation. In general, they can be set up to work as level-sensitive inputs, latched outputs, or strobed inputs or outputs. In Chapter 7 we found that the control register is loaded with an appropriate byte to configure the I/O lines of the A, B, and C ports as inputs or outputs and select between MODE 0, MODE 1, or MODE 2 operations. From Fig. 9.10(a), we see that the control register of the PORT 1 PPI is at I/O address $FFFF_{16}$.

Now that we have introduced the parallel I/O interface, let us trace through the operation of the circuitry in Fig. 9.9 as the 8086 writes a byte to the control register of the PORT 1 PPI. Since the 8255As are located in the I/O address space, this represents an output bus cycle and would be initiated by executing an OUT instruction.

As the output bus cycle begins, $M/\overline{IO}$ is switched to the 0 logic level. $M/\overline{IO}$ is applied to the $\overline{CS_2}$ input of the I/O address decoder and signals that an I/O bus cycle instead of a memory bus cycle is in progress. At the same time, the control register address, which is $FFFF_{16}$, is output on AD_0 through AD_{15} and latched along

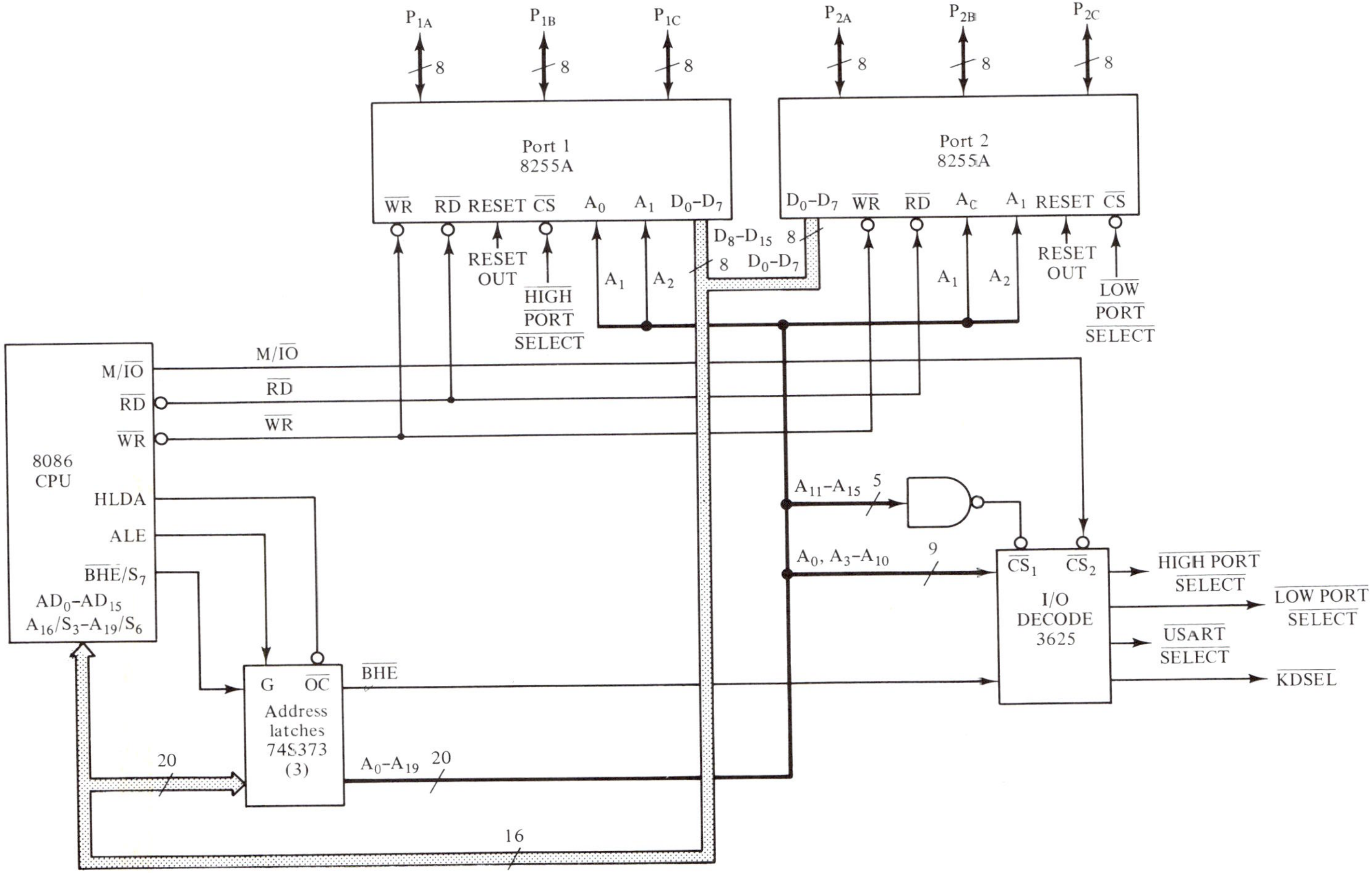

Figure 9.9 Parallel I/O interface circuits.

Port	Address
P_{1A}	FFF9
P_{1B}	FFFB
P_{1C}	FFFD
$P_{1\ \text{Control}}$	FFFF

(a)

Port	Address
P_{2A}	FFF8
P_{2B}	FFFA
P_{2C}	FFFC
$P_{2\ \text{Control}}$	FFFE

(b)

Figure 9.10 **(a)** Register addresses for PORT 1 (*Courtesy of Intel Corporation*); **(b)** register addresses for PORT 2 (*Courtesy of Intel Corporation*).

with $\overline{\text{BHE}}$ into the 74S373 address latches on the trailing edge of the ALE pulse. Expressing this address in binary form, we get

$$A_{15}A_{14} \ldots\ldots\ldots A_0 = 1111111111111111_2$$

Looking at the circuit in Fig. 9.9, we see that bits A_{11} through A_{15} of the address are decoded with a NAND gate to produce the second chip select input $(\overline{CS}_1)$ for the I/O address decoder. These address bits, which are all logic 1 in the address $FFFF_{16}$, cause $\overline{CS}_1$ to switch to logic 0.

With both $\overline{CS}_1$ and $\overline{CS}_2$ logic 0, the 3625 PROM is enabled for operation. Therefore, the rest of its inputs A_0, A_3, through A_{10}, and $\overline{\text{BHE}}$ are decoded to produce one of the four I/O select outputs: $\overline{\text{HIGH PORT SELECT}}$, $\overline{\text{LOW PORT SELECT}}$, $\overline{\text{USART SELECT}}$, or $\overline{\text{KDSEL}}$. Looking at the PORT 1 8255A in Fig. 9.9, we see that its $\overline{CS}$ input is supplied by the $\overline{\text{HIGH PORT SELECT}}$ output of the *I/O address decoder*. The decoding performed by the I/O address decoder is illustrated in Fig. 9.11. Here we see that to produce an active $\overline{\text{HIGH PORT SELECT}}$, signal bits A_3 through A_{10} of the address must all be logic 1, $\overline{\text{BHE}}$ must be logic 0, and A_0 can be either 0 or 1. The address bits are all at the 1 logic level in the address $FFFF_{16}$ and $\overline{\text{BHE}}$ is 0; thus the PORT 1 PPI is enabled for operation.

The last two address bits, A_1 and A_2, are applied to the A_0 and A_1 inputs, respectively, of the 8255As in parallel. It is the code on these lines that selects the internal register of the PPI that will be accessed. These bits must both be logic 1 to select the control register. In our example, the are both 1; however, just the PORT

PROM Inputs					PROM Outputs			
A_5–A_{10}	A_4	A_3	$\overline{\text{BHE}}$	A_0	O_4 $\overline{\text{HIGH PORT SELECT}}$	O_3 $\overline{\text{LOW PORT SELECT}}$	O_2 $\overline{\text{USART SELECT}}$	O_1 $\overline{\text{KDSEL}}$
1	0	1	0	0	1	1	1	0
1	0	1	1	0	1	1	1	0
1	1	0	0	0	1	1	0	1
1	1	0	1	0	1	1	0	1
1	1	1	0	0	0	0	1	1
1	1	1	0	1	0	1	1	1
1	1	1	1	0	1	0	1	1
All other states					1	1	1	1

Figure 9.11 I/O device address decoding (*Courtesy of Intel Corporation*).

1 PPI is enabled. Therefore, its control register is to be accessed. That is, a byte-wide output operation is to be performed over the bus to the PORT 1 PPI's control register.

Later in the bus cycle, the 8086 outputs the byte of data on data bus lines D_8 through D_{15} and then switches $\overline{WR}$ to logic 0. The 0 level on $\overline{WR}$ signals the PORT 1 8255A to read the data off of the bus and put the data into the control register.

Example 9.5

What is the difference between the two I/O address decoder output states during which $\overline{\text{HIGH PORT SELECT}}$ is active 0?

Solution. From the table of Fig. 9.11, we see that for the first state when $\overline{\text{HIGH PORT SELECT}}$ is active,

$$A_{10}A_9 \ldots\ldots A_3 = 11111111_2$$
$$\overline{BHE} = 0$$
$$A_0 = 0$$

Notice that both $\overline{\text{HIGH PORT SELECT}}$ and $\overline{\text{LOW PORT SELECT}}$ are at their active 0 logic level

$$\overline{\text{HIGH PORT SELECT}} = 0$$
$$\overline{\text{LOW PORT SELECT}} = 0$$

and both the PORT 1 and PORT 2 PPIs are enabled for operation. This state corresponds to a word I/O bus cycle during which registers from both PORT 1 and PORT 2 are accessed at the same time.

The second state where $\overline{\text{HIGH PORT SELECT}}$ is active is for

$$A_{10}A_9 \ldots\ldots A_3 = 11111111_2$$
$$\overline{BHE} = 0$$
$$A_0 = 1$$

This state produces just

$$\overline{\text{HIGH PORT SELECT}} = 0$$

Now the PORT 1 PPI is enabled but PORT 2 remains disabled. It corresponds to an I/O bus cycle where a byte operation is performed to a register in the PORT 1 device.

Example 9.6

Write a program that will initialize PORT 2 such that it is configured with P_{2A} set for MODE 0 input operation, P_{2B} set for MODE 0 input operation, and P_{2C} for MODE 0 output operation. Then write a sequence of instructions that will input the contents at P_{2A} and P_{2B} and output their sum to P_{2C}.

Solution. In Chapter 7 we discussed how to configure the ports of the 8255A by forming control bytes and loading them into the control registers. For this example, the control byte needed to configure P2's ports is shown in Fig. 9.12(a). Its value is

$$10010010_2 = 92_{16}$$

This byte must be written to the control register at address $FFFE_{16}$ of the I/O address space. To do this, we must first load the accumulator with 92_{16} and then output it to

D_7	D_6	D_5	D_4	D_3	D_2	D_1	D_0
1	0	0	1	0	0	1	0

(a)

```
MOV   AL,092H       ; LOAD AL WITH CONTROL BYTE
OUT   0FFFEH,AL     ; LOAD PORT 2 CONTROL REGISTER
IN    AL,0FFF8H     ; READ PORT P2A
MOV   BL,AL         ; SAVE FIRST BYTE
IN    AL,0FFFAH     ; READ PORT P2B
ADD   AL,BL         ; ADD INPUT DATA
OUT   0FFFCH,AL     ; WRITE TO PORT P2C
```

(b)

Figure 9.12 **(a)** PORT 2 control word; **(b)** input/output program.

the control register. This is done with the instructions

```
MOV  AL,092H
OUT  0FFFEH,AL
```

Now we can read the first byte of data from the input port at address $FFF8_{16}$ and save it in BL. This is done with the instruction sequence

```
IN   AL,0FFF8H
MOV  BL,AL
```

The byte from the input port at $FFFA_{16}$ is next read into the accumulator with the instruction

```
IN   AL,0FFFAH
```

The two values of input data are now added,

```
ADD  AL,BL
```

and their sum is output to the port at address $FFFC_{16}$.

```
OUT  0FFFCH,AL
```

The complete program is repeated in Fig. 9.12(b).

RS-232C Communications Port

Another important I/O interface in the SDK-86 microcomputer is the *RS-232C serial I/O port.* This port permits a CRT terminal to be connected to the microcomputer. In this way, information can be input from the keyboard of the terminal instead of from the build-in keypad.

The serial port circuitry is shown in Fig. 9.13. Note that the 8251A USART is the communications controller used. In Chapter 7 we introduced this device. Here it is configured by the monitor software to operate in the asynchronous mode. At power-up, the monitor configures the 8251A for 8-bit character length, no parity,

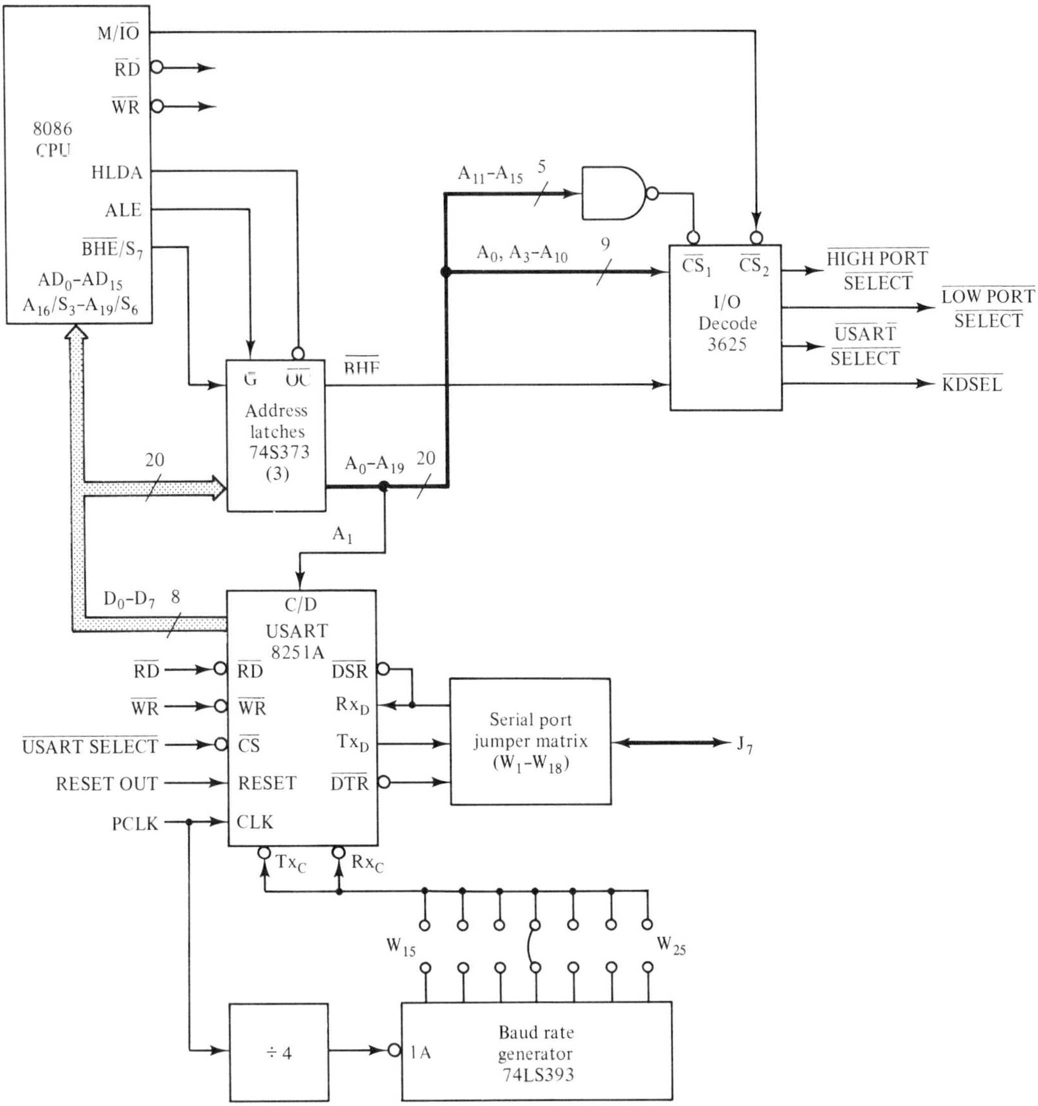

Figure 9.13 USART communications interface.

and two STOP bits. Moreover, it sets up the internal clock divider circuitry such that the externally generated baud clock input signal is divided by 64 within the device.

The 8251A is located in the I/O address space of the SDK-86 microcomputer. The table in Fig. 9.14 shows the logic states of the control signals and corresponding addresses needed to access each of its registers. For instance, execution of an IN instruction to address $FFF2_{16}$ lets the 8086 read the contents of the 8251A's status register. On the other hand, executing an OUT instruction to the same address causes the mode control register to be loaded.

Looking at Fig. 9.13, we find that the chip select input of the 8251A is driven by the $\overline{\text{USART SELECT}}$ output of the I/O decode circuit. Earlier we found that bits A_{11} through A_{15} of the address must all be logic 1 to enable the I/O address decoder for operation. From Fig. 9.11 we find that to produce the $\overline{\text{USART SELECT}}$ output, bits A_4 through A_{10} must all be logic 1 while A_0 and A_3 must be logic 0. Therefore, to input data from or output data to the registers of the 8251A, the address on the bus must be

$$A_{15}A_{14} \ldots\ldots . A_0 = 11111111111100X0_2$$

For X = 0 this gives

$$A_{15}A_{14} \ldots\ldots . A_0 = 1111111111110000_2$$
$$= FFF0_{16}$$

and for X = 1

$$A_{15}A_{14} \ldots\ldots . A_0 = 1111111111110010_2$$
$$= FFF2_{16}$$

Note that an X is in bit A_1 of the address and this signal is applied to the $C/\overline{D}$ input of the 8251A. As shown in Fig. 9.14, the logic level of this bit is used to select between the data registers and status/control registers. Moreover, the fact that data are input or output depends on whether $\overline{RD}$ or $\overline{WR}$ is at logic 0.

Now that we have examined the microprocessor interface of the 8251A let us continue by looking at how the clock signal that sets the baud rate of the receiver and transmitter sections is generated. In Fig. 9.13 we see that the *baud rate generator* is formed by a 74LS393 dual 4-bit binary counter. The PCLK signal produced by the clock generator section of the microcomputer is first divided by 4 and then applied to the 1A input of the baud rate generator circuit. The two counters within the 73LS393 are set up for cascaded operation and seven of its parallel outputs are available for use as the receiver and transmitter clock signals.

In the circuit, both the receiver and transmitter are to run at the same baud rate; therefore, the Tx_C and Rx_C inputs are connected together. Any one of the clock outputs of the baud rate generator can be connected into the clock input by simply installing a jumper in the appropriate location. The baud rate jumpers are labeled W_{19} through W_{25}.

USART Input			Port Addresses	Port Function
A_1	$\overline{RD}$	$\overline{WR}$		
0	0	1	FFF0H	Read USART Data
0	1	0	FFF0H	Write USART Data
1	0	1	FFF2H	Read USART Status
1	1	0	FFF2H	Write USART Control

Figure 9.14 USART register selection (*Courtesy of Intel Corporation*).

Baud rate	Shorting plug position	Output frequency
4800	W_{25}	307.2 kHz
2400	W_{24}	153.6 kHz
1200	W_{23}	76.8 kHz
600	W_{22}	38.4 kHz
300	W_{21}	19.2 kHz
150	W_{20}	9.6 kHz
75	W_{19}	4.8 kHz
110	W_{20}, W_{26}	6.98 kHz

Figure 9.15 Baud rate selection (*Courtesy of Intel Corporation*).

The table in Fig. 9.15 shows the relationship between jumper setting, baud rate generator output frequency, and baud rate of the USART. Remember that the baud rate clock input is divided by 64 within the 8251A. This is the reason that the output frequencies and corresponding baud rates are different.

Example 9.7

If the jumper is installed in the W_{21} position, what is the output frequency of the baud rate generator and baud rate of the USART? Show how the value of the baud rate is derived from the clock frequency.

Solution. Looking at Fig. 9.15, we see that when the jumper is installed at W_{21} the 19.2-kHz clock has been selected and that this results in a baud rate of 300 baud (307.2 baud). The input clock frequency is divided by 64 to give the baud rate

$$\text{Baud rate} = f_{BRG}/64 = 19.2\text{ kHz}/64$$
$$= 300 \text{ baud}$$

The last part of the serial I/O interface in Fig. 9.13 is the RS-232C port. Here we see that this part of the circuit includes the receive data (Rx_D) and transmit data (Tx_D) lines of the 8251A, a serial port jumper matrix, and the connector J_7. The connector is a DB-25S 25-pin female EIA connector. This is the type of connector used at RS-232C ports. The pin assignments of signals at this connector can be changed by jumpers W_1 through W_{18} to support interface to a wide variety of equipment. For instance, to configure it for connection to a stand-alone CRT terminal a jumper should be installed between the W_1 and W_5 positions. This simply connects the receive data line to pin 2 of J_1, the transmit data line to pin 3, and supplies a common signal ground at pin 7. These signal locations are consistent with those identified for the RS-232C interface in Fig. 7.23.

Keypad and Display Interface

The last I/O device that we will consider is the 8279. This device provides the interface to the keypad and display in the SDK-86 microcomputer system. The 8279 keyboard/display control IC was described in detail in Chapter 7. At power-up, the monitor program configures the 8259 at power-up for encoded keyboard scanning with two-key lockout, eight-digit eight-segment display with left entry, and a prescaler of 25.

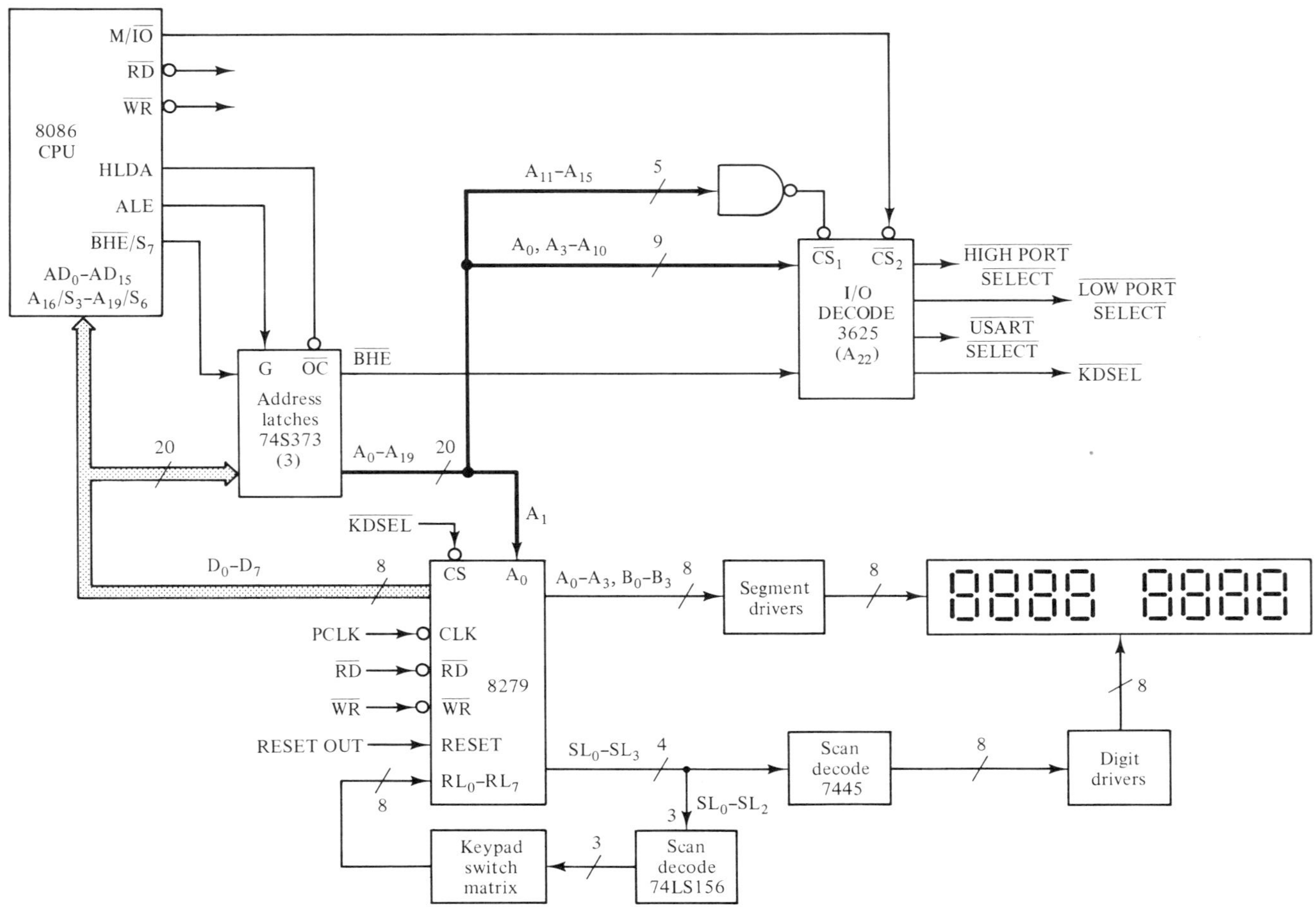

Figure 9.16 Keypad/display interface.

The circuitry involved in the scanning of the keypad and display is shown in Fig. 9.16. Let us begin by examining the microprocessor interface. Just like the other I/O devices we have considered up to this point, the 8279 is located in the SDK-86 microcomputer's I/O address space. Figure 9.16 shows the control signals and addresses for each type of bus access that can be performed by the 8086. For instance, to read data from the display RAM, an IN instruction can be executed to the address $FFE8_{16}$, or to write data into this RAM, an OUT instruction can be executed to the same address. Remember that a read or write display memory command must be issued to the 8279 before executing the IN or OUT instruction, respectively.

Looking at Fig. 9.16, we see that the $\overline{CS}$ input of the 8279 is connected to the $\overline{KDSEL}$ output of the I/O address decoder. Earlier we found that the decoder was chip selected when bits A_{11} through A_{15} of the address are all logic 1 and $M/\overline{IO}$ is logic 0. Figure 9.10 shows that bits A_5 through A_{10} and A_3 must also be all logic 1, while A_4 and A_0 must be logic 0 in order to produce an active $\overline{KDSEL}$ output. Therefore, the address used in an IN or OUT instruction that is used to access the 8279 is

$$A_{15}A_{14} \ldots \ldots . A_0 = 11111111111010X0_2$$

For X = 0 this gives

$$A_{15}A_{14} \ldots \ldots . A_0 = 1111111111101000_2$$
$$= FFE8_{16}$$

and for X = 1, we get

$$A_{15}A_{14} \ldots \ldots . A_0 = 1111111111101010_2$$
$$= FFEA_{16}$$

From Fig. 9.17, we find that bit A_1 of the address determines whether the bus operation to the 8259 is a memory access or status/command operation. When A_1 is logic 0, the on-chip display RAM or keyboard FIFO is being accessed. On the other hand, logic 1 in this bit position corresponds to reading of the 8259's status register or writing of a command to the command register.

Scan outputs, SL_0 through SL_3, of the 8259 are decoded separately in the display and keypad sections. In the display section, a 7445 4-line to 10-line decoder IC is used as the scan decoder. Here we see that just eight of its outputs are used

8279 Input			Port Address	Port Function
A1	$\overline{RD}$	$\overline{WR}$		
0	0	1	FFE8H	Read Display RAM or Keyboard FIFO
0	1	0	FFE8H	Write Display RAM
1	0	1	FFEAH	Read Status
1	1	0	FFEAH	Write Command

Figure 9.17 Keypad/display controller register selection (*Courtesy of Intel Corporation*).

as digit select signals for the display. These signals are buffered by the *digit driver circuit*. Eight bits of segment data are output to the display at ports A and B. They are buffered by the segment driver circuit and then applied to the segment inputs of the display.

The *keypad scan decoder* is a 74LS156 3-line to 8-line decoder. Just three of its outputs are used as row inputs to the keypad switch matrix. The eight outputs of the switch matrix are applied to return line inputs, RL_0 through RL_7 of the 8259.

Example 9.8

All of the keys that attach to one row of the keypad matrix do not work. What signal should be tested first to determine the cause of the malfunction? Assume that all digits of the display work correctly.

Solution. Since the display works correctly, it can be assumed that the scan line outputs of the 8279 are functioning correctly. Moreover, if the problem was at the return line inputs of the 8279, we would expect to find that all keys attached to a column of the keypad matrix do not work instead of all keys in a row. Therefore, the source of the problem would be expected to be in the keypad scan decoder section, and the first signal to be examined should be the row output that connects to the malfunctioning row of keys.

ASSIGNMENT

Section 9.2

1. What is the size of the program storage memory in the SDK-86 microcomputer system?
2. How much RAM is supplied in the data storage part of memory?
3. What happens to the contents of program storage memory when power is turned off? What would happen to the contents of the data storage memory?
4. Where are programs that are keyed in at the keypad stored?
5. What I/O resources are supplied on the SDK-86 microcomputer?
6. What LSI device is used to interface the keypad and display to the 8086 microprocessor?
7. What do the 8255A devices implement in the SDK-86 microcomputer?
8. In Fig. 9.2, what is the logic level of the $MN/\overline{MX}$ pin? What mode of operation does this select?
9. In Fig. 9.2 what is the significance of the jumper connections (W_{36}, W_{37}, and W_{38}) made for the INTR, TEST, and HOLD inputs of the 8086?

Section 9.3

10. If a 12-MHz crystal is used in the SDK-86 microcomputer instead of the 14.7456-MHz crystal, at what frequency will the microcomputer run?
11. What is the frequency of PCLK if the 8084 has a 12-MHz crystal, as indicated in problem 10?
12. Overview what happens when the SYSTM RESET key is depressed.

13. Which devices in the microcomputer system are initialized with the RESET OUT signal?

14. What is the duration of a I/O bus cycle if the wait state jumper is inserted at the W_{30} position?

15. Assuming that all bus cycles are to on-board memory and I/O, what affect on wait-state operation would be found if jumper W_{39} were installed? Explain your answer.

16. Assume that in Example 9.2 the RDY input was found to be fixed at the 0 logic level. Which signal should be examined next?

17. Measurements are taken to determine the duration of the on-board memory and I/O bus cycle to assure that on-board memory accesses are performed without wait states and I/O accesses are performed with one wait state. However, it was found that both bus cycles are always being performed with one wait state. Jumper W_{39} was then checked and found to be removed. Finally, the signals $M/\overline{IO}$, ON BOARD MEMORY, and $\overline{\text{OFF BOARD}}$ were examined. $M/\overline{IO}$ and $\overline{\text{OFF BOARD}}$ were found to work correctly, but the ON BOARD MEMORY output was found to be always logic 0. Which of the following could be the cause?

(a) Jumper W_{39} was not installed.
(b) The AND gate that produces ON BOARD MEMORY is burned out.
(c) The jumper at W_{28} should be moved to W_{27}.
(d) None of the above.

Section 9.4

18. Assume that the address latched at the output of the 74S373 in the circuit of Fig. 9.4 during a memory read cycle is $FF400_{16}$ and $\overline{BHE} = 0$. What is the output of the EPROM address decoder, and which EPROM storage location is accessed?

19. What would be the output of the EPROM address decoder in the circuit of Fig. 9.4 if a bus cycle is initiated to read a word of data out of storage location $000FE_{16}$? Assume that $\overline{BHE}$ is at logic 0.

20. Assume that in Example 9.2 the cause of the malfunction was not found in the reset, clock, or ready logic circuits and the testing of circuitry was continued into the program storage memory section. Additional measurements were taken and it was observed that an address was latched at the outputs of the 74S373, $M/\overline{IO}$ was at the 1 logic level, CS_2 was at logic 0, $\overline{BHE}$ was at logic 0, and A_0 was also at logic 0. However, all outputs of the EPROM address decoder remained at the 1 logic level. What should be done next?

(a) Replace the address decoder IC.
(b) Replace all four EPROMs.
(c) Verify that the address is in the program memory address range $FE000_{16}$ through $FFFFF_{16}$.
(d) None of the above.

21. During the bus cycle initiated by the instruction MOV AH,03FH, what will become the logic levels of the signals $M/\overline{IO}$, $\overline{WE}$, and $\overline{CS_1}$ on the RAM address decoder, and at outputs O_4 through O_1 of the RAM address decoder?

22. Draw a memory map for the SDK-86 microcomputer.

23. Write a simple program that could be used to verify that all RAM in the SDK-86 microcomputer is operating correctly.

Section 9.5

24. What address must be output on the bus in order to write a byte of data into the control register of the PORT 2 8255A?

25. What are the logic levels of $\overline{CS_1}$ on the I/O address decoder, $\overline{CS}$ on the PORT 1 8255A, and $\overline{CS}$ on the PORT 2 8255A when the address found in problem 24 is output on the bus?

26. Assume that I/O PORT 2 is already configured as described in Example 9.6. Write a program that will input the contents of P_{2A}, mask off the four MSBs, and output the result to the four MSBs of P_{2C}. The upper four bits of P_{2C} are not to be affected.

27. Assume that I/O PORT 2 is already configured as described in Example 9.6. Write a diagnostic program that will test output operation at P_{2C} by producing symmetrical square waves at each of its eight output lines.

28. What address must be output on the address bus for the 8086 to read the contents of the receive data register of the 8251A?

29. Write an instruction sequence that will load the transmitter data register of the 8251A with the ASCII character A.

30. What baud rate is produced when the baud rate selection jumper is in the W_{23} position?

31. If the internal baud rate divider of the 8251A was set to 4 instead of 64, what clock frequency would need to be input to result in a baud rate of 110 baud?

32. If the serial port does not work, what should be checked first?

33. If a measurement is taken to observe the clock signal at Rx_C and it is found that the signal is missing, what other signals should be checked to identify the source of the problem?

34. What address and data must be output over the bus to the 8279 in order to set the keyboard/display mode to encoded scan keypad with two-key lockout and eight-digit eight-segment display with left entry?

35. What address and data must be output on the bus to the 8279 to set the clock divider for divide by 25?

36. Write the instruction sequence needed to perform the two programming operations described in problems 34 and 35.

37. Write the instruction sequence needed to read a key code off the top of the key code FIFO.

38. If one segment in one digit of the display never lights, what would you expect to be the cause of the problem?
(a) Bad display unit.
(b) Bad segment driver.
(c) Bad display scan decoder.
(d) None of the above.

39. If all segments in one of the digits of the display never light, which signal (signals) should you check first?
(a) A and B port segment outputs.
(b) Segment driver outputs.
(c) Display scan decoder output for the digit.
(d) Digit driver output for the digit.

40. Draw a map of the SDK-86's I/O address space.

Bibliography

CIARCIA, STEVEN, The Intel 8086, *Byte,* Nov. 1979.

INTEL CORPORATION, *Component Data Catalog.* Santa Clara, CA: Intel Corporation, 1980.

INTEL CORPORATION, *iAPX86,88 User's Manual.* Santa Clara, CA: Intel Corporation, July 1981.

INTEL CORPORATION, *MCS-86tm User's Manual.* Santa Clara, CA: Intel Corporation, Feb. 1979.

INTEL CORPORATION, Peripheral Design Handbook. Santa Clara, CA: Intel Corporation, April 1978.

LEMAIR, IAN, and ROBERT NOBIS, *Electronic Design 19,* Sept. 1, 1978.

MORSE, STEPHEN P., *The 8086 Primer.* Rochelle Park, NJ: Hayden Book Company, Inc., 1978.

RECTOR, RUSSELL, and GEORGE ALEXY. *The 8086 Book,* Berkeley, CA: Osborne/McGraw-Hill, 1980.

TRIEBEL, WALTER A., *Integrated Digital Electronics.* Englewood Cliffs, NJ: Prentice-Hall, Inc., 1979.

TRIEBEL, WALTER A., and ALFRED E. CHU, *Handbook of Semiconductor and Bubble Memories.* Englewood Cliffs, NJ: Prentice-Hall, Inc., 1982.

Answers to Selected Problems

Chapter 1

Section 1.2

1. Computer program.

Section 1.3

5. A computer that has been tailored to meet the needs of a specific application.

Section 1.4

7. Secondary storage is for long-term storage of data that are not in use. On the other hand, the data that are currently being processed are held temporarily in primary storage memory.

Section 1.5

9. Program storage memory is the part of the memory subsystem that contains the program that is executed by the microcomputer. On the other hand, the data that are processed during execution of the program are held in the data storage part of memory.

Section 1.6

11. 4-bit, 8-bit, 16-bit, and 32-bit.

Chapter 2

Section 2.2

1. High-density N-channel MOS (HMOS).
3. 1M byte.

Section 2.3

5. Logic 1 at the MN/$\overline{\text{MX}}$ input selects the minimum mode and logic 0 at this input selects the maximum mode.

Section 2.4

7. Address bus width equals 20 bits and data bus width equals 16 bits.
9. $\overline{\text{INTA}}$ output.

Section 2.5

11. HOLD, HOLDA, $\overline{\text{WR}}$, M/$\overline{\text{IO}}$, DT/$\overline{\text{R}}$, $\overline{\text{DEN}}$, ALE, and $\overline{\text{INTA}}$ in minimum mode are $\overline{\text{RQ}/\text{GT}}_{1};_{0}$, $\overline{\text{LOCK}}$, $\overline{S}_2$-$\overline{S}_0$, QS_1, and QS_0, respectively, in the maximum mode.
13. The 8089 implements the Multibus arbitration protocol that permits multiple processors to reside on the 8086's system bus.
15. $\overline{\text{RQ}/\text{GT}}_{0,1}$

Section 2.6

17. The BIU is used to prefetch instructions from memory and store them in its queue and perform bus cycles to access data operands. The EU extracts instructions from the queue and performs the operation defined in the instruction.

Section 2.7

21. Pointer registers are SP and BP and the index registers are SI and DI. The pointer and index registers generally contain memory addresses, whereas the general purpose registers generally contain data for operations or data that result from an operation.
23. Status flags monitor (record) the processor status that results from the execution of an instruction. On the other hand, the control flags control processor operations or the execution of instructions.

CF = carry-out/borrow-in or no carry-out/no borrow-in for the MSB during an arithmetic instruction

PF = result produced by executing an instruction; has even or odd parity

AF = carry-out/borrow-in or no carry-out/no borrow-in between the high and low nibble in the lower byte of a word; result of an arithmetic instruction

ZF = result produced by executing an instruction is zero or non-zero

SF = the result produced by executing an instruction is positive or negative

OF = an overflow or nonoverflow condition has occurred during the execution of the arithmetic instruction

TF = enables/disables single-step mode of operation

IF = enables/disables external maskable interrupts

DF = determines whether the string count increments or decrements

Section 2.8

25. $V_{Hmin} = 3.9$ V and $V_{Hmax} = V_{cc} + 1$ V
$V_{Lmin} = -0.5$ V and $V_{Lmax} = 0.6$ V

Section 2.9

27. Idle states are performed if the queue is full and the EU does not require the BIU to read or write operands from memory. On the other hand, wait states are initiated in response to slow memory or I/O devices which make the CPU wait for the READY signal to be returned before the processor can proceed to complete the current bus cycle.

Chapter 3

Section 3.2

1. Yes, the 8086 can directly store a word of data starting at an odd address boundary.
3. Code segment (CS) register, data segment (DS) register, stack segment (SS) register, and extra segment (ES) register.

Section 3.4

7. Register addressing mode, immediate addressing mode, direct addressing mode, register indirect addressing mode, based addressing mode, indexed addressing mode, based indexed addressing mode, string addressing mode, and I/O port addressing mode.

9.

	Destination operand	Source operand
(a)	AL	BL
(b)	AX	FF_{16} (immediate value)
(c)	PA = $(DS)0_{16} + (SI)_{16}$	AX
(d)	SI	PA = $(DS)0_{16} + (DI)_{16}$
(e)	PA = $(DS)0_{16} + (BX)_{16} + XYZ_{16}$	CX
(f)	PA = $(DS)0_{16} + (SI)_{16} + XYZ_{16}$	AH
(g)	PA = $(DS)0_{16} + (BX)_{16} + (DI)_{16} + XYZ_{16}$	AL

Section 3.6

11. **(a)** Loads the SI register with the contents of memory address $ABCD_{16}$. **(b)** Loads the memory location pointed to by SI with $ABCD_{16}$.

12.
```
MOV     CX,BX
MOV     BX,AX
MOV     AX,CX
```

13. AL is loaded from address $10000_{16} + 0100_{16} + 0010_{16} = 10110_{16}$.

15. LDS AX,A000H

Section 3.7

16.
```
MOV     DS,0H             ; INITIALIZE DATA SEGMENT
MOV     SI,0A000H
MOV     AX,[SI]
MOV     BX,0C000H         ; POINTER FOR RESULTS
```

```
MOV   DI,0B000H
MOV   DX,[DI]
ADD   DX,AX
MOV   [BX],DX        ; SAVE THE SUM
SUB   DX,AX          ; RESTORE NUMBER
SUB   DX,AX
ADD   BX,2H
MOV   [BX],DX        ; SAVE THE DIFFERENCE
ADD   DX,AX          ; RESTORE NUMBER
MUL   DX
ADD   BX,2H
MOV   [BX],AX        ; SAVE LS PART OF PRODUCT
ADD   BX,2H
MOV   [BX],DX        ; SAVE MS PART OF PRODUCT
MOV   AX,[SI]        ; RESTORE NUMBER
DIV   [DI]
ADD   BX,2H
MOV   [BX],AX        ; SAVE QUOTIENT
ADD   BX,2H
MOV   [BX],DX        ; SAVE THE REMAINDER
```

Section 3.8

19. The new contents of AX are the negative of the old contents.

20.
```
NOT   NUM2
MOV   CL,AL
AND   AL,NUM2
OR    AL,BL
AND   CL,NUM1
OR    AL,CL
```

Section 3.9

21. The original contents of AX must have the four most significant bits equal 0.

Section 3.10

23.
```
MOV   BL,AL
MOV   CL,5
SHR   BX,CL
AND   BX,1
```

Chapter 4

Section 4.2

1.
```
CLI
LAHF
MOV DS, 0H
MOV BX,0A000H
MOV [BX],AH
CLC
```

Section 4.3

3.

Instruction	ZF	CF
Initial state	0	0
MOV BX,1111H	0	0
MOV AX,0BBBBH	0	0
CMP BX,AX	0	1

4. 64

Section 4.4

6.

```
        MOV  AL,1H
        MOV  CL,0H
        MOV  DL,N
NXT:    CMP  CL,DL
        JE   DONE
        INC  CL
        MUL  CL
        JMP  NXT
DONE:   MOV  FACT,AL
```

7. Only instructions 3 and 4 must be modified. The new instructions are:
   Instruction #3 MOV DI,BLK1ADDR
   Instruction #4 MOV SI,BLK2ADDR

9.

```
        MOV  CX,100
        MOV  DS,0H
        MOV  BX,0A000H
        MOV  SI,0B000H
        MOV  DI,0C000H
AGAIN:  MOV  AX,[BX]
        CMP  AX,0H
        JGE  POSTV
NEGTV:  MOV  [DI],AX
        INC  DI
        INC  DI
        JMP  NXT
POSTV:  MOV  [SI],AX
        INC  SI
        INC  SI
NXT:    DEC  CX
        JNZ  AGAIN
        HLT
```

Section 4.5

13. The call instruction saves the value in the instruction pointer (and maybe both segment registers) in addition to performing the jump operation.

14. The intersegment call provides the ability to call a subroutine in either the current code segment or a different code segment.

16. When any of the instructions in the subroutine will change flags.

Section 4.6

19.

```
        MOV    AL,1H
        MOV    CX,N
        JCXZ   DONE    ; N = 0 CASE
        LOOPZ  DONE    ; N = 1 CASE
        INC    CX      ; RESTORE N
AGAIN:  MUL    CL
        LOOP   AGAIN
DONE:   MOV    FACT,AL
```

21.

```
(a)  CLD
     MOVSB
(b)  CLD
     LODS
(c)  SDD
     CMPLS
```

Chapter 5

Section 5.3

1. 0000001111000010_2 = 03C2H; **3.** (a) 00011110_2 = 1EH; (c) 10010001_2 = 91H.

Section 5.4

5.

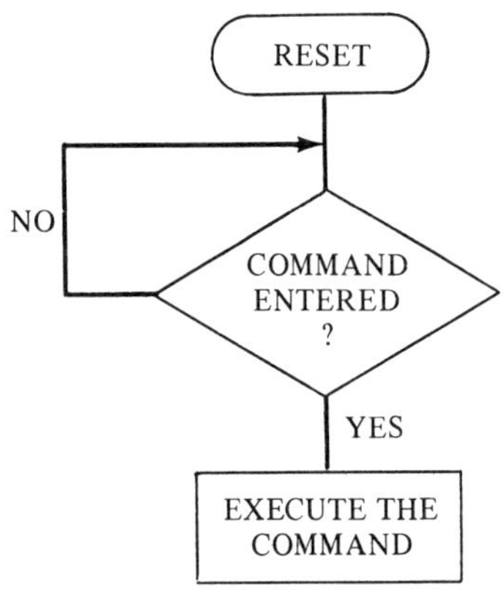

Section 5.5

7. ER CS 10.
ER DS 20.
ER ES 30.
ER SS 40.

9. GO 50, FF. or EB CS 25 GO 0, AF.

Section 5.6

11. Program execution begins at address 260_{16} and ends at address $27A_{16}$.

Chapter 6

Section 6.2

1.

Address	Contents
A001	78
A002	56
A003	34
A004	12

3. $A0000_{16}$ through $AFFFF_{16}$.

5.
```
MOV    DX,0A000H
MOV    CS,DX
MOV    DX,0B000H
MOV    DS,DX
MOV    DX,0C000H
MOV    SS,DX
MOV    DX,0D000H
MOV    ES,DX
```

Section 6.3

7. $\overline{BHE} = 0$, $A_0 = 0$, $\overline{WR} = 0$, $M/\overline{IO} = 1$, $DT/\overline{R} = 1$, $\overline{DEN} = 0$.

Section 6.6

9. During T_1 the 8086 outputs address B0010H on the address bus; asserts $\overline{BHE}$; and asserts ALE. The address for the memory must be latched external to the 8086 using ALE to gate the latch device. The 8086 also asserts the M and DT signals at this time. During T_2 $\overline{WR}$ is inserted and then the 8086 puts the data word onto the data bus. This data remains valid until the end of T_4 and should be written into memory with the rising edge of $\overline{WR}$ early in the T_4 cycle.

Section 6.7

11. Stack is the area of memory used to temporarily store information (parameters) that is to be passed to subroutines and other information, such as the contents of IP and CS, that is needed to return from a called subroutine to the main part of the program.

Section 6.8

13. During T_1 of the bus cycle, the 8086 supplies the address A0000H to the 8282 data latches. It also outputs logic 0 on $\overline{BHE}$ and a pulse to logic 1 on ALE. This pulse is used to latch the address and $\overline{BHE}$ into the latches. Also during T_1, the 8086 sets the $DT/\overline{R}$ line to logic 0. This specifies a read cycle and when applied to the 8286 devices configures them to transfer data from their ports B to ports A. The data to be read from memory is available at the B ports. During T_2, the 8086 switches $\overline{DEN}$ to logic 0 which enables the 8286 devices to transfer data, and during T_3 it reads the word of data on its 16 data lines.

Section 6.10

15. 2K-word read/write memory subsystem (see figure on page 329).

Chapter 7

Section 7.2

1. The address bus carries the address of the I/O port and the data bus carries the data that is transferred between CPU and the I/O port.
3. When in the maximum mode, the 8086 outputs status code $\overline{S_2}\overline{S_1}\overline{S_0}$ = 001 or 010 to inform external circuitry that an I/O operation is in progress.

Section 7.3

5. Execution of this input instruction causes the accumulator AX to be loaded with the contents of the word-wide input port at address $1A_{16}$.

Section 7.4

7. During T_1 of the bus cycle, the 8086 outputs address $A000_{16}$ on the address bus. Then it sets $M/\overline{IO}$ to logic 0 to signal that the address on the bus is an I/O address instead of a memory address. Finally, ALE goes active to latch the address in external circuitry. During T_2, $\overline{RD}$ goes active, logic 0, to signal that an input cycle is to be performed. Then $\overline{DEN}$ is switched to logic 0 to enable the data from the input port at address $A000_{16}$ onto the data bus, and status is output. In the T_3 part of the bus cycle, the 8086 reads the data off the bus and puts them into the AX register. This is followed by $\overline{RD}$ and $\overline{DEN}$ being returned to their inactive 1 level in T_4 to complete the bus cycle.

Section 7.7

11.
```
MOV DS,0H
MOV AL,092H
MOV BX,0100H
MOV [BX],AL
```

Section 7.8

13.
```
IN    AL,01H     ; READ PORT A
MOV   BL,AL      ; SAVE IN BL
IN    AL,03H     ; READ PORT B
ADD   AL, BL     ; ADD THE TWO NUMBERS
OUT   05H,AL     ; OUTPUT TO PORT C
```

Section 7.9

15.
```
MOV   CX,0401H
MOV   AL,[CX]
```

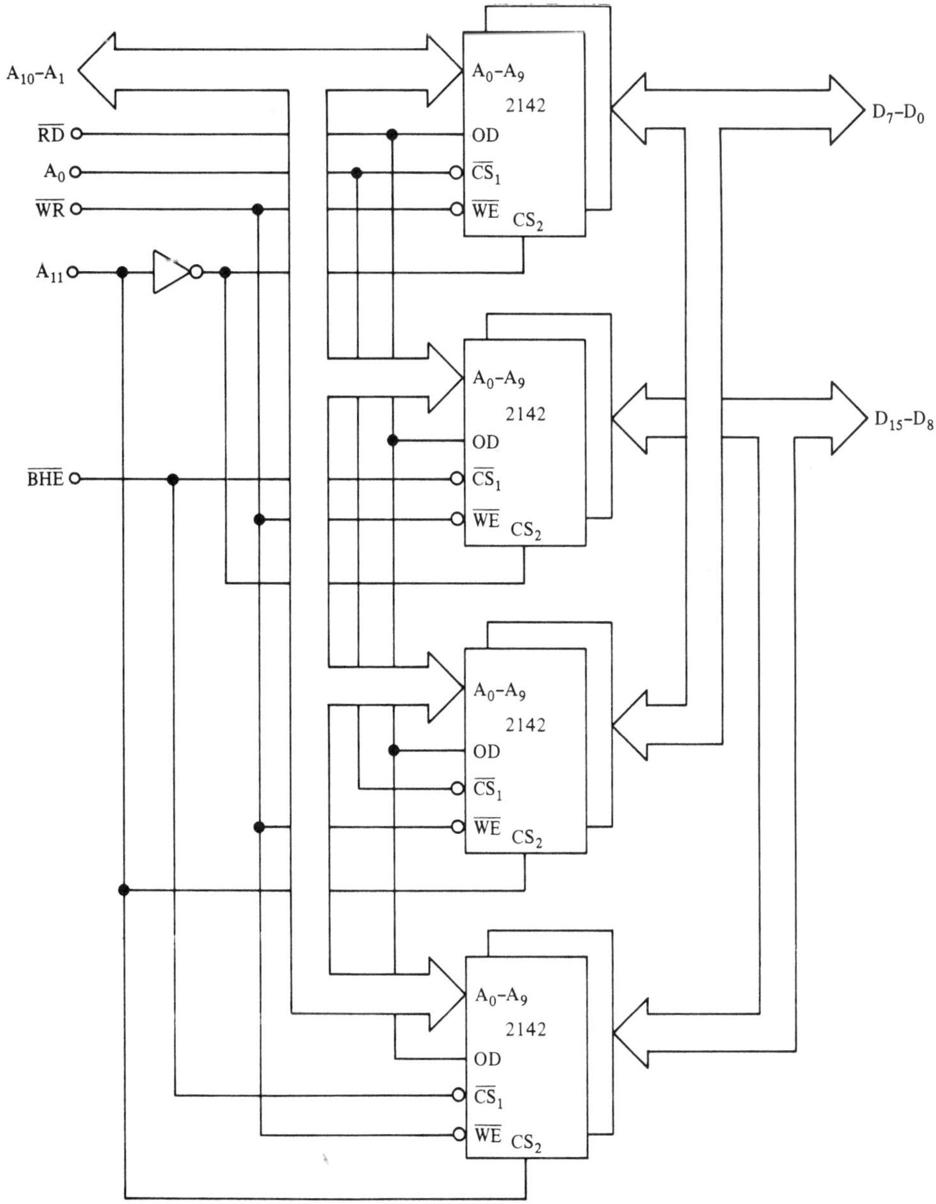

A_{10}–A_1
$\overline{RD}$
A_0
$\overline{WR}$
A_{11}
$\overline{BHE}$
A_0–A_9
2142
OD
$\overline{CS}_1$
$\overline{WE}$
CS_2
D_7–D_0
D_{15}–D_8

```
MOV   BL,AL
MOV   AL,0403H
MOV   AL,[CX]
ADD   AL,BL
MOV   CX,0405H
MOV   [CX],AL
```

Section 7.10

17. **(i)** The microcomputer activates its $\overline{RTS}$ line, which is applied to $\overline{DSR}$ of the terminal **(ii)** The terminal responds by activating its $\overline{DTR}$ line, which is returned to the $\overline{CTS}$ input of the microcomputer; **(iii)** Then the microcomputer sends character bits along with the start bit and stop bits on the TX_D line. These bits are received by the terminal on its RX_D line.

Section 7.11

19. $C/\overline{D} = 0$, $\overline{RD} = 1$, $\overline{WR} = 0$, and $\overline{CS} = 0$

21.
```
MOV   AL,0FFH
MOV   MODE,AL
```

Section 7.12

23. 12 rows × 12 columns = 144 keys

25. P = 30
CLK = (100 KHz) (30) = 3 MHz

Chapter 8

Section 8.2

1. External hardware interrupts, software interrupts, internal interrupts, nonmaskable interrupt, and reset interrupt.

Section 8.3

3. The pointer table contains the starting memory addresses of the service routines for the various interrupts.

Section 8.4

5.
```
•
•
CLI      ; Entry point of noninterruptable service routine and disable interrupts
•
•
•
•
STI      ; Reenable interrupts
IRET     ; Return to main part of program
•
•
```

Section 8.6

7. INTR is the interrupt request signal that must be applied to the 8086 MPU by external interrupt interface circuitry to request service for an interrupt driven device. In a minimum mode system, the MPU signals external devices that the request for service has been granted by outputting a pulse to logic 0 on the interrupt acknowledge ($\overline{INTA}$) line. In a maximum mode 8086 system, an interrupt acknowledge bus status code is output on $\overline{S}_0$ through $\overline{S}_2$ and this code is decoded by the 8288 bus controller to produce the $\overline{INTA}$ signal.

Section 8.8

9. $D_0 = 0$ ICW_4 not needed
$D_1 = 1$ Single device
$D_3 = 0$ Edge triggered
and assuming all other bits are logic 0 gives
$ICW_1 = 00000010_2 = 02_{16}$

11. $D_0 = 1$ Use with the 8086
$D_1 = 0$ Normal end of interrupt
$D_3D_2 = 11$ Buffered mode master
$D_4 = 0$ Disable special fully nested mode
and assuming that the rest of the bits are 0, we get
$ICW_4 = 00001101_2 = 0D_{16}$

Section 8.10

17. INT 20 is a software interrupt whose service routine starts at the address defined by the values IP and CS stored at memory locations 80_{16} and 82_{16}, respectively. When the instruction is executed, first the old values of CS and IP are saved on the top of the stack. Then the IF and TF flags are cleared to 0. Next, IP and CS are loaded from addresses 80_{16} and 82_{16}, respectively. Finally, execution resumes with the first instruction of the service routine.

Section 8.11

19. NMI differs from the external hardware interrupts in three ways:

a. NMI is not masked out with the IF flag.

b. The NMI interrupt is initiated from the NMI input lead while external hardware interrupts are initiated from the INTR input.

c. The NMI input is edge triggered instead of level sensitive. Therefore, its occurrence is internally latched into the 8086 as it is switched to the 1 logic level.

Section 8.12

21.

```
        PUSHF
        PUSH    DS
        PUSH    CX
        PUSH    DI
        MOV     DS,0
```

```
        MOV     CX,100H
        MOV     DI,0A000H
NXT:    MOV     [DI], 0
        INC     DI
        DEC     CX
        JNZ     NXT
        POP     DI
        POP     CX
        POP     DS
        POPF
        IRET
```

Chapter 9

Section 9.2

1. 8K.
3. Program storage memory contents remain intact when power is turned off; data storage memory is lost at power off.
5. Keypad, display, parallel I/O, and serial communications port.
7. Parallel I/O.

Section 9.3

11. 2 MHz.
13. Peripherals.
15. ON BOARD MEMORY will be logic 0. Thus, even if we access onboard memory, the wait states are inserted as per the jumper setting (W_{27} through W_{34}.)
17. b.

Section 9.4

19. $O_4O_3O_2O_1 = 1111$.
21. $M/\overline{IO} = 1$, $\overline{WE} = 0$, $\overline{CS}_2 = 1$, and $O_4O_3O_2O_1$.
24. $FFFE_{16}$.
27.

```
AGAIN:  MOV     AL,0H
        OUT     FFCH,AL       ;WRITE 0s
        CALL    DELAY         ;WAIT A WHILE
        MOV     AL,0FFH
        OUT     FFFCH,AL      :WRITE 1s
        CALL    DELAY         ;WAIT A WHILE
        JMP     AGAIN
DELAY:  MOV     CX,OFFFFH     ;START TIME DELAY
NEXT:   DEC     CX
        JNZ     NEXT
        RET
```

29. MOV AL,'A' ; LOAD AL WITH ASCII 'A'
OUT FFF0H,AL

31. 436.25 Hz.

33. PCLK and the output of the divide by 4 circuit.

39. c.

Index

A

D

E

F

G

H

I

J

K

L

M

N

O

P

Q

R

S